EPHESIANS
ROOTED AND GROUNDED IN CHRIST

The Proclaim Commentary Series

THE PROCLAIM COMMENTARY SERIES

EPHESIANS
ROOTED AND GROUNDED IN CHRIST

NEW TESTAMENT
VOLUME 10

MATTHEW STEVEN BLACK

WENATCHEE, WASHINGTON

Ephesians: Rooted and Grounded in Christ
(The Proclaim Commentary Series)
Copyright © 2021 by Matthew Steven Black
ISBN: 978-1-954858-02-2 (Print)
        978-1-954858-01-5 (eBook)

Proclaim Publishers
PO Box 2082 Wenatchee, WA 98807
proclaimpublishers.com

Cover art: *The Ruins of the Celsus Library at Ephesus*

Typesetting by Laurie Hilsabeck Miller

Unless otherwise quoted, Scripture quotations are from the ESV® Bible (The Holy Bible, English Standard Version®), copyright © 2001, 2016 by Crossway, a publishing ministry of Good News Publishers. Used by permission. All rights reserved.

Scripture quotations marked NASB are taken from the New American Standard Bible®, Copyright © 1960, 1962, 1963, 1968, 1971, 1972, 1973, 1975, 1977, 1995 by The Lockman Foundation. Used by permission.

Scripture quotations marked NKJV are taken from the New King James Version®. Copyright © 1982 by Thomas Nelson. Used by permission. All rights reserved.

Scripture quotations marked NIV are taken from The Holy Bible New International Version®, NIV® Copyright © 1973, 1978, 1984, 2011 by Biblica, Inc.® Used by permission. All rights reserved worldwide.

Scripture quotations marked CSB are taken from the Christian Standard Bible®, Used by permission. All rights reserved. CSB ©2017 Holman Bible Publishers.

Scripture quotations marked NLT are taken from the Holy Bible, New Living Translation, copyright ©1996, 2004, 2007 by Tyndale House Foundation. Used by permission of Tyndale House Publishers, Inc., Carol Stream, Illinois 60188. All rights reserved.

Scripture quotations marked KJV are taken from the King James Version of the Bible.

All rights reserved. No part of this publication may be reproduced, stored in a retrieval system or transmitted in any form by any means, electronic, mechanical, photocopy, recording or otherwise, without the prior permission of the publisher, except as provided by USA copyright law.

Ancient quotations have been at times changed to the ESV as well as some archaic language updated and additional phrases added for clarification. At times verse references (non-existent until recent times) have been interspersed as well to guide the modern reader.

Second Printing, January 2023
Manufactured in the United States of America

Dedicated to my forever family: Living Hope Bible Church of Roselle, Illinois. Thank you for letting me be a shepherd among you.

CONTENTS

INTRODUCTION 21

Background 21
Purpose 22
Author 22
Structure 23
Consider Your Identity in Christ (chs 1-3) 24
Remember Who You Are in Christ 24
Remember Who You Were Without Christ 27
Remember Your New Life in Christ 28
Remember Your Forever Family in Christ 29
Consider Your Responsibility in Christ (chs 4-6) 30
Walk Worthy in the Church 30
Walk Worthy in Your Personal Life 31
Walk Worthy at Home and at Work 33
Walk Worthy in the World 34

1 | EPHESIANS 1:1-14 THE DESTINY OF THE CHURCH 37

Our Destiny is Eternity (1:1-3) 38
An Eternal Citizenship 39
An Eternal Holiness 40
An Eternal Favor 40
An Eternal Blessing 42
Christians Bless God 42
Christians are Blessed by God 43
Our Destiny is Sanctity (1:4-6) 44
Chosen in Christ 45
Chosen for Holiness 46
Chosen for Adoption 47
Chosen for the Praise of His Glorious Grace 49
Our Destiny is Liberty (1:7-10) 50
Free from the Penalty of Sin 52
Free from the Poverty of Sin 53
Free from the Power of Sin 53
Free from the Presence of Sin 55
Our Destiny is Guaranteed (1:11-14) 56
Guaranteed by God's Sovereignty 56
Guaranteed by God's Word 58
Guaranteed by God's Spirit 59

What is Sealing? *60*
The Holy Spirit is a Down Payment of Heaven... *60*

2 | EPHESIANS 1:15-23 ROOTED IN CHRIST'S SUPREMACY 63

Christ is Exalted in Your Salvation (1:15-16) 65
- The Miracle of Faith 65
- The Nature of Faith 66
- The Expression of Faith 67

Christ is Exalted in Your Spiritual Growth (1:16-19) 67
- The Practice of Maturity 68
- The Means of Maturity 68
- The Focus of Maturity 70
  - *Hope – a perspective to brings us to maturity* *70*
  - *Riches – a promise to bring us to maturity* *71*
  - *Power – a power to bring us to maturity* *71*

Christ is Exalted in Your Service (1:20-23) 73
- Christ is Exalted Positionally 73
- Christ is Exalted Personally 74

3 | EPHESIANS 2:1-10 ROOTED IN CHRIST'S GRACE 77

Our Misery Requires God's Grace (2:1-3) 78
- The Shock of Grace 78
- The Human Condition 80
  - *The Misery of Senselessness*.. *80*
  - *The Misery of Sinfulness* *81*
  - *The Misery of Slavery*.. *82*

The Motive of Grace is Love (2:4-6) 85
- God's Love is Engaging 85
- God's Love is Extravagant 86
- God's Love is Empowering 88
  - *United with Christ in His Resurrection*... *88*
  - *United with Christ in His Ascension*.. *89*

We are God's Masterpiece of Grace (2:7-10) 89
- The Focus of our Salvation 89
- The Failure of Works Salvation 90
  - *Saved by Grace Alone* *90*
  - *Saved by Faith Alone* *91*
  - *Salvation is by God's Works Alone* *91*
- The Founder of True Salvation 92
  - *An Act of Creation*.. *93*
- The Fruit of True Salvation 93

4 | EPHESIANS 2:11-17 ROOTED IN CHRIST'S COMMUNITY 95

Remember the Old Hostility (2:11-12).. 96

Remember your Hard Heart 96
Remember our Hostility with God 98
   Alienated from His Kingdom 99

Refocus on A New Hope (2:13-14a) 100
Refocus on Christ's Propitiation 100
Refocus on Christ's Peace 101
   The Walls of Separation 102
   Tearing Down the Wall of Hostility 102

Rejoice in a New Humanity (2:14b-17) 103
A Populated Humanity 103
A Perfect Humanity 103
A Peaceful Humanity 104
   Human Hostility 105
   Divine Hostility 105
   Christ-focused Harmony 105
A Personal Humanity 105

5 | EPHESIANS 2:18-22 ROOTED IN GOD'S FOREVER FAMILY 107

Access to the Triune God (2:18) 109
In Christ We Access a New Kingdom (2:19a) 111
In Christ We Access a New Family (2:19b) 112
From Slavery to Family 112
In Christ We Access a New Temple (2:20-22) 113
Jesus is the Cornerstone 114
The Apostles and Prophets are the Foundation 115
   The Sufficiency of Scripture 116
Jesus is the Chief Cornerstone 118
The Lord is the Architect 118
   God's Temple Individually 120
   God's Temple Corporately 120

6 | EPHESIANS 3:1-13 ROOTED IN GOD'S ETERNAL PLAN 123

The Prisoner for Christ (3:1-2) 124
Paul was willing to suffer for God's plan. 126
Paul's usefulness did not end in prison. 127
Paul had no pity parties. 128
The Prophecy of God's Plan (3:3-6) 129
The Mystery Introduced 129
The Mystery Received 130
The Mystery Unveiled 130
The Mystery Explained 132
The Preachers of the Plan (3:7-11) 133
The Making of the Minister 134
The Smallness of the Minister 134

  The Riches of the Minister... 135
The Purpose of God's Plan (3:10-11)... 136
The Privileges of God's Plan (3:12-13) 136
  The Privilege of Access 137
  The Privilege of Progress... 137

7 | EPHESIANS 3:14-19 ROOTED IN GOD'S PRESENCE 141

A Prayer to Experience The Spirit's Power (3:14-16)........... 142
  Allegiance to the Father.. 142
  Affection for God's Family 143
  Ability from the Spirit.. 146
  The Secret to Experiencing God's Power........................... 147
A Prayer to Experience Christ's Love (3:17-19)....................... 148
  Indwelt by the Loving Christ 149
  Seized with Christ's Love.. 150
A Prayer to Experience God's Fullness (3:19b)......................153
  The Meaning of Fullness 153
  The Pathway to Fullness 154

8 | EPHESIANS 3:20-21 ROOTED IN GOD'S POWER 159

  Paul Writing from Prison 160
The Response to God's Power (3:20-21a) 162
The Resources of God's Power (3:20)....................................... 163
  God's Power is Infinite.. 163
  God's Power is Intentional 164
  God's Power Incomprehensible... 164
  God's Power is Internal 165
The Request for God's Power (3:20) 166
The Reason for God's Power (3:21) 167
  God's Glory Defined 168
  God's Glory in the Church.. 168
  God's Glory in Jesus 169
  God's Glory in Your Family 169
  God's Glory Forever... 169

9 | EPHESIANS 4:1-6 ROOTED IN CHRIST'S UNITY 173

The Request for Unity (4:1)...173
  A Request from a Prisoner.. 174
  A Weighty Request... 174
The Reflection of Unity (4:1-2) 176
  Humility 176
  Gentleness.. 177
  Patience... 178

Forbearance 178
Love 178
The Rigor of Unity (4:3) 179
The Roots of Unity (4:4-6) 181
One Body 182
One Spirit 184
One Hope 185
One Lord 186
One Faith 187
One Baptism 188
One God and Father of All 190

10 | EPHESIANS 4:7-13 ROOTED IN SPIRITUAL GIFTS 193

The Description of Spiritual Gifts (4:7) 194
A Spiritual Gift is Given to Every Believer 194
A Spiritual Gift is a Supernatural Ability 194
A Spiritual Gift is a Stewardship 195
Spiritual Gifts are Merited by Christ 196
The Giver of Spiritual Gifts (4:8-10) 197
Our Victorious General 197
Our Humble General 199
Our Exalted General 200
The Function of Spiritual Gifts (4:11-12) 201
The Officers Who Do the Equipping 201
The Act of Equipping 204
The People Who are Equipped 205
The Purpose for Spiritual Gifts (4:13) 207
Purpose #1 Involvement 207
Purpose #2 Maturity 209
Purpose #3 Christlikeness 211

11 | EPHESIANS 3:14-4:12 THE ABUNDANT CHURCH 213

We Need Encouragement from God (3:14-19) 214
Your View of God 215
A Loving Heavenly Father *215*
A Loving Forever Family *215*
Your Experience of God 216
The Infinite Power of the Spirit *216*
The Infinite Love of Christ *216*
The Dimensions of Christ's Love 218
Christ's Love is Wide *218*
Christ's Love is Long *219*
Christ's Love is Deep *219*
Christ's Love is High *219*

    The Infinite Fullness of God 220
We Need Empowerment from God (3:20-21) 220
    An Infinite Power 221
    An Internal Power 221
We Need Effectiveness from God (4:11-12) 222
    Effective Shepherds 223
    Effective Saints 223

12 | EPHESIANS 4:11-16 ROOTED IN SPIRITUAL MATURITY 227

Industry: Growing in Service (4:11-12a) 228
    Serving Up the Word 228
    Building Up the Saints 229
Unity: Growing in Humility (4:12b) 230
Conformity: Growing in Christ's Image (4:13) 231
Stability: Growing in Responsibility (4:14) 234
    Childlikeness Commended 235
    Childishness Condemned 237
    Spiritual Growth Possible 240
Community – Growing in Fellowship (4:15-16) 243
    The Balance of Fellowship 243
    The Word of Fellowship 244
    The Lord of Fellowship 245
    The Family of Fellowship 245

13 | EPHESIANS 4:17-24 ROOTED IN THE NEW LIFE 247

The New Life is a Life of Separation (4:17-21) 248
    Be Separated from Mindless Living 249
    Be Separated from Careless Living 251
    Be Separated from Godless Living 253
    Be Separated from Heartless Living 254
    Be Separated from Enslaved Living 256
The New Life is a Life of Transformation (4:20-24) 257
    Be Transformed by the Regenerate Life 257
    Be Transformed by the Christ-Centered Life 258
    Be Transformed by the Crucified Life 260
    Be Transformed by the Renewed Life 265
    Be Transformed by the Victorious Life 269

14 | EPHESIANS 4:25-32 ROOTED IN GODLY COMMUNICATION 273

Truthful Communication (4:25) 276
    Hearts that Hate Lies 277
    Mouths that Speak Truth 278
    A Body that Dwells in Harmony 278

Transformed Communication (4:28) 279
Temperate Communication (4:26-32) 279
   Don't Curse Your Anger 279
   Don't Nurse Your Anger 282
   Don't Rehearse Your Anger 284
   Don't Converse About Your Anger.. 285
   Don't Worsen Your Anger 287
   Don't Disperse Your Anger 288
      Grudges 288
      Rage 290
      Anger 291
      Shouting 291
      Slander 292
      Malice 293
   Do Reverse Your Anger 294
      Kindness 294
      Tenderness 295
      Forgiveness 296

15 | EPHESIANS 5:1-7 ROOTED IN SEXUAL PURITY 299

Priorities Matter: Imitate God (5:1) 301
   Our Desire to Imitate God 301
   Our Endeavor to Imitate God 301
People Matter: Love People (5:2) 302
   Our Walk of Love 302
   Christ's Demonstration of Love 303
   The Pleasing Aroma of Empathy 304
Purity Matters: Avoid Sexual Sin (5:3-4) 304
   Sexual Sin is Rotten 306
   Sexual Sin is Selfish 307
   Sexual Sin is Thoughtless 309
   Godly Sex is Celebrated 311
Partnerships Matter (5:5-7) 313
   The Damnation of Immorality 314
   The Deception of Immorality 315
   The Deliverance from Immorality 318

16 | EPHESIANS 5:8-21 ROOTED IN THE SPIRIT'S FILLING 325

The Regeneration of the Spirit (5:8-10) 326
   In Conversion We Have A New Nature 327
   In Conversion We Have a New Behavior 329
   In Conversion We Have a New Master 330
The Roadblocks to Spirit Filling (5:11-17) 331
   Worldliness 331

Sleepiness 334
Wasting Time 336
False Worship 341

The Reality of Spirit Filling (5:18-21) 342
What Spirit Filling is Not 342
What Spirit-filling Is 344
What Spirit-filling Produces 346

17 | EPHESIANS 5:22-24 GOD'S DESIGN FOR WIVES 351

The Beauty of God's Design for the Wife (5:22-24) 352
The Wife is Prized 352
The Wife is Protected 353
The Wife is Pictured 355

The Battle for God's Design for the Wife 356
The Struggle of Worthiness 356
The Battle of Fatherlessness 357
The Unseen Battle 358

The Blessing of God's Design for the Wife 359
The Helper of the Home 359
The Organizer of the Home 359
The Molder of the Home 360
The Evangelist of the Home 360

18 | EPHESIANS 5:25-33 GOD'S DESIGN FOR HUSBANDS 363

Husbands Should be Leaders (5:22-25) 364
Not Superior Leadership 364
Not Selfish Leadership 365
Servant Leadership 365
Spiritual Leadership 366

Husbands Should be Lovers (5:25-33) 367
Husbands Lack Agape Love 368
Husbands Need God's Love 368
God's Love is Self-Sacrificing 369
God's Love is Self-Originating 370
God's Love is Unexpected 371
God's Love is Voluntary 371
Husbands Should Act Out God's Love 371
The Wife Should be Prized 372
The Wife Should be Cleansed 372
The Wife Should be Protected 373
The Wife Should be Provided For 375
The Wife Should be Cherished 377
The Wife Should be Pictured 378

Husbands Should be Learners 380

| Attention 380
     Gentleness 381
     Honor 381

19 | EPHESIANS 6:1-4 ROOTED IN LOVE POWERED PARENTING 385

  The Child's Responsibility (6:1-3) 387
     A Child's Obedience 387
     A Child's Attitude 389
     A Child's Life 389
  The Father's Responsibility (6:4) 390
     The Negative Command 390
     The Positive Command 393
        Tenderness: Love them! *393*
        Discipline: Live for Christ with them! *393*
        Instruction: Counsel them! *394*
  Our Heavenly Father's Love 395

20 | EPHESIANS 6:5-9 ROOTED IN WORKING FOR JESUS 399

  Focus on our Ultimate Master (6:5) 403
     Obeying our Master 403
     Worshipping our Master 404
     Loyal to our Master 405
  Focus on our Ultimate Mission (6:6-7) 406
     A Mission to Please God 406
     A Mission to Serve God 407
     A Mission to be Satisfied by God 408
  Focus on our Ultimate Motivation (6:8-9) 408
     Motivated by More than a Paycheck 408
     Motivated by Our Mutual Master 409

21 | EPHESIANS 6:10-13 ROOTED IN SPIRITUAL WARFARE 411

  Our Strength (6:10) 412
     The Significance of Strength 412
     The Source of Strength 413
  Our Weaponry (6:11) 414
     The Description of Our Armor 414
     The Depiction of Our Armor 415
     The Demand for Our Armor 416
     The Design of Our Armor 416
  Our Enemy (6:12) 417
     The Enemy's Position: Unseen 418
     The Enemy's Princes: Regional Rulers 418
     The Enemy's Power: Decision Makers 420

- The Enemy's Planning: Cosmic Powers ... 422
- The Enemy's Plentitude: Evil Armies ... 423
- The Enemy's Policy: Evil ... 423
- The Enemy's Place: The Spiritual Realm ... 424
- The Enemy's Panic: Time is Short ... 425

Our Victory (6:13) ... 425
- The Protection for Our Victory ... 425
- The Peril in Our Victory ... 426
- The Promise of Victory ... 427

22 | EPHESIANS 6:14-17 ROOTED IN GOD'S ARMOR ... 431

The Belt of Truth (6:14) ... 433
- The Belt's Freedom ... 433
- The Belt's Fastening ... 434
- The Belt's Function ... 435

The Breastplate of Righteousness (6:14) ... 436
- The Breastplate's Forger ... 436
- The Breastplate's Function ... 437
- The Breastplate's Form ... 437
- The Breastplate's Pharmacy ... 438
- The Breastplate's Faith ... 439

The Boots of Peace (6:15) ... 439
- The Boots' Praise ... 440
- The Boots' Posture ... 440
- The Boots' Peace ... 441
- The Boots' Preparation ... 441
- The Boots' Position ... 441

The Shield of Faith (6:16) ... 442
- A Shield of Togetherness ... 442
- A Shield of Trust ... 442
- A Shield of Testing ... 443
- A Shield of Triumph ... 444

The Helmet of Salvation (6:17) ... 444

The Sword of the Spirit (6:17) ... 445
- A Specific Sword ... 445
- A Scripture Sword ... 446
- A Two-Sided Sword ... 447

23 | EPHESIANS 6:18-24 ROOTED IN BLESSING ... 451

The Blessing of Prayer (6:18) ... 452
- Stay Alert with Practical Prayer ... 453
- Stay Alert with Powerful Prayer ... 453
- Stay Alert with Persevering Prayer ... 453
- Stay Alert with Plentiful Prayer ... 454

The Blessing of Preaching (6:19-20) 455
Open Door for Proclamation 455
Open Door for a Prisoner 456
The Blessing of Pastors (6:21-22) 456
Pastor Tychicus 457
Pastor Paul 460
The Blessing of Blessings (6:23-24) 460
Peace 461
Love 462
Faith 463
Grace 463

SELECTED BIBLIOGRAPHY 465

ABBREVIATIONS

Common

cf – Latin "conferatur", compare, or see, or see also
ff – and following (pages or verses)
i.e. – Latin "id est", that is
e.g. – Latin "exempli gratia", for example
c. – Latin "circa", about

Books of the Bible

OLD TESTAMENT

Genesis	Gen	Esther	Est
Exodus	Exo	Job	Job
Leviticus	Lev	Psalms	Psa
Numbers	Num	Proverbs	Pro
Deuteronomy	Deut	Ecclesiastes	Ecc
Joshua	Josh	Song of Solomon	Song
Judges	Jdg	Isaiah	Isa
Ruth	Ruth	Jeremiah	Jer
1 Samuel	1 Sam	Lamentations	Lam
2 Samuel	2 Sam	Ezekiel	Eze
1 Kings	1 Kgs	Daniel	Dan
2 Kings	2 Kgs	Hosea	Hos
1 Chronicles	1 Chr	Joel	Joel
2 Chronicles	2 Chr	Amos	Amos
Ezra	Ezr	Obadiah	Oba
Nehemiah	Neh	Jonah	Jonah

Micah	Mic	Haggai	Hag
Nahum	Nah	Zechariah	Zech
Habakkuk	Hab	Malachi	Mal
Zephaniah	Zeph		

New Testament

Matthew	Mt	Titus	Titus
Mark	Mk	Philemon	Phm
Luke	Lk	Hebrews	Heb
John	Jn	James	Jas
Acts	Acts	1 Peter	1 Pet
Romans	Rom	2 Peter	2 Pet
1 Corinthians	1 Cor	1 John	1 Jn
2 Corinthians	2 Cor	2 John	2 Jn
Galatians	Gal	3 John	3 Jn
Ephesians	Eph	Jude	Jud
Philippians	Phil	Revelation	Rev
Colossians	Col		
1 Thessalonians	1 Thess		
2 Thessalonians	2 Thess		
1 Timothy	1 Tim		
2 Timothy	2 Tim		

INTRODUCTION

A mini-course in theology, centered on the church. That is what Paul's great letter to the Ephesians, written from Rome shortly after the midpoint of the first Christian century, is about. But what a course! What theology![1]

JAMES MONTGOMERY BOICE

The subject of the book of Ephesians is vital to your existence on this planet as God's child. What does it mean to be "in Christ" as an individual and as a congregation? What does it mean to grow in Christ? These are the themes of the book of Ephesians.

BACKGROUND

Paul wrote this letter to the Ephesian congregation in the middle of this pagan city of 300,000 in the ancient world. Ephesus was the most important city in western Asia Minor (now Turkey). It had a harbor that at that time opened into the Cayster River, which in turn emptied into the Aegean Sea. Because it was also at an intersection of major trade routes, Ephesus became a commercial center. It boasted a pagan temple dedicated to the Roman goddess Diana (Greek Artemis; *cf* Acts 19:23–31). Paul made Ephesus a center for evangelism for about three years (*cf* Acts 19:10), and the church there apparently flourished for some time, but later needed the warnings of the letters to the seven churches (Rev 2-3). Ephesus is very much like the cities of this world today. And believe it or not, even in this modern day, our cities are just as pagan as in Paul's day.

---

[1] James Montgomery Boice, *Ephesians: An Expositional Commentary* (Grand Rapids, MI: Ministry Resources Library, 1988), xi.

Purpose

The purpose of Paul's letter is that the Ephesians needed to stop changing with the fads of the world and instead be growing and changing in Christ. The letter to Ephesians could be summarized with Paul's description of body life in chapter 4.

> **Ephesians 4:15b-16** | We are to grow up in every way into him who is the head, into Christ, from whom the whole body, joined and held together by every joint with which it is equipped, when each part is working properly, makes the body grow so that it builds itself up in love.

Don't you want to be growing and changing in Christ? Have you ever felt like you were not making the progress in the Christian life that you desire? Would you like to know how to do that? Paul tells us in Ephesians.

Author

Paul is the author of the book of Ephesians, of which there is almost no dispute. The author identifies himself as Paul (1:1; 3:1; cf 3:7,13; 4:1; 6:19–20). Some have taken the absence of the usual personal greetings and the verbal similarity of many parts to Colossians, among other reasons, as grounds for doubting authorship by the apostle Paul. However, this was probably a circular letter, intended for other churches in addition to the one in Ephesus. Clement (35 AD – 99 AD), an early pastor of the Roman congregation and disciple of the apostle Peter writes of the beloved apostle Paul in his early letter to the Corinthians.

> *1 Clement 5:5-7* | Paul also obtained the reward of patient endurance, after being seven times thrown into captivity, compelled to flee, and stoned. After preaching both in the east and west, he gained the illustrious reputation due to his faith, having taught righteousness to the whole world, and come to the extreme limit of the west, and suffered martyrdom under the prefects. Thus was he removed from the world, and went into the holy place, having proved himself a striking example of patience.

It was under his imprisonment in Rome around 62 AD that Paul likely wrote several letters including Ephesians, Colossians, Philemon, and Philippians, while he was under house arrest (3:1;4:1; 6:20; cf Acts 28:16, 30-31). During this time, Paul had relative freedom in his own rented house, albeit, he was chained to a Roman soldier in the elite

Pretorian guard (Phil 1:13; 4:7). As Luke records: "Paul was allowed to stay by himself, with the soldier who guarded him" (Acts 28:16).

STRUCTURE

Ephesians is divided into two sections. The first three chapters are our identity in Christ, and the final three chapters are our responsibility in Christ. You cannot do what God has called you to do, until you realize what God has called you to be. Your actions always proceed from who you are. Theologians call this the indicative (our identity in Christ) and the imperative (our responsibility to walk according to our identity). Thirteen times in the book of Ephesians we find the phrase "In Christ." Four times Paul says we are seated "with Christ" in the heavenly realm. Three times he says Christ dwells in you or in your heart! Something has changed! We are no longer enemies and strangers to God. We are His children. We are heirs of God and co-heirs with Christ.

Have you ever seen a crawling butterfly? Our kids have a pet caterpillar. They hope to see this caterpillar go into his cocoon for three months, and come out as a butterfly. The caterpillar who was once bound to the ground should be able to fly. Can you imagine if the butterfly with great big wings just crawled on the ground and never wanted to fly? What if he kept saying: "I'm only a caterpillar – I can't fly!" You may be like that caterpillar. God has given you wings of holiness and a Spirit-filled nature, but you are like that crawling butterfly. You have the power to fly in conformity to Christ, but you keep crawling on the ground of old sinful living. You may not be continuing in sin the way you used to, but there are little slave masters in your life that control you. It may be anger. It may be lust. It may be anxiety and worry. It may be irrational thoughts and fear.

Martin Luther said that indwelling sin is like a man's beard, which even though each day it is shaved off and smooth, yet it never stops growing back. Only when the shovel beats the ground on our grave does it stop. Indwelling sin remains in us as long as we live.[2] It is not that a Christian is sinless, but we are sinning less. You say, ok, I want grow and change in Christ. How can I do that? The book of Ephesians tells us.

---

[2] Martin Luther. *What Luther Says: An Anthology* (St. Louis, MO: Concordia Publishing House, 1959), 1303.

Consider Your Identity in Christ (chs 1-3)

We need to realize that we are a "new creation" in Christ (2 Cor 5:17). You are not what you once were. You are (1:3) "blessed... in Christ with every spiritual blessing in the heavenly places." Colossians 2:10 says it a different way: you are "complete in Christ." You lack nothing! You have all you could ever need already in Christ. Paul does not say, you have a few blessings or most blessings, but *every* spiritual blessing in Christ. As far as your soul is concerned, you do not need the perfect spouse to be complete. You are complete in Christ. You do not need a better job to be complete. If you are single, you do not need marriage to be complete! No human being will complete you. No amount of money will complete you. What are you living for? A better house? A better car? Better relationships? These things will not complete you. You are complete in Christ.

Remember Who You Are in Christ

Though in this life we are never sinless, we also can never be what we once were. John Newton, the former slave ship captain who was liable for the imprisonment of tens of thousands of Africans into slavery, and guilty for the death of hundreds and hundreds of them came to Christ and wrote the hymn "Amazing Grace." God changed him. Listen to his words. He said, "I am not what I ought to be, I am not what I want to be, I am not what I hope to be in another world; but still I am not what I once used to be, and by the grace of God I am what I am!"[3] So, it is with every Christian. Though we are not yet what we long to be and what we will be one day when Jesus comes, we can truly say "the old life is crucified with Christ" and that our old life is "dead with Christ." We will never be that person we were before our conversion. We are truly a "new creation." This is the message of Ephesians 1-3.

You are Chosen and Accepted in Christ

You are (1:4) "chosen in Christ before the foundation of the world..." God "predestined you for adoption as sons through Jesus Christ, according to the purpose of his will his will, to the praise of his glorious grace, with which he has accepted us in the Beloved" (1:5-6). God chose you and accepts you in Christ. He did this before the

---

[3] John Newton. *The Christian Spectator*, vol 3 (New Haven, CT: S. Converse, 1821), 186.

foundation of the world. Long before you were born, he loved you. Even while you were dead in your sins (2:1) he still loved you and chose you. And yes "while we were still weak," unable to save ourselves, the Bible says, "at the right time Christ died for the ungodly" (Rom 5:6). We must stop trying to make ourselves acceptable to God! "We love him because he first loved us!" God loves us not because of our good behavior. Even our most righteous deeds, Isaiah says, are like "an unclean thing...like filthy rags." God loves us not because we are good, but because he is good. God is kind and merciful and tender! He sings over you! He rejoices over you, like a nursing mother rejoices over her infant child. You are no longer an outcast. You are no longer rejected. You are loved. You are chosen. You are welcomed and accepted in the Beloved One, Jesus Christ!

You are an Heir of God

Ephesians 1:4 | In him we have obtained an inheritance, having been predestined according to the purpose of him who works all things according to the counsel of his will.

The word inheritance (1:11, 14, 18) evokes thoughts of money or property handed down from generation to generation, with some special person receiving a legacy from a parent or relative. The heir is granted full benefits and ownership privileges and has gratifying knowledge that he is unique, blessed, chosen for honor in some way. "We have redemption through his blood, the forgiveness of our trespasses" (1:7). You don't have to purge your sin in purgatory. You don't have to earn your way back to God through good works. You are forgiven! How? Through redemption.

What is redemption? In the context of Ephesians means to purchase a slave. In the ancient world, 50% of the Roman Empire was in slavery. Those conquered by the Romans were made slaves. Those who could not pay their debts were slaves. Sometimes criminals were made into slaves. Back then, if a man had an inheritance he wanted to give away, but he had no sons, then he would go to the slave market and purchase a slave and make him a son. At that moment of redemption, he received all the rights and privileges of a natural born son. He would receive the full inheritance of a natural born son! God went to the slave market of sin and saw us as slaves of sin. And God gave his Son as the purchase price for our salvation. You see God's grace is free to us, but it is not cheap! It cost God everything! That is why Paul says in Ephesians 1:11, "In him we have obtained an inheritance, having been predestined according to the purpose of him who works all things according to the counsel of his will." We have an inheritance. We who squandered our lives in slavery to sin have become sons and daughters of the living God. We now have all the rights and privileges of his own dear Son. We are heirs of God and co-heirs with Christ.

In the Old Testament God promised Abraham a new home and a new family. He gave him the promised land of Israel. He promised to make his descendants multiply like the sands of the sea and the stars of heaven. That was just a shadow of the greater and genuine things in the New Covenant. Today we not only are heirs of the promised land, but Romans 4:13 says God's promise to Abraham was that he would literally be the "heir of the cosmos." He's not heir only of the promised land, but the whole universe. He would be heir of the entire new heavens and new earth. Through his seed, he would not only bless Israel but through his Seed (Christ) all the nations of the earth would be blessed. And Galatians 3:29 says, "if you are Christ's, then you are Abraham's offspring, heirs according to promise." You have the same inheritance!

You are Sealed as God's Special Possession

You are not your own. You are bought with a price. Glorify God with your whole being!

> **Ephesians 1:13-14** | In him you also, when you heard the word of truth, the gospel of your salvation, and believed in him, were sealed with the promised Holy Spirit, **14** who is the guarantee of our inheritance until we acquire possession of it, to the praise of his glory.

When God saved you, he sealed you with his Holy Spirit. The seal refers to a stamp of ownership. You have the stamp of God's ownership. He can never deny Himself. He has joined you with Christ. That can never be undone. The Holy Spirit is the "guarantee" of your "inheritance." The word "guarantee" was in weddings. The engagement ring was the guarantee of the wedding. It was also used in purchases. The down payment was the guarantee that you would one day in the future get the property. The Holy Spirit is God's engagement ring, his down payment guarantees that one day we will have all of heaven. His Holy

Spirit is his seal of ownership on his special possession. You are holy and set apart for God's kingdom, child of God.

Then in Ephesians 1:15-22, Paul prays that the congregation at Ephesus will have the "eyes of their heart" opened and illuminated to who they are in Christ and to their inheritance, and to the fact that Christ is their Sovereign Lord and Head.

Remember Who You Were Without Christ

In Chapter 2, Paul begins with a very dark thought: what we once were without Christ.

You were Dead in Trespasses and Sins

Paul begins by looking back before the Ephesians' salvation: "And you were dead in the trespasses and sins" (2:1). A trespass is when we break God's law purposely. Like a sign that says: "no trespassing" and we go beyond guarded area. All of us by nature are lawless. We lie, steal, lust, complain, and curse by nature. A sin is to "miss the mark." It means to set out to do what is right, and then to miss it. That's the story of our lives, isn't it? It says we are dead, and then it says we walk in the world, with the wicked one and by our own passions and lusts. The idea of dead is that we have no true tenderness toward God. When it comes to a contrite and broken spirit, we are hard and dead and senseless.

You were Living as a Slave

These verses describe what we were before Christ: living in slavery to sin.

> **Ephesians 2:2-3** | ...in which you once walked following the course of this world, following the prince of the power of the air, the spirit that is now at work in the sons of disobedience — among whom we all once lived in the passions of our flesh, carrying out the desires of the body and the mind, and were by nature children of wrath, like the rest of mankind.

It says we are slaves before we come to Christ: We were slaves of the world: we followed the course or current of the world. It's not talking about the dirt under our feet or the planet, but the "world system." What is now. What is temporary. What is in front of my eyes. Riches. Lust. Power. Popularity. The lust of the eyes. The lust of the flesh. The pride of life. The "world" means the world's "way of thinking." We were slaves to that.

We were slaves of Satan: the prince of the power of the air, the spirit that is now at work in the sons of disobedience. Lucifer is that fallen angel that is presently the governor of the atmosphere- He governs what is philosophically "in" what is "cool" and "hip" as to the philosophies in the realm of wickedness. What is Satan promoting today? He says – let's redefine marriage and make homosexuality a human rights issue, or – let's call the murder of infants in the womb the compassionate "choice" of the mother, or – let's glorify immodesty and make women mere objects and property, or – let's erase the order of God's creation and encourage men to act like women and women to act like men. You see, we used to be in slavery to these philosophies of the wicked one. He blinds the eyes of all unbelievers on the planet. We were enslaved to the wicked one. We were slaves of self and our own wicked heart. Verse 3, "we all once lived in the passions of our flesh, carrying out the desires of the body and the mind, and were by nature children of wrath, like the rest of mankind." We were once governed by our feelings and passions. We were governed by lust, anger, fear, bitterness, covetousness. We wanted what we wanted, and we were willing to sin to get it!

Remember Your New Life in Christ

Then we read the greatest words in the Bible in Ephesians 2:4,

> **Ephesians 2:4-6** | But God, being rich in mercy, because of the great love with which he loved us, **5** even when we were dead in our trespasses, made us alive together with Christ—by grace you have been saved— **6** and raised us up with him and seated us with him in the heavenly places in Christ Jesus.

What is this? Because of God's mercy, when we were dead in sins, He regenerated us. He gave us a new nature. He united us with Christ. He made us alive. We are no longer what we once were. Paul uses the metaphor of a dead person being made alive and resurrected to describe what theologians call regeneration. What is regeneration? The prefix is *re* which means new, and *genesis* which means beginning. Regeneration is a new beginning with God. In Adam all die, but in Christ, all are made alive. We are given a new beginning with God. The curse is erased. Our guilt is gone. Our transgressions are throne as far as the east is from the west.

The Bible has many metaphors for regeneration. We have a new heart. We no longer have a heart of stone. The only hard, stubborn heart is transformed into a tender heart of flesh (Eze 36:25-27). We are no longer stubborn. We have new life – resurrected with Christ! We are no longer dead in sin. We are born again. We are no longer a child of this sinful world. We are a new creation. The old life is passed away. The new life has come. In all the metaphors for regeneration, we are passive. God does it all. I cannot birth myself. I cannot give myself a heart transplant. I cannot resurrect myself. I cannot create myself. God must do it! All the sinner must do is believe!

> **Ephesians 2:8-9** | For by grace you have been saved through faith. And this is not your own doing; it is the gift of God, **9** not a result of works, so that no one may boast.

And yet our entire salvation including our faith, is a gift from God! Of course, there is so much more! You are no longer pagan Gentiles (2:11), cut off from God's family, as 2:12 says:

> **Ephesians 2:12** | … separated from Christ, alienated from the commonwealth of Israel and strangers to the covenants of promise, having no hope and without God in the world.

Now you are "brought near by the blood of Christ" (2:13). You are no longer identified mainly by your race or family on earth where there is hostility between Jew and Gentile. But Christ has "the dividing wall of hostility" (2:14) and created "one new humanity." You are now "no longer strangers and aliens, but you are fellow citizens with the saints and members of the household of God" (2:19). You are part of God's forever or eternal family!

Remember Your Forever Family in Christ

Ephesians 3 speaks of the great mystery of God's hidden plan. Who would have guessed that God would join all the Gentile nations of the earth with Israel into one new family?

> **Ephesians 3:6** | This mystery is that the Gentiles are fellow heirs, members of the same body, and partakers of the promise in Christ Jesus through the gospel.

This goes back to the Abrahamic covenant in Genesis 12 and 15, which says that through Abraham's seed (Christ) all the nations of the earth would be blessed. And so now you are no longer what you once were! You are part of God's forever family, and this was the plan even before the beginning of time, and God reiterated it to Abraham.

You are loved! You are chosen! You are accepted and welcomed by God! You are God's child, and therefore you are an heir of God, you are sealed by God's Spirit! You have a new nature that is empowered to live holy. You are part of God's forever covenant family! That's Ephesians 1-3. That's who you are. And based on who you are – i.e. your identity, God calls you to live up to your responsibilities.

Consider Your Responsibility in Christ (chs 4-6)

Paul begins the second part of Ephesians with a challenge to walk worthy of our identity in Christ.

> **Ephesians 4:1** | I therefore... urge you to walk in a manner worthy of the calling to which you have been called.

Walk worthy! Because you are "in Christ," you need to walk in a manner worthy of His high and holy Name! Paul gives three realms where we exercise Christian maturity: in the church, in close human relationships, and in the world.

Walk Worthy in the Church

So, the first realm where we exercise Christian maturity is the church. In Ephesians 4:1-10, we are called to live in peace with other Christians. In 4:2, we are called to "bear with each other in love." This literally means to lovingly tolerate each other's peculiarities and differences. I know you don't have any peculiarities or irritating habits, but I'm sure I do! We are all like porcupines, and we don't realize we are sticking each other. We sometimes cause offense to brothers and sisters and we don't even know it! When you find offense in the Body of Christ, you ought not to go church hopping and find the perfect church. If you do find the perfect church, don't join it, because it will no longer be perfect!

Then, in Ephesians 4:11-16, Paul tells us *how* to live in Christian maturity in the church community. He basically says you need to listen carefully to the word that is preached by the pastors, teachers and evangelists, and then get busy and serve God by building up your eternal family. This language is all over the New Testament. Over 35 times in the NT we are told to do something for one another in the church. Love one another. Bear with one another. Teach one another. Encourage one another. Here in Ephesians 4:11-13 Paul says that God has given the pastors, teachers, and evangelists to equip the church. Listen to them preach the Word. But doesn't stop there. It says it is the people in the church that is to do the work of the ministry. Your church doesn't just have the elders and pastors as ministers. No, every one of you is a minister of the gospel of Christ.

> **Ephesians 4:11-13** | And he gave the apostles, the prophets, the evangelists, the shepherds and teachers, [12] to equip the saints for the work of ministry, for building up the body of Christ, [13] until we all attain to the unity of the faith and of the knowledge of the Son of God, to mature manhood, to the measure of the stature of the fullness of Christ.

Get to know the people in your church. Do you know each other? Are you in each other's homes? Are you committed to this body of believers? God put you here not to sit and soak up the Word only, but to apply it to each other and speak the truth to each other in love.

Walk Worthy in Your Personal Life

So, the first realm where we exercise Christian maturity is the church. The second is in close earthly relationships. All close relationships will bring difficulty. In Ephesians 4:17 and following, Paul gives us the secret to growing and changing in Christ. This is the blazing center of the book of Ephesians. In Ephesians 4:17 says an unregenerate person cannot carry out the Christian life – "You must no longer walk as the Gentiles do, in the futility of their minds." Why? Because unsaved people (Gentiles):

- Have hearts that are hard like marble (4:18a),
- Are darkened in their understanding and alienated from the life of God (4:18b),
- They have given "themselves up to sensuality, greedy to practice every kind of impurity" (4:19)

You get the picture! Without Christ we are a mess! Those in Christ are totally equipped to live in holiness because we have been... (as 4:24 says, "created after the likeness of God in true righteousness and holiness."

Verse 25 has an important word: Therefore! Therefore, based on your regeneration in Christ, you can change! Look at the verses before:

Ephesians 4:22-23 | ...to put off your old self, which belongs to your former manner of life and is corrupt through deceitful desires, [23] and to be renewed in the spirit of your minds.

Worthy in Communication

Since you are indwelled a new nature in Christ, you can put away: lying (4:25), and sinful anger and holding grudges (4:26) – did you ever go to bed angry and wake up angry? Because you are regenerate in Christ, stop doing that. Don't give any opportunity for the devil to counsel you (4:27). Every time you choose to continue and live in sin, the devil is going to whisper in your ear a lot of hateful things. Count on it. Every time you hold a grudge and are not willing to forgive, you give Satan another opportunity to preach to you his message of hatred (4:28). The thief, if he is saved, should stop stealing. And when is a thief not a thief? When he merely stops stealing? *No.* When he starts working hard and starts to be generous, giving his money away to people in need!

God wants you to grow in Christ right now. You grow by replacing sinful habits with godly habits. Paul applies this to the area of communication. Paul says:

Ephesians 4:29 | Let no corrupting talk come out of your mouths, but only such as is good for building up, as fits the occasion, that it may give grace to those who hear.

Only 7% of our communication is words. 93% are attitudes, gestures, and facial expressions. Someone close to you could ask: "How are you" And you might say (happy attitude) "I'm doing just fine." Or you might say (sarcastic attitude, rolling eyes): "I'm doing just *fine*!" God wants to change you from the inside out – not just your words, but your heart, your attitudes – that the joy and peace of the Lord would be seen even on your face!

Paul gives finally gives us the secret to putting off bitterness and a lack of forgiveness. He gives the "Put off" principle in Ephesians 4:30-32. Put off bitterness, anger, wrath (grudge holding), etc. Bitterness is a cycle of craziness! You replay the insult of offence over and over again, but it doesn't help. Someone said, "Holding grudges and being bitter is like you drinking a bottle of poison and hoping the other person will die." Paul says put off these sinful ways of thinking, like bitterness. Take it off like a filthy garment. Take it outside the city gates and burn it in the garbage pile. Put off these things: bitterness, wrath – boiling over and calming down, anger – grudge holding, clamor – shouting, slander – personal blasphemy, malice – settled hatred against someone. You say, "How do I get rid of these toxic behaviors and emotions?" Paul tells us to be like Christ.

> **Ephesians 4:32** | Be kind to one another, tenderhearted, forgiving one another, as God in Christ forgave you.

Worthy in Holiness

Ephesians 5 begins with reminding us we need to be regenerated in order to experience meaningful change, and for the child of God, we have a new nature that ought to lead us to a life of holiness where we are "imitators of God" (5:1). We are no longer the same.

> **Ephesians 5:8** | For at one time you were darkness, but now you are light in the Lord. Walk as children of light (5:8).

You are a new creation. Live up to this transformation that has occurred in you.

Walk Worthy at Home and at Work

Only if you are regenerated can you live in the home with joy under God's established order. "Wives, submit to your husbands, as to Christ" (5:22) "Husbands, love your wives, as Christ loved the church and gave himself up for her" (5:25).

"Children, obey your parents in the Lord..." (6:1-4) We can only live according to God's order if we are regenerated! You can only have joy in the home if you are not hoping others around you will change. Stop trying to change those around you. Give up on trying to change your spouse. You need to change. Parents you cannot change your children. Plead with them that they will never change until they bow before Christ as Lord and Savior.

Paul then addresses slaves who lived in households. Over fifty percent of the Roman empire were brought into slavery mainly through debt, as prisoners of war, or sometimes through volunteering to be slaves, since living in a wealthy home with all your needs taken care of was desirable in the first century. His instructions to slaves, and really to all people employed whether free or slave is act as:

Ephesians 6:6-8 | ...bondservants of Christ, doing the will of God from the heart, ⁷ rendering service with a good will as to the Lord and not to man, ⁸ knowing that whatever good anyone does, this he will receive back from the Lord, whether he is a bondservant or is free.

Walk Worthy in the World

Finally, Paul says we need to "be strong" in the Spirit of God (6:10). We need to walk worthy of Christ in the world. How?

Ephesians 6:11-12 | Put on the whole armor of God, that you may be able to stand against the schemes of the devil. ¹² For we do not wrestle against flesh and blood, but against the rulers, against the authorities, against the cosmic powers over this present darkness, against the spiritual forces of evil in the heavenly places.

Your problem is not your boss. Your problem if you are married is not your spouse. It's not your parents. It's not the people in the world. Your battle is against Satan!

Paul says we need to walk worthy of Christ in the world. How? Put on the whole armor of God (6:10-18). Every piece of armor is related to the Word of God. If you want to change, you need to be in the word day and night. The gospel shoes, the belt of truth, the breastplate of righteousness, the helmet of salvation, the shield of faith, and the sword of the Spirit are all related to the Word of God. Get into the Word and you will grow and change. Don't just read it. Meditate on it. Apply it to your life. You can have all the knowledge of the Bible (Jas 3:13ff) and still have wisdom that is earthly, feelings-oriented, and demonic. No, apply the Word to your life, and you will grow. Pray through the Word. Pray the Psalms! Pray the promises of God. Pray the commands of God. Tell God you are not able, but he is.

This is how you grow and change. You must be regenerate. You must be in union with Christ or you will never joyfully serve Christ in the Spirit. You can carry out the commands and responsibilities of Scripture because of the life transforming change God brought you when you were born again.

Conclusion

How we want to grow in Christ! How can we stop from being "crawling butterflies" and start flying? Remember who you are in Christ. And then walk worthy of your calling. Let me close with 1

Thessalonians 5, which summarizes the hope of our sanctification and the theme of Ephesians:

> *1 Thessalonians 5:23-24* | Now may the God of peace himself sanctify you completely, and may your whole spirit and soul and body be kept blameless at the coming of our Lord Jesus Christ. ²⁴ He who calls you is faithful; he will surely do it.

Amen and amen!

1 | EPHESIANS 1:1-14

THE DESTINY OF THE CHURCH

Blessed be the God and Father of our Lord Jesus Christ, who has blessed us in Christ with every spiritual blessing in the heavenly places, even as he chose us in him before the foundation of the world.

EPHESIANS 1:3-4

What should be the direction and vision for a local assembly? What is our destiny? Alice in Wonderland came to a fork in the road. Icy panic stung her as she stood frozen by indecision. She lifted her eyes toward heaven, looking for guidance. Her eyes did not find God, only the Cheshire cat leering at her from his perch in the tree above. "Which way should I go?" blurted Alice. "That depends ..." said the cat, fixing a sardonic smile on the confused girl. "On what?" Alice managed to reply. "On your destination. Where are you going?" queried the Cheshire fiend. "I don't know ..." stammered Alice. "Then," said the cat, with grin spreading wider, "it doesn't matter." It matters to the Christian. Every Christian has a destiny in the kingdom of God. We are a pilgrim people, a people on the move—our destination matters. Where are we going as a church? It's important. The primary words of Ephesians 1 are "in Christ."

The epistle of the Ephesians was delivered by Tychicus to a number of churches (6:21) – the first being Laodicea and the final being

Ephesians. This is why some scholars consider this to be the letter Paul refers to as his letter to the Laodiceans, yet the epistle rightly bears the name "to the Ephesians".

God has his hand on his church. Jesus promised: "I will build my church, and the gates of hell will not prevail against it" (Mt 16:18). The church will continue until the end of time. One of the oldest products ever continually manufactured in the world is the Beretta firearm. They began production in 1526. The printing press was barely a decade old. But there is coming a day when Beretta will cease manufacturing. That is the day when Jesus comes. But there is never a day when the church will end. The church of Jesus Christ will last forever.

OUR DESTINY IS ETERNITY (1:1-3)

We have gone from "in Ephesus" to "in Christ." We have moved our citizenship from a temporary place to an eternal dwelling. It is the apostle Paul who helps the Ephesian believers how to have this eternal, enduring perspective.

> **Ephesians 1:1-2** | Paul, an apostle of Christ Jesus by the will of God, To the saints who are in Ephesus, and are faithful in Christ Jesus: ² Grace to you and peace from God our Father and the Lord Jesus Christ.

Paul was most certainly an apostle of Jesus by the will of God. Originally Saul of Tarsus, he had a dramatic conversion on the Damascus road. Saul, which is Paul's given name, was born into a Jewish family in Tarsus (Turkey) around the year AD 8; he was also a Roman citizen, a fact that would play a large role later in his life. Schooled as a Pharisee, he was a tent maker by trade, but was most noted for his hatred of Christians. He believed the teachings of Jesus violated the Mosaic Law and zealously harassed, and even jailed, anyone who followed those teachings.

The first scriptural mention of Saul is found in Acts 7:58, as he is a bystander watching his fellow Jews stone Stephen to death. An aggressive persecutor of Christians in Jerusalem, Saul sought and received permission from the high priest to proceed to Damascus for the purpose of imprisoning more followers of Christ. Most Christians know the story of what happened on the Damascus road: the bright light that knocked Saul down, the voice of Jesus, Saul's blindness and immediate response to the calling of Christ.

Saul's sudden change confused those around him, because he was known as one who hated Christians, who went about seeking them out to eliminate those individuals he genuinely considered as breaking Jewish law. Suddenly he was transformed from despising the followers of Jesus into fervently espousing the gospel of that same Jesus. No one could have anticipated this conversion; it is one of the great miracles of mankind.

Why would Jesus select the likes of Paul? There were certainly other devoted followers of Jesus available in those early days of the Church — followers ready to give their lives to proclaim Jesus Christ as savior of the world. But Jesus picked and converted this Pharisee, known as Saul, saying, "This man is a chosen instrument of mine to carry my name before Gentiles, kings and Israelites" (Acts 9:15). God selected this man who had a strong hatred of all Jesus stands for, a man who went into the houses of Christians and "dragging out men and women," then "handed them over for imprisonment" (Acts 8:3). This man became God's chosen instrument to spread the message of Jesus across the Middle East and parts of Europe. Why Saul? The answer is simple: grace! God chose to take someone totally undeserving, a "chief of sinners" to expand the kingdom of Jesus. Paul would end up writing thirteen New Testament books and ultimately sacrificing his life for Christ in AD 64 under the reign of Emperor Nero. It was worth it to Paul to give his life for a the message of grace and peace in Jesus.

An Eternal Citizenship

Through the grace and peace that this world cannot give, I have all that I need to remain faithful to Christ. Everyone that Paul was trying to reach was living in and for Ephesus. Here is a heathen city, just like the city of Nineveh—totally wicked and unregenerate—completely given over to idolatry and wickedness. By ancient standards, Ephesus was a mega-city of over 300,000 people. By comparison, the city of Rome was around two to four million in population. Ephesus was the capital city of the Roman province Asia Minor and the home of one of the Seven Wonders of the Ancient World: the temple of the goddess Diana. But now these former pagans in Ephesus were now in Christ.

We find in the book of Acts that Paul had labored among the Ephesians for three years—by far his longest time in one church (Acts 19; 20:31). The church was probably begun by Aquila and Pricilla (when they were kicked out of Rome with the rest of the Jews in AD 41), but it is Paul who labors among them and brings them together as a church—a unified body under Christ. Aquila and Pricilla would have ministered in Ephesus from AD 41 until Paul's arrival in AD 54, just before the Jews were permitted to return back to Rome under the reign of Nero in AD 54.

Paul would later hand the Ephesian church over to young Timothy after planting the church, and so when you read 1 and 2 Timothy, you are reading a letter originally intended for the Pastor of the Ephesian church who succeeded Paul. The apostle John is also traditionally held to be one of the later pastors at Ephesus (around AD 64 when Paul was beheaded).

An Eternal Holiness

The Ephesian church has such a rich history. Yet they were brought out of paganism. Look at what these former idol worshipping heathens are called in our text:

> **Ephesians 1:1** | Paul, an apostle of Christ Jesus by the will of God, To the saints who are in Ephesus, and are faithful in Christ Jesus.

Paul and the Ephesians are certainly a strange pair. It wasn't Paul's idea to be an apostle or the Ephesian pagans to be saints. But this strict Jew and these wild pagans had one thing in common – at one time they were lost, dead in their sins, without God. In Ephesus, everyone was faithful to Diana. She was the goddess of fertility. And there were many gods in the Roman empire. In your town, there are just as many gods. People serve work, or family, or money, or pleasure! But now these pagans were saints, or "holy ones". They were cleansed from their sins and made righteous in the sight of a holy God. Saints are not super Christians, such as in Roman Catholicism where you have to have performed miracles, etc. Every Christian is a saint. Paul was writing to ordinary people who had put their faith in Jesus, and because of that they were made holy and righteous as saints.

An Eternal Favor

The church is built on two gospel pillars of God's favor which Paul uses as a greeting: grace and peace.

> **Ephesians 1:2** | Grace to you and peace from God our Father and the Lord Jesus Christ.

Grace is God exercising his free pleasure to unworthy sinners. The principle of grace is found on every page of the Bible. Grace is the source and fountain of God's unmerited favor to wicked and defiled people who are worthy of nothing else but to be destroyed by God's wrath in the eternal refuse pile of hell, and yet God shows them free grace—it's God's pleasure to show you his favor. Grace is God giving you heaven, when all you deserve is condemnation. Grace has been called "favor you receive but to which you have no right or title in any shape or form, and of which you are entirely unworthy and undeserving."[4]

Charles Haddon Spurgeon said, "Grace is the free favor of God, the undeserved bounty of the ever-gracious Creator against whom we have offended. Grace is the generous pardon, the infinite, spontaneous loving-kindness of the God who has been provoked and angered by our sin, but who, delighting in mercy, and grieving to smite the creatures whom he has made, is ever ready to pass by transgression, iniquity, and sin, and to save his people from all the evil consequences of their guilt."[5]

Paul introduces grace here in the very beginning of his letter, but he spends the rest of chapters applying it to our daily struggles against sin and self and to our most intimate relationships in life. Paul never just presents theological truths about God—no, Biblical truth arrives in action. So many times we talk about grace in this "happy-go-lucky," nonchalant, superficially sweet tone. No, grace is known by those who smell the battlefield. Grace is known by those who fight for righteousness. They are crucified to the world and crucified to self. Grace is a living, breathing, transforming principle that makes its mark on every area of our lives. Truth is alive.

Paul also greets the Ephesians with peace. Peace in its very essence is a reconciliation. This reconciliation is not invented by man, but by designed God. The idea is a bringing together of a man at war with God restored to a right relationship. The man has stopped fighting. And yet, this peace does not merely mean "cessation of war, rest, and quiet."[6] Surely it means that, but that's not all it means. It's not that we've

---

[4] D. Martyn Lloyd-Jones. *God's Ultimate Purpose: An Exposition of Ephesians 1* (Grand Rapids, MI: Baker Books, 1978), 37.

[5] Charles Haddon Spurgeon. *Metropolitan Tabernacle Pulpit, 3115*. 506.

[6] Lloyd-Jones. *Ephesians 1*, 17.

simply stopped fighting against God. The actual idea in the Greek language is "a union after a separation,"[7] i.e., reconciliation.

God calls us rebels to put down our weapons and be united to Christ. Perhaps you are fighting him right now. Recognize this natural aggression in your own heart. It exists most obviously in the lost person, but it still remains in the saved person. God calls us to put down our weapons. It's time for surrender. Come to Jesus with a broken heart. Come to the Lord bleeding and wounded, ready to be brought into a renewed relationship with him. Christ will give you peace. If you have peace with God, you have something the world cannot touch. The stock market may crash, but you are reconciled. Tragedy strikes, but you are redeemed. Bankruptcy, sickness, poverty, persecution, all these things come upon us, but we have a clean conscience. We are right with God. And no one and nothing can take that away. This is what God has done.

An Eternal Blessing

Our ultimate blessing is not sought after in this world's fame, fortune, or favorability, but in Christ. All in Christ are blessed with every kind of spiritual blessing through Jesus. We have so much to praise God for.

> **Ephesians 1:3** | Blessed be the God and Father of our Lord Jesus Christ, who has blessed us in Christ with every spiritual blessing in the heavenly places.

Christians Bless God

Praise is the mark of true Christianity. We are always praising God, because God's work in the heart always makes its way to our lips. We are genuine Christians. Christians may never be happy in circumstances, but they are always happy in God. They are always saying, "Blessed be the God and Father of our Lord Jesus Christ." Can you say that in your life right now? Vital, living Christianity is always marked by *praise*! This is the starkest contrast between the children of heaven and the children of hell. Paul says that one of the primary marks of those who are unregenerate, in Romans 1:21, is that they are not "thankful." Do you find yourself fighting against the message today, hanging on to bitter thoughts? Come to Christ, and he will sweeten your

---

[7] Ibid., 37.

soul with praise. Praise is not just a sentimental response to God; it is a command. "Rejoice in the Lord always, and again I say, rejoice" (Phil 4:4). All true Christians will have a happy spirit in God.

In our English translation, verses 3 through 14 are stretched out over several sentences, but when Paul wrote this, it was one sentence of over 200 Greek words! Paul is brimming over with powerful words in trying to describe all the spiritual blessings we have in Christ, and it is as if he almost gets lost in his praise. Each word is bursting with meaning, and it is all one long continuous thought. This is doctrine that fills our hearts with praise! So after the doctrine of verses 1 and 2, we see nothing but doxology. Doxology is our response to doctrine! This is an important point: you and I have not truly understood doctrine, until it results in doxology!

It is so clear in this text that our pleasure comes by blessing God. We should bless God, because God has created us to praise him. We are created to reflect God's glory. You need to come to the realization in your life that the only way you are going to find true happiness, is if you find your happiness and pleasure in pleasing God. Man's chief end, the reason God created us, is to glorify God and to enjoy him forever.

Christians are Blessed by God

It was God's design to "bless us in Christ with every spiritual blessing in the heavenly places." We are blessed specifically "in Christ." Those who are in Christ Jesus have lives filled with God's blessings, with all the good gifts from God. If there is anything good in your life, God alone produced it! God's blessings come from his sovereign hand! He is the Strategist, the Designer, and the Engineer of our salvation! All that is good about our life, our past, our present, our future—we can attribute it all to God! This also means that everything you could possibly need to live out the Christian life, you already have if you are in Christ. Let me encourage you, that however little or much you have, you are blessed in Christ! You have all you need to please God and more than you need to bless God.

We are blessed "in heavenly places." As Christians we live a "paradoxical, two-level existence—a dual citizenship. While we remain on earth, we are citizens of earth. But in Christ our primary and infinitely more important citizenship is in heaven. Christ is our Lord and King, and we are citizens of his realm, the heavenly places."[8] Fix your eyes on the author and finisher of our faith. Let us live, not like we're going to be here forever, but like we're going to be there forever, as you live like that then you will experience the fullness and the richness of all the blessings that you have in Christ.

This verse does not say that God blesses us, but that he "has blessed us." The idea is that it is already fulfilled—it is accomplished. It is a moment, an event, a point on the horizon line of history. It's already taken place. All that we need in this life, we will find in what Christ has already given us in our salvation. He is all we need for the here and the now. It's all accomplished. Everything we need to live was given to us when God called us to faith in Christ. It's done!

2 Peter 1:3 tells us that God's "divine power has given unto us all things that pertain to life and godliness." It is not that God *will* give us "all things pertaining to life and godliness," but that he has *already* given them to us. God has already blessed us with "all spiritual blessings in heavenly places." Our resources in God are not simply *promised*; but they are in actuality already *possessed*. So, God cannot give us more than his Son. Are you saved? Is the Son of God your all? You don't need to receive something more, but you need to do more with what you already have.

God has blessed us "with *all* spiritual blessings." We have to ask ourselves the question—how are we blessed with *all* spiritual blessings? How far do these blessings go? Paul in the rest of this chapter gives a survey of the multitude of blessings we have—and we have all of them: election, adoption, redemption, sanctification, forgiveness, and resurrection in Christ—if you get a hold of these blessings, they'll change your life!! And no blessing is left out—all that God has promised has been secured by Christ, so that at this moment we have all we need to be all that Christ wants us to be.

OUR DESTINY IS SANCTITY (1:4-6)

God promises that whoever he justifies, he is predestined to be conformed to the image of his Son (Rom 8:28-29). Theologians call this the doctrine of sanctification. This is exactly what Paul teaches the Ephesians. We are chosen in Christ to become like Christ.

---

[8] John F. MacArthur Jr., *Ephesians*, MacArthur New Testament Commentary (Chicago: Moody Press, 1986), 9.

Chosen in Christ

Ephesians 1:4a | ...even as he chose us in him before the foundation of the world...

God has chosen us. This speaks of the doctrine of election. Before you were born, before your father or mother, before the creation of the universe, God chose you.

When I was younger, I moved from Chicago to Louisiana. I was the strange city boy. I can remember a game of stick ball on the playground, and I was the last one picked. God doesn't choose us because of anything in us. It is because of his goodness and glory he chooses us. Remember the words of Jesus: "Fear not, little flock; for it is your Father's good pleasure to give you the kingdom" (Lk 12:32). It is according to his kind will that he chose you.

We come to what has been called the eternal counsel of redemption. We have often called it God's plan of salvation. There was a counsel, a plan, a compact in eternity past. This verse brings us there into the mind of God before the creation of the world. At that time, God had a plan to create man. And he knew that once he created human beings that they would fall—they would sin against him—they would be cut off from him. God knew that. In eternity past he planned the way, and how we would be purchased back and be forgiven and redeemed. And there was a counsel in eternity past, and the Father and the Son and the Holy Spirit, all one God, three distinct personalities, equal members of the Godhead, met as it were together to determine how men and women would be saved and forgiven. And they agreed together; they made a compact together.

We are chosen in Christ. Christ for his part would in due time enter into this world, put on a robe of humanity, and suffer and die for them, take the punishment that they deserved for all eternity because of their rebellion against God and because of sin—he would purchase these people from the slave market of sin. He would be their representative. He would by his grace grant them faith and repentance. So based on all those conditions, the Father made an agreement to give these people to the Son. And the Son therefore came and suffered and died for them. He substituted himself for them and paid an immeasurable price.

Chosen for Holiness

Ephesians 1:4 | ...even as he chose us in him before the foundation of the world, that we should be holy and blameless before him.

God has chosen us not just to be saved from the penalty of sin, but to live free from the power of sin here and now in holiness. Holiness means to be "separated, set apart" for God's special purposes. We are called saints. Holy ones. We are not chosen to be taken out of this world but elect in Christ for a life of holiness in this wicked world (1:4-6). The Bible is full of assurances that all who are "in Christ" are chosen by God. We are chosen to be inwardly holy and outwardly blameless. He accomplishes the outworking of our holiness through the indwelling Holy Spirit (Eze 36:25-27; Phil 2:12-13).

1 Thessalonians 5:24 | He who calls you is faithful; he will surely do it.

Isaiah 41:9-10 | You whom I took from the ends of the earth, and called from its farthest corners, saying to you, "You are my servant, I have chosen you and not cast you off"; [10] fear not, for I am with you; be not dismayed, for I am your God; I will strengthen you, I will help you, I will uphold you with my righteous right hand.

Romans 8:28-29 | And we know that for those who love God all things work together for good, for those who are called according to his purpose. [29] For those whom he foreknew he also predestined to be conformed to the image of his Son.

Jude 24-25 | Now to him who is able to keep you from stumbling and to present you blameless before the presence of his glory with great joy, [25] to the only God, our Savior, through Jesus Christ our Lord, be glory, majesty, dominion, and authority, before all time and now and forever. Amen.

Philippians 1:6 | And I am sure of this, that he who began a good work in you will bring it to completion at the day of Jesus Christ.

2 Thessalonians 2:13 | God chose you as the firstfruits to be saved, through sanctification by the Spirit and belief in the truth.

Ephesians 2:10 | For we are his workmanship, created in Christ Jesus for good works, which God prepared beforehand, that we should walk in them.

1 Corinthians 1:8-9 | God will sustain you to the end, guiltless in the day of our Lord Jesus Christ. God is faithful, by whom you were called into the fellowship of his Son, Jesus Christ our Lord.

You may live in the sin-city of Chicago, but you are chosen, set apart, separated unto God among his people for his purposes. We not only have justification; we also have sanctification. God does not simply justify you (give you a right standing before him); it is his will that you would be experiencing holiness and blamelessness here. Not sinlessness—but blamelessness. Those whom God has chosen, he's given them his Spirit, from the time they believed to the time they are delivered into glory, there is a work called sanctification that is going on in the lives of everyone whom the Lord has justified. And that work of sanctification is the Lord progressively changing you for the rest of your life more and more into the image of his Son. We are not only a changed people—praise be to God—we are a changing people. He changed me when he saved me, and he's changing me today, and he'll be changing me for the rest of my life because I have not arrived, I never will arrive until the day comes that I'm glorified and with the Lord forever. So the rest of my time on this earth is going to be a time of growing. It's a time of being in the school of Christ, it's a time of being purified, it's a time of the Lord changing me more and more into the image of his dear Son and my Savior. That's Christian growth, and that's what the Lord is doing in the life of every person that he's chosen, once he's saved them and brought them to faith in Christ.

Chosen for Adoption

The god of this world is no longer our father. God has brought us to himself and made us his children! The highest expression of God's love in the universe is that he would give us the adoption of sons so that all the rights and privileges won by Christ would be ours. "Behold, what manner of love the Father has bestowed upon us, that we should be called the children of God" (1 Jn 3:1).

Ephesians 1:5a | In love [5] he predestined us for adoption to himself as sons through Jesus Christ...

Adoption in Paul's day would happen when the head of a family would adopt a son (often a grown man) in order to pass on the family name and inheritance.[9] Often this would occur by going to the slave market to pay the purchase-price in order to release them from their bondage.[10] Once the slave was purchased, adoption could take place.

Adoption for the Christian means that the true and living God, the Creator of the heavens and the earth, by grace has made believers members of his family with all the rights and responsibilities that go with that status (Rom 8:14-17, 23, 29; Gal 3:25-4:7; 1 Jn 1:12, 3:1). Do you understand that we are God's dear children? This did not happen by our natural birth. I have had a mother and a father on this earth, and how grateful I am for them, but they themselves gave me no right to be called into God's family. It is only by the divine purpose and plan of God that I have been born into God's family! I am a child of God, not just by creation, but by regeneration, and through my adoption I now have all the rights and privileges of a child of God. I'm a joint-heir with Christ (Rom 8:17)

It was always God's plan to bring you into his family as an adopted son or daughter. Predestination speaks of God's plan. This is something God has intended. In other words, God has a plan in every event that comes to pass. He has a pattern for every thread on the fabric of history. He has destined all things that come to pass. This plan is referred to in this verse as *"predestination."* It is *"pre"* because God lives outside of time and before time. If God intends something, it must come to pass—it is automatically destined through his omnipotence. God knows all things, and he has always known all things. It is not that God predicts all things, but he predestines them. He is the cause of all things that come to pass. This is what in this verse is called predestination. Listen to Spurgeon explain: "Predestination is both a doctrine of Scripture and of common sense that whatever God does in time he planned to do in eternity."[11] In other words, predestination is simply the architectural plan of history. It is the plan that God formed before time, the blueprint of history. In a more personal way we can say, like Jeremiah, before I was born, God chose me for his family, his plan, and his purposes (Jer 1:5).

---

[9] Bryan Chapell, *Ephesians* (Phillipsburg, NJ: P & R Publishers, 2009), 25.

[10] R. C. Sproul, *The Purpose of God: Ephesians* (Scotland: Christian Focus Publications, 1994), 27.

[11] Charles H. Spurgeon. *Adoption*. Sermon delivered on Sunday evening February 10, 1861.

The wonderful truth of adoption is that because of your faith in Christ, you are adopted into God's forever family and now have all the rights and privileges of a true child of God. When the Father looked upon his Son at Jesus' baptism, he said, "This is my beloved Son in whom I am well pleased" (Mt 3:17). Because of adoption, this is now what he says about you.

To add to this, the grace you receive in adoption includes an inheritance. You are an heir of God and a co-heir with Jesus. All things are yours because of Christ. As God's child, you are pitied, protected, provided for and disciplined as a true child of God. You can stray, but God will always track you down. He will never leave or forsake you (Heb 13:5). The unrelenting covenant love (*hesed*) described throughout the Old Testament that God has for Israel is now yours.

Chosen for the Praise of His Glorious Grace

There was nothing in us that made us appeal to God. In fact, we were rebels in his sight. We were dead in trespasses and sins—his enemies. Yet it was God's highest pleasure to adopt us. One of the most important doctrines in Scripture is that of God's sovereign pleasure. His sovereign pleasure is what makes him God. God had our adoption in mind when he created the world. It was the best thing that God could do. It was his highest pleasure to do it.

> **Ephesians 1:5b-6** | ...according to the purpose of his will, **6** to the praise of his glorious grace, with which he has blessed us in the Beloved.

God elected us in order that he might give us all the blessings and benefits of adoption. That we, the vilest sinners on the face of God's earth, would be the sons and daughters of the living God and have all the rights and privileges of God's children. And what we find out in this verse, is that it is God's purpose for our lives to incessantly praise God. That we would live lives that do nothing but praise God and that we would live lives that do nothing but draw attention to the greatness and majesty and glory of God.

One thing that unleashes God's grace in our lives is the realization of our own unworthiness. That is grace. We are shamefully dirty people compared to God's righteous and holy character. We are unworthy to be breathing God's air at this moment. We deserve only the deepest miseries that only an omnipotent God could deliver to such wretched creatures. Words cannot describe our wretchedness in God's sight.

Only an everlasting hell can demonstrate the fierceness and violent hatred God has for those who continually defy him. John Bunyan said:

> Sin is the dare of God's justice. Sin is the rape of God's mercy. It is the jeer of his patience, the slight of his power and the contempt of his love.[12]

Anything God is pleased with is founded on the work that Jesus Christ, the beloved Son of God accomplished of his own free will and pleasure. All that is good comes from the beloved Son Jesus Christ. Five times in Scripture, God the Father reveals his supreme pleasure. He proclaims from his throne in Heaven: "This is my beloved Son in whom I am well pleased" (Mt 3:17, 17:5; Mk 9:7; Lk 9:35; 2 Pet 1:17). God is satisfied, utterly happy and content in the person of his Son. He delights in him (*cf* Psa 2).

Christians who lived in the time of the Reformation had a Latin phrase that summarized our purpose for living: *Soli Deo Gloria*—God's glory alone. That is all that matters. We have one burning and shining purpose dear brethren – that we would live to the glory of God demonstrated only in the grace of Jesus Christ. You cannot rightly glorify God in any way unless you know the grace of Christ in your own soul. God is not pleased with any one of us in and of ourselves. God has one only in whom he is pleased—that is his beloved Son. This text tells us that we are blessed in the Beloved. God's grace is found in Jesus, God's mighty Son and our mighty Savior—God's grace is the only thing that we can grasp that will bring God glory through our lives!

OUR DESTINY IS LIBERTY (1:7-10)

We have gone from being in slavery to sin, to freedom in Christ.

Ephesians 1:7a | In him we have redemption through his blood...

We come now to the centerpiece of the entire Bible. All throughout the Old Testament, God promised a redeemer. God promised to send Christ. It is clear from the Scripture that the Redeemer of mankind is the same in all ages. Redemption in Jesus Christ is the scarlet thread of the Bible. In the Old Testament He was called the Seed of the woman, the Prophet, the Seed of Abraham, the Son of David, the Branch, the Servant of the Lord, the Ancient of Days, the Great King, the Holy One

---

[12] John Bunyan. *Works, Volume 1*, ed. Henry Sebbing (London: John Hirst, 1861), 228. Note: the quote is paraphrased and shortened.

of Israel, the Sun of Righteousness, the Prince of Peace, and the God of the whole earth. In the New Testament, we see that God fulfills all His promises, and the Word becomes flesh, and his name shall be called Jesus "for he shall save his people from their sins" (Mt 1:21).

All of the sacrifices of the Old Testament foreshadow what we see in this verse. All the Old Testament prophets "searched and inquired carefully, [11] inquiring what person or time the Spirit of Christ in them was indicating when he predicted the sufferings of Christ and the subsequent glories" (1 Pet 1:10-11). When we come to this verse, it is as if all the angels in heaven were peering through the clouds in anticipation—Abraham and Moses, Isaiah and Ezekiel—they all anticipated this *redemption*. Job said: "For I know that my redeemer lives, and that he shall stand at the latter day upon the earth" (Job 19:25).

The word redemption in our text means "to purchase something from the marketplace, and also to loosen or set free from bondage and slavery".[13] The term is used of freeing from chains, slavery, or prison. In the theological context, the term "redemption" indicates a freeing from the slavery of sin, the ransom or price paid for freedom. This idea is often used in the Gospels, which speak of Christ who came "to give his life as a ransom for many" (Mt 20:28; Mk 10:45).[14]

During New Testament times the Roman Empire had as many as six million slaves, and the buying and selling of them was a major business. If a person wanted to free a loved one or a friend who was a slave, he would buy that slave for himself, and then grant him freedom, testifying to the deliverance with a written certificate.[15]

This word "redemption" is used to designate the freeing of a slave in that way. It is an emancipation—a setting free from the slave master of sin. Redemption is Christ purchasing freedom for us with his own blood on the Cross. We are locked up in the shackles of sin, and Christ frees us, by buying our freedom through his own substitution. He paid the redemption price to buy for himself sinners who would make up his church—his elect people. "[Jesus] entered the Most Holy Place once for all by his own blood, having obtained eternal redemption" (Heb 9:12b).

---

[13] John H. Sailhamer, Tremper Longman, and David E. Garland, *The Expositor's Bible Commentary, Volume 10* (Grand Rapids, MI: Zondervan, 2017), 461.

[14] Walter A. Elwell and Barry J. Beitzel, "Redeemer, Redemption," *Baker Encyclopedia of the Bible* (Grand Rapids, MI: Baker Book House, 1988), 1827.

[15] MacArthur. *Ephesians*, 18.

That ransom sets us, the people of God, free from the *penalty* and *power* of sin, and one day we will be free even from the very *presence* of sin!

Free from the Penalty of Sin

God provides redemption in Christ in order to wipe out the record of our sin. Christ gives his blood as the payment price to buy us from the bondage sin. This speaks of our justification.

> **Ephesians 1:7b** | In him we have redemption through his blood, the forgiveness of our trespasses...

He walks right into the shopping center of the world – into the slave market. And as it was in New Testament times, he goes to this place where the slaves are—these people that had been conquered or had been in debt. But Christ goes to the spiritual slave market where all of us are in bondage to sin with an impossible debt to pay, and he substitutes his life for us. He pays the price of that slavery with his blood. Christ gave his blood to redeem us from the bondage, the guilt, the enslaving power, consequences, and the effects of sin. He has even redeemed our bodies so that when he comes again, we will receive a perfect, glorified body, free from the bondage of sin.

The liberty we have from the massive price Jesus paid is the forgiveness of our trespasses. By nature, we are enslaved to sin. Over and over, we break God's law. God's justice cries out for our condemnation. But Christ's blood cries out for our forgiveness. Because of Christ's payment, we are now free from the penalty of sin. "There is now therefore no condemnation for those who are in Christ Jesus" (Rom 8:1). No one can accuse us any longer. The only thing for us to do is rejoice.

> *Romans 5:1-2* | Therefore, since we have been justified by faith, we have peace with God through our Lord Jesus Christ. ² Through him we have also obtained access by faith into this grace in which we stand, and we rejoice in hope of the glory of God.

John Calvin said, in preaching on this very text from Ephesians 1:7 in Geneva in 1558, "God puts our sins out of his remembrance and drowns them in the depths of the sea, and, moreover, receives the payment that was offered him in the person of his only Son."[16]

---

[16] John Calvin, *Commentaries on the Epistles of Paul to the Galatians and Ephesians* (Bellingham, WA: Logos Bible Software, 2010), 202.

Free from the Poverty of Sin

Not only has God removed the penalty and cleansed us by his grace. While before we were swimming in sin, now we are swimming in grace. Before we were poor wretches, unable to pay for the great debt of sin, but now we are enriched with God's grace.

> **Ephesians 1:7c-8a** | ...according to the riches of his grace, **8** which he lavished upon us.

Our trespasses that once characterized us have been wiped away. We are clean, washed, forgiven. In the place of our sin is lavished the perfect riches of Christ's righteousness, rewards and inheritance. It's all ours in Christ. We who were once poor in sin are now rich in faith.

Free from the Power of Sin

God's grace was poured out upon us in all wisdom and insight. Our once fallen minds were renewed by the power of the Holy Spirit working faith in our minds. This speaks of our sanctification when we grow in wisdom and insight to know his purpose and his will each day for our lives.

> **Ephesians 1:8b-9** | ...in all wisdom and insight **9** making known to us the mystery of his will, according to his purpose, which he set forth in Christ.

Before we were justified, our broken wills were utterly subject to the power of sin. We chose sin at every turn. Even when we made choices that appeared good from an external standpoint, because we had no higher internal purpose than to glorify self these choices were ultimately sinful as well. Now, the power of sin is broken. We have been given the deposit of the Holy Spirit.

Our spirit has been united with the Holy Spirit (Eze 36:26-17) who now causes us to "walk in his statutes and keep his judgments." All was hidden because of the corruption of sin in the human heart. We were unable to see God clearly, only wanting to "suppress the truth in unrighteousness" (Rom 1:20). We were enemies of God, fighting against his constant appeal to us. "All day long" he spread his arms out to us, but we kept rejecting him (Isa 65:2). But there came a day when he made known to us the mystery of his will.

His purpose, which he set forth in Christ was to renew the whole creation, beginning with the minds and hearts of his people. This great redemption was set forth from the beginning. Abraham would bless all nations through Christ who would be born through his family lineage. The blessing of Abraham, through Christ, is to be renewed to our original holiness by the power of the blessed Holy Spirit. In Christ you are no longer a slave to sin. God's grace is also his empowerment.

> *Romans 6:6–14* | We know that our old self was crucified with him in order that the body of sin might be brought to nothing, so that we would no longer be enslaved to sin. [7] For one who has died has been set free from sin. [8] Now if we have died with Christ, we believe that we will also live with him. [9] We know that Christ, being raised from the dead, will never die again; death no longer has dominion over him. [10] For the death he died he died to sin, once for all, but the life he lives he lives to God. [11] So you also must consider yourselves dead to sin and alive to God in Christ Jesus. [12] Let not sin therefore reign in your mortal body, to make you obey its passions. [13] Do not present your members to sin as instruments for unrighteousness, but present yourselves to God as those who have been brought from death to life, and your members to God as instruments for righteousness. [14] For sin will have no dominion over you, since you are not under law but under grace.

Transformative wisdom and insight are gifts of the Holy Spirit that empower us to live a holy life, free from the domination of sin. It is not God's will for any of his children to live in sin of any kind. He will bring about whatever it takes to make his children holy so that they might daily die to sin, renew their minds, and learn to keep in step with the Holy Spirit. God will most definitely accomplish this in every single one of his people, though it will always be a very imperfect process (Phil 1:6).

God's will and plan of salvation was such a mystery until Christ came. The Old Testament saints could not have comprehended the substitutionary atonement of Christ and his resurrection with the clarity we have, yet it was all there in the ceremonies, prophecies, and in the Psalms and poetry. His salvation is also naturally hidden from the natural or unregenerate heart, which is from birth hostile to God (Psa 58:3). Also, the idea of the Gentiles being grafted into Israel as "one new humanity" was also a great mystery. All who are in Christ can now understand the mystery of salvation through the wisdom and insight that comes through the Spirit. No longer is our mind totally depraved. We have the light and insight of the Spirit.

1 Corinthians 2:12-14 | Now we have received not the spirit of the world, but the Spirit who is from God, that we might understand the things freely given us by God. [13] And we impart this in words not taught by human wisdom but taught by the Spirit, interpreting spiritual truths to those who are spiritual. [14] The natural person does not accept the things of the Spirit of God, for they are folly to him, and he is not able to understand them because they are spiritually discerned.

Because of sin, man is blinded, and Christ, his kingdom, and his plan are all a mystery. The significance of who Christ is as Creator and Savior is all a gigantic *blind spot* for every unregenerate person in this world. Christ is a mystery to lost people. Oh, they can understand the historical figure in a historical context. What they cannot do is see Christ for who he is, as the Son of God, the Creator of the world, and the only mediator between God and man. The person and work of Christ is a mystery to the lost person. They do not understand Jesus Christ, for if they did, they would let go of all their worldly aspirations, repent of their sins, and follow him. The Father in heaven revealed the wisdom of Christ to Peter, and so he can reveal this wisdom to us.

Matthew 16:15-17 | Jesus said to his disciples, "But who do you say that I am?" [16] Simon Peter replied, "You are the Christ, the Son of the living God." [17] And Jesus answered him, "Blessed are you, Simon Bar-Jonah! For flesh and blood has not revealed this to you, but my Father who is in heaven.

We give glory to God that through the Word and the Spirit, lost people can receive God's grace and have the wisdom and insight of the Spirit lavished upon them that they might turn this mystery of his salvation and miracle of salvation.

Free from the Presence of Sin

The plan of God is to remove sin from all creation and unite all things in Christ, so that there will be perfect unity and harmony with all sentient beings in heaven and earth. This verse refers to our glorification, when the very presence of sin will cease forever.

Ephesians 1:10 | ... as a plan for the fullness of time, to unite all things in him, things in heaven and things on earth.

The redeemed see that a new order is coming. Sin will be no more. One day we will be completely set free. We will be set free from sin and sorrow. The former things will soon pass away. All creation is moving toward its consummation in him, as described in by Paul in Romans.

> *Romans 8:19–21* | The creation waits in eager expectation for the sons of God to be revealed ... the creation itself will be liberated from its bondage to decay and brought into the glorious freedom of the children of God.

Thus, all redeemed souls, all the universe, and all the faithful angelic hosts — literally everything in heaven and on earth — everything material, everything spiritual, everything within, without, above, and below — will be united in Christ. This is the blessing of the universe! It is this day that all creation is groaning for: a day when we shall all be set free from the very presence of sin.

We will fight to grow in holiness our entire lives while we live on this sin cursed earth. But when we have run the race and fought the good fight, we will enter into the presence of the Lord forever. We will be glorified. In his presence, our soul rest will at last be complete, as sin and its devastation will cease to assail us. There can be no evil in his presence. Though now we are surrounded on all sides by sinfulness, though now sin continues to cling to our hearts, on a day not too distant we will go to a place where sin is no more. In our glorification we will at last be granted freedom from the very presence of sin. Our glorification is coming. It is the day we trade the persistent presence of sin for the perfect presence of the Lord. We *will be saved* from sin's presence.

OUR DESTINY IS GUARANTEED (1:11-14)

We see three guarantees in these verses that display God's ownership of us: his sovereignty, his Word, and his Spirit.

Guaranteed by God's Sovereignty

God's sovereign plan of salvation carries on in both the Old and New Testament peoples. They are actually one people of God who have been chosen by the sheer sovereign love of God. It was the infinite heart of God that led him to control all events in a way that would bring salvation to humanity and bring glory to himself. Jonathan Edwards was greatly comforted by God's control of all things, so much that he wrote:

The doctrine has often appeared exceedingly pleasant, bright, and sweet. Absolute sovereignty is what I love to ascribe to God.[17]

It is this teaching that Paul so clearly expressed in his letter to the Ephesians.

> **Ephesians 1:11** | In him we have obtained an inheritance, having been predestined according to the purpose of him who works all things according to the counsel of his will.

By the sovereign plan of God, Christians have obtained an inheritance. Here, inheritance is another word for our salvation. An inheritance is obviously something you did not earn. And our salvation is totally and completely earned by Jesus Christ. Your heaven is not earned by your works, your baptism, your faithfulness to the activities to this church, your family, or any earthly connections you have. Salvation is an inheritance. It is utterly and thoroughly *free* and given by God's sovereign mercy and love.

God's plan for us is personal—it is part of a larger plan that includes the entire universe of God's creation. This plan not only includes absolutely all things that ever take place in heaven, on earth, and in hell; past, present, and even future—this plan pertains to believers and unbelievers, angels and demons, all-natural processes like hurricanes, tornadoes, tsunamis. God controls every molecule on earth and ever molecule in the universe. Everything is his. It all belongs to him. The Mississippi runs down stream because God fastened it that way before the world began. If you stepped in a puddle this morning, God predestined that puddle to be there. The guiding principle of God's sovereignty in salvation is his love and mercy toward totally undeserving sinners.

There is also here a beautiful and interesting distinction of pronouns between verses 11 and 13. He speaks of the Jews (we have... been predestined, vs 11) and then the Gentiles, (but you...when you heard...the gospel...believed in him, vs 13). What a delight to see God's predestination of the Jews so gloriously present in the New Testament. In all of their rebellion, he chose to love them and treat them as his own dear children. Certainly, he had to send them to foreign nations in captivity for many years. When they returned, it seems they were entirely

---

[17] Jonathan Edwards. *The Works of Jonathan Edwards, Volume 1*, ed. Edward Hickman (Edinburgh: The Banner of Truth Trust, 1974), xii, xiii.

free from the pagan idols. And now that Christ has come, God's plan has worked all things according to the counsel of his own will. This plan has united Jew and Gentile in Christ. Paul is celebrating the miracle of the salvation and union in Christ which Jews and Gentiles share. This is a miracle to which he will give full exposition in 2:11–22.[18]

The chosen people of Israel were not chosen because of anything in them. They were not more holy, more numerous, or more distinguished than any other nation. Moses tells the people in Deuteronomy,

> *Deuteronomy 7:6–7* | The Lord your God has chosen you out of all the peoples on the face of the earth to be his people, his treasured possession. The Lord did not set his affection on you and choose you because you were more numerous than other peoples, for you were the fewest.

> *Deuteronomy 9:5–7* | It is not because of your righteousness or integrity that ... the Lord your God is giving you this good land to possess, for you are a stiff-necked people. Remember this and never forget how you provoked the Lord your God to anger in the desert.

So it is that no Gentile was ever chosen because of any righteous characteristic. All are chosen, both Jew and Gentile, out of God's tender-hearted mercies. Therefore, no one has anything to boast in except in Christ. This was Paul's emphasis whenever he spoke of the Christian's election and calling.

> *1 Corinthians 1:26–31* | Consider your calling, brothers: not many of you were wise according to worldly standards, not many were powerful, not many were of noble birth. [27] But God chose what is foolish in the world to shame the wise; God chose what is weak in the world to shame the strong; [28] God chose what is low and despised in the world, even things that are not, to bring to nothing things that are, [29] so that no human being might boast in the presence of God. [30] And because of him you are in Christ Jesus, who became to us wisdom from God, righteousness and sanctification and redemption, [31] so that, as it is written, "Let the one who boasts, boast in the Lord."

Guaranteed by God's Word

Ephesians 1:12-13a | ...so that we who were the first to hope in Christ might be to the praise of his glory. [13] In him you also, when you

---

[18] R. Kent Hughes, *Ephesians: The Mystery of the Body of Christ*, Preaching the Word (Wheaton, IL: Crossway Books, 1990), 39–41.

heard the word of truth, the gospel of your salvation, and believed in him...

The Jews who first heard the Word and put their trust in Christ for salvation have a testimony that is to the praise of God's glory. Something that we have to understand when we look at the Scriptures is that in order to be a Christian you have to hear the word of truth and believe. This word of truth that is being spoken of is the gospel. In order to be saved, the Jews, who were the first to hope in Christ, had to respond to the good news that Jesus Christ substituted himself for their sins. Anyone who fully surrenders to the gospel that saves will be born again. We know that Romans 1:16 is true – the gospel is the power unto salvation. This gospel is what saves: the blood of Christ! You cannot be saved by anything that you can do or have done. Nothing but Christ. We must understand that even though we heard and believed it wasn't our work. Jesus makes it clear in John 6:29 that it is the work of God for us to believe the one that was sent. This idea is clear from the context when Paul writes that God chose us before the foundations of the earth (1:4). Our salvation, Israel's salvation, from beginning to end, was the work of God. The way God does this is through hearing his word, specifically the gospel of your salvation as the Holy Spirit acts to transform our hearts. Simply put, God's Word, applied by God's Spirit brings about salvation. This is all to the praise of his glory among all peoples, Jews or Gentiles, that the Word engenders faith.

Guaranteed by God's Spirit

Ephesians 1:13 | In him you also, when you heard the word of truth, the gospel of your salvation, and believed in him, were sealed with the promised Holy Spirit.

God himself lives inside of you. You have it better than Moses who met with God at the burning bush and at the Tent of Meeting. You have it better than all the high priests of the Old Testament that entered into the Holy of holies. We have God in us. His Spirit has sealed us, and through him we have power over sin and assurance and hunger for the Word of God and deep hope for the world that Jesus will bring in when he returns. Until then, the Scripture says we are sealed with the promised Holy Spirit.

What is Sealing?

This idea of sealing comes from what a King used to do to document hundreds and thousands of years ago. The King would melt wax on a scroll of some sort of document and he would put his signet ring on it to seal it. This is what is being spoken of here. Now there are three reasons for this sealing.

With the king if someone had gotten a document with a law they didn't just go through with it unless it was really from the king that's why the seal proved this. Our seal states that God has said that we have eternal life and that comes straight from God. So it is an authentic thing. The sealing of the document shows that that document actually belonged to the king and that it was his property. The sealing of the Spirit shows that we are actually God's property. That we are not children of anyone else except for God. This seal also protected the document from being tampered with or harmed. If someone tampered with and changed something in the document, then the seal would be broken. The same is with us. Once we have been sealed, we cannot be tampered with or taken from God. It has been shown what God's intent for our lives is and it cannot be altered.

The Holy Spirit is a Down Payment of Heaven

We are marked with God's down payment. The Holy Spirit is our seal of ownership.

> **Ephesians 1:14** | ...who is the guarantee of our inheritance until we acquire possession of it, to the praise of his glory.

The word "guarantee" has the idea of down payment. This is essentially a down payment of our heavenly inheritance which will assure us of our future in Christ. I believe this story explains it rather well. A wealthy man called his faithful assistant into his office one day and said, "I've put your name in my will, and someday you'll receive $100,000. Since it may be a while before you get that legacy, I want to make you happy now by paying you the interest on that amount each year. Here is a check for $1,000 as a starter." The surprised clerk was doubly grateful. The prospect of the inheritance was certainly good news, but the money he received in advance gave him complete assurance that someday the entire $100,000 would be his.

The word "guarantee" also has the idea of an engagement ring. Not only does it mean a down payment but in the truest sense this word speaks of a ring you would give at betrothal. The Holy Spirit is the engagement ring for the believer who upon conversion is engaged to Christ and has become his bride for the future wedding feast. Now if a guy goes to a girl and says: "*Hey I love you,*" she shouldn't go crazy and make all her future plans. However, if he says, "*Hey, I love you! Will you marry me?*" and gives her a diamond ring, that's a commitment. The same commitment that God has made to Christians by giving us the Holy Spirit. This commitment will one day be redeemed.

Conclusion

Our full destiny will become clear when we stand before God and are fully reconciled. Christ will come forward and based on his sacrifice God will declare: "Righteous! No condemnation!" Those who are Christians will also have the proofs of the Holy Spirit working in their lives. Any crowns we receive will be cast at Jesus feet. We will say: *It was all of grace.* We will be able to testify how God changed our hearts and set us on Christ the solid Rock. I can't wait for that day. The whole church, Old Testament and New, are destined for that glorious day.

Most of us struggle so often, day by day, because we cannot yet see our full destiny. Our view of God's glorious grace gets obscured by some temporary thing. The only way forward is diligently focusing on the promises of God and remembering who we are. We are destined for glory. Our destiny is eternity, sanctity, liberty, and it is all guaranteed. Ephesus was a place of sin and slavery and much insecurity. We as believers in Christ are not in slavery to sin. We are in Christ. We are rooted in Christ. And our destiny is guaranteed in Jesus, because we trust in him.

2 | EPHESIANS 1:15-23
ROOTED IN CHRIST'S SUPREMACY

> *God seated Christ at his right hand in the heavenly places, far above all rule and authority and power and dominion, and above every name that is named, not only in this age but also in the one to come. And he put all things under his feet and gave him as head over all things to the church, which is his body, the fullness of him who fills all in all.*
>
> EPHESIANS 1:20-23

What's the greatest thing about your life? For the Christian, the best thing is that Christ has first place in your life. Our text here in Ephesians is a celebratory prayer for the full salvation of the believer. It's all done by Christ and for Christ. When Christ is exalted in the life of the believer, there is truly something to celebrate in prayer.

Remember at the transfiguration Peter, James, and John got to see the unveiled Christ—they saw the Lord in a way that no person living on earth had ever seen him in the history of the world—they saw his glory transfigured before them. It took their breath away. It left them in a state of awe. We come to a similar place today. We come to a place in Scripture that unveils the rightful place of Jesus Christ on the throne of Almighty God because he is Almighty God. We are about to see Jesus "highly exalted" (Phil 2:9). I ask you all to bow the knee of your life before him right now. If you are going to grow as a Christian, you must be rooted in the supremacy of Jesus Christ.

This passage of Ephesians lets us into how Paul talked to people and helped them along in Christ. Our text here is a prayer. He's writing this probably two decades after his conversion. What a wonderful prayer of the apostle Paul for the Ephesian believers. Instead of being self-focused, prayer keeps him others focused and God-centered. Paul is writing from a rented house where he is under house arrest, chained to a member of the Emperor's Praetorian Guard day and night: six soldiers in a twenty-four-hour period, four hours for each soldier. He is not complaining but rejoicing. He is blessing God, exulting in the supremacy, and concerned about the Ephesians. Again, this letter was likely a circular letter that was passed on throughout the churches in Asia Minor. They had been pagans, but now were brought into the family of God. Paul prays for them as such.

Ephesus was one of the idol-worshipping capitols of the world. Multitudes of people from all over the world would come to Ephesus to see this goddess in the Ephesian temple—the goddess Diana. These people were just like you and me. We think we know God and worship God, but Paul says these people had been "dead in their trespasses and sins" and that they had been "children of wrath" like the rest of mankind. What happened in their lives was nothing short of a miracle. God opened their eyes. They were awakened. They were transformed. They were brought low by the working of God's Spirit applying the gospel to their hearts. They confessed to God that they were liars, thieves, adulterers, and blasphemers. And they rested on the mercy of Christ to forgive them.

Paul heard about this all the way in Rome, a thousand miles away from Ephesus. He had ministered among them four or five years earlier. How does Paul respond? Does he just say, "*Oh, that's great? Nice to hear that. I guess I'll go on with my pity party in this filthy Roman prison.*" No, he says, "*Now more than ever, now that these people have come to faith in Christ, I need to pray for them.*" And in praying for his Christian family in Ephesus, he ends up in a beautiful strain of exaltation of the Lord Jesus Christ. Often praying for others can be what lifts our eyes to the glories and power of Jesus.

CHRIST IS EXALTED IN YOUR SALVATION (1:15-16)

Ephesians 1:15-16 | For this reason, because I have heard of your faith in the Lord Jesus and your love toward all the saints, **16** I do not cease to give thanks for you, remembering you in my prayers.

Paul heard about God's fingerprints on these Ephesian saints, and he began to pray for them. He heard about God's salvation in their lives. They were saved by grace alone through faith alone in Christ alone. That's something to celebrate. Paul felt a personal responsibility to pray constantly for them. There is power in prayer. We ought to pray for every saint in our local assembly. It was Paul's practice to pray for these saints without stopping. Paul mentions two marks that demonstrate that we have been joined to Christ. He mentions a God-ward mark (faith in Christ) and a man-ward mark (love to the saints). In short, those who live for Jesus are always loving his people. It is these two marks: love for God and love for others – that push him toward prayer.

The Miracle of Faith

Paul begins his prayer with thanksgiving for the faith the Ephesians have in the Lord Jesus. Paul said, *I heard about your faith and love in the Lord Jesus, and it caused me to pray and to rejoice.* What was it that would cause Paul to rejoice? The love and faith in the Ephesian church was something that God had done. Not long before, these Ephesians were pagans. Their girls had been temple prostitutes. They had been enslaved to superstitions. They had been selfish and self-consumed. But now there was this radical faith, and Paul heard about it, and it cause him to rejoice.

John Calvin regarded the faith necessary for salvation as a miracle: "We could not have one single spark of faith, or of light unless God had worked in us already!"[19] Paul says here in our text in Ephesians 1:15, "When I heard about your faith and love in Christ, I did not cease to give thanks to God for you." When a gift is given, a person gives thanks. Faith and love are gifts of God. A man is totally unable to love God or cling to him in faith in his own natural power. There is need of a miracle.

---

[19] John Calvin. *Sermons on Ephesians* (Banner of Truth: Carlisle, PA, 1973), 91.

Calvin went on to say that if a person could believe on their own, we should boast in man instead of God: "If every man was able to believe and have faith of his own accord or could get it by some power of his own, the praise for it ought not to be given to God. For it would be but mockery to acknowledge ourselves indebted to him for what we have obtained, not from him, but from elsewhere."[20] If love and faith come naturally from our own hearts, why should we thank God for that? Is faith a miracle or is it a responsibility for all people? The answer is yes and yes. There is always a tension in God's sovereignty and man's responsibility. We must begin by giving God the glory for our faith. We have nothing to boast in.

The Nature of Faith

When we speak of faith, we are not referring to mere intellectual acknowledgment. True faith has been defined as "radical dependency" that is more akin to trust and surrender than mere understanding.[21] It is not a mere acceptance of Jesus. "The devils believe and tremble" (Jas 2:19). Faith is more than information. Faith is a radical trust. Christians through a miracle of God's grace are given new eyes that cause them to cast themselves on God – we become radically dependent on Jesus. Saving faith means that we trust and treasure Jesus Christ. It is not when you were baptized or signed a card or responded to an invitation to accept Christ. Your conversion took place when you abandoned yourself to Christ by faith and became radically dependent on him. It's not complicated. It's so simple Jesus compares it to the trust of a child. When did that happen in your life? What happened to the Ephesians, has happened to us.

Now Paul had been among them for 3 years, but he had been gone for a while. Many people were coming to faith in Christ that he did not know. He heard of their radical conversion from paganism to *passion* for Christ. We ought to be looking for this in our children. We ought to be looking for this in each other. Not some mere mental assent, but a deep, moving, flowing, radical faith. "For as the body apart from the spirit is dead, so also faith apart from works is dead" (Jas 2:26). In Matthew 7, many come to Jesus in the Day of Judgment, who had faith

---

[20] Ibid., 83.
[21] David Powlison, *Seeing with New Eyes: Counseling and the Human Condition through the Lens of Scripture* (Phillipsburg, NJ: P & R Pub., 2003), 5.

without works. They had religion, but they were lawless in their heart. They were without the law and compulsion and power of Christ in their hearts. Christ tells us his verdict ahead of time: "Depart from me, I never knew you" (Mt 7:21ff).

The Expression of Faith

Faith is alive! It bears fruit. Paul rejoices that faith is expressed in a glorious love toward all the saints. Paul had spent three years with the Ephesians. He knew many of them by name. It's one thing to observe things yourself. Paul observed their love but also heard of their love from many others. They did not merely speak of love but actually lived it out so that others could see their good works and glorify their Father in heaven (Mt 5:16). This is how saving faith always works itself out. The great commandment teaches us that we are to love God by loving our neighbor. Our Lord said this is how the world will recognize true followers of Christ: "By this all people will know that you are my disciples, if you have love for one another" (Jn 13:35). Indeed, John says:

> 1 John 4:20 | If anyone says, "I love God," and hates his brother, he is a liar; for he who does not love his brother whom he has seen cannot love God whom he has not seen.

Paul said he was thanking God, he was rejoicing concerning their love unto all the saints. There are a lot of local churches in the body of Christ, but God looks down and he says, "I see one Church." There is a lot of division even among those denominations and God says, "But I see one Church." We seem to have the incredible ability to build walls in the body of Christ. When Jesus Christ and the apostles and those that have gone before us have spent countless effort and energy, not to mention blood to tear down those walls and build bridges.

Do you have a commitment to the Lord's people? I'm not talking about one day a week for worship but every day. Are you committed to being a disciple and discipling others? You must have a deep love toward *all* the saints. You must care where they are spiritually.

CHRIST IS EXALTED IN YOUR SPIRITUAL GROWTH (1:16-19)

Paul heard about God's fingerprints on these Ephesian saints, and he began to pray for them. Paul felt a personal responsibility to pray constantly for them. There is power in prayer. We ought to pray for every saint here. It was Paul's practice to pray for these saints without stopping.

> **Ephesians 1:16-17** | I do not cease to give thanks for you, remembering you in my prayers, ¹⁷ that the God of our Lord Jesus Christ, the Father of glory, may give you the Spirit of wisdom and of revelation in the knowledge of him.

The Practice of Maturity

Paul cannot go and visit the Ephesians. He's under house arrest far away in Rome. But Paul has a practice that helps the Ephesian church grow in maturity: he prays. And what is his prayer? That God may give the Spirit... in the knowledge of Christ, or as one translation puts it: "That you might know him better" (1:17b). It is amazing to consider what God does for us in our immediate salvation. Yet there is more to salvation than just having your sins forgiven. God wants us to "know him better!" We are to be constantly growing. "But grow in the grace and knowledge of our Lord and Savior Jesus Christ" (2 Pet 3:18). God does not want you to remain immature in Christ.

A tree doesn't produce fruit until the roots are down deep. An architect does not build until he understands architectural engineering and structures. I don't let my twelve-year-old operate on my three-year-old. If my three-year-old needs an operation, I send them to a mature expert. Are you in a place where you are growing in Christ? Oh that "the God of our Lord Jesus Christ, the Father of glory, may give you the Spirit of wisdom and of revelation in the knowledge of him" (1:17). Do you know him better? You must look into God's Word and not be a forgetful hearer. You desperately need the assistance of the Holy Spirit. He has to give you the wisdom and revelation to know Christ better. Flesh and blood cannot change you. The Father in heaven through the Spirit must give you eyes to see. It's not just about knowing the Word, but the Spirit revealing God to you through the Word. Don't be superficial about your devotional life. Seek for your roots to grow deep by the filling of the Spirit, the renewal of the Word, and the intimate knowledge of walking with Jesus. Go deep!

The Means of Maturity

Paul is talking to Christians here, so he is not speaking the initial opening of our eyes that occurs at conversion. He's saying we need to pray for our eyes to be opened more! It is the Spirit that does this work. We need God's Spirit of wisdom and revelation.

> *Ezekiel 36:26-27* | And I will give you a new heart, and a new spirit I will put within you. And I will remove the heart of stone from your flesh and give you a heart of flesh. ²⁷ And I will put my Spirit within you, and cause you to walk in my statutes and be careful to obey my judgments.

The Fear of the Lord

What Paul is getting at is the concept of "the fear of the LORD." Worshipping God and acknowledging his awesome presence in all your thoughts, words and deeds is the essence of fearing God.

> *Proverbs 9:10* | The fear of the LORD is the beginning of wisdom, and the knowledge of the Holy One is insight.

In other words, to have wisdom is to see everything from God's perspective! People who have authentic wisdom consider everything from God's point of view. Paul said it this way in Colossians 3.

> *Colossians 3:1-3* | If then you have been raised with Christ, seek the things that are above, where Christ is, seated at the right hand of God. ² Set your minds on things that are above, not on things that are on earth. ³ For you have died, and your life is hidden with Christ in God.

Revelation is knowledge that only God can impart. God's Word is the source of all wisdom and the Spirit of God inspired that Word. You can know a lot about me. You can make a lot of external observations about me, but in order to really know me, I have to reveal myself to you. In order to know a person, that person has to open up to you. That is what this word "revelation" means. God has revealed himself to us. This is not just knowing about God but knowing him intimately and knowing him better day by day. That this wisdom and revelation leads to a greater "the knowledge of him" – literally, "that you might know him better."

When is the last time you poured your heart out to God in prayer? When is the last time your heart was filled with amazement in the Scripture? This should be a daily activity for you. Or are you just coasting along? Wake up! Open your heart. Clear out all the clutter in your heart and soak up the knowledge of Christ.

The Focus of Maturity

In order to grow and change in Christ and get to know Christ better and better, we need to have a constant focus. Just like we plan for our meals each day, we need to plan on feasting on Christ each day.

Hope – a perspective to brings us to maturity

The great focus of the Christian begins with seeing the hope of all God has called us to. Hope in the Scriptures is no wish or wishful thinking. No hope is an earnest expectation of a certain reality. Hope for the Christian is a certainty. God has opened our eyes to his plan—the hope of his calling is not in this world. It's focused on another world! This world will lead you to destruction, but we can focus on the hope of a world with Christ as Head, and where he dominates our thoughts.

> **Ephesians 1:18a** | having the eyes of your hearts enlightened, that you may know what is the hope to which he has called you...

Our hope is not found in this life. We don't get the promises here and now. We get some benefits, but the vast majority are in the world to come. Consider Hebrews 11. We see a paradox at the end of the chapter.

> *Hebrews 11:32-40* | And what more shall I say? For time would fail me to tell of Gideon, Barak, Samson, Jephthah, of David and Samuel and the prophets— [33] who through faith conquered kingdoms, enforced justice, obtained promises, stopped the mouths of lions, [34] quenched the power of fire, escaped the edge of the sword, were made strong out of weakness, became mighty in war, put foreign armies to flight. [35] Women received back their dead by resurrection. Some were tortured, refusing to accept release, so that they might rise again to a better life. [36] Others suffered mocking and flogging, and even chains and imprisonment. [37] They were stoned, they were sawn in two, they were killed with the sword. They went about in skins of sheep and goats, destitute, afflicted, mistreated— [38] of whom the world was not worthy—wandering about in deserts and mountains, and in dens and caves of the earth. [39] And all these, though commended through their faith, did not receive what was promised, [40] since God had provided something better for us, that apart from us they should not be made perfect.

No one in the Hall of Faith received what they were looking for on this earth. We long for Christ. This world stands against Christ and against us. Stop looking on earth for what can only be found in the presence of Jesus. Paul says in Romans 8:18, "the sufferings of this present time are not worth comparing with the glory that is to be revealed to us."

Our hope is in the world to come! Yes, there are tremendous things we can look forward to in this world, but it's all the world to come peeking through! God's blessings are that He "makes all things new". He bears fruit through us! We see people transformed. We see our children walking with God! Those are the blessings of the world to come manifesting themselves here!

There is an emphasis in churches today to replace our eternal hope with a present earthly hope. Churches are replacing the hope of the gospel with a utilitarian message that allows you to have "your best life now". And this is not only being seen in the prosperity churches. The hope becomes that we can have a better life by utilizing the things of this world. Our life is enriched brothers and sisters by the hope we have in Christ right now.

Riches – a promise to bring us to maturity

God has opened our eyes to his promise—the promises of the world leave you empty!

Ephesians 1:18b | ...what are the riches of his glorious inheritance in the saints.

Here on earth, we must live for a realm in which Jesus Christ has no competition. There are no idols when we see Jesus Christ face to face, and we come into our inheritance. Only Christ! Live for those things that are to come. Sometimes we get a peek into the world to come. When people are enlightened by the Spirit and receive Christ by faith, you are witnessing the power of the world to come. When your prayer life is filled with the unction of the Spirit, you are touching the face of God! When you see submission in marriage from the heart, even though it is hard, you are observing Christ's exaltation in that brother or sister. Glory! Joy! This is the power of the world to come. Focus on these things! Focus on a place where Christ is God alone.

Power –a power to bring us to maturity

God has opened our eyes to his power—the arm of the flesh will fail you!

Ephesians 1:19-20 | ...and what is the immeasurable greatness of his power toward us who believe, according to the working of his great might [20] that he worked in Christ when he raised him from the dead and seated him at his right hand in the heavenly places.

This is the same power that raised Christ from the dead. Focus on these things will lead you to maturity. Paul was describing how powerful we are, so he used every word for power he could think of. There are four different Greek words used for power in verse 19.

Dunamis: "The immeasurable greatness of his power [*dunamis*]." We derive the English word dynamite from *dunamis*. It refers to inherent power.

Energeia: "According to the working [*energeia*]." That word is the basis for the English word *energy*. It refers to operative power.

Kratos: "The working of his mighty power [*kratos*]." Sometimes *kratos* is translated "dominion." It refers to ultimate power or authority.

Ischus: "His mighty [*ischus*] power." It refers to *endowed power*. It means power that is designated to us by another.

Who is the power given to? His power is directed "toward those who believe." There is no hope for those who lack faith. If you do not entrust yourself through a holy surrender to God, there is no power for you. You must surrender your life. You are impotent in your own power. There is absolutely no meaningful power in the flesh. Have you ever tried to plug something into a dead power outlet? Spiritually, we are plugged into the infinite outlet of endless energy in Christ.

Paul was saying that God has given believers unbelievable power. Many Christians claim they don't have enough strength or power. That's why Paul prayed for the believer to know the power available to him. Have you experienced the working of that mighty power? If you know Christ, then you know and have tasted of the power of God. What kind of amazing power is this? It's the power...

Ephesians 1:20 | that he worked in Christ when he raised him from the dead and seated him at his right hand in the heavenly places...

The same power that God demonstrated when he raised his Son from the dead is the same power right now that works in you. You have no real power in yourself that is of yourself. The power that works, that matters, that transforms, and that empowers is the power that comes from Jesus Christ. Focus on that power and you will grow in maturity.

It's not only the power of the resurrection, it's the power of the ascension. Remember when Christ ascended to the right and of the Father and God "seated him at his right hand" in the heavenly realm? Not only do you have infinite energy to do what God wants you to do, he also gives you all authority to do what God wants you to do.

CHRIST IS EXALTED IN YOUR SERVICE (1:20-23)

We have every reason to submit to Christ because of his highly exalted position. Jesus Christ has no rivals. He has no equals. He's exalted for a purpose: that he might fill his church. When Christ is exalted in the lives of his people, he is incarnated: seen and felt through your life. He wants to "fill all in all" (1:23).

Christ is Exalted Positionally

Christ is seated at the right hand of God. He is at the highest place of authority and honor in the presence of the Father. God's raised his Son to the highest place of honor and glory, with all authority. And his place of honor is so far above any other name, because no one comes close or compares to Jesus. There's no comparison.

> **Ephesians 1:20-21** | ...that he worked in Christ when he raised him from the dead and seated him at his right hand in the heavenly places, ²¹ far above all rule and authority and power and dominion, and above every name that is named, not only in this age but also in the one to come.

Historically and theologically, this speaks of his resurrection and ascension. It's not speaking of geography or location. It's speaking of authority and position. This is a means of saying that Christ sits in the place of God as God. He is deity. Everything will be under his control, even His enemies. Every knee will bow, and every tongue confess that Jesus Christ is *kurios* (LORD). This is the Greek translation in the Septuagint for *Yahweh*, or the God of Genesis. Jesus Christ is Yahweh. Every tongue will confess that. The God of Genesis came to earth incarnate in humanity and was crucified for your sins and for mine.

Christ is exalted above everyone in heaven and earth and under the earth in this present age. That is, Christ is exalted in history. He is exalted in the metaphysical realm. He's exalted in the realm we see and the realm we don't see. Christ is exalted in the present time of rebellion and spiritual warfare, and he will be exalted when sin is wiped off the face of the earth forever and ever for the ages to come.

Christ is Exalted Personally

Christ is exalted as Head of the church. The Father put him there. The Son accomplished redemption for the church through his blood, and the result is that all things are placed under his feet. This is in direct correlation with the Genesis 3:15 prophecy that though the Seed of the woman would be wounded, the Seed would also crush the serpent's head, and put all things under his feet, illustrating the crushing judgment reserved for those who stand against Christ's headship.

> **Ephesians 1:22-23** | And he put all things under his feet and gave him as head over all things to the church, **23** which is his body, the fullness of him who fills all in all.

Christ opposes and crushes those not submitted under his feet, but he also fills those who are submitted with the fullness of him who fills all in all. If Christ is not exalted personally in your life, how will the world know him? We who are called to salvation must submit to him in all things – that's the pathway to fullness. We are to be filled with him that he might be our collective Head. He must uncover every idol in our life. He must be our Lord and Head in all things pertaining to us, his church, and his bride.

Christ is most seen in his exalted form in this temporary time of earth that we live in through his church. He is seen in his people, in you and in me. He is seen in us. And when Christ is exalted in us, when they see us, they see *him*. Glory to his name! He is supreme!

Conclusion

Here are two challenges for you in this text: 1) are you saved, growing spiritually and serving? 2) Are you praying for your own spiritual growth and the growth of others?

The first challenge is about spiritual growth. Are you growing spiritually? Are you serving joyfully under the exalted Christ? Is Christ exalted in your life? What kind of fruit are you producing for the kingdom? Is your character changing to be more like Christ day after day?

The second challenge is about your prayer life. This passage is a prayer of praise. Paul says in this passage: Because of what God has done in your lives, I want to give praise to him! Do you praise God in your prayers? We are called to praise God for what he has done and what he is doing in our lives and in the lives of others. God is working in you. Lift up your eyes and see. If you see what God is doing, you will praise him.

3 | EPHESIANS 2:1-10
ROOTED IN CHRIST'S GRACE

For by grace you have been saved through faith. And this is not your own doing; it is the gift of God, not a result of works, so that no one may boast. For we are his workmanship, created in Christ Jesus for good works, which God prepared beforehand, that we should walk in them.

EPHESIANS 2:8-10

God's grace is breathtaking. We talk about salvation sometimes in such a casual or forensic way. It's all textbook talk. In the passage before us, God's grace is seen up close and personal. It brings deep emotion and affection to God when we magnify it. Sometimes we are so amazed at a person's testimony of salvation that we give undue honor to the person. No. We should not do that. We are just sign posts. No one honors and glories in signposts. We glory in what the signpost is pointing toward. We honor the God who has transformed us. We need to see what God can do up close so that we can turn around and give glory and praise to our great God for his great love in Christ.

How great is the love of Christ? The Puritan Richard Sibbes famously said, "There is more mercy in Christ than sin in us."[22] Paul

---

[22] Richard Sibbes. *The Bruised Reed and Smoking Flax* (London: Gooch Booksellers, 1630), 16.

asked, "Who shall separate us from the love of Christ?" (Rom 8:35). His answer: Nothing. God's love and mercy are infinitely greater than our sin. God's mercy and grace is breathtaking. We talk about salvation sometimes in such a casual or forensic way. It's all textbook talk. In the passage before us, God's grace is seen up close and personal. It brings deep emotion and affection to God when we magnify it. Sometimes we are so amazed at a person's testimony of salvation that we give undue honor to the person. No. We should not do that. We are just sign posts. No one honors and glories in signposts. We glory in what the signpost is pointing toward. We honor the God who has transformed us. We need to see what God can do up close so that we can turn around and give glory and praise to our great God.

Have any of you ever seen the Sears Tower? Many people have only seen it from a distance. It's a whole lot different when you get inside it. I can remember going up to the sky deck where people looked like ants on the sidewalk below. There's a big difference between seeing the Sears Tower up close and just seeing it from a distance. Most of us have seen God's love for us from a distance. We know it's there; we understand that God is love—that he loves sinners, but I want to look up close at it and be awed by it. In order to see the brightness of God's love, we need to see the darkness and brokenness of the human condition.

OUR MISERY REQUIRES GOD'S GRACE (2:1-3)

God begins this passage with a very dark and miserable atmosphere in order to magnify the glory of his grace. Theologians have often noted that the first three verses of Ephesians 2 are some of the darkest verses in the Bible. We are found in such misery, that without the grace of God, we would be lost forever.

> **Ephesians 2:1-3** | And you were dead in the trespasses and sins ² in which you once walked, following the course of this world, following the prince of the power of the air, the spirit that is now at work in the sons of disobedience— ³ among whom we all once lived in the passions of our flesh, carrying out the desires of the body and the mind, and were by nature children of wrath, like the rest of mankind.

The Shock of Grace

Grace is shocking. Those who experience the "fullness of him who fills all in all" (1:23) were once "dead in their trespasses and sins" (2:1).

Those you see assembled here once lived very far from God. Had you gathered us ten or twenty years ago, or some of you just a year or five ago, we would have gathered for entirely different reasons. We once lived lives that were dead to God. We were unfeeling toward him. We ignored him and lived as if he didn't exist.

This text tells us that there is hope. God came to save those who were in the worst condition. He didn't come to call the righteous, but sinners to repentance. Man today is in such a horrible state, and he is in a very unsafe and catastrophic situation. Man has misdiagnosed his problem. A misdiagnosis of a disease would be catastrophic—disastrous! Imagine you go into the doctor with an illness, and he gives you the wrong medicine. Or you need the right ventricle of your heart operated on, and instead the doctor cuts open the left. Or imagine you go into the doctor for a kidney transplant, and instead he operates on your spinal cord. That would be disastrous! Imagine you enter an emergency room with chest pain. The doctor tells you it's only a chest cold. You can see that misdiagnosis is fatal!

Most of us picture us throwing out a lifeline to mankind. We just need to get them to latch on to the lifeline. Dear friend, man cannot latch on to the lifeline because he is not sick or struggling with the lifeline. He is dead on the bottom of the ocean floor. There are many people that would take offense to this. They say they know God, but the Bible describes them differently. "They have a zeal of God, but not according to knowledge" (Rom 10:2). They have "a form of godliness but deny the power thereof" (2 Tim 3:5). Listen to Jesus' disturbing words in Matthew 7.

> *Matthew 7:21-23* | Not everyone who says to me, 'Lord, Lord,' will enter the kingdom of heaven, but the one who does the will of my Father who is in heaven. ²² On that day many will say to me, 'Lord, Lord, did we not prophesy in your name, and cast out demons in your name, and do many mighty works in your name?' ²³ And then will I declare to them, 'I never knew you; depart from me, you workers of lawlessness.'

Many who think they know God have never known him, because they are dead in the trespasses and sins in which they walk. So, Paul brings us to verse one, and he gives us that unmistakable diagnosis. He says, here is the cause of all your problems! Here is the reason for all the war, the sadness, and the sickness; all disease and all death have its root in this. Paul says: You were "dead in trespasses and sins." This is an ugly subject, but we cannot know the greatness of God's love and grace except on the backdrop of the ugliness of sin. Grace is only as amazing as sin is awful and vile.

The Human Condition

The apostle Paul gives a breathtaking and controversial description of the human condition. It's controversial because many believe that man is basically good. Paul is clear, as was his Lord Jesus Christ, that man is at his core, fundamentally bad. Paul says, "And you were dead in the trespasses and sins in which you once walked..." You had no way of coming to God on your own. Romans 3 tells us:

> Romans 3:10-12 | None is righteous, no, not one; [11] no one understands; no one seeks for God. [12] All have turned aside; together they have become worthless; no one does good, not even one.

The Misery of Senselessness

Paul tells us that by nature we are dead in his trespasses and sins (2:1-2a; 1 Cor 2:14). How awful it is to be blind or deaf: to not see or hear the obvious. But how much greater it is to be spiritually blind and deaf to God. By nature, we are born not feeling the degree of shame for transgressing against the glory of God. Paul says in verses 1-2a, "And you were dead in the trespasses and sins 2 in which you once walked..." The word "dead" is being used as a metaphor here, and it means to have no power or ability and to be completely "senseless". A dead person has no ability to do anything concerning this world. He cannot make money. He cannot have a family. He cannot write a book. He is dead. He has no senses. He cannot see, hear, smell, or feel anything. In the same way, the natural man is dead toward God because of his sins. We live in a way that is so contrary to our Creator, that we have no feeling for him. We are not concerned enough to stop what we are doing. Our concern is dead.

Have you ever been to a funeral? A funeral is sad because there has been a loss of life. The person you once knew is not with you on earth anymore. You see their body. There's no life in it. How do you know that life has departed? No life means no perception. When death comes all sensory perceptions are gone. A strawberry pie with whipped cream will not stir the appetite of one who has no life. They cannot enjoy it. When you're dead you lose all sensory perception. The dead can't see.

The dead cannot hear. They cannot talk. They cannot taste. They cannot think or perceive anything!

> *1 Corinthians 2:14* | The natural person does not accept the things of the Spirit of God, for they are folly to him, and he is not able to understand them because they are spiritually discerned.

He is senseless when it comes to sensing the need to please God. He does not feel the weight of his sin because he does not see the beauty of God. He is not compelled at all to adore him. He does not see the need to serve him. He is spiritually dead. Isaiah didn't realize he was a man of unclean lips until he was awakened to see by God. He said, He said,

> *Isaiah 6:5* | Woe is me! For I am lost; for I am a man of unclean lips, and I dwell in the midst of a people of unclean lips; for my eyes have seen the King, the Lord of hosts!

He does not sense the atrocity of his sin. He is blind and dead to the need to live for God. Instead, he lives completely for himself, breaking God's law, trespassing the purpose for which God created him. What a sad reality! Man is dead to God. He has no sense at all that he should worship him. Instead, he is very content to live his life totally centered around self. This is the reality of who man really is.

The Misery of Sinfulness

Paul tells us we are dead in trespasses and sins. We were spiritually dead people walking. Though we were dead to God, we were very much alive to our trespasses and sins. It was our rebellion to God that kept us dead in regard to knowing the beauty of God.

> **Ephesians 2:1** | And you were dead in the trespasses and sins...

When I was a teenager I trespassed onto a friend's property, knocking on my friend's window in the middle of the night. Immediately I knew I had made a mistake. My friend's large Cajun uncle considered me to be an intruder and called the police. I proceeded to jump into the Tickfaw River that runs into Lake Ponchatrain. As the police searched for the "intruder," I was ducking under the swampy water. As the police drove away, I jumped out of the water, relieved that I had avoided arrest. But when it comes to our trespasses against God, no one escapes arrest. We have all trespassed against God's law.

Dead in Trespasses

What does it mean to trespass? Not only do we miss the mark when we try to do good, but we actually choose to do evil. We trespass. God says about certain things, "Do not enter", but we enter. He says, "No trespassing," but we trespass. Theologically, the word trespass has the idea of breaking God's law. 1 John 3:4 tells us "sin is the transgression of the law." God says, "I am all wise, and these are my all-wise judgments – live by them." But we in pride and in smug audacity deviate from the all-wise engineering of God, and we break his law and his instructions.

Dead in Sins

The word "sins" here means to "miss the mark". We all try to reach God's mark of perfection, but we constantly miss His mark. Paul says "there is no distinction: for all have sinned and fall short of the glory of God (Rom 3:22-23). Paul is saying there is no difference between Jew or Gentile, the religious or pagan person. All have missed God's mark. The spiritually dead are content to trespass God's law regularly and continually. They are self-deceived, thinking that breaking God's law will bring blessing and benefit, when it brings the opposite.

The Misery of Slavery

We were created to be servants of God, but we have indentured ourselves to follow other masters. Three are named in this passage: the world, the wicked one, and our own whims.

Enslaved to the World

> **Ephesians 2:1-2a** | And you were dead in the trespasses and sins ² in which you once walked, following the course of this world....

Man follows the world: "following the course of this world" (2:2). This world is the sworn enemy of God. 1 John 2:15 says "If any man love the world, the love of the Father is not in him." The world is the environment that we live in – which happens to be utterly in opposition to God's holiness. It says *now* is all that matters – now is all you have. Your life is ultimately eternally inconsequential, so do what you like. It is a world system that is opposed to God. The whole world is in darkness and opposes God. This is part of encourages human beings to continue in their rebellion against God. It is the "group think" of our communities that oppose God.

Enslaved to the Wicked One

Ephesians 2:2b | ... following the prince of the power of the air, the spirit that is now at work in the sons of disobedience—

Man follows the wicked one. Satan is called "the god of this world" – he is a prince or a governor in this world. He controls the power of the air or atmosphere of evil thought, the spiritually evil philosophies that are now at work in the children of disobedience. Satan is only at one place at one time, but he is crafty and intelligent, and he controls the spirit or outlook of the sons of disobedience. In other words, Satan sets the tone for what is in fashion. Satan the spirit being that is now at work in the sons of disobedience and controls both the sinful world system and the false religious system. All religious systems that do not hold Christ as being the exclusive way to the Father, "the way, the truth, and the life", are controlled not by God, but by the wicked one. Jesus said to the Pharisees who were far more religious than most people: "You are of your father the devil, and your will is to do your father's desires" (Jn 8:44). This dark ruler who roams the unseen spiritual realm is Satan. He is the one who brings evil influences to bear upon the world of men.

Enslaved to Our Own Desires

Ephesians 2:3 | Among whom we all once lived in the passions of our flesh, carrying out the desires of the body and the mind, and were by nature children of wrath, like the rest of mankind.

Unregenerate man follows his own whims. We all once lived in the passions of our flesh. It's the universal past experience of all Christians. Whether a person was raised in a Christian home or in an unbelieving home, we all were lost and needed conversion. It was the desires and passions of the body that drove us. Our physical appetites were many: sex, food, rest, pleasure, socialization, and so many more. We were controlled by our bodies. But there were also desires of the mind. We were ego driven, people-pleasing, power hungry, etc. We were mastered by fear, anger, despair, jealousy, hatred, and pleasure. Self-focused, we lived in our power and for our own pleasure to the neglect of God and others. This kind of self-centered life is in direct rebellion against God, independent of his love, his guidance, and his good commands.

We were by nature, children deserving and inviting God's just and right wrath. Rebellion was not merely learned by the nurture and culture and example of our own families, but it is by our own fallen, rebellious human nature. It's still true that "sin came into the world through one man, and death through sin, and so death spread to all men because all sinned" (Rom 5:12).

Man without Christ is destined for God's wrath. The word for wrath has the idea: "to grow ripe for something". It is God's growing, intensifying opposition to sin. One day, God who is pure, holy, and just will send his Son to come "with flaming fire, taking vengeance on those who know not God" (1 Thess 1:8). Let me say, it does not get worse than this! Oh, dear sinner, wake up to your misery!

Until we come to know Christ through personal faith and fellowship, we remain abiding under the wrath of God, like the rest of mankind. There is no one exempt from the full fury of God's wrath. Until we see our need of Christ, we cannot have God's wrath removed from us. It's not enough to have the knowledge and good doctrine of proper biblical teaching. We can have the most pristine gospel propositions memorized without actually coming to know Christ. We don't get a prescription from the doctor and eat the paper script with the doctor's signature. No, we want the medicine that will heal our body. When we go to a nice restaurant, we don't eat the menu. We don't savor the paper pictures of the food. No, we savor and taste and eat the actual food. So it is, we need to feel our real need of Christ and "taste and see that the Lord is good" through personal faith in Jesus. Until that moment of repentant faith and personal surrender to Jesus, we remain under God's righteous wrath.

Here biblically is man's condition. The Father had to predestine me in love because I would never have initiated anything. Without Christ I have no hope for a number of reasons: I was *dead*. (I was positively, spiritually "dead" and unable to help myself. I needed to be raised up by God in order to live. I was *disobedient* (2:2b) – slave to my desire, the devil, and the world. I was *depraved* (Isa 64:6; Phil 3:8). I wasn't unable to do anything. I was dead in sin. I was so full of sin there was no room for obeying God. Bottom line: I was my own god. I was *doomed* (2:3b) – I was a child of wrath unable to redeem myself. I could not help myself.

THE MOTIVE OF GRACE IS LOVE (2:4-6)

There is nothing in any of us that can cause God to love us. He does not love us because we are good. He loves us because he is good. Here we find the two most important words in the Bible, "But God"! Martyn Lloyd-Jones said, "These two words, in and of themselves, in a sense contain the whole of the gospel."[23]

If it wasn't for God's sovereign drawing (Jn 6:44), we would never come to Christ. No one has ever sought God on their own without God first seeking them (Rom 3:11-12). No one ever found God; God wasn't lost. God found us: we are lost. That's how God's love is: it finds us where we are.

God's Love is Engaging

Ephesians 2:4 | But God, being rich in mercy, because of the great love with which he loved us...

"But God!" God intervened and interrupted my depravity and sinful, selfish condition. God meets us where we are. We are spiritually poor and bankrupt, and God is rich in mercy and great in his love. While we were yet sinners, Christ died for us! Like Jesus coming to the tomb of Lazarus, Jesus comes to us. And just as in John 11, as he groaned for Lazarus's family and wept, even knowing that he would raise them from the dead, he weeps for us today. He comes with compassion and power. What rich mercy and great love he has for us.

He engages me in my unescapable sin. Ephesians 2:3 paints a terrifying picture of where we all are by nature and by choice. If the chapter ended with verse 3, we would all be in trouble, "we all once lived in the passions of our flesh, carrying out the desires of the body and the mind, and were by nature children of wrath, like the rest of mankind" (2:3). If God dealt with us according to even just one of our sins, we would be lost forever. We say with David in Psalm 130:3, If you, O LORD, should mark iniquities, O Lord, who could stand?" God has not dealt with us the way we deserve. He meets us right where we are. He does not leave us in the prison of our sin but gives us an escape. We deserve his wrath and punishment, but we get his rich mercy and his great love.

---

[23] Lloyd-Jones, *Ephesians 2*, 59.

He engages me in my blind, incapable rebellious nature. Never would we have sought after God—ungrateful people. We were lost, but we thought we were ok. We were self-sufficient. We thought we didn't need God. We went right on sinning day after day. How many sins did we commit in even one day? God has not dealt with us after our sins. He engages us where we are. Where were we? We were dead in trespasses and sins. We were influenced and controlled by Satan "the prince of the power of the air." Not all lost people are indwelt by Satan or by demons, but they are all subject to his influence through the corrupt world system. We were the "children of disobedience." And where was our life, day in and day out? Verse 3: "we all once lived in the passions of our flesh, carrying out the desires of the body and the mind." This was our life day in and day out.

He engages me in hell-bound destiny. And what is Paul's conclusion in verse 3? Because of our very nature—because of our inborn guilt and sinful tendencies, we were worthy of nothing else but God's wrath. We "were by nature children of wrath, like the rest of mankind." We were objects of God's condemning judgment. God is holy. He is beautiful in his holiness. He holds back all wickedness from himself. He cannot have it in his presence. He must punish it. If God did not do this, He would not be good. If we did not punish murderers and thieves and immoral people, our society would quickly dissolve into something that was also not good. God is good, righteous, and holy, and sin must be met with his most fierce wrath. To love good is to hate evil. God is supreme good, and so He must be supremely opposed to evil. We are caught up in trespasses and sins, and therefore "children of wrath". We see how God's love is engaging. He meets us right where we are. He loves us because he wants to.

"But God!" If it weren't for God's rich mercy and great love, I would remain in the same radically depraved, dark, and doomed condition. Without God's grace and kindness, my heart, my mind, and my will would remain corrupted by sin and selfishness, with a heart that is bent inward.

God's Love is Extravagant

God's love is so extravagant, that he sent his Son who lived, died, and rose again to unite us with himself. God didn't just send well-wishes. He sent his Son. He got personally involved. That's quite extravagant. If I go to the hair club for men, I don't want a bald man applying the product. I need someone totally invested. God the Father is extravagantly invested when it comes to our salvation. He lavished his great love upon us by sending his Son.

> **Ephesians 2:4-5** | But God, being rich in mercy, because of the great love with which he loved us, ⁵ even when we were dead in our trespasses, made us alive together with Christ—by grace you have been saved—

What is it that caused God to bring us back from the spiritually dead? His rich mercy, or in other words, his extravagant love demonstrated by the death, burial and resurrection of Christ. I was dead in my trespasses, and Christ took on flesh to die so that he could make me alive together with him. This was God's plan from the beginning.

> *Romans 8:32* | He who did not spare his own Son but gave him up for us all, how will he not also with him graciously give us all things?

Martin Luther said we all carry in our pocket Christ's nails. Who crucified Christ? You did! I did! Christ died "for us". Are you aware that you have Christ's nails in your possession? Look at the love God has for us in Christ. That brutal cross shouts God's love to us. Remember for hours the crushing darkness of God's wrath was upon Christ. He was hanging between heaven and earth. His mouth was not complaining about the wicked sinners like you and me who put him there. As Isaiah 53:7 says, "He was oppressed, and he was afflicted, yet he opened not his mouth; like a lamb that is led to the slaughter, and like a sheep that before its shearers is silent, so he opened not his mouth." But Christ did open his mouth. He was not completely silent. Listen to his words to his Father on your behalf. They are recorded in Luke 23:34. Listen to what comes from the Savior's mouth, "Father, forgive them; for they know not what they do."

What kept Christ on that cross? What was it that held him there? Love that originates in the Trinity itself was what held him on that cross. As he bore every ounce of the wrath of God for you, he became your eternal shield. As felt every ounce of agony, there was one thing that made it all worth it to him. He loved you. He loved me. He loved you long before you came into this world. He will love you when ten thousand ages have passed. Christ's love for you held him there on the cross.

Martin Luther tried everything to try to gain God's favor. He slept on hard floors. Going without food, even climbing a staircase to Rome on his hands and knees—but it was to no avail. His teachers in the monastery told him that he was doing enough to have peace with God, but he had no peace. His sense of sin was too great. Luther one day turned to Romans 1:16, "the just shall live by faith". God's grace opened up His heart to understand it. God gives to the needy sinner the righteousness which he needs by faith. Luther no longer felt the wrath of God, but the love of God. The love of God entered his heart and life and changed the world.

God's Love is Empowering

We were dead in our trespasses, But God made us alive and raised us up with Jesus Christ. A fundamental change has occurred. We who were powerless are now pulsating with infinite, divine power. We are empowered by our union with Christ. Look what God did for us in Christ.

> **Ephesians 2:6** | and raised us up with him and seated us with him in the heavenly places in Christ Jesus

In C. S. Lewis' book, *The Lion, the Witch, and the Wardrobe* the wicked witch had brought a perpetual winter to Narnia. She kept turning all her subjects to stone. But Aslan comes and breathes into them new life. God's love brings new life. St. John said when we come to know Jesus, "we pass from death to life" (Jn 5:34). The same power that raised Christ from the dead now dwells in you (Rom 6:10). The old has passed and the new has come. You are a new creation (2 Cor 5:17). Paul lays out the clear truth in his letter to the Romans.

> *Romans 8:10-11* | But if Christ is in you, although the body is dead because of sin, the Spirit is life because of righteousness. [11] If the Spirit of him who raised Jesus from the dead dwells in you, he who raised Christ Jesus from the dead will also give life to your mortal bodies through his Spirit who dwells in you.

United with Christ in His Resurrection

When Christ died, I died. When Christ was raised from the dead, I was raised. When Christ ascended and was seated with God in the heavenly places, I ascended with Jesus. What's that mean? It speaks to the power of holiness and the power of headship. Christ's resurrection takes away all my excuses to continue in sin. He's completely defeated it – not just theoretically or theologically, but personally in my own life. I am raised up with Christ. My sinful impulses are put to death with Christ. The Spirit has put new impulses in me. I'm no longer bound and enslaved by sin. Christ has raised me up over the power of sin.

United with Christ in His Ascension

And then we see Christ's ascension. I'm seated with God in heavenly places in Christ. I'm enthroned with God. That speaks to Christ's headship in my life. Christ's ascension takes away any sense of unworthiness that might keep me from doing God's will. I now function from a position of authority. I am now God's instrument. Christ is my divine head, and I'm seated with him right now in his throne in heavenly places. Because of my union with Christ, I can be confident that God's going to do what he has eternally planned to do in my life.

WE ARE GOD'S MASTERPIECE OF GRACE (2:7-10)

I used to work in a museum of sacred art. There were some very famous, priceless masterpieces there. One that I enjoyed was a Rembrandt entitled, "The Head of Christ". That painting was hardly two feet high. It was just a practice piece for Rembrandt, yet it is a priceless painting because of the fame and brilliance of the author. So it is with our salvation. Our lives are priceless because of what God has done and is doing in us. You are God's masterpiece, and he's going to be showing you off as a trophy of his grace for eternal ages to come. God's brilliance and fame is seen in what God has done in you.

The Focus of our Salvation

It goes without saying that Jesus is the focus of our salvation. One of my favorite Old Testament words is *hesed*. It almost always means: "God's covenant love". New Testament words used to express that concept are found in this verse: riches, grace, kindness – and all of this is found "in Christ Jesus."

> **Ephesians 2:7** | ...so that in the coming ages he might show the immeasurable riches of his grace in kindness toward us in Christ Jesus.

For all the ages to come, the focus will be Jesus, Jesus, Jesus. It's all about him. How rich is Jesus' grace? It's immeasurable grace. Our lives in eternity will be an aroma of Christ's kindness. God wants to show off his grace and kindness toward us in Christ Jesus.

The Failure of Works Salvation

The masterpiece of God's grace cannot happen through human merit. The gospel is God's gospel (Rom 1:1-5). It was his idea from beginning to end. No human would ever come up with the gospel (good news). It is not even possible through human design or power. The best of our good works could not even come close to attain salvation. Eternal salvation is by grace.

> **Ephesians 2:8-9** | For by grace you have been saved through faith. And this is not your own doing; it is the gift of God, **9** not a result of works, so that no one may boast.

Salvation by works has already failed. I need grace because one sin is all it takes to fail. How many sins did it take for Lucifer to be cast out of heaven? One! You might say, "I'll live a good life to make up for it!" You can't live a good enough life. One sin separates you forever from a holy God. You committed that first sin a long time ago. Through Adam, sin has come upon all people (Rom 5:12). It's too late. We cannot make up for our sin through works. There is only one way to get to a good standing with God the Father: Jesus is the only way (Jn 14:6). That's a gift of grace.

Saved by Grace Alone

> **Ephesians 2:8a** | For by grace you have been saved...

Is there anyone who can claim that he or she is already saved by works, so far in life? Is there any human that is without the need of God's grace? Has anyone lived without sinning? Look at your life; examine your conscience; observe your words, your thoughts, your imaginations, your motives; for all these things will be brought to account on the Last Day. Is person a man on earth that "does good, and does not sin" (Eccl 7:20)? I need God's grace. Scripture declares that "there is none that does good, no, not one" (Rom 3:10). I need God's grace. "All we like sheep have gone astray; we have turned everyone to his own way" (Isa 53:6). I need God's grace. "The saying is trustworthy and deserving of full acceptance, that Christ Jesus came into the world to save sinners, of whom I am the foremost" (1 Tim 1:15). Can you agree that we all need God's grace? Works salvation failed even before I was ever born. I was conceived in sin (Psa 51:1). I desperately need God's grace.

Saved by Faith Alone

Ephesians 2:8b | For by grace you have been saved through faith.

That right standing with God is only available to those who trust in Christ. If you want justification, you must come by faith. What is justification? Justification means to be "declared righteous" before God now and at Judgment Day by virtue of the imputed merits of our crucified Savior, Jesus Christ.[24] "He [*God*] made him [*Jesus*] to be sin for us, who knew no sin; that we might be made the righteousness of God in him" (2 Cor 5:21, KJV). To be justified is to have a right standing with God based on the glorious exchange of your filth and sin for Jesus' righteousness. You can imagine on Judgment Day and God says to you, "Well done my good and faithful servant" (Mt 25:21). Stunned, you will be thinking, "well done?" I did my best, but it wasn't much! But you be quiet on that day. Because Jesus with the nail prints in his hands will do all the talking.

When we hear that we must come to Jesus by faith, that means a personal surrender of your whole self to his person, his work, his lordship. Faith is a complete trust of your heart, mind, will, and destiny to Jesus. It's not something you need to work up. You cannot have faith in faith. Faith must have an object. Jesus Christ is the object of our faith. The message is that Jesus suffered and died for my sins and rose again. Your response is to repent from trusting in yourself or anything else and place your trust in Christ alone.

Salvation is by God's Works Alone

Ephesians 2:8c-9 | And this is not your own doing; it is the gift of God, [9] not a result of works, so that no one may boast.

You've not thought up this salvation: it's from God – it's his gift to you. You don't need to work it out. The only works salvation that will save us is the work of Jesus Christ. He lived his life on our behalf. He was born under the law and fulfilled the law perfectly. His righteous life

---

[24] S. Lewis Johnson. *Discovering Romans: Spiritual Revival for the Soul* (Nashville: Zondervan), 60. Cf. Deut. 25:1; 1 Kings 8:32; Isa. 5:23; Rom. 2:13; 3:4; 4:3-25; 5:17

replaces my sinful life when we put our trust in him (2 Cor 5:21; Rom 5:1). This salvation is not of your or my own doing – it's the gift of God. My works are worthless.

Works cannot take away my sins. Good works are the result of God's salvation, they are not and could not be the requirement for salvation. The best any of us can do is nothing to boast about. Yet if it were possible to earn salvation by works, we would have something to boast about. Yet and still the glaring truth is that no amount of good works can take away my sin. I can never balance the weights. A billion lifetimes of my own self-righteousness can never take away one iota of sin. Only Jesus, the sinless Savior, who lived perfectly and fulfilled every aspect of the law can take away my sin. Only he who satisfied the righteous wrath of a holy God can take away my sin. Jesus alone is worthy of my boast and praise.

The truth is, no sinner can ever be worthy. I think of the scene in the book of Revelation 5 – the multitude of the redeemed are crying out: "Who is worthy to break the seals and open the scroll?" (Rev 5:3). Who is worthy and able to redeem humanity? Who is worthy to carry out eternal salvation, the divine plan of redemption? Jesus alone! My only boast is in Jesus Christ. Salvation is a gift of God, not of my own self-righteous works, lest there be reason for human boasting. We sinful humans have nothing to flaunt. All we have is shame. We are sinners. My only boast is in Jesus who gave me the eternal gift of salvation and replaced my shame with his righteousness. "Far be it from me to boast except in the cross of our Lord Jesus Christ, by which the world has been crucified to me, and I to the world" (Gal 6:14).

The Founder of True Salvation

Ephesians 2:10a | For we are his workmanship, created in Christ Jesus...

Paul here says God is the great Artist, and we are his canvas. This work of salvation in us is literally God's workmanship, his masterpiece. He's the Author, the Artist, the Founder. God creates us anew by the Word of God. This is God's sovereign choice. "Of his own will begat he us with the word of truth" (Jas 1:18, KJV). Salvation is a miracle. It is God's creative act in the new birth. John 3:3 Jesus tells us, "Except a man be born again, he cannot see the kingdom of God."

An Act of Creation

The new life comes out of a radically transformed heart that God has created. When Paul says that "we are his workmanship" we can deduce that he's not talking about our physical body but our spiritual being, our innermost being. He's done something new there through an act of creation. As Ezekiel 36:26 says, "A new heart also will I give you, and a new spirit will I put within you: and I will take away the stony heart out of your flesh, and I will give you a heart of flesh." That's an act of creation. That's a sovereign act of God.

Think of the creation of man back in Genesis. God breathed into man the breath of life, and man became a living soul (Gen 2:7). In the same way, when we are saved, God breathes into us the breath of his Holy Spirit, and we become alive. We are "quickened by the Spirit" (1 Pet 3:18, KJV). God breathes into us and fills us with the Spirit, and for the rest of our lives we are possessed of his Spirit doing his very bidding. We read in Genesis 1:1, "In the beginning God created the heaven and the earth." And what does verse 3 say? "And God said..." God spoke, and he created. "Through faith we understand that the worlds were framed by the word of God" (Heb 11:3). We see the spiritual parallel in 2 Corinthians 5:17 – "if any man be in Christ, he is a new creature: old things are passed away; behold, all things are become new." Listen to the Lord. "And he that sat upon the throne said, Behold, I make all things new" (Rev 21:5). Real change in your life is not possible without the foundational change of a new heart. The house of your life must be built on the solid rock of Christ's transformative work in your heart. All else is the sinking sand of self-righteousness and self-effort. Trying to change without God's Genesis power of creation is like trying to perform heart surgery upon yourself. It's impossible.

The Fruit of True Salvation

> **Ephesians 2:10b** | ...created in Christ Jesus for good works, which God prepared beforehand, that we should walk in them.

We are not saved by good works, but we are saved for good works. These good works are prepared by God for all true believers planned before the foundation of the world. He chose everything in your life that you might be "conformed to the image of his Son" (Rom 8:29). Way before you were born, Christ planned salvation for you. He chose you.

He even chose your good works. He called you to holiness and service. A truly saved person will demonstrate genuine salvation through a life of good works. Good works come from God. Paul is even more specific with the Philippian church when he says: "work out your own salvation with fear and trembling, 13 for it is God who works in you, both to will and to work for his good pleasure" (Phil 2:12-13). God has mapped out your good works beforehand. No matter what you are facing this week or this year, the Lord is sovereignly directing your steps. King David rejoiced in this truth when he said,

> *Psalm 37:23-24, NKJV* | The steps of a good man are ordered by the Lord, and He delights in his way. 24 Though he fall, he shall not be utterly cast down; for the LORD upholds him with is hand.

God establishes our steps, and he delights in our way. We can never fall away from the Lord, because like a good Father, he holds our hand. We do not walk alone. His goodness and steadfast love follow you all the days of your life (Psa 23:6). You may stumble but he will keep you from falling away (Jude 24-25). You are watched over and cared for by the Shepherd of Israel.

Conclusion

What shall we say to these things? Christ has made our salvation possible. When we were dead, he made us alive. When we were cast out, he enthroned us with him. When we had no just standing with God, Christ became our righteousness. When we had no direction, he predestined and established our steps. I have nothing left but to celebrate. My only boast now is in Christ. I didn't do this, God did it through. He gets the praise. He gets the glory. All praise be to the one who sits on the throne and to the Lamb. Hallelujah!

4 | EPHESIANS 2:11-17
ROOTED IN CHRIST'S COMMUNITY

Remember that you were at that time separated from Christ, alienated from the commonwealth of Israel and strangers to the covenants of promise, having no hope and without God in the world. But now in Christ Jesus you who once were far off have been brought near by the blood of Christ.

EPHESIANS 2:12-13

"I love Jesus; I just don't care for the church." "I don't need the hypocrites in the church to help me follow God." "My relationship with God is private; I don't need other people to tell me how to worship my God." Sometimes we get wounded by the church. Church is sometimes bad. How do we get to the place where we are not focused on each other but focused on Jesus? We need to begin by remembering.

We all have trouble remembering. We weren't always part of God's family. We weren't always touched with God's Holy Spirit. We weren't always satisfied by Christ and his word. There was a time when we were far away from God. We are told in this text to remember. Remember! Ponder! Meditate on this! Paul tells us: based on the fact that you have been moved from the lowest position in the universe to the highest one, you need to think about the pit you just crawled out of, and keep thinking about it, and never forget it! We are witnesses of God's miracle of salvation. Don't forget where you came from. Paul tells us here to remember because we are so prone to forget.

REMEMBER THE OLD HOSTILITY (2:11-12)

There was a great war going on in the churches of the first century. Jews and Gentiles were at odds. The brilliant Greeks where there were all the philosophers said that anyone who was not a Greek was an ignorant Barbarian, including the Jews! And the Jews said that anyone who wasn't a son of Abraham was a dog. We all have our divisions and disagreements. The questions is: Why can't we all get along? The answer is clear from our text! We don't remember where we came from.

Normally, you would think Paul would say, "Listen, based on all this great stuff, *rejoice!*" He doesn't say that. He says the opposite. He says "Remember." He says, you need to remember (ponder, let it grip you) that not too long ago, you were on the side of the great cliff on the edge of hell, and every breath you took was enough to cause you to lose your balance and fall into the abyss—you were that close to hell! You were "without Christ" and without "hope" and "without God in the world". You were so far away from Christ.

Our culture today says in essence, "Don't remember." "Don't worry, be happy." Your happiness is all that matters. That philosophy, my friends, is the death knell of your happiness. If you try to please yourself, you will most certainly be miserable. Your flesh cannot be pleased. You were not created for you. You were created for God. If you want to be really, really happy, you need to see how far God has brought you to himself.

Remember your Hard Heart

It wasn't so long ago when I was lost in sin and my heart was hard. God had not yet cut and circumcised my heart by his Spirit. I was like the hard soil: the seeds of the gospel did not penetrate the depth of my heart because I was hardened by devil. I was spiritually dead. What a calloused heart I had. The apostle says we ought to remember this.

Ephesians 2:11 | Therefore remember that at one time you Gentiles in the flesh, called "the uncircumcision" by what is called the circumcision, which is made in the flesh by hands.

There was a great division between the Jews and the rest of the world. They were to be separated from all the other nations. They were to humble, holy, and hungry for God. The sign of this was circumcision. Circumcision was the sign of God's covenant. Everyone part of the covenant community was to be circumcised. It was an outward sign of an inward reality. It was to show that the hard heart was cut out and new heart was put there. It was a sign that the people were sensitive to God, that they were cut and circumcised in their heart. The Jews were to be a blessing to the world. They were to bless all nations with the message that Messiah was coming.

Did they bless all nations? Think about Jonah. The last thing he wanted to do was give hope and life to those Ninevites! The Jews were given the Word of God in order to bless all nations and to bring them to God. Instead, they were overcome by spiritual pride on one side of the spectrum and by becoming like the pagans in their idolatries on the other side.

The Jews called the Gentiles "uncircumcised". That was a derisive name. That was like calling them trash. The Jews of 2,000 years ago actually taught that it wasn't lawful for them to help a Gentile mother at childbirth because that would be helping to bring another dog into the world. If a Jewish daughter or son married a Gentile, the family held a funeral service. They never recognized their own children again. The children were in effect dead.

The Jews were called out of this world to be holy, but they were also to be humble! They lost that, and trusted in the outward sign instead of the inward reality. You trust in the outward, and you will become proud. They trusted in their outward circumcision, but they missed the whole point. Look at a few places in the Scriptures:

> *Deuteronomy 10:16* | Circumcise therefore the foreskin of your heart, and be no longer stubborn.

> *Deuteronomy 30:6* | And the LORD your God will circumcise your heart and the heart of your offspring, so that you will love the LORD your God with all your heart and with all your soul, that you may live.

Before we knew Christ, we were divided against our family. Many of us were racists. Some Christians still lean toward racism. The most segregated time of the week is Sunday morning in most churches. That's sad. Wherever there is division, there is pride and unbelief. And God doesn't dwell with the proud. "God resists the proud but gives grace to the humble" (Jas 5:5).

Remember our Hostility with God

Often, we think of people in the world as being basically good and kind. Thankfully God has given us a conscience to remind us of his good law. He's written it in the hearts of all people through the conscience. Despite having a conscience, the truth about humanity is that we tend to ignore our conscience. We are willing to run over our conscience because we want what we want (Jas 4:1-4). There is a problem in the human soul, and it's not because we merely make mistakes or have had a psychological misdeed. No, we have rebelled against a good God. How we have lacked in taking sin seriously in our generation. John Bunyan took it very seriously. He said that sin "is the dare of his justice, the rape of his mercy, the jeer of his patience, the slight of his power, and the contempt of his love."[25] Paul says: remember the sin that alienated you from God and his people and separated you from Christ.

> **Ephesians 2:12** | Remember that you were at that time separated from Christ, alienated from the commonwealth of Israel and strangers to the covenants of promise, having no hope and without God in the world.

If Ephesians 2:1-10 tell us we were helpless, our text here tells us how hopeless we were. In every conceivable way, we were far away from God. There was a time when as Gentiles we were separated from Christ, alienated from his kingdom (the commonwealth of Israel), strangers to his covenant, without hope, and without God in the world.

We did not know the warning of Acts 4:12, "Neither is there salvation in any other: for there is none other name under heaven given among men, whereby we must be saved." The Gentiles were totally separated from the Savior. The Jews were waiting for Christ to come. They

---

[25] John Bunyan. *The Works of John Bunyan, Volume 1* (London: Blackie and Son, 1866.), 65.

were sacrificing bulls and goats as a picture of Christ's covering of sins. Believing Jews were truly united to Jesus Christ.

Remember when you thought Christians were crazy and ignorant? Remember when for the life of you, you could not understand why they wanted to go to church. Maybe Christmas and Easter. Maybe once a month. But once, twice, three times a week? What? Do you live at church now? What's so attractive. You couldn't understand. We need to remember where we came from: "remember that you were at that time separated from Christ."

Alienated from His Kingdom

Out of all the heathen people in the world, God chose Abraham and made of him and his children a commonwealth, or in other words, a kingdom. The word commonwealth means "citizenship". The Jews were citizens in God's kingdom with God himself ruling over them.

God was in the business of saving Gentiles. In order to follow the Lord in the Old Testament, the Gentile had to follow the Lord by uniting in some way to the kingdom of Israel. So though Gentiles were "alienated from the commonwealth of Israel", it is also true that God saved many Gentiles in the Old Testament. Think of some of them:

Caleb was not an Israelite but a Kenizzite, descended from the Edomites, i.e. Esau (Num 32:12, Josh 14:6, 14). Ruth was a Moabitess. Rahab the harlot was from Gentile Jericho, and she was the great Grandmother of David. Naaman was a General in the Syrian Army. Remember Elisha cured his leprosy in the river, and Naaman became a believer in the LORD. We think of Nebuchadnezzar and the 500,000 Gentile Ninevites who put their faith in the Lord. Yet these conversions were not the norm. For almost the entirety of the Gentiles, they were living separated and alienated from the nation of Israel. They worshipped Zeus and Diana and gods of stone made with hands.

And this is how so much of the world is today. They live each day living outside the influence of God's rule and reign in their lives. You remember when you were not part of God's covenant people? You remember when you were building your own kingdom? Remember when you were not concerned about souls all around you that were headed straight to hell? You were not concerned to tell them of our Great Substitute, our Savior, our Sovereign, and our Great God and King, King of kings, and Lord of lords.

Remember when you were outside of God's redemptive favor? Remember when even if you had a Bible you didn't want to read it? It was foolishness to you? The Bible tells us about how he calls people out of the world and into a covenant and relationship with him. Remember when you had no idea of the covenant with Noah, with Moses and Israel, with David as King, and all of those pointed to our covenant relationship with Christ? Remember when we never thought of how Christ in covenant love died for us? Remember?

My ancestors in Scotland were strangers to God's covenants. They worshipped rocks and trees. We were without hope and without God in the world. We may be hostile toward men, but it is because we are hostile toward God. We cannot make peace with God on our own. He must come after us. He must seek after us. And he has. But God has given us a new hope. We were dead in trespasses and sins. We were outside of God's plan, we didn't care about his word, we hated each other. We fought. Our marriages were falling apart. We were destroying ourselves and destroying others.

REFOCUS ON A NEW HOPE (2:13-14A)

Who is it that can turn all this hostility into hope? Jesus! God is all about turning hostility into hope! How? Paul must have marveled at the great unity that was in the Ephesian church. There was a massive division between Jews and Gentiles in his day. Paul was a Jew, and he knew the deep division from all sides. There was cultural division, social division, and spiritual division. Historically, this is a division that had existed as long as Israel had been a people.

But now you have both Jew and Gentile together, worshipping the same God, bowing their knee to the same Lord, and loving each other. How did this happen? Through Jesus Christ! Through his propitiation, his power, and through his peace.

Refocus on Christ's Propitiation

> **Ephesians 2:13** | But now in Christ Jesus you who once were far off have been brought near by the blood of Christ.

This is the language of the temple and sacrifices. For years God taught them that there was a price to be paid for sin. And there is. Each of us is going to have to pay for our sins, or there must be a sinless sacrifice to pay. Someone has to pay that price. You can pay it yourself, or you can let someone else. But who would be that kind? Who would pay that price for you? The Old Testament saints sacrificed the innocent lamb. The only worthy sacrifice that God will accept on your behalf is Jesus. John the Baptist said, "Behold the Lamb of God who takes away the sin of the world" (Jn 1:29).

One day all of us are going to bow our knee. You can bow the knee now and be Christ's eternal servant or bow the knee later and be his eternal enemy. Which will it be? Can you say, "I once was his enemy... but now in Christ Jesus you who once were far off have been brought near by the blood of Christ" (2:13)? Christ's blood refers to the theological concept of propitiation, which means a satisfaction of the righteous wrath of a good judge. God is angry with sinners every day. His wrath abides and remains upon all who are not in Christ. Our condemnation keeps us far away from God. God is so holy that he cannot dwell with sin or sinners. The only thing God wants to do with you is arrest you, prosecute you and condemn you to the righteous sentence of eternal damnation. But wait. Out steps Christ. He was born of a woman, born under the law. Unlike anyone else in humanity, he kept the law perfectly. Not only did he satisfy the justice of God's law, but he satisfied the justice of my condemnation for breaking his law.

Refocus on Christ's Peace

Christ's propitiation results in peace with God. Our peace does not come from a treaty or a gifted negotiator. Our peace is not a document but a person. The person of Jesus Christ.

> **Ephesians 2:14** | For he himself is our peace, who has made us both one and has broken down in his flesh the dividing wall of hostility...

These verses are illustrating our peace through the walls in the Jewish temple complex. There are various walls outside the temple that separated various peoples. The priests from the people, then the people were divided Jews first and then Gentiles. Jews were separated Male and Female. One thing was in common though. They were *all* outside of God's presence. None were allowed. This wall of hostility may separate us from our neighbor, a family member, a boss, but ultimately the wall separates us from who? From God.

The Walls of Separation

Our text says that God has made both groups here, both Jew and Gentile, to be one in Christ. Now this distinction doesn't mean much to us today, but it was massive in the ancient world. Jews saw Gentiles as dogs! If a Jew saw a Gentile mother giving birth, they could not help that young mother because they did not want to help bring another Gentile dog into the world. Talk about conflict. In Christ's day, in the temple, there were barriers. Of course, the main emphasis in the temple was in the very center.

First, we see God himself in the center, represented by the Holy of holies. Outside of that was that was the court of the priests. Then there was the court of Jewish men. After that was the court of Jewish women. Finally, on the very outside there was a five-foot wall where you had the court of the Gentiles, who the Jews referred to as "dogs." They could not pass that wall, or they would be put to death. There were signs that said this in Greek and Latin.

Tearing Down the Wall of Hostility

When Christ died, he destroyed that wall of distinction. There was an unnecessary distinction at this time. The point God was making in the temple is that none of us is able to approach him. Only the high priest, a picture of our Lord Jesus Christ, could go into the Holy of Holies on our behalf, and that once a year. Some have even said that the high priest may have needed a rope around him in order to drag him out in case of death. Neither the Jews or the Gentiles could approach God on their own. The Jew was certainly closer because he had the Word of God, he had the promises of God, but those promises were not applied for the majority of the Jews. Most of them lived and died in self-righteousness and in unbelief. They had a spirit of slumber!

But in Christ, all the walls of division have been torn down. How? "In his flesh..." Indeed, Christ "has broken down in his flesh the dividing wall of hostility" (2:14). In Christ's incarnation, he became flesh and substituted his life for us. He settled our account with God. Christ is our peace! He is our Mediator. He is our Advocate. His nail pierced hands settle the argument in God's courtroom. Satan cries out against us day and night against the saints of God (Rev 12:10), but Christ has cast him down! Christ has conquered him! All that Satan says is true about us, but it's all been put on Christ. We have peace with God. Christ himself is our peace. It's an emphatic statement. Christ settled our hostility with the Father.

REJOICE IN A NEW HUMANITY (2:14B-17)

Ephesians 2:14-15 | For he himself... has made us both one and has broken down in his flesh the dividing wall of hostility ^{15} by abolishing the law of commandments expressed in ordinances, that he might create in himself one new man in place of the two, so making peace.

In saving us, God was bringing about a holy union with himself through Christ.

Ephesians 1:9-10 | Making known to us the mystery of his will, according to his purpose, which he set forth in Christ ^{10} as a plan for the fullness of time, to unite all things in him, things in heaven and things on earth.

A Populated Humanity

Ephesians 2:14b | For he himself... has made us both one and has broken down in his flesh the dividing wall of hostility

God has made us one and broken down anything that might divide us. He's chosen us out of every "people, language, family, and nation". We may have nothing else in common, but we love Jesus. We are united in Christ. He settled the hostility between Jew and Gentile. No longer do ethnic divisions divide us. There are no socio-economic divisions. We are one in Christ. He has torn down the wall of hostility! "For as many of you as were baptized into Christ have put on Christ. ^{28} There is neither Jew nor Greek, there is neither slave nor free, there is neither male nor female, for you are all one in Christ Jesus" (Gal 3:27-28).

A Perfect Humanity

Ephesians 2:15 | By abolishing the law of commandments expressed in ordinances, that he might create in himself one new man in place of the two, so making peace.

Christ has done it all. Christ has come and abolished the hostility between you and God. You can't fulfill the Law, but Christ did. You cannot live holy without Christ. If you want to be reconciled to God, you must turn to Christ. If you want to be reconciled to men, you must turn to Christ.

Christ settled the hostility between us and his Father. He did this by keeping the Mosaic Law perfectly. He obeyed the law actively and passively for us. Listen to verse 15, We've been brought near... Christ himself was our peace... in what way? How did it happen? He did it... "by abolishing the law of commandments expressed in ordinances, that he might create in himself one new man in place of the two, so making peace, 16 and might reconcile us both to God in one body through the cross, thereby killing the hostility." The hostility God had towards us was put on him. The hostility we had with God was fully satisfied for you and all who come to Him by faith. Do you realize how great a hostility it was God had toward you? Think of eternity with His holy wrath fully fixed against you. "For he made him who knew no sin to be sin for us, that we might become the righteousness of God in him" (2 Cor 5:21).

Christ abolished the law and ordinance to bring a peace. He completed the Law perfectly by fulfilling all the types and shadows of the Old Testament. All the sacrificial laws, All the dietary laws, All the ceremonial laws, All the moral law. Christ did it all. No longer do we have the shadow of sacrificial laws, dietary laws, ceremonial laws. No longer do we have the condemnation of the moral law. "Christ is our peace."

What does this mean? Because Christ abolished the standard of law keeping for me since he kept it for me, I can never be more righteous than I am right now. I will never have more of a right standing than I have right now. All who know Christ are part of this perfect humanity.

A Peaceful Humanity

> **Ephesians 2:16** | And might reconcile us both to God in one body through the cross, thereby killing the hostility.

Notice both Jew and Gentile needed to be reconciled to God. They were both out of sorts with God. The Jews had religion, but for most of them, they didn't have Christ. They were also alienated from Him, even though they were near. They had the Word, but their hearts were unchanged. I know this verse is about soteriology, the doctrine of salvation, how we are reconciled to God. Christ killed the hostility of the law on the Cross. He killed the hostility of all the ethnic groups and families of the earth by bringing us together in the church. Now the only thing that some of us have in common is our love for Jesus!

Human Hostility

We have all our divisions. There so much envy and strife, jealously and pride, hurt feelings and bitterness and even rage. When we have a conflict, we think of it on an earthly level like the hostility between the Jews and Gentiles with walls of separation and partition outside of the temple.

Divine Hostility

God is put off by our sin. The conflict of Jews and Gentiles was not primarily on an earthly level! The sins of Jews and Gentiles separated them from God. The Jews and Gentiles were all outside of where the mercy seat was in the holy of holies. They may have been separated from one another, but their biggest problem is that the vast majority of them were separated from God.

Christ-focused Harmony

But what does this peace look like when it is lived out in the church? When we have our eyes on each other, there is always hostility. When we turn to God there is harmony. The more we get our eyes off ourselves and onto the needs of others and helping them walk with Christ, the more harmony is in the church. God's heart is that we have the unity that Christ has purchased on the cross. This is experienced as we have our eyes on Jesus. Hostility will come when we focus on each other. Harmony comes when we fix our eyes on Jesus.

A Personal Humanity

Ephesians 2:17 | And he came and preached peace to you who were far off and peace to those who were near.

I never stop being amazed at the fact that Christ loves me personally. This verse says that Christ has come and personally preached peace to us: both the far off seekers – perhaps without any Christian background – and those who are near, perhaps those raise in a Christian home or environment. The peace that Christ preached is the same peace of Christ proclaimed by the prophets and Christ himself. It is the message of Christ's lordship and kingdom that is made possible by his blood. Christ died for sinners that I might come under his lordship and be reconciled, having access to God.

The Father wants us to personally hear the voice of the Son of God in our own heart through his sufficient Word. Jesus said: "My sheep hear my voice, and I know them, and they follow me" (Jn 10:27). At the transfiguration, in the presence of the two greatest prophets, God says, "This is my beloved Son, in whom I am well pleased, hear him" (Mt 17:5).

Conclusion

Whether you realize it or not, you need the divine community of the church. The church is very human. It's messy. But we need the church. The church is the living organism. Christ promises: "I will build my church, and the gates of hell shall not prevail against it" (Mt 16:18). In the next chapter we are going to see how much we need each other as a body. God has ordained the church, a fellowship of the flawed, to carry out his purpose and will in the world. When we consider the biblical teaching on the church, we realize the church is vitally important for growing in Christ. Like a branch that grows because of its connection to the tree, we thrive when we stay connected to the church as we are each connected with Christ.

5 | EPHESIANS 2:18-22
ROOTED IN GOD'S FOREVER FAMILY

In him you also are being built together into a dwelling place for God by the Spirit.
EPHESIANS 2:22

The other day I put my key in the lock and it didn't work. I had no access. Thankfully my friend, who has rescued me from many perils, showed up and let me in the door! A door without any access is a very frustrating situation. Before I knew Christ, access in my life was limited because of my own poor choices. I was on probation because of wrong decisions. And this is where we all are before Christ. We are dead in our trespasses and sins with no access to God! Only through the regenerating grace of God can we have access restored by the Cross of Christ. The pathway to redemption is stained with Jesus' blood! And this is what we find in Ephesians 2:18-22.

Everything the world has to offer is at our fingertips. Right here, right now—it's all yours. Through the television you can access any sports arena in the world. You can experience the Olympics across the world or view a press conference in Europe. Through the telephone we have access to anybody on the planet.

We live in an age of amazing access. We have access to journey the entire world. Through mass transportation, I can hop on a plane tonight and be in Barcelona tomorrow morning. We can travel to India or Africa and be back in a few days. And today, you can have access to it all whether you can afford it or not. A credit card grants us access. Don't worry, if you've been turned down, you'll have five more offers in the mail tomorrow. All this access feels like it's free, but it's not. 19% interest is way more than any of us can afford. Why are so many so willing to pay such a high price? Because access is important. People want immediate access to whatever their heart desires. You want a book, a car, a house? You don't even have to leave your home. It's all available from Amazon or eBay.

Think about all the access we have. We have access to the best medical advances in the history of the world. You can have major surgery without scars! 100 years ago, it was unheard of for diabetics to live beyond a few years after diagnosis. Now we have tests for everything and specialist doctors for every ailment known to man. Today through new medical advances deaf people are getting their hearing back, doctors are transplanting hearts, and there are even face transplants available.

Through the internet, you can look through the lens of the Hubble telescope and see hundreds of thousands of light years from your back yard. Or you can look right in your own back yard. We have access to satellite maps of the entire globe. We have access to more information today than in the history of the world. Things that used to take days and weeks to find can now be accessed in a matter of seconds. We live in an age of unprecedented access. Everyone has a car, a computer, an iPod, a cell phone. We've never been more connected. We've never had more access.

And yet, as connected as we are to our world, we are missing the most important connection of all. Money can buy just about anything, but it cannot buy you a ticket to heaven. You cannot buy access to God on the internet. People are so connected, but most of our connections are amazingly superficial. You see, no matter how connected you are in this life, no matter how much information you can put into your head, no matter how many cell phones, laptops, and iPods you have, all this access will one day come to an end. We are all part of the ultimate statistic. Ten out of ten people die. With all the access we have, we are missing the ultimate access we need. You see death is coming. It's ugly. Death is a result of sin. You see Romans 5:12 tells us "by one man sin entered into the world, and death by sin; and so death passed upon all men, for that all have sinned."

What a joy today that we can say: We are sons and daughters of the Most High God! If you are to grow and change in Christ, you must know your position in Christ. That position gets you privilege and access. Christ has given you access to God which gives you amazing privileges. It's what you were made for! If you are in Christ, you are now part of: God's kingdom. God's family. God's temple.

ACCESS TO THE TRIUNE GOD (2:18)

Ephesians 2:18 | For through him we both have access in one Spirit to the Father.

Here is the great Trinitarian doxology of this passage. We have access through Christ, in the Spirit, to the Father. D. A. Carson says, "The gift of the Holy Spirit brings the conscious presence of God to the individual."[26] I love the way Jonathan Edwards describes the roles and economy of the holy Trinity:

> The Father is the deity ... in its direct existence. The Son is the deity generated by God's understanding, or having an idea of Himself ... The Holy Ghost is the deity ... breathed forth in God's infinite love to and delight in Himself. And I believe the whole Divine essence does ...subsist both in the Divine idea and Divine love, and that each of them are properly distinct persons.[27]

So what does the Trinity mean to us? Why is the Trinity important? First of all, unless we worship God in the way he has revealed himself to us, we are idolaters. Secondly, to truly do what we were made to do – to soar, and to freely accomplish all that God wants us to accomplish, we must look into the face of God. We must be conformed to his likeness. Edwards put it this way:

> God is glorified within Himself these two ways: (1) By appearing ... to Himself in His own perfect idea of Himself, or in His Son, who is the brightness of His glory. (2) By enjoying and delighting in Himself, by flowing forth in infinite... delight towards Himself, or in his Holy Spirit.... So God glorifies Himself toward the creatures also in two ways: (1) By appearing to...their understanding. (2) In communicating

---

[26] D.A Carson, *New Bible Commentary: 21st Century Edition* (4th ed.) (Leicester, England; Downers Grove, Ill., USA: Inter-Varsity Press, 1994), Eph 2:11–22.
[27] Jonathan Edwards. "An Essay on the Trinity," in Treatise on Grace and Other Posthumously Published Writings, ed. Paul Helm (Cambridge, UK: Clarke, 1971), 118.

Himself to their hearts, and in their rejoicing and delighting in, and enjoying, the manifestations which He makes of Himself.... God is glorified not only by His glory's being seen, but by its being rejoiced in. When those that see it delight in it, God is more glorified than if they only see it. His glory is then received by the whole soul, both by the understanding and by the heart. God made the world that He might communicate, and the creature receive, His glory; and that it might be received both by the mind and heart. He that testifies his idea of God's glory doesn't glorify God so much as he that testifies also his approbation of it and his delight in it. [28]

Remember the Son exegetes (makes known) the Father to us (Jn 1:18). He manifests and reveals all we know about God to our understanding. Look at the mercy of God in Christ! Look at the love of God! Look at the wrath of God poured out on Christ. All that we know about the Father is revealed in Christ (Jn 14:9). Christ gives us access to the Father. He makes it possible through His death. He is the *Logos* – the very fullness of deity in bodily form. He is so compassionate that he takes on our nature! In this he is revealing the infinite compassion of the Father to us.

And the blessed Holy Spirit stirs our affections up for God. He stirs up the deep waves of love and enjoyment and addiction to God. "Whom have I in heaven but thee? and there is none that I desire upon earth beside thee" (Psa 73:25). It is by the Son and the Spirit that we have access to the Father. We could never understand the way to the Father except through Christ! We could never love God without the Spirit stirring in us infinite yearnings for God.

Look around you and consider the Body of Christ. God's done this. He's put us together as one body in Christ. Not only could we not accomplish this, but none of us would have wanted it in our old, selfish nature. Aren't you glad God knows a whole lot more than us?! God is calling out a people for his name. He is saving one person at a time and putting them together into one Body for his purposes. He's given us access.

God takes a group of sinful people—people like you and like me—people who have loved their sin, and he cleans them up. He makes them holy through the blood of his Son, and he makes them desire holiness—hungering and thirsting after righteousness. He puts them together to

---

[28] John Piper. *Think: The Life of the Mind and the Love of God* (Wheaton, IL: Good News Publishers/Crossway Books, 2010), Kindle Locations 451-459.

serve him and to do his will on this earth. That's why we gather together. We live life together. We are united by the Spirit of God. We are one body in Christ today. God is putting this masterpiece he calls the church together. He's given us access! What does this access to God look like? First, it looks like a kingdom.

IN CHRIST WE ACCESS A NEW KINGDOM (2:19A)
We are No Longer Illegal Immigrants

Ephesians 2:19a | So then you are no longer strangers and aliens, but you are fellow citizens with the saints...

We were like illegal immigrants with no rights. A "stranger" was an illegal immigrant. An "alien" or foreigner was like a temporary resident on a passport. You only had so much time and limited rights.

We used to enjoy God's creation and God's benefits. He fed us. He gave us our breath and our life. In Him we live and move and have our being. But we were just illegal immigrants on God's earth. Before we were in Christ our home country and eternal abode was hell and our father was the devil. We loved lies. We loved pride. We loved this world and its possessions.

You are no longer an illegal immigrant with no rights. What right have you to ask God for anything? You have every right. You are no longer a foreigner and illegal immigrant. You are fellow citizens with the saints. There was a time when we were strangers and foreigners in the church. But now we are strangers and pilgrims in the world! Now we are fellow citizens with the saints! The Old Testament theocracy has been replaced! We now have access to God. We now have rights!

At the time of the writing of this letter, the Roman Empire is at the zenith of its splendor. There are no signs of its coming decline or fall. Yet Paul sees this other kingdom – and it's not Jewish or Roman. It's made up of every tribe, tongue, people, and nation. It is international and includes every language and family of the earth. Here is something a thousand times more splendid than the greatest kingdoms of the earth.

We no longer have to show a green card or a passport! We have birth certificates to the kingdom that will last when all other kingdoms and nations fall.

Philippians 3:20 | But our citizenship is in heaven, and from it we await a Savior, the Lord Jesus Christ.

Romans 8:17 | We are heirs—heirs of God and fellow heirs with Christ.

Now we can say to anyone in Christ:

1 Peter 2:9 | But you are a chosen race, a royal priesthood, a holy nation, a people for his own possession, that you may proclaim the excellencies of him who called you out of darkness into his marvelous light.

We have access, because we are now full-fledged citizens of the heavenly Jerusalem, of God's kingdom. We have rights afforded to us!! We have authority to call the kingdom of Jesus our home. We identify with his people and his nation!

IN CHRIST WE ACCESS A NEW FAMILY (2:19B)
We are No Longer in Slaves

Now the language becomes more intimate. We are not just members of the same country; we are members of the same family.

Ephesians 2:19b | ...but you are fellow citizens with the saints and members of the household of God.

From Slavery to Family

This language is significant, because 50% of the Roman Empire were slaves. This would have significance for a great number of the Ephesian Christians, many of whom were slaves. Sometimes we act like the prodigal son: "make me one of your hired servants" (Lk 15:19). We are no longer in the slave status saints of God. We are family members.

Purchased from the slave market of sin. We were once enslaved to our sins. We had many masters. No longer should we live as slaves. We have been adopted as sons and daughters of the living God. We have all the rights and privileges of sonship.

As a member of God's family, you have security. You need to know if you are saved, you are not yet whole. You are still broken. You are part of the Body of Christ. This place is not a show case for saints. If you are looking for that, you're at the wrong place. We are a place for broken people. If you are yearning to be loved and where people will meet you where you are then you are at the right place. We want so badly at the church to be a place where you don't have to put on a mask. Leave your masks behind. The church is a place where sinners struggle.

You need to know that you are accepted in the church. You can struggle. We must lean on each other. We are a family, a Body. Like a family every member is different. The children in our families are different from each other. Just when you think you have your parenting skills perfected, God throws you a curveball. And that's how it is in the family of God – we are all so different. Paul compares us to a body in 1 Corinthians 12.

The church does not consist of one particular denomination or family of churches, but all those people, men, women, and children who have been truly converted by the Holy Spirit of God – who have embraced the Cross of Calvary – who have gone through that narrow gate to "forsake all and follow Christ". This is membership in his family. You can no longer be a friend of the world and be part of the family of God. To be a friend of the world is to be an enemy of God.

We were once as Ezekiel describes as an abandoned half aborted child left to die in the street. God has picked us up and made us his own. Then, what makes the family of God so special?

There is a family *language*: Praise and prayer. Day and night, we pray to the Lord without ceasing. And we say, "Let everything that has breath praise the Lord."

There is a family *likeness*: Christ in us, the hope of what we will be like in glory. As part of God's family, bear his likeness. We no longer look like the sinful selfish Adam.

There is the family *location*: heaven and earth. The church triumphant in heaven and the church militant on earth.

There is a family *love*: in Christ and for one another.

There is a family *legacy*: the Name above all names.

IN CHRIST WE ACCESS A NEW TEMPLE (2:20-22)
We are No Longer in the Trash Heap

Ephesians 2:20-22 | ...built on the foundation of the apostles and prophets, Christ Jesus himself being the cornerstone, [21] in whom the whole structure, being joined together, grows into a holy temple in the Lord. [22] In him you also are being built together into a dwelling place for God by the Spirit.

Paul tells us we are God's temple! Peter tells us we are living stones in God's temple! Consider 1 Peter 2.

> *1 Peter 2:4-5* | As you come to him, a living stone rejected by men but in the sight of God chosen and precious, ⁵ you yourselves like living stones are being built up as a spiritual house, to be a holy priesthood, to offer spiritual sacrifices acceptable to God through Jesus Christ.

Saints of God, we are no longer part of the trash heap. We are bricks in God's temple. We members of God's temple. God wants us to soar with the gifts he has given us, but you must be founded on the right foundation. You are built on Christ and the apostles – the Word of God.

Jesus is the Cornerstone

> **Ephesians 2:20** | ...built on the foundation of the apostles and prophets, Christ Jesus himself being the cornerstone...

Jesus is the cornerstone of the foundation. A cornerstone was the first piece of the foundation laid, and the pinnacle of the building was measured by it, and the entire foundation was measured by it.

> *1 Corinthians 3:11* | No one can lay a foundation other than that which is laid, which is Jesus Christ.

When Paul talks about the cornerstone, he is delving into ancient prophecy. There would be a cornerstone laid for God's people. It is Jesus Christ. Way back in Psalm 118 we get intimations of it. In fact this is where Paul is quoting from...

> *Psalm 118:22-23* | The stone that the builders rejected has become the cornerstone. ²³This is the LORD's doing; it is marvelous in our eyes.

Jesus applied this verse directly to himself (Mt 21:42). He says in John 14:6, "I am the way the truth and the life." All the weight of biblical prophecy and divine promise rest on the cornerstone of the person and work of Jesus Christ. Without the gospel of Jesus, the whole house falls. Without Christ we are damned.

> *Galatians 1:9* | As we have said before, so now I say again: If anyone is preaching to you a gospel contrary to the one you received, let him be accursed.

Unfortunately, not everyone aligns with the cornerstone. Some accept Christ; some reject him. Jesus is the "stone the builders rejected"

(Mk 12:10; *cf* Psa 118:22). When news of the Messiah's arrival came to the magi in the East, they determined to bring Him gold, frankincense, and myrrh. But when that same news came to King Herod in Jerusalem, his response was to attempt to kill him (Mt 2:16-18). From the very beginning, Jesus was "a stone that causes people to stumble and a rock that makes them fall" (1 Pet 2:8).

How can people reject God's chosen, precious cornerstone? Simply put, they want to build something different from what God is building. Judgment is promised to all those who reject Christ: "Anyone who falls on this stone will be broken to pieces; anyone on whom it falls will be crushed" (Mt 21:44). You may know all theology and all the information correct and have all the Christian service, and even all the preaching. But is Christ your all? Is your life built on the chief cornerstone?

The Apostles and Prophets are the Foundation

When I lived in Spain, we had the privilege of transforming a 300-year-old Basque farmhouse into a Christian camp and conference center. Buildings 300 years ago were built differently than today. Many of those buildings were built stone by stone. Those stones rest on each other with only clay in between them. Do you know why that building is still standing today? Because it is built on solid rock. Christ is the cornerstone, and his weight is distributed amongst the apostles. Ephesians 2:20 gets specific. Christ's church is...

> **Ephesians 2:20a** | ...built on the foundation of the apostles and prophets...

What does it mean that the church is built on the foundation of the apostles and prophets? The word "apostle" means one who is sent out—specifically the Twelve apostles who were sent out and commissioned by the Lord personally, to write the New Testament and to expound the message of the gospel—the teaching and doctrine of Jesus Christ, inspired by the Holy Spirit. There are no "capital A" apostles anymore. Certainly, there were more than the Twelve during the first century, such as Paul, Apollos, and James as well as others. The foundation is laid, and it cannot be laid again. Surely there are "little a" apostles today, that is "sent out ones". There are those who are pastors of pastors and leaders of the leaders. We are grateful for such men. Yet there are no popes or any real authority like the apostles had, only gifting and influence from the exercise of those gifts for the good of the Body. We celebrate those "sent out ones".

The prophets were also foundational and are no longer are functioning today. They sometimes spoke revelation from God (Acts 11:21–28) and sometimes simply expounded revelation already given (as implied in Acts 13:1, where they are connected with teachers). They always spoke for God but did not always give a newly revealed message from God. The prophets were second to the apostles, and their message was to be judged by that of the apostles (1 Cor 14:37).[29]

The word order (apostles first, prophets second) suggests that Paul means New Testament apostles and prophets, the prophets being those to whom and through whom the Word of God was proclaimed. In support of this meaning, 3:4, 5 says that the "mystery of Christ ... has now been revealed by the Spirit to God's holy apostles and prophets" (*cf* 4:11).[30]

While the formal offices of Apostle and Prophet are no longer functioning, all who preach and teach the word rest on the apostolic and prophetic foundation. The gifts of pastors and evangelists have their full weight on the authority of the apostles and prophets through the Word of God that they gave us. There was a special attestation to the ministry of the apostles and prophets.

> *Hebrews 2:3-4* | How shall we escape if we neglect such a great salvation? It was declared at first by the Lord, and it was attested to us by those who heard, ⁴ while God also bore witness by signs and wonders and various miracles and by gifts of the Holy Spirit distributed according to his will.

> *Hebrews 1:1-2* | Long ago, at many times and in many ways, God spoke to our fathers by the prophets, ² but in these last days he has spoken to us by his Son.

The Sufficiency of Scripture

One thing about true believers is they love the message of the apostles. They love the apostles' doctrine. They search the Word of God and they scorch it into their hearts. There is one thing your life as a

---

[29] MacArthur. *Ephesians*, 142.
[30] Charles Hodge, *An Exposition of Ephesians* (Wilmington, DE: Associated Publishers and Authors Inc., 1972), 52.

Christian must be built around—the study of the Word of God. It is as Jesus said, quoting Deuteronomy 8:3.

> *Matthew 4:4* | Man shall not live by bread alone, but by every word that comes from the mouth of God.

The Scriptures are profitable. We have everything we need for life and godliness (2 Pet 1:3) in the message of Christ's apostles and prophets.

> *2 Timothy 3:16-17* | All Scripture is breathed out by God and profitable for teaching, for reproof, for correction, and for training in righteousness, [17] that the man of God may be competent, equipped for every good work.

We need the apostles' doctrine in order to be changed from glory to glory into the image of Christ (2 Pet 3:11). The apostles and prophets are the foundation for the church for any meaningful change. There are many models of change in this world, but all are vain and ineffective outside of the Scriptures. There are many erroneous understandings of the human heart. Consider some of those proposed by secular psychology.

The *blank slate model*. You are simply a product of your environment. The idea is to change your environment. That only works if there is not something sinister on the inside. The Scripture says our problem is not our environment. It's our heart.

The *psychoanalysis model*. It's your parents' fault. There's something in your past that makes you messed up. The goal is talk about your past.

There is *the biological model*. You are simply a mix of chemicals. You just need some pills.

There is *the self-esteem model.* There's nothing wrong with you. You need to love yourself. That just ignores the problem!

The only reasonable model is *the biblical model*. We take responsibility for our sin. We are rebels against God. We need forgiveness. We need to appropriate Christ's awful and wonderful payment for our sins. We need to trust Christ. And then, he gives us the Scriptures. The truth sets us free. We need a change of nature: regeneration gives you the power to change. We need a renewing of our mind in the Word of God. We need the foundation of the apostles' doctrine that points us to Christ, our chief cornerstone.

Jesus is the Chief Cornerstone

Ephesians 2:20b | ...built on the foundation of the apostles and prophets, Christ Jesus himself being the cornerstone...

Scripture describes Jesus as the "cornerstone" of our faith. Since ancient times, builders have used cornerstones in their construction projects. A cornerstone was the principal stone, usually placed at the corner of an edifice, to guide the workers in the measurement of the entire building. The cornerstone was usually one of the largest, the most solid, and the most carefully constructed of any in the edifice. Paul describes Jesus as the cornerstone that his church would be built upon. He is foundational. Once the cornerstone was set, it became the basis for determining every measurement in the remaining construction; everything was aligned to it. As the cornerstone of the building of the church, Jesus is our standard of measure and alignment. As the cornerstone, Jesus ensures the stability of the whole system of our salvation. Jesus was and is the only plan of salvation. The idea is first found in Isaiah.

Isaiah 28:16 | Therefore this says the Lord God: 'Behold, I lay in Zion a stone for a foundation, a tried stone, a precious cornerstone, a sure foundation.

The cornerstone was the most important stone of the building and of the foundation. Christ as the cornerstone taught the apostles and prophets who made up the rest of the foundation, and very importantly were the authors and expounders of the New Testament. For the world he is a rejected stone, but for us, he is our cornerstone.

The Lord is the Architect

Ephesians 2:21 | In whom the whole structure, being joined together, grows into a holy temple in the Lord.

The idea is that God has put you in the place you are! My desire is to see each of God's people be right where God has placed them in his holy temple, his church. James Montgomery Boice, beloved pastor of Fourth Presbyterian in Philadelphia makes a wonderful point regarding God's placement of his people in his temple, the church.

> We are told in 1 Kings 6:7 that when the great temple of Solomon was constructed, "it was with stone prepared at the quarry, so that neither hammer nor axe nor any tool of iron was heard in the house while it

was being built." To my knowledge, no building in history was ever built in this way. Its construction was almost silent, so holy was the work. Silently, silently, the stones were moved and added and the building rose."[31]

No noise. No hammers. So, it is with the Spirit of God. As the Lord says in John 3:7-8, "Do not marvel that I said to you, 'You must be born again.' 8 The wind blows where it wishes, and you hear its sound, but you do not know where it comes from or where it goes. So, it is with everyone who is born of the Spirit."

God's Spirit has raised you to life and made you a living stone in his temple. The test of regeneration is not a sinner's prayer, but the omnipotent transformative work of the Spirit raising you to life. What a mysterious work it is.

Paul says we ae joined, literally "being joined". This is in the passive tense. It means God picked you out and chose you. Anyone who is a builder knows this. The builder carefully chooses his materials. Yet he chose us not based on our fitness, but on our unfitness. He came not to save the righteous, but to call sinners to repentance.

The word "joined" also means jointed—shaped. God has made you and gifted you for service to him. We are joined "together." You cannot please God alone. You need the rest of the body. Now what you can do is hide your sin and come to church and not grow, or you can be vulnerable to other people and grow and change. But you cannot do this alone. The work of God cannot and will not go forward alone.

You are God's home. Atmosphere is important. Atmosphere changes everything. God has moved into my heart. My inner man is radically different. When I got married, a radical change took place. I became one with my wife. The plain walls got decorated. The beauty of a woman's touch was evident. Not only that, I began to dress better. A woman's opinion about clothing is identifiable to those outside the home who observed my fashion. Not only that, but her influence was also seen in my character. Her gentleness and tenderness rubbed off on me. Her orderliness and carefulness could be seen not only in my character but in how I managed my life and how I treated others. I was kinder, more thoughtful, more diligent in serving others. Now if a woman can have that kind of effect on a man from the outside, how much more can the indwelling God by his Spirit radically transform us

---

[31] Boice. *Ephesians*, 93.

from the inside? In salvation, I become the dwelling place of God. That's not to say God is confined to a space. Of course, God remains omnipresent. The heavens cannot contain him. Yet the mystery of salvation tells me that when I am indwelt by the Spirit, I am "filled with all the fulness of God." He's in all places, but he is also fully in me. Behold the wondrous mystery of the indwelling Spirit. God has moved in to your heart and soul! You ought to be different now. If you take a fish out of water, what happens to the fish? It cannot survive. Atmosphere is important. So it is with the Christian. Now the born-again Christian's air is the Spirit of holiness. Have you ever gone into a nice restaurant, and the only table available was smoking? Atmosphere is important.

God's Temple Individually

You are God's temple individually. The Spirit of God lives in you. His ministry is to fill you, guide you, produce his fruit of salvation in you, keep you away from sin and keep you walking in the love of Christ.

> *1 Corinthians 6:19* | Do you not know that your body is a temple of the Holy Spirit within you, whom you have from God? You are not your own.

God is going to enlighten you and reveal his Word to you personally each day by his Spirit if you let him.

God's Temple Corporately

1 Corinthians 12 teaches us that we are members of one Body with Christ as the head. In 2 Corinthians Paul turns to the image of a temple and how we are each a part of collective whole as God's temple.

> *2 Corinthians 6:16* | What agreement has the temple of God with idols? For we are the temple of the living God; as God said, "I will make my dwelling among them and walk among them, and I will be their God, and they shall be my people."

Each one of us is uniquely placed in God's temple. Peter says, "you yourselves like living stones are being built up as a spiritual house, to be a holy priesthood, to offer spiritual sacrifices acceptable to God through Jesus Christ" (1 Pet 2:4). You are not a finished temple. You are growing in holiness and love and faith. You are no longer part of the trash heap of throwaway stones, but you are a living stone. You are part of God's temple. You have a new functionality. Before you knew Christ, your life was being wasted. Now every good work is ordained beforehand that you should walk in it.

Conclusion

Christ has given us access to the God, and we are now his kingdom, his family, and his temple. What an amazing privilege access to God is! A great visual illustration of our access to God is found in Matthew 27:51, where we read: "And behold, the curtain of the temple was torn in two, from top to bottom. And the earth shook, and the rocks were split." It was as if Jesus' cry "It is finished" shook the earth, split the rocks, and tore the thick temple veil in two "from top to bottom." We know it is supernatural because huge, handwoven tapestries aren't usually "torn in two" and "from top to bottom."

What we don't know is to which veil Matthew is referring. Is it the inside veil that separates the Holy Place from the Most Holy Place or the Holy of Holies (the sanctuary where the Ark of the Covenant was kept and where only the high priest could enter only once a year on the Day of Atonement), or is it the outside veil that would have hung at the gate dividing the Court of the Jews from the Court of the Gentiles? If it is the outside veil it is a more dramatic and public spectacle, as that veil was eighty feet high and visible to all. If it is the veil to the entrance of the Holy of Holies it is less public but no less dramatic or theologically rich. The point of the torn veil is that we now we have access to God through Christ!

> *Hebrews 4:16* | Let us then with confidence draw near to the throne of grace, that we may receive mercy and find grace to help in time of need.

6 | EPHESIANS 3:1-13
ROOTED IN GOD'S ETERNAL PLAN

To me, though I am the very least of all the saints, this grace was given, to preach to the Gentiles the unsearchable riches of Christ, 9 and to bring to light for everyone what is the plan of the mystery hidden for ages in God, who created all things, 10 so that through the church the manifold wisdom of God might now be made known to the rulers and authorities in the heavenly places.

EPHESIANS 3:13

We are learning in Ephesians chapters 1-3 who we are in Christ. This is Paul's method in all his writings. We must know who we are in Christ before we can do what God wants us to do. You are not simply a citizen of this earth. You cannot keep your focus here on the things that are passing away. We can grow only as we keep our eyes on the heavenly kingdom.

Ephesians 3 is all about God's eternal plan for me. One of the things that seems to severely distract me from God's plan, and I believe all of God's people, is suffering. It comes in many forms. Sleepless nights, worries and anxieties, the aching and throbbing of your heart because of finances, the sheer terror of what could happen with your health, the agony of broken relationships – even physical or emotional abuse, and a thousand other things. It may come from watching a loved one, friend or child go through deep suffering.

If you live on earth, trials, tragedies, and incomprehensible pressures are as frequent as water. Suffering is common to man. How can we make sense of suffering? One of the biggest misconceptions is that either God doesn't love us, or he's forgotten about us. Neither could ever be the case. Those are lies from hell. God has an amazing plan that was hidden for all the ages but is today made known through Christ.

So, what are we to make of suffering? What do I do when all the pressures of the bills, your health, my family and loved ones, conflicts, and everything else start to add up? Some don't know what to do. You may even be experiencing panic attacks and severe anxiety because you don't know what to do with suffering. You may be experiencing many sleepless nights and tear-filled days. Life hurts, doesn't it?

And you must be wondering, is this God's plan for me? You may be asking then: What should I do with my pain? Paul answers question this in Ephesians 3:1-13 by lifting us above the pain of this life to focus on God's eternal plan.

We see how Paul addresses suffering – his suffering, and how it might have been confusing to the Ephesian believers. It was distressful to consider that this apostle was in prison. We see this in verse 1 and verse 13, "For this reason I, Paul, a prisoner for Christ Jesus on behalf of you Gentiles— 13 So I ask you not to lose heart over what I am suffering for you, which is your glory." Everything in between verses 1-13 tell us about God's infinite plan for us so that all our suffering can work for God's glory. We often want to lose heart because of our suffering or the sufferings of those we love. We must not lose heart. Paul himself was placed under house arrest in Rome for the purpose of reaching the Gentiles with the gospel of Christ. This is all part of God's eternal plan to save the world through Christ.

THE PRISONER FOR CHRIST (3:1-2)

God used Paul in a mighty way, even though he was under house arrest, chained to a Roman soldier day and night. Pain did not stop Paul from rejoicing. As Christians, we use pain as a platform for gospel ministry. Suffering does not limit us, rather, it expands our empathy and our ability to connect with other sufferers. Paul was a prisoner for

Christ under house arrest while writing this, a point upon which he focuses his hearers' attention.

Ephesians 3:1 | For this reason, I, Paul, a prisoner for Christ Jesus on behalf of you Gentiles.

It was worth it to Paul to be a prisoner for Christ because of the eternal mystery that was being revealed in the gospel, that the Seed promised in Genesis 3:15 was now revealed: Christ would crush the serpent's head in the act of being crushed and crucified himself. Through death Christ would conquer death. Paul was now in prison for proclaiming that Messiah had come. Specifically, he was under house arrest in Rome, in a house he rented at his own expense, chained twenty-four hours a day to members of the Emperor's Praetorian Guard (Acts 28:17-31). It was during this time he wrote the "Prison Epistles": Philippians, Ephesians, Colossians, and Philemon, from around 60-62 A.D.

But let's back up a bit. This imprisonment was no surprise. The Holy Spirit had revealed it to Paul years before. Before his imprisonment, near the end of his Third Missionary Journey, probably around the year A.D. 56 or 57, Paul and his traveling companions were making their way from Asia Minor to Jerusalem, primarily by boat. Their intention was to deliver funds to the poor Christians in Jerusalem, who were enduring a famine. On their way, they stopped in Miletus, where Paul met with the elders from the nearby church of Ephesus. During this meeting, Paul revealed that the Holy Spirit had warned him that he would be imprisoned when he arrived in Jerusalem. We read his prophetic words in Acts 20.

> *Acts 20:22-24* | Compelled by the Spirit, I am going to Jerusalem, not knowing what will happen to me there. I only know that in every city the Holy Spirit warns me that prison and hardships are facing me. However, I consider my life worth nothing to me, if only I may finish the race and complete the task the Lord Jesus has given me – the task of testifying to the gospel of God's grace.

In many cities Paul visited, believers prophesied his coming imprisonment. But the Holy Spirit compelled Paul toward this imprisonment. Paul knew that these prophecies were not intended to dissuade him from his course, but rather to prepare him for his coming hardships. A riot

"For this reason" introduces the cause of Paul's prayer (which really begins in 2:14) and refers back to the group of unifying truths Paul has just discussed in chapter 2—including the truths that the person in Christ becomes new (2:15); that all believers are in one body (2:16); that the Gentiles, who were once far away, now become near when they believe (2:17); that all believers are equally citizens of God's kingdom and members of his family (2:19); and that all believers are being built into God's temple and dwelling (2:21–22).[32]

Paul was willing to suffer for God's plan.

There is a purpose for Paul's pain. He knew that no matter what he suffered as a prisoner for Christ, it was worth it because it was part of God's plan to bring a multitude of Gentiles into Christ's kingdom.

If we are to follow Christ, we also ought to expect suffering. God has a wonderful purpose for pain in your life. C.S. Lewis said that "pain is God's megaphone to rouse a deaf world."[33] God uses pain in our lives. God works in us through affliction to transform us, to cleanse us, to humble us and make us gentle, sympathetic and compassionate toward others so that we can be useful. Pain advances of the gospel. Paul used pain as a platform for gospel ministry. We read in Philippians 1,

> *Philippians 1:12-14* | I want you to know, brothers, that what has happened to me has really served to advance the gospel, [13] so that it has become known throughout the whole imperial guard and to all the rest that my imprisonment is for Christ. [14] And most of the brothers, having become confident in the Lord by my imprisonment, are much more bold to speak the word without fear.

When John Piper had surgery because of prostate cancer – he said, "I don't want to waste my cancer." We must not waste our suffering. We must use it to advance the gospel. Whether we are a prisoner because of the gospel, or simply bound by sickness or tragedy or pressure – we must not waste our suffering. Pain is a test of our Christianity. Really when we get down to it, pain is a test of our Christianity. How we react to pain tells us how committed we are to Christ. Remember the words of Peter.

---

[32] MacArthur. *Ephesians*, 86.
[33] C. S. Lewis, *The Problem of Pain* (New York: Simon & Schuster, 1996), 83.

1 Peter 4:12-13 | Beloved, do not be surprised at the fiery trial when it comes upon you to **test** you, as though something strange were happening to you. ¹³ But rejoice insofar as you share Christ's sufferings, that you may also rejoice and be glad when his glory is revealed.

When you are sick or going through tragedy, rest in the grace of God and use it to advance the gospel. Pain brings attention to us. We were not made to get the attention. We must deflect attention to God and give him glory for his grace. We need to accept pain as a part of God's plan. Paul says in Philippians 4,

Philippians 4:11-13 | I have learned in whatever situation I am to be content. ¹² I know how to be brought low, and I know how to abound. In any and every circumstance, I have learned the secret of facing plenty and hunger, abundance and need. ¹³ I can do all things through him who strengthens me.

Paul's usefulness did not end in prison.

God gives us grace for ministry that is far greater than our pain and suffering. It is our responsibility to steward the grace of God that he gives us for ministry.

Ephesians 3:2 | assuming that you have heard of the stewardship of God's grace that was given to me for you...

Paul assumes his hearers have heard his testimony of a transformed life – from persecutor to preacher of Christ. He helps them to remember that whatever suffering he's going through is nothing compared to the glories he was presently experiencing through the Holy Spirit. Paul was in prison. Surprisingly, this did not hinder his ministry. He assumes the Ephesians have already heard of the amazing dispensation of God's grace that was given to Paul for the Ephesians and all the churches.

The word stewardship (*oikonomia*) has the idea of an administration or dispensation of something that was dispensed to Paul. Look at the word, and it is easy. We are all familiar with what it is to dispense something. This dispensation was the power Paul received to carry out his ministry. We are all given grace to carry out God's ministry. Later in Ephesians Paul says: "But grace was given to each one of us according to the measure of Christ's gift" (4:7). Peter tells us we all have exactly the gifts we need to carry out our ministry for the Lord no matter what our circumstances are.

1 Peter 4:10-11 | As each has received a gift, use it to serve one another, as good stewards of God's varied grace: [11] whoever speaks, as one who speaks oracles of God; whoever serves, as one who serves by the strength that God supplies—in order that in everything God may be glorified through Jesus Christ. To him belong glory and dominion forever and ever. Amen.

Paul was a prisoner for Christ. It did not stop him from being useful. What is it that stops you from being useful for Christ? Is there any circumstance that ought to hinder a child of God from using his or her gifts for the kingdom?

Paul had no pity parties.

3:2b | ... God's grace that was given to me for you...

Paul wasn't overly focused on himself. Even in prison, he was focused on the grace that has no barriers. God gave Paul a stewardship of grace to be given to the Gentiles, bringing them into the kingdom of God. This dispensation or measure of God's grace was far more than Paul needed for his own personal suffering and more than enough to preach the gospel to Gentiles.

Don't let your suffering keep you from ministering to others. Remember Paul's jail ministry. He had just been beaten, but he didn't say "Woe is me!" He sang with passion to God. And when the earthquake shook the prison, he started evangelizing the Philippian jailer.

What was Paul dispensing? What was Paul to be a steward and a manager of? Look at it here: He speaks of "the stewardship of God's grace that was given to me for you" (3:2). He was dispensing the grace of God. He was to be a manager, a steward of God's favor toward men. Wow! Imagine all the things people manage today—restaurant managers, sports team managers. They all have so much to think of to make sure everything goes right. Paul says he's been made the manager of something completely different. God used Paul as a dispenser of his grace—his unmerited favor in Christ, i.e., the gospel. I too have been given the grace of God, and I am to give it out freely.

Christians are grace dispensers. Squeeze them, and grace comes out. Put a tea bag in hot water, and the hot water draws the tea out. Put Christians in hot water and whatever is in their hearts comes out. When you suffer, don't stagnate or get bitter. Instead, get busy serving God. Paul had no pity parties. When he felt he had to address his pain, he quickly turned the attention to God's grace. No fussing and complaining here.

I knew a girl when I was in college named Becky Vaughn. A grease fire started in her kitchen when she was a little girl – literally exploded in her kitchen and knocked her and her mom out in 1978 when Becky was two years old. By the time they pulled her and her mother out they were severely burned. Becky was worse off, and not only burned but severely disfigured over 90 per cent of her body. Her father was my pastor in college, and he tells the story of struggling with God and praying for each of little Becky's fingers in the ICU only to watch them fall off. Why would God allow this? Peace did not come to that family until they realized that this pain did not keep them from ministry, this pain was part of God's ministry for them. Once day Becky's brother John, when they were younger asked, "Mommy, why can't Becky play the piano like I do." Mrs. Vaughn replied, "Son, God gave Becky the exact hands that she needs to fulfill his will for her life, and God gave you the hands you need to fulfill his will for your life." Wise words!

THE PROPHECY OF GOD'S PLAN (3:3-6)

Paul is in prison, but he's not glum or depressed. He's not concerned about his limits due to his incarceration. His eyes are on the eternal plan of God to save both the Jews and all the nations of the world. Listen to his words, written while chained to a Roman soldier.

> **Ephesians 3:3** | How the mystery was made known to me by revelation, as I have written briefly.

The Mystery Introduced

What does Paul when he calls the gospel a "mystery" that was made known to him only by divine "revelation" (3:3)? Have you ever seen the unveiling of a new make for a car? They have the car somewhat hidden, but you can see the shape of it. The car is draped with a covering, but you can see something amazing is underneath. That's how the story of redemption is in the Bible. In the Old Testament, the full understanding of the gospel of Jesus' birth, life, death, and resurrection is veiled. You can see the form. Moses tells us he's coming as the "Seed of the woman" (Gen 3:15). Micah tells us he'll be born in Bethlehem (Mic 5:6). Isaiah tells us he'll be "wounded for our transgressions" (Isa 53:6). Hosea tells us he'll be raised from the dead "on the third day" (Hos 6:2).

Hosea also tells us that the people of the nations that were called "no mercy" will be called "the children of the living God" (Hos 2:1). You can see the form and the shape, but you can't see the story of redemption in living color until Christ comes.

The Old Testament garbed the New Testament church in mystery. A mystery is a divine secret that only God can reveal. It is something that was in shadow form in the Old Testament but is now revealed by God. No one would ever know it if God hadn't revealed it. Augustine famously said: "The New Testament is in the Old concealed. And the Old Testament in the New is revealed."[34]

The Mystery Received

Paul gets into his testimony. He assumed most everyone knew who he was. He was a Pharisee of Pharisees, but he was marvelously and miraculously transformed into a follower of Christ on the Damascus Road. He explains how he was chosen to be the one to unveil the mystery (along with the other New Testament writers).

Ephesians 3:3 | How the mystery was made known to me by revelation.

The Bible uses the term, "mystery" to refer to something veiled that is now uncovered. Paul is the vessel that God uses to unveil the glories of the gospel. This was told him immediately at his conversion.

Acts 9:15-16 | The Lord said to him [Paul], "Go, for he is a chosen instrument of mine to carry my name before the Gentiles and kings and the children of Israel. [16] For I will show him how much he must suffer for the sake of my name.

The one who called himself "the chief of sinners" and the "least of the apostles" was chosen to unveil the prophecies of the Old Testament Scriptures. Now the full gospel of the person and work of Jesus Christ was no longer a mystery that was hidden.

The Mystery Unveiled

Paul says, the "sons of men" had not ever seen what you and I take for granted in the New Testament age today.

---

[34] Augustine of Hippo, "A Treatise on the Merits and Forgiveness of Sins, and on the Baptism of Infants," in *Saint Augustin: Anti-Pelagian Writings*, ed. Philip Schaff, trans. Peter Holmes, vol. 5, A Select Library of the Nicene and Post-Nicene Fathers of the Christian Church, First Series (New York: Christian Literature Company, 1887), 35.

Ephesians 3:4-5 | When you read this, you can perceive my insight into the mystery of Christ, ⁵ which was not made known to the sons of men in other generations as it has now been revealed to his holy apostles and prophets by the Spirit.

The reason Paul has such insight into the transforming power of the gospel (as he has shown in the first two chapters of Ephesians) and how we are "in Christ" and "chosen", "adopted", and "made alive", is because it has been "revealed" to Paul "by the Spirit" as one of "his holy apostles and prophets". What we today see through the apostles' writings (i.e. the New Testament) is something that the Old Testament prophets and people of God had hints of, but never knew in all its fullness. St. Peter says we are far more privileged than even the glorious prophets of the Old Testament.

> *1 Peter 1:10-12* | Concerning this salvation, the prophets who prophesied about the grace that was to be yours searched and inquired carefully, ¹¹ inquiring what person or time the Spirit of Christ in them was indicating when he predicted the sufferings of Christ and the subsequent glories. ¹² It was revealed to them that they were serving not themselves but you, in the things that have now been announced to you through those who preached the good news to you by the Holy Spirit sent from heaven, things into which angels long [*or stoop*] to look.

The angels are bent over stooping down to look at this. The prophets and even the angels have watched it unfold from the beginning. Consider the exile from the Garden of Eden and the promise of Messiah (Gen 3:15). God promises the Seed of the woman, though wounded, will crush the serpent's head. Will Messiah come? Years and years pass by, and it seems God has forgotten. Will he come? The angels are stooping down to see.

Moses and the prophets would be amazed at all the privileges we have. Moses had to wear a veil because of the glory of God he experienced, but we experience a greater glory. Peter says "they were serving not themselves but you" (1 Pet 1:12).

The Jews of old could only get near to God by going to the temple, and even then, there were curtains and walls that kept them out. Since Christ came, we know that we are the temple of the Holy Spirit (1 Cor 6:19).

The saints of old looked forward to how Christ would come by offering lambs and bulls and goats. We, as New Testament saints, have been cleansed by the blood of "the Lamb of God, who takes away the sin of the world" (Jn 1:29).

Can you imagine when the people of Jesus' time actually saw the advent of Christ? The incarnation, substitutionary death, and the resurrection of Christ had been hidden in Old Testament prophecy, but now it was revealed. It's not about "smells and bells" anymore. It's not about keeping Gentiles and unclean people out of the holy place. It is not about cleansings and purification rituals. The showbread of the tabernacle and temple are gone. The lights of the Menorah candles are no longer needed! There is no basin in our place of worship. We do not need to take a bath before we meet God. No more do we need to put bells along the bottom of our robe so that if we die in God's presence our friends can drag us out of the Holy Place. We no longer have the bells of worship and the smells of incense and burnt offerings. You don't need to become Jewish to follow the Lord. The reality has come. The ceremonies and blood-soaked altars are done away with because they are fulfilled in Jesus.

The Mystery Explained

One of the greatest revelations of the gospel mystery is that the Gentiles are brought into the covenant with Israel and are now "members of the same body". The Israel of the New Testament includes both Jews and Gentiles.

> **Ephesians 3:6** | This mystery is that the Gentiles are fellow heirs, members of the same body, and partakers of the promise in Christ Jesus through the gospel.

Consider the scandal of this part of the mystery. Gentiles are now fellow heirs. These people were hated by the Jews. They were the rejects. There was no greater hurdle in the ancient Jewish mindset. It would be like saving Nazis and Jewish people and putting them together.

What the mystery reveals is something we all need to remember. It's not about ceremonies – it's about souls. God predicted in the Old Testament that the Gentiles and all the nations of the world would be brought in through Abraham's seed. Truly, "Abraham will certainly become a great and mighty nation, and all the nations of the earth will be blessed through him" (Gen 18:18). It was no accident, surely, that the promised land was a bridge connecting Europe, Asia, and Africa, and that the great arterial highways of international commerce, communication, and conflict passed through it. God had always intended that his chosen people would become a spiritual blessing to all mankind—a truth that had too easily been forgotten. Even in the captivities and dispersions of the Jewish people from their land, God intended for his chosen people to have a redemptive impact on other nations. The book of Acts makes it abundantly clear that Jewish communities around the world formed a natural springboard for global evangelism.[35]

The new equality of the Gentiles was a bitter pill for most Jews to swallow. For centuries they had prided themselves on being God's chosen people. They had nurtured a growing contempt for Gentiles and wallowed in religious and racial snobbery. They had considered themselves to be God's favorites. Now all this superiority was shattered. It turned out that all along God had loved the Gentiles just as much as He had loved the Jews (witness the events in the book of Jonah, for instance). Now God was proving this truth in an astonishing way by bringing Jews and Gentiles together in a new body that ignored the special privileges the Jews had enjoyed for some thousand years. Gentiles were not going to be added to the existing corporate body of the Jewish people, the nation of Israel. There would be an entirely new body to which Jews and Gentiles would be added on equal terms.[36]

THE PREACHERS OF THE PLAN (3:7-11)

God does not choose the most qualified to preach his gospel. In fact, his ministers' only qualification is a gift of grace. Paul often alludes to this by saying that God chooses the weak and the foolish (1 Cor 1:24-26) and that his ministers merely plant and water, but it is God who gives the increase (1 Cor 3:6). Here he returns to this theme of the secret behind the success of God's ministers: God's power.

---

[35] John Phillips, *Exploring Ephesians & Philippians: An Expository Commentary*, The John Phillips Commentary Series (Kregel Publications; WORDsearch Corp., 2009), Eph 3:5-6.
[36] Ibid.

The Making of the Minister

> **Ephesians 3:7** | Of this gospel I was made a minister according to the gift of God's grace, which was given me by the working of his power.

It wasn't Paul's idea to serve Jesus Christ. Minister means "servant"—*diakonos*. Paul was busy persecuting Christians, and one day on the Damascus road, he was "called out". Jesus appeared to him, and he was born again. Christ went after him. If Christ does not go after a sinner, that sinner will not be saved. Paul's conversion was unique, and at the same time it wasn't. Few today will have a vision of Jesus like Paul did, but everyone who comes to know Jesus Christ will have a spiritual encounter with him. The Bible calls this the "drawing" to salvation, or the effectual "call" to salvation. Jesus said, "No one can come to me unless the Father who sent me draws him. And I will raise him up on the last day" (Jn 6:44).

Paul focuses not on his own strength or brilliance, but on the working of God's power. This is the only hope of any gospel minister. No minister has ever changed one person's heart. We are merely the mail carriers. God is the one who does the work. As Paul says, God must first work in the preacher's heart. Paul was made a minister by the gift of God's grace, not by his own brilliance or planning.

The Smallness of the Minister

> **Ephesians 3:8a** | To me, though I am the very least of all the saints, this grace was given...

Paul is using a play on words here. He takes the Greek word for "least" or "smallest" and adds an ending that comes out with the word "leastest". Some think he was playing off his Latin Name Paulus, which means Little or Least. The idea is: "I am little by name, little in stature, I am truly the least of all Christians. I am "Small Paul". He believed himself to be the "chief of sinners" and the "least of all apostles".

There are those who say that this is a bit of pious hyperbole. Paul is not *still* the least of all the saints. He is an apostle, a scholar, a missionary, a faithful servant, and a willing sufferer for Christ. Surely there are worse Christians than he! But such assertions expose a worldly way of reckoning our status before God that the apostle will not accept. If our best works merit us nothing, and therefore all of Paul's righteous deeds and sacrificial actions are not to his credit, then the only entries on Paul's spiritual ledger are those of debt.[37]

The Riches of the Minister

What does Paul or any gospel minister have to give to the nations? He is to proclaim nothing less than the unsearchable riches of Christ. The minister has a profound responsibility:

> **Ephesians 3:8b-9** | ...to preach to the Gentiles the unsearchable riches of Christ, **9** and to bring to light for everyone what is the plan of the mystery hidden for ages in God who created all things,

This plan is for everyone. No one is outside the grace of God. No one is without hope. This is God's plan hidden for the ages. No matter how spiritually impoverished and depraved a person is, we preach Christ, in whom are unsearchable riches that will satisfy our soul's every longing. God's Son is able to save the filthiest, most hopeless sinner. He can humble the proud and give grace to the humble.

Humanly speaking, Paul was a pauper. He owned nothing. Everything he had was either destroyed by those who persecute him or simply given to those in need. He counted all things as "refuse" for the cause of Christ (Phil 3:8). So how can Paul speak of riches? Paul is speaking of the riches of Christ's sacrifice that infinitely pays all our sin.

Paul makes the effect of Christ's sacrifice and the greatness of God's grace all the more obvious. Paul should have the least status, the least privilege, the greatest debt of any Christian, and yet God has called him to preach to the nations. The unsearchable riches of Christ (the word "unsearchable" implies "inscrutable" or "incomprehensible") that Paul is called to proclaim are evident in their application to his own account. The greatness of his debt makes the magnitude of Christ's riches all the more plain. That is why Christian maturity is never afraid of repentance and, in fact, desires it. Seeing our sin for its true magnitude makes the grace of God all the more great and precious to us. That is why, as the apostle Paul approaches the end of his life, he emphasizes his sin all the more, saying not only that he is the least of the saints, but that he is the chief of sinners (1 Tim 1:15).[38]

---

[37] Chapell, *Ephesians*, 142.
[38] Ibid.

Christ's blood gives us the riches we need. His blood paid my debt. He who knew no sin became sin for me that I might become the righteousness of God in him (2 Cor 5:21). What riches of grace I have been given in Christ.

THE PURPOSE OF GOD'S PLAN (3:10-11)

Paul says that the reason that he will make plain the mystery of the Gentiles' inclusion in God's covenant promise to Israel is to enlighten angelic rulers and authorities in the spiritual realm.

> **Ephesians 3:10-11** | so that through the church the manifold wisdom of God might now be made known to the rulers and authorities in the heavenly places. ¹¹ This was according to the eternal purpose that he has realized in Christ Jesus our Lord.

Were these good or bad angels that are being enlightened? It doesn't say, but it's likely both. The elect angels praise God when they see God's grace toward the church from every tribe, language and family. The fallen angels see how just their own damnation is. What is clear in all of these passages is that God is using the church to display his glory to those who operate in the heavenly places.

God's wisdom is here called "manifold" or literally "multi-colored", a word (in the Septuagint) used to describe Joseph's coat of many colors. In this one phrase Paul enfolds previously mentioned ideas of God's predestinating will, sovereign election, and unfolding mystery. All reflect a divine wisdom working to meld into the church sinners made perfect in Jesus from every tribe, people, and nation.

This manifold wisdom of bringing together into one redeemed body those who were so universally fallen and so particularly different is according to the eternal purpose and plan revealed in Christ's life, death, and resurrection. Those who come to Jesus must come to him as Christ (Savior) and Lord.

THE PRIVILEGES OF GOD'S PLAN (3:12-13)

What glorious privileges we have as God's children, chief among them is access to God. This is the reason the Ephesians should never lose heart, no matter how hard life might seem with Paul in prison. God is in control, and he is always near to his children.

The Privilege of Access

Ephesians 3:12-13a | ... in whom we have boldness and access with confidence through our faith in him. ¹³ So I ask you not to lose heart over what I am suffering for you.

No matter how distant God seems to be from your circumstances, we ought to have boldness and confidence in our full access to God's presence. We can draw near to him and to his rainbow-circled, cherubim-guarded, highly exalted throne. We can come without pomp and ceremony, without formal and ritualistic preparations, without mediators of any sort. We can come directly to Him at any time, day or night, with the confidence of a son or daughter. No one on earth, in heaven, or in hell can bar our way. Such is God's love for us.

The Greek word translated "confidence" in Ephesians 3:12 means "confident assurance." One would not have this confident assurance if he entered a neighbor's house uninvited, opened the refrigerator, pulled up a chair to the table, and helped himself to supper. But one would have this confident assurance in his father's house because that is where he belongs, and he knows he is welcome there.

The Greek word translated "boldness" here usually means "free speech," as in 2 Corinthians 3:12. The right of free speech is the privilege of every citizen in a democracy. But Paul had a higher meaning in mind. In the New Testament the word means every believer's right to come directly to God, having no other priest, mediator, or advocate than the Lord Jesus Christ. What arrogance for a religious system to interpose man-made functionaries between the child of God and his Father's smile. The only mediator needed is Christ; in other words the Christian has access "by the faith of him" (3:12).[39]

The Privilege of Progress

Ephesians 3:13 | So I ask you not to lose heart over what I am suffering for you, which is your glory.

In suffering we often feel God has forsaken us. The opposite is true. In all our suffering he is preparing us for our eternal glorification with him. Every hurt and difficulty prepares us to meet Christ face to face. We are progressively being conformed to his image. That's what Paul

---

[39] Phillips, Eph 3:12.

calls "your glory" in this verse. Literally Paul is speaking of the final part of our salvation: glorification. When a person is saved, they are on a journey that cannot be thwarted. Glorification speaks of the moment when we are fully glorified, body and soul, and completely conformed into the image of Christ at his second coming. When you are saved, God sees you complete in Christ. He sees you as his spotless Bride because of the blood of Christ. Yet on earth we still fight against our sinful desires and propensities. Yet there is coming a day when we will be transformed into Christ's perfect likeness.

To state it plainly: our present suffering results in our future glory. Suffering, persecution, and tribulation are those things which demonstrate that you are truly a Christian. If you are saved, then Christ is saving you from your sin. He is testing you and forming the heart of Christ in you. He's doing this for some through marriage, through jobs, through relationship problems, through tragedies, through powerful insults hurled your way. Are you really a Christian? Can you forgive? Can you live holy when you are not being treated well? Paul was in prison when he wrote this epistle. Our suffering is for Christ's glorious image being formed in us day by day. Paul's suffering, and all of our suffering is for our present sanctification and our future glorification.

Conclusion

God has caused history to unfold like a great drama upon a cosmic stage. The angels are the audience. We are the actors. Satan is there to do everything he can to resist and thwart God's purposes. This drama unfolds across the centuries as Adam and Eve, Noah, Abraham, Moses, David, Isaiah, John the Baptist, Jesus, Peter, Paul, and all the other participants of Christian history, both the great persons and the minor persons, are brought on stage to play the part God has assigned them and speak words that come from hearts that love him. Adam proved that God's way is the best way, and he repented of his sin and trusted in the coming of Jesus. So did Eve and Noah and all the others. All these endured as seeing by faith him who is invisible, and they looked beyond the distresses of this life for their reward.

Now you and I are the players in this drama. Satan is attacking, and the angels are straining forward to look on. Are they seeing the "manifold wisdom" of God in you as you go through your part and speak your lines? They must see it, for it can be seen in you alone. It is there—

where you work and play and think and speak—that the meaning and end of history is found.[40]

---

[40] Boice, *Ephesians*, 106.

7 | EPHESIANS 3:14-19
ROOTED IN GOD'S PRESENCE

I bow my knees before the Father... that according to the riches of his glory he may grant you to be strengthened with power through his Spirit in your inner being.
EPHESIANS 3:14, 16

Have you ever felt powerless? I can remember as a child growing up in the winding roads of Louisiana where my most faithful transportation was a Huffy bicycle. I used to go everywhere on that bike. It never failed me... until I was going at top speed at about 15 miles an hour by Michael Barnes' house. Here's the thing – Mike had a big dog. I don't even remember what kind of a dog it was. I just remember one thing about it. It had big teeth. Everything about this dog was big! I couldn't go fast enough. I remember thinking I wanted to grow up. I didn't want to be this dog's meal. Terror raced through my veins as this dog started running next to me and gnawing at my twirling feet that couldn't peddle fast enough! My Huffy bike failed me. Obviously, I survived. I don't remember how I got out of that, but the fact that I'm here today proves I lived through it!

Then came 1987. I begged my mom for a used 1980 C-70 Honda passport moped! She vowed never to get me one of those. It went too fast. But we lived a mile deep into the woods in Louisiana and a moped could be quite helpful. She broke down and got it for me! It wasn't in the greatest shape. It had a part missing from the carburetor, so any time I wanted it to go I had to actually place my hand over the carburetor so that the gas would get suctioned into the engine. I finally rigged the carburetor with a rubber band and a piece of cloth, and I could go anywhere. What's my point? What good is the moped if it has no power? What good is it if it has a broken carburetor and you can't get fuel to the engine?

In the same way, the Christian life is like a car. What good does it do you if you have a beautiful, sophisticated automobile if you don't have the key? No key, no power. Well in the Christian life we have all we need! We've learned about the sufficiency of Jesus Christ, and the believer's resources available in Christ. Ephesians 1-3 speak of who we are in Christ – all the resources we have in Christ, and 4-6 what we are to do – our vocation. The first three chapters explain our position. The last three, our vocation, or our calling. We cannot do what God intends for us to do, unless we be what God intends for us to be.

Sandwiched in the middle of these great chapters is the empowerment of it all. In other words, I know *who* I am in Christ. I know *what* he wants me to do. But *how* do I do it? If chapters 1-3 are *enlightenment*, then chapter 3:14-21 is *empowerment*. I want to be empowered through worship. This is Paul's prayer. This is a passage that tells us how the Christian life works through worship. Paul was dedicated to helping these Christians turn on the power of their Christian lives. He knelt in prayer for this very reason. He wanted the Ephesian believers to experience worship through God's power, Christ's love, and his infinite fullness.

A PRAYER TO EXPERIENCE THE SPIRIT'S POWER (3:14-16)

Since we have no power in and of ourselves, we begin by praying to the Father in heaven, like Paul did, for power.

Ephesians 3:14 | For this reason I bow my knees before the Father.

Allegiance to the Father

Kneeling was not the ordinary position for the Jew. They were accustomed to standing and rocking back and forth like they do at the Wailing Wall today. Bowing the knees would be done at an extraordinary event, like Solomon did at the dedication of the temple. And what it pointed to was allegiance and wholehearted commitment. Paul says,

"I am committed to God to praying for the most important work that can be done in you. I'm praying that you'll not just understand your position. I pray you'll turn on the power!" Because God is our heavenly Father, we do not come to Him in fear and trembling, afraid that He will rebuff us or be indifferent. We do not come to God to appease Him as the pagans do to their deities. We come to a tender, loving, concerned, compassionate, accepting Father. A loving human father always accepts the advances of his children, even when they have been disobedient or ungrateful. How much more does our heavenly Father accept His children, regardless of what they have done or not done? Paul approaches the Father with boldness and confidence, knowing that he is more willing for his children to come to him than they ever are of going to him. He knows that God has been waiting all the while with a Father's heart of love and anticipation.[41]

Affection for God's Family

Not only did Paul have an allegiance to the Father, but he also had an affection for his fellow believers.

> **Ephesians 3:14-15** | For this reason I bow my knees before the Father, **15** from whom every family in heaven and on earth is named.

There are different families in heaven and earth – the family of redeemed saints in heaven, the family of redeemed saints on earth, families of angels – classes of cherubim and classes of seraphim. We all have one commonality – We have a loving relation with our precious Father in heaven. We are loved by him and reflect his identity in our lives. The cherubim reflect him as flames of fire, so glorious is he. We reflect him with fire in our hearts. Now this is who we are, but how do we turn it on?

It's a super big family, "from whom every family on heaven and earth is named." We need to remember that a great host of believers has already made it safely to heaven, and when we are all together on the last day, there will be "a great multitude, which no man could number, of all nations, and families, and people, and languages" (Rev 7:9). We are a called-out people! In other places in Scripture we as the family of God are called "the elect of God"—the "household of faith"--the "body of Christ"—"the bride of Christ"—the "living temple"—the "sheep

---

[41] MacArthur. *Ephesians*, 101.

that never perish"—this is the final redeemed Church, "without spot or wrinkle"—the final number of believers that God brings to perfect holiness in the perfect righteousness of Jesus Christ. This is the group of called out people that will be resurrected on the Last Day to meet the Lord in the air.

It's a supernatural family! Membership in the family of God does not depend on any earthly relationship. It does not come by your physical or natural birth but by a supernatural birth—a new birth. Preachers cannot impart it to their hearers. Parents cannot give it to their children. You may be born in the godliest family in America and grow up under the strongest preaching any church can supply and yet never belong to the family of God. You see, Jesus said, "Except a man be born again, he cannot see the kingdom of God" (Jn 3:3). No one but the Holy Spirit can make you a living member of this family. It is his special function and prerogative to bring into the true Church all those who will be saved. Those who are born again are born "not of blood, nor of the will of the flesh, nor of the will of man, but of God" (Jn 1:13).

There is a family language: prayer. Paul said, "I bow my knees unto the Father of our Lord Jesus Christ, of whom the whole family in heaven and earth is named" (3:14-15a). J.C. Ryle said:

> A habit of prayer is one of the surest marks of a true Christian. All the children of God on earth are alike in this respect. From the moment there is any life and reality about their religion, they pray. Just as the first sign of life in an infant when born into the world is the act of breathing, so the first act of men and women when they are born again is praying. This is one of the common marks of all the elect of God.[42]

There is a family likeness: Christ in us! Christ is in you if you are part of the family of God. You are his body. You are his hands and his feet in this world. When he returns a second time in power and glory, "we know that, when he shall appear, we shall be like him; for we shall see him as he is" (1 Jn 3:2). Of course, we don't have to wait to be like him. Every day we should be more and more resembling the Lord Jesus since all who know Christ are "predestinate to be conformed to the image of his Son, that he might be the firstborn among many brethren" (Rom 8:29).

---

[42] J. C. Ryle (1816-1900). *A Call to Prayer—with Study Guide* (Pensacola, FL: Chapel Library) Kindle Edition.

There is a family location: heaven and earth. Remember, two places, and only two, contain the family of God. The Bible tells us of no third habitation. There is no such thing as purgatory, despite what some may falsely teach. Oh no! Two places, and only two. Some of God's family are safe in heaven. They are at rest in that place which the Lord Jesus expressly calls "Paradise" (Lk 23:43) They have finished their course. They have fought their battle. They have finished their appointed work. They have learned all that God wanted them to learn on earth. They have taken up their cross and followed Jesus 'till the end. They have passed through the waves of this wicked world and have reached the harbor, and by God's grace were kept unspotted from the world. They are no longer troubled by sin and temptation. They have said goodbye forever to finances and anxiety, to pain and sickness their broken body. They will never cry again for God has wiped away all tears from their eyes. Some of God's family are still on the earth. They are scattered everywhere in the midst of a world, a few in one place and a few in another. All are following Jesus according to the grace that is working in them. We are running the race, doing the work he has left us to do, fighting the good fight of faith, daily taking up our cross, striving and fighting and battling against indwelling sin, walking in the Spirit, resisting the devil, crucifying the flesh, struggling against the world, witnessing for Christ. The early church had nick names for those in heaven and on earth. Those in heaven were called "the church triumphant", and those on earth—"the church militant". One day we will all be triumphant in heaven, having won the final victory, but until then, we continue the holy war, the spiritual battle of life and remain the church militant.

There is a family love: It is the Father's love that draws us to Christ. He will not fail in bringing lost sinners to himself. God so loved the world (Jn 3:16). Those he saves, he will save perfectly. He will not fail. He cannot lose even one sheep. Dear, dear beloved child of God. God's love for you is so great that even when you were yet in your sins—like the lost, prodigal son far away from home, you had gone astray—turning to your own way—wasting your substance on riotous living—it was then that he loved you. The Father's love for you was pulsating for you even when you were in your sins. It was in your sins that the Father sent his only begotten Son as a ransom for all your sins. It was the Father's everlasting love that sent the Holy Spirit down into your heart to open your eyes, to bring you to your right mind, to shed his love abroad in your heart.

Ability from the Spirit

Paul knew that God's power had no limit. The supply of power God promises is from the Spirit and it has no end. Paul prays that God would enable them to employ the fullness of that power. Because believers are the habitation of the triune, all-powerful God of the universe, Paul prays that their unlimited energy from him would be manifested.[43]

> **Ephesians 3:16** | For this reason I bow my knees before the Father…that according to the riches of his glory he may grant you to be strengthened with power through his Spirit in your inner being.

To start with, if you're going to really be effective, and want God's power to be released, you need to have spiritual stamina to be victorious over temptation, to be victorious over the world, the flesh, and the devil. You have to have a strong inner man to resist temptation in your flesh. The only way you can ever have a strong inner man is when the Spirit of God strengthens you. God offers infinite strength. Paul is piling on the words to describe the infinite power of the Spirit to live a joyful, holy, victorious Christian life apart from the temptation of the world. I need God's strength. I need him to grant it to me. Jesus says, "Without me you can do nothing (Jn 15:5). God has immeasurable resources. None of us can make ourselves Christians. None can conform ourselves to the image of Christ. It is "according to the riches of his glory" (3:16). He must grant it. If you're going to really be effective, and want God's power to be released, you need to have spiritual stamina to be victorious over temptation, to be victorious over the world, the flesh, and the devil. You have to have a strong inner man to resist temptation, a strong inner man to resist the flesh. And the only way you can ever have a strong inner man is when the Spirit of God strengthens you. Paul's desire is that we might "be strengthened with power through his Spirit in your inner being." We see the outer nature perishing away. One day if live long enough we're all going to look like raisins. We are perishing outwardly. But inwardly, we ought to be being renewed and

---

[43] MacArthur. *Ephesians*, 101-102.

refreshed and renovated. We have everything we need in the Word of God and in surrender to the Spirit.

> *2 Corinthians 4:16* | So we do not lose heart. Though our outer nature is wasting away, our inner nature is being renewed day by day.

It's easy to feed the flesh when things become hard. But instead, we need to apply God's Word when things get difficult. Give attention to your inner being, your soul, who you are. Your inner man used to be addicted to sin. When you feel the desolation of loneliness, don't check out with media. Go to Christ and build up your inner man. Don't ignore problems in your life. Don't check out. Don't feed your flesh. Work out spiritually. Feast on the word. Meditate on it and work on your inner form more than your outer form. "Bodily exercise profits" but it profits "little" (1 Tim 4:8). Godliness profits for now and eternity.

God wants to give you the strength "according to his riches." I hear Apple, Inc. has a surplus of like 500 billion dollars. Now Apple CEO Tim Cook can give investors "from his riches". But he runs out after 500 billion (circa 2006). God gives "according to his riches". That is "on the scale and in proportion to the wealth that he owns". How much does God own? Everything. Let me challenge you, when you are hurting, rely on the riches of God's Word and His power in the Spirit to be conformed to the image of Christ. Apply God's Word to your life instead of checking out! Don't check out! Work out (spiritually). "No soldier gets entangled in civilian pursuits, since his aim is to please the one who enlisted him" (2 Tim 2:4).

Does your face shine like Moses? Moses had a time with God up on Mount Sinai. When he came down from Mount Sinai, he needed a veil to cover his face. Do you shine with Christ? Do you have a prayer closet where there is a burning bush of God's presence? Are you feeding on the Word and yielding to the Spirit?

The Secret to Experiencing God's Power

The power of Christ is so radical and explosive that it ought to be coming out of us in every area of our life. But what is the secret to the power? How can I get it? How can I turn it on? What good is it if I have a sophisticated automobile but I don't know how to turn it on? It has to do with God's love.

We all like secrets. Do you remember the Rubik's Cube? I grew up in the 1980s. Rubik's Cube is a 3-D mechanical puzzle invented in 1974 by Hungarian sculptor and professor of architecture Ernő Rubik.

In 1980, when I was six years old, the Ideal Toy Company purchased the patent and began mass producing them. The craze of the Rubik's Cube took off. It is widely considered to be the world's best-selling toy. As of January 2009, 350 million cubes had been sold worldwide.

There's a secret to the Rubik's Cube. I'm sure you're expecting me to solve it right here. Well, I don't want to show off. But when I was a kid with all of six years under my belt my brothers would give me the Rubik's Cube all mixed up, and I would go away or a while and when I returned, I had solved the Cube! All the sides matched perfectly. It looked like I was a child prodigy – a genius!

Everyone wanted to know – "What's your secret?" I can tell you I wasn't a genius. I was still in my depraved state, and I was very good at deception. I realized that it was much, much easier to take the Cube apart to solve it than to spend hours figuring out which way to turn the confounded little cube.

Look I don't have any secrets for the Rubik's Cube, but I do have one for the power of God to be unleashed in your life. So many people are trying to get a short cut to the power of God. It's not going to happen. Jesus said, "Without me, you can do nothing" (Jn 15:5).

Now the secret to God's power being unleashed in your life is simply this: you need to have a deep sense of God's love for you. You need to seize upon the love of Christ. How can I have this great power? It is as we will see today, by knowing the love of Christ.

A PRAYER TO EXPERIENCE CHRIST'S LOVE (3:17-19)

Ephesians 3:17-19 | so that Christ may dwell in your hearts through faith—that you, being rooted and grounded in love, **18** may have strength to comprehend with all the saints what is the breadth and length and height and depth, **19** and to know the love of Christ that surpasses knowledge, that you may be filled with all the fullness of God.

God says we ought to be "rooted and grounded" in Christ's love (3:17). The soil and foundation of our life ought to be that the Lord Jesus Christ loves me. It is at the Cross where we see the ocean of God's love poured out for us. Jesus cried out, "My God, my God, why have you forsaken me?" And the answer is: for you. He did it all for you! Look at what Paul says: Let the soil of God's life be God's love for you! Let your life be *filled* with God's love for you!

Indwelt by the Loving Christ

Ephesians 3:17 | so that Christ may dwell in your hearts through faith...

The word "dwell" means to make oneself at home. The word is a compound "kata-oikeo" "*kata*" means "down" and "*oikeo*" means home. Is Christ "down-home" in your heart? Is he comfortable? Is the Holy Spirit pleased or is he grieved?

Now remember, this is a progression. The "so that" means first start working out in the inner man. Be doing spiritual exercises. If not, you will not sense the indwelling Christ. Some of you feel distant from God today. Theologically, this phrase is about the indwelling Christ and the union that we have with him. What Paul is praying is that Christ would have *control* over our heart. Is Christ at *home*, controlling your thoughts, controlling your life, communing intimately with you?

There is a book called *My Heart, Christ's Home* by Robert Boyd Munger –perhaps you own it. This is a great book to read to your children. Munger likens the Christian's heart to a house. And the question is, "Is Christ comfortable there?" The heart like a home has a library and then a dining room and then a living room and then a workshop and finally a closet.

The Library – what do you think on? What do you take into your heart? The library is the control room, that's where all the data is stored. All the information is stored, and that's like your brain. And when the Lord comes into your house, what does he find in the library? What does he find in the control room? You might have a TV in that room. What does he find? Is it trash and triviality, pornography and materialism? What does he find? What occupies your mind? Whenever Christ comes in and is comfortable – he renews our mind and comforts our heart with peace. He clears out the garbage books and throws out the trash and replaces it with the Word of God. Truly the blessed man's "delight is in the law of the Lord, and on his law he meditates day and night" (Psa 1:2).

The Dining Room – This is the room of appetites where your desires and appetites are satiated. And Christ wants to know what do you long for? What's on your menu? What do you order? What really satisfies you? The Lord wants to replace all the illegitimate stuff with the will of God so that that alone would satisfy you. We say with David: "Whom have I in heaven but you? And there is nothing on earth that I desire besides you" (Psa 73:25). "The law of your mouth is better to me than thousands of gold and silver pieces" (Psa 119:72).

The Living Room – The living room is a place of conversation and being together and cultivating relationship. And in this particular story Munger describes how Christ comes into the living room and sits there and sits there and sits there and sits there and nobody ever shows up. What ever happened to prayer? And what ever happened to communion? And what ever happened to fellowship? And what happened to relationship? Do you have a prayer closet? Do you get alone with God?

The Workshop – What are you making? What are you doing with your life? What's your legacy? We've got all these gifts – what are we doing with them? And the answer is most are making toys. And Christ wants to fix it so that you're producing something that has eternal value.

The Closet – In Munger's book he gets through the whole house, but he says there's a terrible stench coming from somewhere. And it's a closet. So the Lord, picking up the scent, goes to the closet and in there is something foul, something dead and it's the place of hidden personal sins. And he throws the door open. And Munger says, "This is too much! I am not going to give him the key."[44] I mean, give me a break. I gave you the library, the dining room, the living room and the workshop and everybody knows in every house if you find the right closet, God only knows what you'll discover in there. God wants your closet. He wants to clean out your personal sins. He wants to sanctify you completely. Listen to the sweet words of our Lord Jesus, "If anyone loves me, he will keep my word, and my Father will love him, and we will come to him and make our home with him" (Jn 14:23).

Seized with Christ's Love

> **Ephesians 3:18-19a** | that you...may have strength to comprehend with all the saints what is the breadth and length and height and

---

[44] Robert Boyd Munger; Andrea Jorgenson. *My Heart Christ's Home: A Story for Old and Young* (Kindle Locations 171-172).

depth, **¹⁹** and to know the love of Christ that surpasses knowledge...

The Lord wants us to comprehend – *katalambano* – to seize upon– to leap and take hold of – to dive for –the love of Christ. Rigorously grasp his love. Do whatever it takes to grasp it. Be greedy for it! It is God's will for "all the saints" to experience the love of Christ in all its fullness. It is not for the elite. It is for you. The simplest Christian ought to be seized with the love of God! Oh, how wide, how long, how high, and how deep is the love of Christ! Does it seize you? Jonathan Edwards wrote at age 19 a set of 70 resolutions to go over each day. He had one concerning God's Love for him. Listen to it:

> Resolved, to examine carefully, and constantly, what that one thing in me is, which causes me in the least to doubt of the love of God; and to direct all my forces against it (Resolution 25).

We ought to have a God sized love! Charles Simeon, the old Puritan, called these four measurements of God's love, "the Four Magnitudes".

It is a love *wide* enough to embrace the world (Jn 3:16). There is no limit to who God will reach. Christ's love is not narrow, but wide! It extends to all families of the earth. It is upon every continent and in every culture. The hymns of Christ are sung in Zulu and in Chinese, in Swahili and in English. Those of every culture sings of Christ's love. The poor sing of Christ as well as the rich. The love of Christ extends not only for his elect, but even for those who would be damned. He cries over Jerusalem says, "How often would I have gathered you as a hen gathers her chickens, but you would not" (Lk 13:34). Spurgeon said it best: "God has honest tears of grief" for those who are not his chosen Bride.[45]

It is a love *long* enough to last forever. As Ephesians 1:4 says, God's love is so long that it extends to eternity past when he chose us in Christ. From eternity past, God planned to send his Son to save you on that brutal cross. God says, "I have loved you with an everlasting love" (Jer 31:3). Before you were formed in your mother's womb, God set his love upon you. It's a love so long it also covers eternity future, "so that in the coming ages he might show the immeasurable riches of his grace in kindness toward us in Christ Jesus" (2:7). As Spurgeon said, "It is so

---

[45] Charles Spurgeon. *Metropolitan Tabernacle Pulpit*, Vol 12, Sermon 707, "Heavenly Geometry" (London: Passmore & Alabaster, 1866), 469.

long that your old age cannot wear it out, so long your continual tribulation cannot exhaust it, your successive temptations shall not drain it dry; like eternity itself it knows no bounds."[46] When long trillions of ages have passed, God's love will be so fresh and powerful that you will feel like you've just come into the kingdom. So great is the *joy* and the *power* of God's love!

It is a love *deep* enough to take Christ to the very depths to reach the lowest sinner. Christ took hell for you. Look how low he reached to reach you. When we were dead in our sins God loved us (Eph 2:1-3). Indeed, "when we were without strength" God love us and "Christ died for us" (Rom 5:6). How deep is God's love? John Newton was the scum of the earth. He was a slave ship captain. In 1748 someone gave him a copy of Thomas aKempis' "Imitation of Christ." In May of that year there was a violent storm that made him consider as he called it "the uncertain continuance of life". He put his trust in Christ! Such a murderer, liar, and blasphemer. So deep is the love of Christ that Christ would go to the depths of the cross and take your sin upon him – robed in the maggot infested garment of your iniquity. All your filth was put upon him. He came so low!

It is a love *high* enough to take broken sinners like you and me to heaven. He loves you so much that what he has begun in you he promises to finish (Phil 1:6). He gives us every spiritual blessing in Christ (1:3). He seats us in victory in the heavenlies! So high is the love of Christ that he makes us "heirs of God and joint – heirs with Christ" (Rom 8:17). You will reign with him and you do reign with him. Says Stott:

> The love of Christ is broad enough to encompass all mankind (especially Jews and Gentiles, the theme of these chapters), 'long' enough to last for eternity, 'deep' enough to reach the most degraded sinner, and high enough to exalt him to heaven.[47]

Look how Christ exchanged his crown of majesty for a crown of thorns. He exchanged his throne and his scepter for a cross – and it was all for you! God wants you to soar. This is the secret to loving others. It is to be seized and to be taken by and grasping the love of Christ for

---

[46] Ibid.
[47] John Stott. *The Message of Ephesians: God's New Society*, (Downers Grove, IL: InterVarsity Press, 2014), 137.

you. Oh how wide, how long, how high, and how deep is the love of Christ. Does it seize you?

A PRAYER TO EXPERIENCE GOD'S FULLNESS (3:19B)

Ephesians 3:19b | that you may be filled with all the fullness of God.

We are asking that God – the eternal God, the almighty God, the creator God, the sustainer God, the God of the universe, the God who made it all, the God who fills all to fill me? That's incredible. We are that we all are "his body, the fullness of him who fills all in all" (1:23).

The Meaning of Fullness

The word πληρωμα (pleroma), fullness, is a word that is used many times in the New Testament to speak of total fullness. The Bible speaks of people being filled with anger, filled with rage, filled with all goodness or filled with the Spirit. The word "filled" according to the Greek lexicon is "to fill a vessel or hollow place; to cause to swell; to satisfy; supply abundantly with something, impart richly; to complete, make perfect, accomplish an end". What it means that you are dominated and controlled by something or someone. Can you say you are "dominated with all the domination of God"? You might say, "When I get that job or that relationship, I'll be happy!" The truth is you'll not be happy till you are filled with all the fullness of God. God's got to have complete control! I wonder if we truly know the fullness of God. A. W. Tozer famously lamented:

> If the Holy Spirit was withdrawn from the church today, 95 percent of what we do would go on and no one would know the difference. If the Holy Spirit had been withdrawn from the New Testament church, 95 percent of what they did would stop, and everybody would know the difference.[48]

You don't need to wait for this to happen. I had this immediately when I came to know Christ. You already have "all spiritual blessings in Christ" (1:3). The fullness of God in the simplest experience is the awareness of God's presence and love for you.

A couple years ago I had the privilege of taking Jill and the kids to the Glow Show in Elgin. Basically, there are all these larger-than-life

---

[48] A. W. Tozer in Lyle Dorsett. *A Passion for God: The Spiritual Journey of A. W. Tozer* (Chicago: Moody, 2008), 80.

hot air balloons. When I looked at those massive balloons it reminded me of the fullness of God. In order to fly in the balloon, you have to get into the basket. In the center of the basket above your head is a massive flame that creates the hot air that makes the balloon rise. Now there is no way you and I can fly on our own. But with the fire of the hot air balloon you can rise above the clouds. But you have to get into the basket, take off the weights, and turn on the fire. As you ascend into the atmosphere, the things on earth seem so small. You fill that vessel with the warmth that blazing fire, and you ascend to the heights. Can you say, "It is well with my soul" not because of your efforts, but simply because of God's love for you holding you up – carrying upward to heights and horizons you could never have dreamed of?!

This is not to say that we can contain God. Solomon realized this when he asked, "But will God indeed dwell on the earth? Behold, heaven and the highest heaven cannot contain you; how much less this house that I have built" (1 Kgs 8:27). So, said Solomon at the dedication of the temple.

When Jill and I were newly married we traveled to the Pacific Ocean on the Oregon coast. I had never seen the ocean before. How vast and wide and deep it was! I cusped my hands and filled them with the ocean water. In an instant I could say my hands were filled with the fullness of the Pacific Ocean. Because Christ is infinite, he can hold all the fullness of deity. But whenever one of us finite creatures dips the tiny vessel of our life into him, we instantly become full of his fullness. We can always open to hold more and more of his fullness. And the more fullness of God we receive the more we can receive.

To be filled with God does not mean to simply be filled with emotion, although that may feel deep emotion. Many people think they have been filled with God who don't even know him. Don't confuse emotions with Spirit-filling. We are told that we all are "his body, the fullness of him who fills all in all" (Eph 1:23). And again: "...in him [Christ] the whole fullness of deity dwells bodily, and you have been filled in him, who is the head of all rule and authority" (Col 2:9–10).

The Pathway to Fullness

The word, fullness, is a word that is used many times in the New Testament to speak of total fullness: Jesus being filled with grief, a vessel being filled with oil, a Christian being filled with the Spirit, a believer being filled with joy. There are really at least three ways that we are "filled with all the fullness of God." Satisfaction, Surrender, Reflection.

Be Satisfied in God

Only in Christ can a person find complete rest and satisfaction. "In your presence there is fullness of joy; at your right hand are pleasures forevermore" (Psa 16:11). Jesus said, "Come to me, all who labor and are heavy laden, and I will give you rest" (Mt 11:28). Jesus said it this way, "Blessed are those who hunger and thirst for righteousness, for they shall be satisfied" (Mt 5:6). To be filled with the fullness of God speaks of the sufficiency of God. When we are filled with God, we lack nothing. We are filled to the overflowing. David knew this fullness and sang about it in the Psalms. Listen to his lyric to God: "Your steadfast love is better than life, my lips will praise you" (Psa 63:3). Out of all the best things that life has to offer, God's love is infinitely better and more satisfying. Spurgeon said:

> It is not every kind of knowledge that will fill a man. Many forms of knowledge make a man more empty than he was before... Here is the heart craving for something to love. Oh, but when you love Christ, you have a heart's love that will satisfy you for all time! Where can such sweetness be? Your heart shall never go a-hungering again. His charms shall hold you fast.[49]

The flesh is the way to foolishness and misery. It leads to "confusion and every vile practice" (Jas 3:16). "The way of transgressors is hard" (Pro 13:15). If you want to be assuredly miserable, give in to your anger, fear, despair and foolishness. The great chapter on life in the Spirit shows that the person with a fleshly mindset cannot please, but when we walk in the Spirit there is truly "life and peace" (Rom 8:6-8). Or as James says, the person walking with the Spirit's "wisdom from above" will always gain "a harvest of righteousness and peace" (Jas 3:18). Being drunk with wine or any other thing we make an idol, leads to excess and debauchery, but instead, we should "be filled with the Spirit" (Eph 5:18). This is what it is to be filled with all the fullness of God.

When you experience God's fullness, every idol is forsaken because you don't need the lesser things of this world now that you are satisfied

---

[49] Charles Spurgeon. *Metropolitan Tabernacle Pulpit*, Vol 29, Sermon 1755, "The Top of the Ladder" (London: Passmore & Alabaster, 1882), 685.

in Christ. Being filled all God's fullness means Christ is our everything, and we can say with Paul, "For to me, to live is Christ and to die is gain" (Phil 1:21).

Be Surrendered to God

Another pathway to fullness is a total surrender to God. That's the life of faith. We "have been filled in him, who is the head of all rule and authority" (Col 2:10). If Christ is the head, that means all the rest of the Body must surrender to his total control. D.L. Moody understood this fullness when he said, "The world has yet to see what God can do with and for and through and in and by the man who is fully and wholly consecrated to him. I will try my utmost to be that man."[50] He would often say at his meetings: "Why don't you turn your life over to Christ? He can do more with it than you can."[51] When we are possessive over anything, as if it belongs to us, whether it be possessions or rights, that thing becomes an idol. It is only when we surrender everything to God and yield all to his ownership that we can be truly happy. We are not owners, but managers. God owns everything. I own nothing.

Be Reflecting God

Man was made to be an "image bearer" of God. In the days of the heathen kings of old, a regent would show his authority by placing statues of himself in every town. The king's image would designate the borders of the kingdom and the king's ownership of the land. That's kind of what we are. We are God's image bearers. We designate God's ownership. We are to shine our light. Back in the garden of Eden Adam and Eve desecrated that image. We mutilated that image. Being filled with all the fullness of God means God restoring that image again as we are "being conformed to the image of Christ" (Rom 8:29). It is becoming more and more like him in your character.

Conclusion

The power, the love, and the fullness of God: these are profound experiences of worship! When we dive into God, we worship. We worship whatever we are impressed with. We promote whatever we are impressed with.

---

[50] D.L. Moody in Roberts Liardon. *God's Generals Dwight L. Moody* (New Kensington, PA: Whitaker House, 2008), 4.
[51] Ibid.

When I was six years old, I had open heart surgery. The surgeon said I needed a ventricular septal defect (VSD). It's done to correct a hole between the left and right ventricles of the heart. I wasn't impressed with the big words, but I was impressed with my scar. I remember as a little boy, I showed everyone my scar.

I was also impressed with the television show *Happy Days* and its main character, Arthur Fonzarelli, or "The Fonz" as he was called. His character was a stereotypical greaser who was frequently seen on his motorcycle, wore a leather jacket, and typified the essence of cool. He would always walk into a room and say, "Ay!" I had the "Fonzie" leather jacket at six years old. *Happy Days* impressed me. I would often put my thumbs up and say, "Ay" just like Fonzarelli. I imitated what I was impressed with.

As a kid I was also impressed with John Rambo and the film *First Blood*. Where I lived in Louisiana, we all went out and bought "Rambo" knives wore camouflage for years. I imitated what I was impressed with.

All that to say, you promote and imitate what you are impressed with. That's what we do when we worship. Now that I know Christ, I am so impressed with him. I worship him. I want to imitate and promote him. Who could ever give us such power, show us such love, and fill us so completely? To him be all the glory, now and forever! Amen!

8 | EPHESIANS 3:20-21
ROOTED IN GOD'S POWER

To him be glory in the church and in Christ Jesus throughout all generations, forever and ever. Amen.
EPHESIANS 3:21

When I was just a child, my big brother David planted a little twig in the back yard. Weeks passed, and finally my father noticed it. It was a little tiny tree. He didn't want a tree in our back yard, so each week he mowed it with the lawn mower. My father was persistent. But there was more time my father couldn't mow in Chicago than when he could mow, and my father had to leave the little twig alone. He must have soon given up, because that little twig is a beautiful Maple tree at 5900 Stuart Lane. It's so big you can see it from Google Earth! That little tree was far, far bigger than anything my brother or my father could have imagined.

So it is with the plans God has for us. In the first three chapters of Ephesians, we have the blueprint of the inner man – who we are in Christ. But chapters 3-6 is all about how we live it out. The plans he has for us has to do with living in unity in the Body, living in giftedness in the Body, and living in victory (by replacing sinful habits) in the Body. He wants to help you to deal with the past. That's all in chapter 4. The first part of chapter 5 is all about the transforming power of regeneration. We are radically different on the inside, so we can live radically different on the outside. So, there is the marriage relationship picture in chapter 5. God wants to change marriages in his Body. In chapter 6, we find, he wants to radically your children here. He wants to change your job relationships. He wants to change the world! That's going to take amazing power.

There may be some chains in your life. There are some impossible situations in your life and perhaps in your heart. And some of what you are looking at looks so distant from the reality that we have in Christ. There are some radical changes that we can commit to if we could only see them clearly. This passage speaks the infinite power of God that is available to us so that we can make real and meaningful change in our lives right now.

This passage does not say, "Now unto those who suddenly get their act together." No. If it depends on us, we are in deep trouble. Our hope is not in ourselves. But if we look to Jesus there is hope for us. And what he has for us and wants for us is far, far beyond anything we could ever ask or imagine.

> **Ephesians 3:20-21** | Now to him who is able to do far more abundantly than all that we ask or think, according to the power at work within us, ²¹ to him be glory in the church and in Christ Jesus throughout all generations, forever and ever. Amen.

I don't know how it could be any more positive and overflowing than these verses. Here is one of the great doxologies in the Bible, perhaps the greatest in the Bible. This is a hymn of praise directed toward God. Paul is praising God with all his might, with all his soul.

Paul Writing from Prison

Paul is not sitting in a church service or in a comfortable study. Instead, the apostle is sitting in a prison in or near the barracks of the Praetorian Guard – the band of elite Roman soldiers assigned to guard the Roman Emperor. Paul may have been in rented quarters at his own expense – chained to Roman soldiers twenty-four hours a day. He is awaiting trial before the Roman officials and has suffered this specific imprisonment for two long years.

Paul is confined as he writes this doxology. He is unable to travel abroad. He is unable to preach the gospel outside the prison or to plant new churches. He is not even able to check on the previous churches he has planted except through the word of others. All Paul can do is sit and wait. The word that describes Paul: *unable*!

We cannot imagine the great difficulty for a man of such energy and zeal and industry to be in such a holding pattern with God. But as he waits, he is not a defeated man. He is not downcast. He is not discouraged. He is not deflated. To the contrary Paul is positive, upbeat, and actually triumphant. He is praising God and full of faith and hope.

Paul is a prisoner, that is a fact not in dispute. But the next chapter, he says he is a prisoner not of his circumstances – nor is he a prisoner of the Roman Empire – He states it for what it is – he is: "a prisoner for the Lord" (4:1). He knows that it is divine providence that provides the very chains around his wrists. He is confined in these chains by the invisible hands of God. He is not confused – he is not confounded – he is confident!

Here we find the mountaintop of Ephesians. Paul states here exalted purpose of all that we do is to bring greater glory to God in our lives, both individually and as a church. This is doxology that sits on the greatest theology in the whole Bible. He has already been praising the Triune God. We are chosen by the Father. Before God saved us, he chose us for a purpose: "to the praise of his glorious grace, with which he has blessed us in the Beloved" (1:4,6). Then we see the second Person of the Trinity: it's in Jesus that "we have redemption through his blood, the forgiveness of our trespasses, according to the riches of his grace" (1:7). Christ redeemed us and forgave us, "that we who were the first to hope in Christ might be to the praise of his glory" (1:12). Then we learned that we are sealed and secured and transformed by the "promised Holy Spirit" (1:13), all "to the praise of his glory" (1:14). Glory to the Triune God! The glory of God is the highest purpose of our great salvation. A prominent theme of the book of Ephesians is that we exist for the glory and greater praise of God.

He is worthy of glory and praise because of his incredible ability and power. Should you ask God to save the lost, he is able to do exceeding abundantly above and beyond all that you could ask or imagine. Ask God for guidance in your life, and God is able beyond your comprehension. As you have need, God is able to do exceedingly abundantly beyond anything you could imagine. As you long to be transformed into the image of Christ, he is able to do immeasurable greater than all you could ask or think.

We are going to see: the *response* to God's power, the *resources* of God's power, the *request* for God's power, the *reason* for God's power.

THE RESPONSE TO GOD'S POWER (3:20-21A)

Ephesians 3:20-21a | Now to him who is able to do far more abundantly than all that we ask or think, according to the power at work within us, [21] to him be glory...

We believe and promote a God-centered church. When you come to a God-centered assembly, you are going to hear about God. You are not going to get entertained. We believe that the joy of being in awe of God far exceeds the superficial mindless entertainment of the world. We do not promote a man centered church. God's glory and attributes must be at the blazing center of worship. All God's people are expendable. If any leader in the church moves or passes away, the church of Jesus Christ will happily go on. He said, "I will build my church, and the gates of hell will not prevail against it" (Mt 16:18). We are not dependent on any man. No man has brought us here together. We live and breathe for God's glory alone.

Paul says: "Now to him who is able..." (3:20). Why now? Now means: based on all that you've seen of God already in Ephesians, consider his power and give him glory. Think about all that God is and is doing and can do, and based on that, see his power and give him glory.

This word *now* pulls together the first three chapters. Paul builds to this mountain peak so that we can stand on the tallest ground, having surveyed the doctrines of election and predestination, the doctrines of forgiveness and redemption, the doctrine of regeneration and transformation, the doctrine of God's free grace apart from works, and even the doctrine of God's omnibenevolence and immeasurable love.

For example, Paul has prayed that you would know the love of Christ which is immeasurable and incomprehensible! That the Spirit would strengthen you in your inner being, That Christ would be "down home in your hearts" That you would know "all the fullness of God". How Paul? How can I do this? Step onto this mountain peak and survey all this. "Now to him who is able to do far more abundantly than all that we ask or think, according to the power at work within us..." (3:20-21a).

As a result of all of this, there is a doxology in response to this lofty vision of this great God - "Now unto him who is able be glory. As you survey how God saved you, at this time and at this place we must say

"To God be the glory!" Let God have all the glory. It's not God and man, but may God alone have all the glory! He did it all – He deserves it all!

We were passive, being "dead in trespasses and sins" (2:1-3). Without the Father drawing us, no person can come to Jesus (Jn 6:44). We were totally unable to respond to God. You didn't save yourself. God saved you (2:8-9). To God alone be the glory! Aren't you glad God took the initiative to act upon our dead soul and to carry out his glorious plan?

There can only be one reasonable response: "to him be glory." This "him" refers to God our Father. Paul (in 3:14) bows his knees to God the Father. Prayers are normally addressed to the Father. So prayer is "to the Father", through the Son and in the power and energy of the Holy Spirit of God who enlivens us. This is high and holy ground. The highest purpose of your existence is that you would ascribe honor and glory and thanksgiving to God. When you say, "Thank you, Lord" and "Glory to God" you are living out your divine purpose. This is how we pray, praise, and serve God! "Now to him who is able... be glory"! All we do is all to the glory of God (1 Cor 10:31). Soli Deo Gloria – to God alone be the glory.

THE RESOURCES OF GOD'S POWER (3:20)

Ephesians 3:20b | Now to him who is able to do far more abundantly than all that we ask or think ...

God's Power is Infinite

God is able! The context of this is prayer, and the promise of prayer is access to the inexhaustible resources that are in God. Essentially, Paul has one message now: God's capacity to answer you infinitely exceeds your ability to ask him! Ask all you want, all you can, everything you can even imagine, and God's capacity to answer you is infinitely greater than you can ask or imagine. God's ability to answer you is far, far above anything you could ever ask or imagine.

Now we need this because let's all be honest: we are only human. We cannot do in our life and in our churches, what needs to get done. We want to see sinners converted. We want to see saints growing. But this cannot be done with human power. "Not by the might of armies, nor by human power, but by my Spirit says the Lord" (Zech 4:6). We need God's power, as Jesus said, "Without me you can do nothing" (Jn

15:5). "Unless the LORD builds the house, those who build it labor in vain" (Psa 127:1).

God is not limited by our limitations. This is why Paul over and over says things like: "God chooses the weak things of this world... that no flesh should glory in his presence" (1 Cor 1:27). In fact, he says, "I will boast all the more gladly of my weaknesses, so that the power of Christ may rest upon me" (2 Cor 12:9-11). Not only is God not limited by our limitations when we pray, but the weaker you are the more glory God gets.

God's Power is Intentional

> **Ephesians 3:20c** | Now to him who is able **to do** far more abundantly than all that we ask or think ...

The word "to do" means "to make, cause, effect, bring about, accomplish, perform, provide, or create". God's power is intentional. He has a purpose. God is able to bring about and accomplish his will, which is to work everything to conform you to Jesus Christ. This points to God as an active worker in our lives with infinite power in our lives. God is at work in you "both to will and to do of his good pleasure" (Phil 2:13). God is always at work in the lives of his beloved children. He is never idle. He is always at work. And he is able to accomplish all his plans for them.

God's Power Incomprehensible

> **Ephesians 3:20d** | Now to him who is able to do far more abundantly than all that we ask or think ...

God's power is incomprehensible. God is "able to do far more abundantly than all we ask or think." We can't imagine or comprehend what God can do. The human mind is too limited to understand or seriously contemplate it. God is unlimited in himself. God has an inexhaustible supply of grace and power to be at work within us. God is unrestricted even by our feeble and fleeting prayers. We cannot even ask or imagine in prayer what God is going to do for us. God goes infinitely farther than anything we could ever ask or imagine. God has infinite power to act upon our tiny, finite prayers. This is why he says in Jeremiah 33:3, "Call to me and I will answer you, and will tell you great and hidden things that you have not known." You cannot even imagine or begin to comprehend the surprising display of his power toward you. God is so much greater than even our prayers. He goes over and above and beyond – even the greatest prayers that come to him. He invites us: "Ask, and it will be given to you; seek, and you will find; knock, and it will be opened to you. For everyone who asks receives, and the one who seeks finds, and to the one who knocks it will be opened" (Mt 7:7–8).

Paul piles superlative upon superlative upon superlative to describe God's incredible power.

> *Ephesians 3:20, NKJV* | Now to him who is able to do exceedingly abundantly above all that we ask or think, according to the power that works in us.

He is able to *do*.
He is able to do *what we ask*.
He is able to do *all* that we ask.
He is able to do all that we ask or even *imagine*!
He is able to do *above* all that we ask or imagine!
He is able to do *abundantly* beyond all that we ask or imagine!
He is able to do *exceedingly* abundantly above all that we could ask or think!
He is able to do exceedingly abundantly beyond all that we ask or think, *according to the power working in us*!

There is no exaggeration in this. Human language fails to properly convey the magnitude of God's incredible power. God is sufficient for all you are facing. This verse is testimony of God's abundant sufficiency for everything we are and everything we face.

God's Power is Internal

> **Ephesians 3:20e** | Now to him who is able to do far more abundantly than all that we ask or think, according to the power at work within us.

God's work is "according to the power at work within us." There is a power exploding forth inside of us. It is the same power that raised Jesus from the dead (Rom 8:11). It is the power that comes forth from the Person of the Holy Spirit (1:13-14), who indwells us. It is glorious to see God working under us and above us and before us and behind us, isn't it? But oh how we feel the loving touch of God when we read that his power is at work within us.

Who is going to accomplish this? The Triune God! God is able to do this. His Spirit will strengthen you, Christ will dwell in you, and God will fill you! The power comes directly from the *Spirit* of God within you: "that according to the riches of his glory he may grant you to be strengthened with power through his Spirit in your inner being" (3:16). The Spirit ministers the very presence of *Christ* to you, "so that Christ may dwell in your hearts through faith" (3:17). And the result is "that you may be filled with all the fullness of *God*" (3:19). The Triune God is able to do so much more than anything you could ask or need!

When I was a child of fourteen, I got in trouble with the law, and I was in deep trouble. The judge gave me two options: juvenile detention or a probational work program. One of our kind neighbors stepped up. He was a business owner. He owned a world-renowned propeller shop (New Orleans Aircraft Propeller) near the Louis Armstrong New Orleans International Airport. I was sweeping floors there for $2.65 an hour. I was just glad to get out of trouble. But my expectations of the good Mr. Downs wanted to do for me were low. One day, Mr. Downs' friend pulled up in a restored World War II fighter plane. Mr. Downs asked me, "Do you want a ride?" His pilot took me high into the sky. He asked me, "Do you want to roll"? I had just seen the movie Top Gun, and of course I said, "Yes!" There I was flying upside down, suspended in the air above New Orleans. God's power is like that. It far exceeds our expectations! Over and above and beyond the greatest abundance – this is the power the God has promised you.

THE REQUEST FOR GOD'S POWER (3:20)

We are to ask knowing God's capacity far exceeds our ability to ask.

> **Ephesians 3:20** | Now to him who is able to do far more abundantly than all that we ask or think, according to the power at work within us.

Bring on whatever you want to ask God. God's ability to give far exceeds your ability to ask in prayer. Do you understand that God is super abundantly more than able to answer your most difficult requests and even beyond what you could imagine asking? He can answer your most difficult request without breaking a sweat!

"Is anything too hard for the LORD?" (Gen 18:14). Can Sarah, at 90 have a baby long after the change of life has occurred? Yes! Jeremiah proclaimed: "Ah, Lord God! It is you who have made the heavens and the earth by your great power and by your outstretched arm! Nothing is too hard for you" (Jer 32:17). Nothing is impossible for God. When God created the universe, He did it out of nothing!

Sometimes there are things we hold back asking God for in prayer. We hardly have the courage to ask God for something, so we think it without even saying it. God even answers what's in our imagination, beyond what we could ever imagine. We are to ask knowing God's desire for you is greater and higher than your own desire.

Even you asking shows that God is at work in you. But remember God's plan for you is always bigger and greater than whatever you ask. And his power is at work in you to do what he has planned. God's invested in you. God's more concerned about your welfare more than you are! Your requests hardly touch what God's wisdom has for you. Keep asking. Keep conforming your requests to the will of God.

The Hoover Dam was built during the Great Depression. It had been years in the planning to tame the floods of the Colorado River. They wanted to build hydro-electric facilities. It was a way these engineers would tame the Wild West. The Hoover Dam is a marvel of Engineering, and it is done during the Great Depression. It is the largest use of concrete in the world up to this point, with massive armies of workers. It was treacherous work. They had to dynamite areas. They didn't know if concrete would set properly. Hoover Dam in the summer can get up to 120 degrees F. There were cliffs that were a thousand feet tall, and they were sitting on a board pouring concrete. They worked 12 hours a day. A total of 3.25 million cubic yards of concrete were poured. Today the Hoover Dam provides power to about 1.3 million people. Unlike the great Hoover Dam, God's power cannot be contained. It is far greater! And it is at work within you.

The Hoover Dam harnesses 9.2 Trillion gallons of water at any given moment, but God's power is far greater! His ability to conform you to Christ is far more than you can comprehend, "according to the power at work within us..." (3:20) God is not stingy with his power. His power is at work. The reason for his power being revealed in you is mentioned in the next verse: his glory!

THE REASON FOR GOD'S POWER (3:21)

Ephesians 3:21a | To him be glory ...

God's Glory Defined

Paul exclaims: to God be the glory! But what exactly is glory? God displays his power in you so that you might praise him and give him glory. The chief end of man is indeed "to glorify God and to enjoy him forever" (Westminster shorter catechism, Question 1). The word "glory" means "to give the right opinion of." This is a theme that weaves its way through Ephesians and through the Bible: "to the praise of his glory"!

There are two ways God's glory is spoken of in the Bible. There is his resident glory and his reflected glory. God's resident glory is the display of God's attributes and Person which is immutable and all wise and incomprehensible. In that way God's glory cannot be added to. But when Paul says "to him be glory in the church" – he's talking about God's reflected glory. We are to reflect the glory of God and display it. We glorify God by acclaiming, blessing, and reflecting his Person by becoming more and more like Christ (Rom 8:29). He wants to form Christ in me in such a way that we can shout: "to him be glory in the church and in Christ Jesus."

God's Glory in the Church

Ephesians 3:21b | To him be glory in the church...

The church is to bring glory to God through Christ Jesus. To be in Christ Jesus is to be regenerated. It is to be born again. It is to be united to Christ by his Holy Spirit. It is to be sealed by the Spirit so that your life reflects Christ and your heart burns with the love of the Father. You love what God loves and hate what he hates. Are you giving glory to God in Christ Jesus? Oh, that you would be to the praise of his glory in every area of your life.

Chapters 4-6 describe how this is going to take place in the church, in your family and in the world. Chapter 4 speak of your unity, sanctification and giftedness in the church. It also speaks of godly communication. Chapter 5 speaks of how you can bring glory to God in your life and in your marriage (if you are married). Chapter 6 speaks about how you can bring glory to God if you have children as well as bringing glory to God in your spiritual warfare in the world.

Paul speaks both of the church local and the church universal. You cannot be a healthy Christian if you are a lone ranger Christian. You cannot be healthy if you are born again but unbaptized, connected to a local assembly. You are not connected to Christ's Body in a healthy way. You cannot be healthy as a Christian if you are not accountable through church membership. If you are not a church member, genuine church discipline in your life is not a possibility. You may be an attender but if you are not a member something is missing. I say this because Jesus wants to display his glory through you as you are connected in vital union with other believers in covenant accountability.

God's Glory in Jesus

Ephesians 3:21c | To him be glory in the church and in Christ Jesus.

It is "in Christ Jesus" that God's glory is displayed. Jesus uniquely brings glory to the Father. Christ exegetes the Father (Jn 1:18). He is the image of the invisible God (Col 1:15). He gives the perfect opinion of God. God pours his power out upon us and is at work in us in order that we might fulfill our purpose of bringing glory to the Triune God.

God's Glory in Your Family

Ephesians 3:21d | To him be glory in the church and in Christ Jesus throughout all generations.

What does Paul mean "throughout all generations"? God wants to display Christ Jesus in your family, that is "throughout all generations". In all generations, God has his glory displayed by sinners saved by grace! Ten generations of my wife's family have known and served Christ. Does your family have a spiritual family tree? Is there multigenerational godliness in your legacy?

God's Glory Forever

Ephesians 3:21e | To him be glory in the church and in Christ Jesus throughout all generations, forever and ever. Amen.

He This work of God's glory is an eternal work. How long is this to go on? "... forever and ever. Amen." It is to go on in your family and in your children's family and in your grandchildren's family. We are all about multi-generational discipleship! And it is to go on until the last generation is on earth! Until the end of time. And then when time is over, the praise of God's glory is to go on and on forever and ever (and ever and ever and ever and ever and ever). Amen.

Amen! Yes, Lord I want this more than anything Let it be so! Amen! To God be the glory in all generations. In my generation. In the generations to come! Use me Lord! This is the purpose of God's amazing power. God can split a Red Sea. God can open the barren womb of a 90-year-old woman. God can heal the sick, make the blind see, and raise the dead. God can form Christ in you.

Let it be that God is glorified through Christ. Let it be in my church, in me, in my generation, throughout all generations. Forever and ever and ever and ever and ever. Amen! Amen! Amen!

Paul later concludes Ephesians as "an ambassador in chains" (Eph. 6:20). Is he complaining? Is he down and out? No, he's soaring in the heavenlies. He's seated with Christ Jesus. He's reigning over sin death and hell. He's a victor. Why? Because God is able. I'm not able. I'm weak. But God is able. He is able. He can do it. He will do it. He is the Author and Finisher of my faith. He is the One who "works to will and to do of his good pleasure" in me (Phil 2:13). Wherever Paul is he is an ambassador. With or without chains, Paul is praising God and giving this great doxology. God is able! He is abundantly able. He is exceedingly abundantly able to do far more than all we ask or imagine! To him alone be the glory in Christ Jesus throughout all generations for ever and ever and ever and ever. Amen!

Last week someone gave us a grandfather clock. The clock is the new center piece of our living room! Jill painted and rearranged furniture. I don't recognize my house. But the clock has a prominent place! Rearrange your life and make God's love and fullness working out his incredible power for you the centerpiece of your life. Give him all the honor and glory in your life. That's the life of true happiness and satisfaction.

Conclusion

Here we have one of the greatest benedictions in the Bible. And Paul piles on superlative upon superlative. God is able. God "is able to do exceedingly, abundantly above all that you could ever ask or imagine." He'll get you to where you need to go: conformity to Christ.

If you needed to get from here in Chicago to across the ocean, say the coast of Scotland or something, you could choose one of many modes of transportation. You could use the old reliable and dependable tennis shoes. Better yet, you could obtain some roller skates and roll there! You could go to Amish country and grab a horse and buggy. Or perhaps you could ride a bicycle—that's what my kids love to do. How many of you though instead of these things would just rather take a car or train?

All of these modes might be fine until you reach the ocean. Actually, I googled a map from here to London once and I found that it will take you step by step from here to the New York Harbor. Step 30 is "Turn left on the long wharf" in New York Harbor." Step 31 is "swim across the Atlantic Ocean". This kind of trip might be possible on Google, but in real life it's neither possible nor advisable! What you need is a ship, or better yet a plane!

Over two hundred years ago (1799), no one could ever have dreamed of flying a plane anywhere because there was no such thing as an airplane. The best they could do then (beginning in 1783) was the hot air balloon. No one living back then could even come close to imagining a 747 which can carry 500 people up to 8000 miles in one trip, all in less than a 24-hour period! No one could have imagined that kind of power! And friends, we have not begun to imagine the potential of what God can do in your life. Living your life without the power and presence of God is like trying to swim across the Atlantic Ocean. To try to be what God wants you to be without his power and presence is neither possible nor advisable.

When compared to a horse and buggy, the power and potential of a 747 is beyond comprehension. How much greater is God's awesome power? As we close this benediction, just think of the awesome potential of God's power. His power is limitless. We can't even imagine the things that God can do.

9 | EPHESIANS 4:1-6
ROOTED IN CHRIST'S UNITY

There is one body and one Spirit—just as you were called to the one hope that belongs to your call— one Lord, one faith, one baptism, one God and Father of all, who is over all and through all and in all.

EPHESIANS 4:4-6

We are told in the New Testament that the church is like a body with many different parts. You might illustrate it with the many sides of a diamond, and yet it's one diamond. The other night we had a bunch of people over and we had a guitarist and a violinist. Before we sang there was "organized chaos". We were all tuning our instruments to the piano. Have you ever been to an orchestra when they all tuned together, and you wondered what a strange cacophony of sound? But it was necessary. We are going to tune our spiritual instruments so that we can be unified as God's church. How can we get in tune today?

THE REQUEST FOR UNITY (4:1)

Ephesians 1-3 tell us who we are in Christ. In fact, Eph. 1:3 sets the stage for the first three chapters. It says we've been called and elected by God (1:4), called by the Father (1:3), redeemed by the Son (1:7), sealed by the Spirit (1:13-14), raised from death to life (2:1-10), joined to the Body of Christ (2:11-22), filled with the strength of the Spirit, the love of Christ, and the fullness of God (ch 3). Based on these riches in Christ, Paul implores Christians to: "walk in a manner worthy of your calling" (4:1).

A Request from a Prisoner

Now remember, at the time Paul wrote this letter to the Ephesian church, he was under house arrest in a rented house chained to a Roman soldier from the Emperor's famous Praetorian guard (Acts 28:17-31). The year is around 60 A.D., and this is Paul's first imprisonment. This imprisonment is the very occasion for writing the letter to the Ephesians and the other "prison epistles". John McRay has written about what it would have been like for the Apostle in prison.

> Roman imprisonment was preceded by being stripped naked and then flogged, a humiliating, painful, and bloody ordeal. The bleeding wounds went untreated; prisoners sat in painful leg or wrist chains. Mutilated, blood-stained clothing was not replaced, even in the cold of winter.[52]

We assume Paul had it better than most prisoners since there were many that would visit him, tend to his wounds (such as Dr. Luke) and care for his needs. Even so, Paul is in very difficult circumstances while writing this letter, but he is not at all concerned with himself. He does not mention how horrible the conditions are—he is selfless.

A Weighty Request

Paul begged and urged God's people in this way in all his writings. "I *beg* (urge, beseech) you therefore, brothers, by the mercies of God, to present your bodies as a living sacrifice..." (Rom 12:1). "We *implore* (beg) you on behalf of Christ, be reconciled to God" (2 Cor 5:20).

> **Ephesians 4:1** | I therefore, a prisoner for the Lord, urge you to walk in a manner worthy of the calling to which you have been called.

The therefore of Ephesians 4:1 marks the transition from positional to practical truth, from doctrine to duty, principle to practice.[53] After telling us who we are in Christ in chapters 1-3 of Ephesians, Paul tells us what we should do: "walk worthy". "Worthy" means to have worth

---

[52] John McRay. *Paul: His Life and Teaching* (Grand Rapids, MI: Baker Publishing Group, 2003), Kindle Locations 2876-2880.
[53] MacArthur. *Ephesians*, 116.

or value. But it is more than that. It means to have a worth equal to one's position.[54] The word "worthy" has the root of "weight" or "balance". Feel the weight of your position. Balance your glorious identity in Christ with a life that equals your high calling! We are to equalize our behavior in accord with our identity. We are to live up to our position. We are to live in the reality of who we are in Christ.

What a high and holy calling we are called to. Walk worthy we must. But what is this calling? A key part of this calling is the Christian hope, which works like this. Because King Jesus has conquered death itself, all who give him their faithful allegiance are assured that the same victory will be theirs as well. This is the 'calling' to which they must 'live up'. At every moment, in every decision, with every word and action, they are to be aware that the call to follow Jesus the Messiah, and give him their complete loyalty, takes precedence over everything else.[55]

Here Paul was writing to the church at Ephesus, a very prosperous church. We might call it one of the mega churches of the ancient world. Jerusalem and Antioch were the first really large churches. But Ephesus was definitely one. The Ephesian church was established by Paul on his third missionary journey. You could read about that, if you want to, in Acts 19. Paul actually lived in Ephesus for two years. He carried on his ministry there. This was a well-established church. This church knew Christian doctrine backwards and forwards. Ephesus was once a large, seaport city; and it's significant that it is not a seaport city today.

In Ephesus there is acre after acre after acre of gorgeous Roman architecture. There are huge colonnaded streets; there are huge, paved streets that lead throughout the city. It's the great megachurch of the New Testament.

Ephesus is the church that left its first love. What happened physically to the city of Ephesus also happened to the church in Ephesus. During the days of the apostle Paul, Ephesus was a harbor city. Today it's almost a mile inland and the reason is the river that runs through it has been silting all these years – moving it farther and farther away from the coast. So, Ephesus was inundated with the silt of the River

---

[54] Boice, *Ephesians*, 121.
[55] N.T. Wright, *Paul for Everyone: The Prison Letters: Ephesians, Philippians, Colossians, and Philemon* (London: Society for Promoting Christian Knowledge, 2004), 43.

Cayster and it filled in the Ephesian harbor. Spiritually in the church at Ephesus, the same thing happened: the silt of sin came into the church. And while the church was strong, and the city was strong, and things were good for it, it was being filled up little by little with the silt of sin.

> *Revelation 2:1-5* | To the angel of the church in Ephesus write: 'The words of him who holds the seven stars in his right hand, who walks among the seven golden lampstands. ² "'I know your works, your toil and your patient endurance, and how you cannot bear with those who are evil, but have tested those who call themselves apostles and are not, and found them to be false. ³ I know you are enduring patiently and bearing up for my name's sake, and you have not grown weary. ⁴ But I have this against you, that you have abandoned the love you had at first. ⁵ Remember therefore from where you have fallen; repent, and do the works you did at first. If not, I will come to you and remove your lampstand from its place, unless you repent.

Paul and John urged Ephesus to be unified together and in their love for Christ. He made the strongest request possible: walk worthy of your high calling in Christ. How easy it would be for us to drift off from Christ despite deep reservoirs of Scriptural knowledge: to lose our first love and leave our knowledge cold and lifeless. May it never be! This passage drips sweet with the life-giving signs of the Spirit: humility, unity, gentleness, patience, tolerance, and love. Paul could have gone on I'm sure.

THE REFLECTION OF UNITY (4:1-2)

Now Paul gives a number of traits that we are to be unified in. Essentially, this is the character of Christlikeness. All these traits are used to describe Christ. Christ brings back each Christian into the original image of God intended from the beginning (Gen 1:26).

> **Ephesians 4:1-2** | I therefore, a prisoner for the Lord, urge you to walk in a manner worthy of the calling to which you have been called, ² with all humility and gentleness, with patience, bearing with one another in love...

Humility

I love how the Spirit says, "All humility." All the virtues of the Christ-life flow from humility. It makes sense since "God resists the proud but gives grace to the humble" (Jas 5:5). Humility is said to be "the personal quality of being free from arrogance and pride and having an accurate estimate of one's worth."[56] Humility was despised in the ancient Greco-Roman world as a slave-like quality. What was admired was the *mega-souled* or "great-souled" man who was complete and self-sufficient.[57] In God's new humanity, the church, humility is the grandest virtue. We see the perfect display of humility in Philippians 2 where Christ humbled himself. He became of "no reputation" displaying perfect humanity. The New Testament links this virtue to childlikeness and poverty of spirit.[58] Perhaps one of the clearest illustrations of humility is the one who sees the greatness of God and trembles before his Word and power, living in a spirit of humility (Isa 57:15). Since God opposes the proud and gives grace to the humble, humility would logically fit as the foundation of all virtue (1 Pet 5:5).

Gentleness

The virtue of gentleness (sometimes translated *meekness*) is not weakness. It is rather strength under control. There is nothing spineless or timid about it.[59] It is the ability to submit to difficult and even unjust circumstances, trusting God's promises of ultimate deliverance and salvation. Those who are meek will suffer injustice, poverty, or oppression with a calm, controlled spirit of strength.[60] Have you ever seen a big ugly dog with a little rascally puppy? The puppy's growling! But we all know the big ugly dog could destroy the rascally pup in about half a second. So, it is with gentleness or meekness. It's strength under control. The great Old Testament example of meekness is Moses. "Now the man Moses was very meek, above all the men which were upon the face of the earth" (Num 12:3). Moses was a man who completely relied on God rather than his own strength. The most notable and glorious example of gentleness is Christ. Jesus said, "Take my yoke upon you and learn from me, for I am gentle and humble in heart" (Mt 11:29). Here is God in human flesh, and he allows those he created to fasten

---

[56] Gary Hardin, "Humility," ed. Chad Brand et al., *Holman Illustrated Bible Dictionary* (Nashville, TN: Holman Bible Publishers, 2003), 792.

[57] William Barclay, *The Letters to the Galatians and Ephesians* (Philadelphia: Westminster Press, 1958), 159.

[58] Siegfried Rudolf Dunde, "Humility," *The Encyclopedia of Christianity* (Grand Rapids, MI; Leiden, Netherlands: Wm. B. Eerdmans; Brill, 1999–2003), 611.

[59] Hughes, *Ephesians*, 123.

[60] Robert L. Plummer, "Meekness," ed. Chad Brand et al., *Holman Illustrated Bible Dictionary* (Nashville, TN: Holman Bible Publishers, 2003), 1098.

him to the cross with nails. He could have destroyed the world, but he meekly suffered injustice, knowing and directing the very circumstances by which this meekness would result in the salvation of the world.

Patience

Patience is a joyful perseverance. It's not mere endurance, but joyful endurance. The person who is patient has the ability to joyfully wait on God in awful circumstances. The antiquated term is "long suffering" because it is a kind of hopeful hurting. Patience has to do with tolerance and longsuffering that endure injuries inflicted by others, the calm willingness to accept situations that are irritating or painful. God himself is "slow to anger" (Psa 86:15) and expects his children to be the same. Just as believers should never "think lightly of the riches of God's own kindness and forbearance and patience" (Rom 2:4), they should themselves manifest those attributes of their heavenly Father.[61]

Forbearance

Now Paul says we are to forebear with one another. This is the virtue of tolerating each other – putting up with others. We are all porcupines. You may not know it, but like a porcupine, you will offend people from time to time and not even know it. You will stick someone. This is the liability of living in community. We all have quirks and idiosyncrasies. Christians are willing to put up and tolerate with each other. That means we keep a tender, forgiving heart, covering offences with love. That means forgiving seventy times seven times, and then some. The person with a forbearing spirit is always committed to godly conflict resolution.

Love

Agapē love is the form of love that most reflects personal choice, referring not simply to pleasant emotions or good feelings but to willing, self-giving service. "God demonstrates his own love toward us, in that while we were yet sinners, Christ died for us" (Rom 5:8). True *agapē* love is a sure mark of salvation. "We know that we have passed out of death into life," John says, "because we love the brethren.... Everyone who loves is born of God and knows God" (1 Jn 3:14; 4:7). By the

---

[61] MacArthur, *Ephesians*, 167.

same token, as John repeatedly makes clear throughout the same letter, having a habitually unloving spirit toward fellow Christians is reason for a person to question his salvation (see e.g., 1 Jn 2:9, 11; 3:15; 4:8, 20).[62] This kind of self-sacrificing love is so high and divine that it cannot be fulfilled apart from the Holy Spirit, the source of this and all the other manifestations of spiritual fruit. "The love of God has been poured out within our hearts through the Holy Spirit who was given to us," Paul explained to Roman believers (Rom 5:5).[63]

All of the virtues listed: humility, gentleness, patience, forbearance, and love are all fruits of a heart conquered by Christ. This ought to be the normal state of the believers' heart and is in stark contrast to the noisy unrest of the flesh-dominated heart at the end of the chapter, described as bitter and angry (4:31-32). Instead, Paul describes the believer as putting on a life of similar virtues as the beginning of the chapter: instead of anger, put on tenderness, kindness, and forgiveness.

THE RIGOR OF UNITY (4:3)

Ephesians 4:3 | ... eager to maintain the unity of the Spirit in the bond of peace.

The word "eager" could also be translated endeavor, and it means to spare no effort. It's a very, very strong exhortation. It means to labor to the point of exhaustion. The NIV translates it: "make every effort" which comes from a root word which means to *make haste*, and thus gives the idea of zealous effort and diligence. We see the rigor of maintaining the unity we have in Christ. "Do your utmost to keep the unity of the Spirit — this is urgent!"[64] Unity takes work. The Christian life is hard work. And yet, it is not the hard work of self-propagation or self-righteousness. It is the work that comes from the power of the Spirit: "that according to the riches of his glory he may grant you to be strengthened with power through his Spirit in your inner being" (3:16). This work of the Spirit is described as well in another place: "Work out your own salvation with fear and trembling, 13 for it is God who works in you, both to will and to work for his good pleasure" (Phil 2:12b-13).

---

[62] MacArthur, *Galatians*, 165.
[63] Ibid.
[64] Hughes, *Ephesians*, 125.

Let's consider the unity mentioned here. This unity is from the Spirit. It cannot be manufactured through the flesh. We are to work through the reviving, life-giving power of the Spirit toward this unity. Access the power of the Spirit (Gal 5:16). God gave us this unity, and we are called to maintain it or guard it. Christ put you in the Body. He gave you the Spirit. It is this very unity of the Spirit for which Jesus so earnestly prayed in the Upper Room shortly before His betrayal and arrest:

> *John 17:11, 21–23* | And I am no longer in the world, but they are in the world, and I am coming to you. Holy Father, keep them in your name, which you have given me, that they may be one, even as we are one.... that they may all be one, just as you, Father, are in me, and I in you, that they also may be in us, so that the world may believe that you have sent me. ²² The glory that you have given me I have given to them, that they may be one even as we are one, ²³ I in them and you in me, that they may become perfectly one, so that the world may know that you sent me and loved them even as you loved me.

We are to work hard to keep close fellowship with the Lord Jesus, and through that, we will have close fellowship with other believers. This takes work. It's easier to isolate or become a lone ranger Christian since that takes no effort. Fellowship takes vulnerability, teachability, and humility, inviting God's worship, presence, and fear into every moment of life (Pro 1:7). We are called to be disciples, or "learners" with a childlike spirit, hungry for truth and growth in Christ (2 Pet 3:18).

Unity is maintained in a number of ways. We maintain unity by supporting the systematic and practical preaching from the Word of God in the local church. We uphold unity through prayer, hospitality, and living life together, caring for one another. We maintain unity by confronting conflict in a godly way. When conflict arises, we are to go to our brother privately and diligently work toward restoration. If this is unity is not possible privately, we are to go with an impartial witness or two. If still unity is not possible, we are to bring it before the elders of the church (Mt 18:15-20). If unity is not present in the Body, there cannot be proper worship. Instead of ignoring the conflict, we are to go as quickly as possible, leaving our gift at the altar, and reconcile with our brother quickly (Mt 5:24). This does not mean we should skip worship if there is conflict in our lives. But it does mean that as soon as possible, we speak to the person and set up a time to get things right.

There have been times when I have sought a brother out with tears before a church service so that I could be right with God when I worship. This unity entails that we be impartial and not jump to conclusions. We have to think the best until solid evidence proves otherwise. Indeed, anyone who begins to judge before he has all the facts is foolish (Pro 18:13, 18). In summary, work hard in biblical conflict resolution...immediately (Mt 5), privately (Mt 18), and with due process of all the facts and all sides (Pro 18:13, 18).

The result of diligently accessing the power of the Spirit is that we actually do maintain the unity of the Spirit in the bond of peace. The peace here is not one of an absence of war. Often the confrontation of problems brings conflict. Yet it is how we handle those problems that really brings the peace that comes from unity. Will we confront those problems or leave them be? Peace is not possible without the confrontation of idols and the problems that come from heart idolatry. And *how* we confront problems matters as well. Will we confront them with anger and bitterness (4:31) or with kindness, tenderness and forgiveness (4:32)? The peace here comes from a right relationship with God through Christ, living in joyful reconciliation. Nothing less than true fellowship is what this peace is, and in it is fullness of joy (Psa 16:11). This unity brings the peace of true happiness and contentment in Christ. The Christian ought to want the joy of this peace more than he wants to breath. Anything less than knowing Christ and the peace and joy that comes from him is just dung and refuse in comparison (Phil 3:8).

THE ROOTS OF UNITY (4:4-6)

Ephesians 4:4-6 | There is one body and one Spirit—just as you were called to the one hope that belongs to your call— **5** one Lord, one faith, one baptism, **6** one God and Father of all, who is over all and through all and in all.

Believers are one. They always have been one, and they always will be one. They are not divided. How is that? Our unity as believers in the Body of Christ is based on the unity of the Godhead. Here in this passage we have seven collective marks of unity among all believers: one body, one Spirit, one hope of your calling, one Lord, one faith, one baptism, one God and Father of all, sovereign – over all, omnipotent – through all, omnipresent – in you all.

You will notice that these seven unities are founded on the Trinity – one Spirit, one Lord, One God and Father of all Christians. The order is given this way because we experience God this way. The Spirit draws us, we yield in repentant faith to the Son who reveals and gives us access to the Father. We are brought into the one Body, by one Spirit, living for one glorious hope of future glorification. The Son is the one Lord who embodies our one faith, with faith we identify with through the one baptism by water. And then we see one God and Father of us all who sovereignly works in and through the believer for that worthy walk of unity.

One Body

Ephesians 4:4a | There is one body...

This is the one Body that does the work of Christ on earth. Christ departed, but sent his Spirit to baptize all who believe and bring them into his Body, of which he is the Head. All who are part of the Body have Jesus Christ as the Head and Lord of their life. They build one another up in love and carry out the will of their Head. Jesus said, "I will build my church, and the gates of hell shall not prevail against it" (Mt 18:16). The gates of hell cannot hold back those to whom God is calling out of darkness. This is our "forever family" that God planned before the foundation of the world. The Spirit places people into the Body of Christ.

The Body is organic. It isn't put together piece by piece. It isn't that you add two more fingers—add another arm. Now put an ear on that head. The Body grows organically together with each part dependent on the other. The systems in the Body are connected. They are mutually dependent. You cannot separate them. How are you going to separate your respiratory system from your nervous system? God says just like the physical Body cannot be separated because it is organically one, so every believer is part of one Body. We see this taught wonderfully in 1 Corinthians 12.

> *1 Corinthians 12:12-25* | For just as the body is one and has many members, and all the members of the body, though many, are one body, so it is with Christ. [13] For in one Spirit we were all baptized into one body—Jews or Greeks, slaves or free—and all were made to drink of one Spirit. [14] For the body does not consist of one member but of many. [15] If the foot should say, "Because I am not a hand, I do not

belong to the body," that would not make it any less a part of the body. [16] And if the ear should say, "Because I am not an eye, I do not belong to the body," that would not make it any less a part of the body. [17] If the whole body were an eye, where would be the sense of hearing? If the whole body were an ear, where would be the sense of smell? [18] But as it is, God arranged the members in the body, each one of them, as he chose. [19] If all were a single member, where would the body be? [20] As it is, there are many parts, yet one body. [21] The eye cannot say to the hand, "I have no need of you," nor again the head to the feet, "I have no need of you." [22] On the contrary, the parts of the body that seem to be weaker are indispensable, [23] and on those parts of the body that we think less honorable we bestow the greater honor, and our unpresentable parts are treated with greater modesty, [24] which our more presentable parts do not require. But God has so composed the body, giving greater honor to the part that lacked it, [25] that there may be no division in the body, but that the members may have the same care for one another. [26] If one member suffers, all suffer together; if one member is honored, all rejoice together.

The Body is not united on earthly similarities. The basis of our unity in the Body is not racial. There is diversity of cultures. Revelation 5:9 tells us that God has redeemed a people out of every "kindred, and tongue, and people, and nation." The basis of our unity is not circumstantial either. In the twin epistle to Ephesians (Colossians), Paul writes virtually the same truths.

Colossians 3:11 | Here there is not Greek and Jew, circumcised and uncircumcised, barbarian, Scythian, slave, free; but Christ is all, and in all.

The unity that we have is not based upon the fact that we are free or not free. It is not based upon whether we are rich or poor. It's not based on your gifts or skills or abilities. It has nothing to do with your circumstances. If you are a believer and have no money, you are on the same level as a millionaire in the congregation. With God there is no respect of persons (Rom 2:11). What is money compared to the precious and priceless blood of Christ? And you were all bought with that precious blood and placed into one Body (1 Cor 6:20).

The world has superficial unity based on human abilities or circumstances. A sports team can have a pep rally. When I worked for MCI phone services during my college days, we had pep rallies for the biggest sellers. That's earthly. That's natural. This is something supernatural. God has placed us into this one Body when we believed on him and he baptized us into the Body by his Spirit (1 Cor 12:13). Pastor John MacArthur summarizes this passage well.

> Humility gives birth to gentleness, gentleness gives birth to patience, patience gives birth to forbearing love, and all four of those characteristics preserve the unity of the Spirit in the bond of peace. These virtues and the supernatural unity to which they testify are probably the most powerful testimony the church can have, because they are in such contrast to the attitudes and the disunity of the world. No program or method, no matter how carefully planned and executed, can open the door to the gospel in the way individual believers can do when they are genuinely humble, meek, patient, forbearing in love, and demonstrate peaceful unity in the Holy Spirit.[65]

One Spirit

Ephesians 4:4b | There is one body and one **Spirit**...

When we are saved, we are baptized into Christ's Body by the Spirit. This is the Spirit's sovereign work of regeneration, where he takes out the heart of stone, and puts in the heart of flesh—a heart that is soft, alive, and teachable (Eze 36:25-27). When we are regenerated there is a change of principle for every child of God.

> *Romans 8:2* | For the law of the Spirit of life has set you free in Christ Jesus from the law of sin and death.

Not just death, but the power of sin and death. No longer am I totally captivated by the things of the flesh. Now I am captivated by the things of the Spirit.

> *Romans 8:5* | For those who live according to the flesh set their minds on the things of the flesh, but those who live according to the Spirit set their minds on the things of the Spirit.

I am no longer in bondage to the "law of sin" but I am now bound to the "law of Christ". The indwelling Christ lives in me by his Spirit, and I am now a servant to Christ by his Spirit. Paul tells us that we are sealed with God's stamp of ownership – the Spirit who regenerated us.

There is not one Holy Spirit for the Bible churches and one for the Baptists and one for the Presbyterians. No one can call Jesus Lord

---

[65] MacArthur. *Ephesians*, 128–129.

except by the revelation of the Holy Spirit. This Holy Spirit reveals Christ, he regenerates us; he convinces us of sin. Nobody has ever been convinced of sin and seen the cross of Christ lifted up without the Holy Spirit. Jesus said about the Holy Spirit in John 14:16, "He shall glorify me." The Holy Spirit always points to Christ as the answer for our sins. Ephesians 1:13 tells us we were "sealed with that Holy Spirit of promise." Where were we sealed? Into the Body of Christ. The Spirit is the "the earnest of our inheritance until the redemption of the purchased possession" (Eph 1:14). Every believer who comes to that knowledge, no matter what local church he happens to be a part of has come to faith by only one Holy Spirit. This one Holy Spirit fills the one Body of Christ. Indeed, God the Father has given the fullness of Christ to all believers.

> *Ephesians 1:22-23* | He put all things under his feet and gave him as head over all things to the church, ^{23} which is his body, the fullness of him who fills all in all.

So, there is one Holy Spirit for all who have Christ Jesus as their head in local churches scattered throughout the world. He's our Comforter, Counselor, and Keeper. He expresses the love poured out from the Father. He unites us to each other.

One Hope

> **Ephesians 4:4c** | There is one body and one Spirit—just as you were called to the one hope that belongs to your call.

This one hope is not a wishful desire. Instead, the word "hope" refers to a certain and absolutely sure expectation. This certain and sure hope is referring to our hope of glorification when the believer is completely delivered not only from the penalty and power of sin, but the very presence of sin. What a day that will be. The timing of our glorification is at the moment of Christ's Second Coming and is also referred to as our final redemption. Our calling to salvation is ultimately a calling to Christlike eternal perfection and glory. In Christ we have different gifts, different ministries, different places of service, but only one calling, the calling to "be holy and blameless before him" (Eph 1:4) and "to become conformed to the image of his Son" (Rom 8:29), which will occur when we see the glorified Christ (1 Jn 3:2). It is the Spirit who has placed us in the one Body and who guarantees our future glory of finally being completely conformed to Jesus.[66]

Salvation can be spoken of in three ways: past, present, and future. Our *past* salvation refers to our conversion – the moment of salvation, which is like a line of demarcation in my life. God was calling me from birth, and responded in various ways, but there came a decisive moment where I was delivered "from the domain of darkness and transferred ... to the kingdom of his beloved Son" (Col 1:13). Our *present* salvation is referred to by theologians as sanctification. It is that daily being conformed into the character of Christ. My goal can never be to change my circumstances, but for God to change my heart and character to Christ's. There was paradise lost. In Christ, paradise is regained! The image of God was marred at the fall of mankind into sin. In Christ, the image of God is restored. That's what God is doing in sanctification. Our *future* salvation is referred to as glorification– this occurs at the Second Coming! Not only will the penalty and power of sin be defeated as it is now, but the very presence of sin will be gone. Sin will finally be once and for all eradicated for believers. Final redemption may come at any moment, when the trumpet sounds, and Christ returns. Lift up your heads, for your redemption draws nigh (Lk 21:28). That's our one hope, our certain expectation.

One Lord

Ephesians 4:5a | One Lord, one faith, one baptism.

To say we have one Lord, that "Jesus Christ is Lord", is to say there is no other Lord and Savior. He is the exclusive way to the Father (Jn 14:6). Paul with all the apostles acknowledged this.

Philippians 2:10–11 | At the name of Jesus every knee should bow, in heaven and on earth and under the earth, and every tongue confess that Jesus Christ is Lord, to the glory of God the Father.

To say Jesus is *kurios* – was radical. For a Jew to confess Jesus as the *one Lord* was tantamount to confessing him as one with the Father, for Jews daily prayed the *Shema* (Deut 6:4; *cf* Rom 10:9–12; 1 Cor 8:4–6).[67] Polycarp, the 86-year-old bishop of Smyrna and a disciple of John the Apostle, was martyred in 156 A.D. Ironically, Polycarp was charged

---

[66] Ibid., 130.
[67] Carson, *Ephesians* (New Bible Commentary), 1237.

with atheism because he denied the false gods of Rome and he refused to call Caesar "Lord". He was commanded to recant the Christians who were called atheists. The phrase "away with the atheist" was meant to be directed at the Christians since they did not believe or worship the pantheon of gods, but only the one true and living God, creator of the world. The proconsul did not want to sentence Polycarp to death. The great pastor and bishop was well liked. All he had to do was say the words "Away with the atheists" and "Caesar is Lord," and he would be free.

Polycarp responded: "Eighty and six years have I served him, and he never did me any injury. How then can I blaspheme my King and my Savior?"

The proconsul said: "I have respect for your age. Simply say, 'Away with the Atheists' and be set free." Polycarp solemnly said, "Away with the Atheists"—pointing to the pagan crowd."

The proconsul continued..."I have wild beasts; I will throw you to them, unless you change your mind." But Polycarp said: "Call for them!"

"I will have you consumed by fire, since you despise the wild beasts, unless you change your mind," the proconsul responded.

Again, Polycarp replied, "You threaten with a fire that burns only briefly and after just a little while is extinguished, for you are ignorant of the fire of the coming judgment and eternal punishment, which is reserved for the ungodly. But, why do you delay? Come, do what you wish."[68]

Dear brothers and sisters, the very foundation of our faith, that the one Lord, Savior, and Master of the life of every Christian is Jesus Christ. We bow our knees to him as God, King, Substitute, and Savior!

One Faith

Ephesians 4:5b | One Lord, one faith, one baptism.

Jude talks about earnestly contending for the faith (Jude 3). Now sometimes there are controversies in the churches over issues. I think of this historically in the life of George Whitefield and John Wesley.

---

[68] Jefford, Clayton, Kenneth Harder, and Louis Amezaga. *Reading the Apostolic Fathers: An Introduction.* (Peabody, MA: Hendrickson Publishers, 1996), 85ff.

Whitefield preached an emphasis of sovereign grace and election as to the mystery of who comes to Christ. Of course, Wesley had the mindset and emphasis of free will. But God was using them in sweeping two continents with revival —in Great Britain and in the American colonies.

During this time Wesley would write very critical articles in the public papers about these differences in emphasis. Even though Whitefield was a younger man, he died twenty years before John Wesley. And somebody asked Wesley "You know, I'd really like to know, do you think you're going to see Whitefield in heaven?"

And in that moment, when we are really talking about what the Christian faith is, we see something in Wesley's reply. Wesley said, "No I don't think I'll see him in heaven." Of course, there was a great gasp before Wesley continued, "I won't see Whitefield in heaven, because when I get there, I'll be so far back from the throne, and he'll be so near the throne, I won't be able to see him!"[69]

You see Wesley knew that the one faith that we hold is not his version of Wesleyan Methodism. Did Whitefield and Wesley believe the gospel that Christ died for their sins? That he was buried and rose again? Yes and amen! That's the one faith that all believers everywhere have.

One Baptism

Ephesians 4:5c | One Lord, one faith, one baptism.

There are differences over the interpretation of this "one baptism". Generally, it is referring to Spirit baptism, but it almost was always confessed in a public way.

> *Romans 6:3-5* | Do you not know that all of us who have been baptized into Christ Jesus were baptized into his death? ⁴ We were buried therefore with him by baptism into death, in order that, just as Christ was raised from the dead by the glory of the Father, we too might walk in newness of life. ⁵ For if we have been united with him in a death like his, we shall certainly be united with him in a resurrection like his.

---

[69] Giles Buckingham Willcox. *The Pastor Amidst His Flock* (New York: American Tract Society, 1890), 166.

Water baptism was always united with faith in Christ in the early church since it was at the baptism ceremony that the new believer would confess his or her faith in Christ. The one baptism of verse 5 is best taken to refer to water baptism, the common New Testament means of a believer's publicly confessing Jesus as Savior and Lord. This is preferred especially because of the way Paul has spoken specifically of each member of the Trinity in succession. This is the Lord Jesus Christ's verse, as it were: one Lord, upon whom we trust with our one faith, and whom we confess at our one baptism.

Water baptism was extremely important in the early church, not as a means of salvation but as a testimony of identity with and unity in Jesus Christ. Believers were not baptized in the name of a local church, a prominent evangelist, a leading elder, or even an apostle, but only in the name of Christ (*cf* 1 Cor 1:13–17).[70]

To be clear, this verse is not speaking of mode or timing of baptism, though these are addressed in other places. For example, water baptism does not save (1 Pet 3:21). Only people who accept the message of the gospel should be baptized (Acts 2:41). Our Lord demonstrated the mode of baptism when he came up out of the water after he was immersed by John the Baptist (Mt 3:16). So much more could be said, but it is true that godly believers have had various practices regarding mode, whether immersion or sprinkling or pouring as well as timing, whether after conversion or pedobaptism (though not, as the heretical Roman Catholics believe, for any kind of salvation). I hold strongly to a baptism by immersion of believers only. Yet there are some godly and true believers who hold to a closer identification of baptism with the circumcision of the Jewish people of old. Though I do not agree with this interpretation, I still love and fellowship with all those who preach the true gospel, that we are saved by grace alone, through faith alone, in Christ alone, to God's glory alone. All of this way of salvation is revealed to mankind by the Scriptures alone. Water baptism is a picture, a dramatization of the reality of being united with Christ by the Spirit of God. It is my opinion that believers should not separate over the shadows and ceremonies as long as they hold to the substance of true salvation by Christ alone, apart from works (Eph 2:1-10).

---

[70] MacArthur. *Ephesians*, 130.

One God and Father of All

Ephesians 4:6 | One God and Father of all, who is over all and through all and in all.

The basic doctrine of Judaism has always been, "The Lord is our God, the Lord is one!" (Deut 6:4; *cf* 4:35; 32:39; Isa 45:14; 46:9), and God's oneness is just as foundational to Christianity (*cf* 1 Cor 8:4–6; Eph 4:3–6; Jas 2:19). Yet the New Testament also reveals the more complete truth that the one God is in three Persons—Father, Son, and Holy Spirit (Mt 28:19; Jn 6:27; 20:28; Acts 5:3–4).[71]

God the Father is often used in Scripture as the most comprehensive and inclusive divine title, though it is clear from many New Testament texts that He is never separated in nature or power from the Son or the Holy Spirit.[72]

Four attributes of God the Father are given: Creator (Father of all), sovereignty (over all), omnipotence (through all), and omnipresence (in you all). Of course, each member of the Trinity has these attributes.

All had their work in the creation of the world. Jesus is called the "everlasting Father" or perhaps better translated "Father of eternity" in Isaiah 9:6. He is the "Word" from the beginning by which all things were made (Jn 1:1-3; Col 1:16). The Spirit hovered over the waters in Genesis 1 and brought order out of chaos (Gen 1:2).

All are sovereign and in control of all things. We are told that even at this moment Jesus "upholds the universe by the word of his power" (Heb 1:3; *cf* Col 1:17). The Spirit as well is sovereign in salvation (Jn 3:8).

All are omnipotent. Jesus demonstrated his omnipotence many times while on earth, commanding the wind and the waves (Mk 4:35-41), and raising the dead by his command (Jn 11:38-44). The Spirit is also omnipotent, bringing the earth into existence (Gen 1:2) as well as wielding the power of the Most High in the conception of Christ in the womb of the virgin Mary (Lk 1:35). Mighty signs and wonders were performed by the apostles by the power of the Holy Spirit (Rom 15:19).

All are omnipresent. The Bible says numerous times that Jesus is at the "right hand of the Father" (Mk 14:62; 16:19; Acts 2:33; 7:55; Rom 8:34; Eph 1:20; Col 3:1; Heb 1:3; 1 Pet 3:22) and is present wherever

---

[71] Ibid., 131.
[72] Ibid.

two or three believers are gathered (Mt 18:20). The Spirit as well, more obviously, is omnipresent. In Psalm 139:7 asks, "Where can I go from your Spirit? Or where can I flee from your presence?" The answers that follow define the omnipresence of the Holy Spirit.

And yet, this creed highlights God the Father's attributes to emphasize his role in the Trinity as the Father of all the saints. This is a family. Being able to call God our Father is to recognize that all Christians belong together as brothers and sisters and share the same forever family with God as God is our Father, and *above all and through all and in all* (*cf* Rom 11:36).[73] John Stott sums it up well.

> There can be only one Christian family, only one Christian faith, hope and baptism, and only one Christian body, because there is only one God, Father, Son, and Holy Spirit. You can no more multiply churches than you can multiply Gods. Is there only one God? Then he has only one church. Is the unity of God inviolable? Then so is the unity of the church.... It is no more possible to split the church than it is possible to split the Godhead.[74]

Conclusion

How do you identify the Lord's true church? Think about the famous Stradivarius violins. Today, literally hundreds of thousands of Stradivarius violins are being sold even though only 512 are known to be in existence today! Each one of the originals is worth from one to three million dollars. Knowing this, I decided to do a search on the online auction site eBay recently and not surprisingly I found 82 for sale with the highest price being an amazing $24,000. There's a great need for authentication! So, it is with Christians! Many say they know Christ, but do they have the identifying marks?

Last week, my family and I spent time in Amish country. Two days ago, we were dining in an Amish home with no electricity and no telephone. The man's name was Joe Wingart, and he thought there might be some relation to Jill's family in the Old Country – Switzerland. We were chasing "fainting goats" after dinner. We also checked out flying peacocks, feeding chickens, and watching the team of horses plow the field. The children even got to hold a litter of pug-nosed puppies! One

---

[73] Francis Foulkes, *Ephesians: An Introduction and Commentary*, vol. 10, Tyndale New Testament Commentaries (Downers Grove, IL: InterVarsity Press, 1989), 120.

[74] Stott, *Ephesians,* 151.

thing about the Amish is that there is a conformity to each other or a non-conformity however you want to look at it. But as you examine it, you realize the Amish have only attained a man-made unity. All Amish are European. It cannot spread to different cultures because it is a superficial manmade conformity.

The church is different. It is not a man-made conformity, but a supernatural unity! It is diverse, but it is united. It is made up of every "tribe, tongue, people, and nation". But the church is the Body of Christ. When Saul of Tarsus was persecuting the Church, the Head of the Church confronted him and interrogated the future Apostle with the words: "Saul, Saul, why do you persecute me?" How incredible to be united with our Head and King, Jesus. That's where our unity with each other comes from.

There are several mothers who are with child in our congregation. The argument that always occurs when a child is born is: "Who does the baby look like?" Is it Mommy or Daddy? Of course, at first, they all come out looking like raisins. They need to stretch out a bit! But one thing is true about the child of God. There are those identifying characteristics that disclose our supernatural origin. We are touched by the Triune God – One Spirit, One Lord, One God and Father. Oh, those who know that triune God all have the same likeness – conformed to Jesus – and the same language – prayer and praise – and the same love – what an all-consuming love! And we have these seven identifying marks: one body, one Spirit, one hope, one Lord, one faith, one baptism, one God and Father! Let us be sure we are not playing games with God, but that we truly are marked by him with his fingerprints. God grant us mercy that it be so.

10 | EPHESIANS 4:7-13
ROOTED IN SPIRITUAL GIFTS

But grace was given to each one of us according to the measure of Christ's gift.
Ephesians 4:7

I love Spring! You can see the flowers blooming everywhere! Actually, I love to see all the various colors of the flowers together. The flowers are of every variety of the brilliant colors of the rainbow! God's church is beautiful in that same way. Every one of us is different—with different functions and gifting and abilities, yet we are all one Body. And in that one Body, God gave each one of us differing spiritual gifts. In Ephesians 4:7-13, we're going to see God's plan for your place in the Body of Christ.

Wholeness is important. Wholeness means all parts are functioning well. Fifteen years ago, I was so excited to purchase several beautiful bushes for only ten cents apiece. I was proud of myself for finding such a bargain. I planted them in our back yard in the Spring. They were all barely alive. But I took personal interest and care for those bushes, carefully watering them. By the first year, I was just glad that these bushes even survived and began to blossom. Each year the bushes grew more and more. Today, they are beautifully manicured and look like I paid hundreds of dollars for them. This reminds me of how every believer has everything he or she needs to grow in Christ, if they are properly discipled and cared for. Every believer has the gifts that are essential not only for one's own spiritual growth but also the growth and strength of the Body.

As we look at the Body of Christ, we have to realize that every part is vital. Think of it in the realm of flight. There are thousands of pieces in a Boeing 747. Take off a wing and you will see how vital each part is. Take off the landing gear. Take out one of the engines. Every part is important.

The church in Ephesians is described as a Body with all its different members and functions. Or we could think about it like a car or a computer or a space shuttle or any kind of machine with millions of different little parts, but all one united whole. When God saves us, he gives us differing spiritual gifts and unites us to one Body. In order to explore our spiritual gifts, we're going to look at what this Ephesians passage says, but there are at least three other important passages that harmonize with this one: 1 Corinthians 12, Romans 12, and 1 Peter 4.

THE DESCRIPTION OF SPIRITUAL GIFTS (4:7)

Ephesians 4:7 | But grace was given to each one of us according to the measure of Christ's gift.

A Spiritual Gift is Given to Every Believer

Who in the Body of Christ has a spiritual gift? Each one of us. No one gets "cheated" out of a spiritual gift! Every Christian has received at least one spiritual gift from God which he is responsible to use for the good of the church and for the glory of God.

A Spiritual Gift is a Supernatural Ability

What is a spiritual gift? It is described here as a gift of God's grace "according the measure of Christ's gift" that is given to each believer. Christ's gift to us is his atonement and resurrection power that he gives to us. In most places in the Bible, the word grace means God's unmerited favor. But in some places, it means supernatural gifting and ability. Here it refers to ability. We have a special empowerment from God to edify the Body of Christ.

We are going to look at our four passages on spiritual gifts and find out that a spiritual gift is a supernatural ability that manifests the power of the Spirit of God in your life and always strengthens the faith of fellow believers. So a spiritual gift is a supernatural ability that manifests the power of the Spirit of God in your life.

Paul wrote to the Corinthians about spiritual gift and tells them and us, that we should not be uninformed. We need to be educated in the fact and function of spiritual gifts. We cannot just ignore this subject.

> *1 Corinthians 12:1* | Now concerning spiritual gifts, brothers, I do not want you to be uninformed.

A Spiritual Gift is a Stewardship

Again in 1 Corinthians 12, Paul is talking about spiritual gifts, and he actually gives his own definition.

> *1 Corinthians 12:7* | To each is given the manifestation of the Spirit for the common good.

Paul defines spiritual gifts here as "the manifestation of the Spirit" that is to be exercised and used for the "common good." Since these gifts are in the context of the congregation, we can say that your spiritual gift is always for the "common good" and edification of the entire Body. A spiritual gift is clearly a supernatural ability given by the Spirit of God that is also a stewardship to be used for the betterment of the Body of Christ.

Let me be clear about spiritual gifts. A spiritual gift always ministers God's Spirit to someone else. You may be a good cook, but not have the gift of hospitality. You may be gifted in music, but there is a way to sing where it is a manifestation of the Spirit and a way in which it is just a performance. You may be a good mechanic, but a person with the gift of mercy and the gift of helps is going to fix someone's car in a way where it is a manifestation of the Spirit. Your spiritual gift is a supernatural ability that manifests the Spirit and builds up the Body of Christ. Paul testifies to this and gives glory to God.

> *1 Corinthians 15:10* | But by the grace of God I am what I am, and his grace toward me was not in vain. On the contrary, I worked harder than any of them, though it was not I, but the grace of God that is with me.

It was the grace of God in Paul that worked in him to labor. The apostle Peter goes further and tells us not only that we have all received a gift as believers, but that every believer has a responsibility to use his gift as a stewardship from God.

> *1 Peter 4:10-11* | As each has received a gift, use it to serve one another, as good stewards of God's varied [multi-colored] grace: [11] whoever speaks, as one who speaks oracles of God; whoever serves, as one who serves by the strength that God supplies—in order that in everything God may be glorified through Jesus Christ. To him belong glory and dominion forever and ever. Amen.

Indeed, spiritual gifts are stewardships of God's grace. Peter gives us two categories of gifts: those who speak and those who serve. There are speaking gifts and serving gifts. But whatever kind of gift you have, you are to use it! Paul, in Romans, tells us the same thing: every Christian has a spiritual gift, and we are responsible to use them!

> *Romans 12:6* | Having gifts that differ according to the grace given to us, let us use them.

Again, the spiritual gifting you have is a supernatural ability resulting from God's grace that is to be used for the common good of the Body of Christ.

Spiritual Gifts are Merited by Christ

We learn something further in Ephesians 4:7. It is by merit of what Christ has done we are told that every believer is given spiritual gifts.

> **Ephesians 4:7b** | But grace was given to each one of us according to the measure of Christ's gift.

Christ set us free from our slavery to sin by his own gift to us on the cross. By the power of his resurrection, he gave us supernatural abilities. Enabling grace is measured out to be consistent with what is necessary for the operation of Christ's gift. The term *dōrea* (gift) focuses on the freeness of the gift (*cf* Mt 10:8; Rom 3:24).[75] Paul is emphasizing that Christ died for a purpose. It's implied that he died to give you the gift of eternal life, yes. He died to give you right standing with God, yes. But he also died to give you power to serve him in building up the Body through rich discipleship in serving and teaching. How does one measure Christ's gift? Look at the gifting of the Body of Christ. Jesus has

---

[75] MacArthur. *Ephesians*, 135.

given us all the exact measure of power and grace to do what we need to advance his kingdom and grow into his image.

So, we've seen from our four passages (Ephesians 4, Romans 12, I Corinthians 12, and 1 Peter 4) that a spiritual gift is a supernatural ability that manifests the power of the Spirit of God in your life. At least one spiritual gift is given to every believer based on the merit and measure of Christ's gift to us: his substitutionary atonement and resurrection power.

THE GIVER OF SPIRITUAL GIFTS (4:8-10)

> **Ephesians 4:8** | Therefore it says, "When he ascended on high he led a host of captives, and he gave gifts to men."

Our Victorious General

Christ has the right to give spiritual gifts. Ephesians 4:8 is a quote from a song of triumph, Psalm 68, a psalm Paul tells us is about Jesus. This Psalm is speaking of the victory that David experienced as they battled forward with the Ark of the Covenant in front of them. Imagine the great pillar of fire burning before them. God fought for David. Psalm 68 describes God coming down from Mount Sinai into his sanctuary in the Tabernacle, with his presence manifesting from the Ark of the Covenant, there above the Mercy Seat. David says, God, like a mighty general, defeats his enemies, takes them captive, and even gives some of those rebels as gifts to for the expansion of his own kingdom. Paul applies this Psalm to Jesus, emphasizes this majestic military victory, transforming rebels into gifts for his church.

> *Psalm 68:18* | You ascended on high, leading a host of captives in your train and receiving gifts among men, even among the rebellious, that the LORD God may dwell there.

Those that kept God's people in captivity were taken captive, and David made an open show of some of them after coming back from war. In the ancient world, when conquering generals returned home, they would bring a procession of prisoners of war as a sign of their victory. They would "lead captivity captive" in this parade and in celebration, give the gifts and spoils of war to the all the people.

Paul says, Christ is the true David, the ultimate Conqueror. Jesus is our glorious General. Christ storms the gates of hell, and no one can stop him from taking captivity captive. He plunders the strong man's goods (Mk 3:27). Christ is the one who ascended the hill of victory. Christ is the one who brought the spoils and led the captives free.

The image Paul is painting would be a very familiar scene that all the Ephesians would have been familiar with in the ancient military world of the Roman armies. When the Roman Caesar put down a rebellion within the kingdom, he would take the rebels captive, and usually the kings and generals and commanders of the rebellious nations would be put in chains. The Romans would march them through Rome and celebrate with triumphal entry into Rome. They would come captive in chains showing that they had been conquered. Paul takes that picture, pulls it out of the Old Testament and the Roman culture, and applies it to Christ's victory for his church.

In the same way, Jesus Christ as our King has taken away our captivity—he has taken of the devil's spoils. Jesus is the Conqueror. He's already conquered his enemies. He's already redeemed his elect children. He's already shared with them the spoils of his victory, and he's given them their marching orders. Now get that in your mind. The King has already come. He's conquered the enemies that he had on the cross. And by the cross he redeemed, paid for, and purchased, a Bride. Remember the words of Jesus regarding his victory for his church.

> *Matthew 16:18* | I will build my church, and the gates of hell shall not prevail against it.

What does this mean for you? Christ has taken you out of the hands of the wicked one, cleansed and empowered you as a gift to his church. He gives each one of us as a gift to his Body. Each of us has a spiritual gift or gifts. We do not choose our gifts; God has that job, as verse 7 says, "...grace was given to each one of us according to the measure of Christ's gift", and verse 8 says, God "gave gifts unto men". Take those two words: "grace" and "gifts", and you realize these are gifts that God sovereignly gives us by his Spirit. God raises us up and puts his people into his service. It is God through Christ that places us exactly where he wants us in the Body of Christ. You don't decide how or where you are going to minister in God's harvest field.

In our fleshly excitement in the church at times we think we need to call people to programs and tasks in the church. Programs are good and important. But the church is not a group of human programs. The church is the temple of the Holy Spirit. That's why we want people not to be merely working, but to manifest the power of God's Spirit in a ministry given to them by God in the context of the local church.

I read about a famous preacher by the name of Dr. D. Martyn Lloyd-Jones in London. He was at first an assistant to G. Campbell Morgan at the Westminster Chapel of London. But before becoming a preacher, he was a medical doctor. For years he worked in a medical practice. When God called him to preach, Lloyd-Jones sensed God's calling into the pulpit ministry. Let us consider his own testimony.

> When I came here, people said to me: 'Why give up good work – a good profession – after all, the medical profession, why give that up? ...'Ah well!' I felt like saying to them, 'if you knew more about the work of a doctor, you would understand. We but spend most of our time rendering people fit to go back to their sin!' I saw men on their sick beds, I spoke to them of their immortal souls, they promised grand things. Then they got better and back they went to their old sin! I saw I was helping these men to sin, and I decided that I would do no more of it. I want to heal souls. If a man has a diseased body and his soul is all right, he is all right to the end; but a man with a healthy body and a diseased soul is all right for sixty years or so and then he has to face an eternity of hell. Ah, yes! We have to sometimes give up those things which are good for that which is the best of all – the joy of salvation and newness of life.[76]

Of course, David Martyn Lloyd-Jones no longer wanted to fix people up so that they could go back to sinning. He had to do something to change the hearts of men. He never practiced medicine again. God called him into a very fruitful pulpit ministry where he revived thousands with Holy Spirit filled line upon line Biblical preaching with power. He was compelled to stir up his spiritual gifts, which happened to be speaking gifts. You do what God is calling you to do. It is God who sovereignly gives you the gifting. He is the fountainhead, and no one else.

Our Humble General

Ephesians 4:9-10 | (In saying, "He ascended," what does it mean but that he had also descended into the lower regions, the

---

[76] Iain Murray. *D. Martyn Lloyd-Jones: The First Forty Years, 1899-1939* (Carlyle, PA: Banner of Truth, 1982), 80.

earth? **¹⁰** He who descended is the one who also ascended far above all the heavens, that he might fill all things.)

Paul is expanding the imagery of Psalm 68 and applying it to Christ's incarnation and ascension. The fact that he "ascended" implies that he descended in the incarnation to the "lower regions" of the earth, which is another way of indicating the humiliation of coming to earth (*cf* Jn 3:13). His descent to earth meant that he set aside the independent exercise of his attributes (such as his omnipresence), submitting the exercise of them to the Father's will (*cf* Phil 2:6-8), and went down, down, down in the incarnation, and then went even further down in his death, actually becoming sin for us (2 Cor 5:21). He was buried (1 Cor 15:2) and placed into that tomb in the earth for three days. But then he burst up in exaltation — so that now he fills the whole universe as a conquering King and joyously lavishes gifts upon his children. He bestows abundant gifts to his Church and gives his people power to fulfill their gifts. The gifts and enabling grace which we have, have been given to us as Christ apportioned them. They came from the conquering King. They are given with great expectation on his part, for he expects us to use them to bring power and victory in the church.[77]

Our Exalted General

Ephesians 4:10 | He who descended is the one who also ascended far above all the heavens, that he might fill all things.

Christ's victorious ascension has a purpose: "that he might fill all things" (4:10). Our King will set things right again in the entire universe. Paul is here returning to his theme in chapter 1, where he says that Christ's death was the plan of God "to unite all things in him, things in heaven and things on earth" (1:10). So here, Paul says that the power and authority of Jesus will soon be manifested in the entire universe when the presence of Christ will fill all things and unites everything in all realms: seen and unseen.

How is this filling of the universe with the sovereign presence of Christ taking place? It began when Jesus ascended, and the church was empowered to accomplish its mission because at his ascension, Christ sent the Holy Spirit to, first and foremost, indwell and fill all believers (Jn 16:7-13). Ascending in ancient days was connected to the

---

[77] Hughes, *Ephesians*, 132.

enthronement after victory. The sign of Jesus' enthronement and victory was his pouring out his Holy Spirit to gift every member of his church.[78] This is the beginning of Christ's reclaiming of the entire universe.

By saying Christ "might fill all things", he is saying nothing in all the cosmos is untouched by Christ. At his ascension, God made clear that every square inch of the universe belongs to Christ, beginning with his church. So just as Christ has filled his church with his presence, so Christ's presence will, quite soon, fill all things.

This "filling all things" is the ultimate fulfillment of the Abrahamic covenant. Paul says in another place that "the promise to Abraham and his offspring" was that "he would be heir of the world" (Rom 4:13). Paul returns to this theme when he says the creation groans for the fullness of Christ to fill the universe.

> *Romans 8:19-21* | For the creation waits with eager longing for the revealing of the sons of God. [20] For the creation was subjected to futility, not willingly, but because of him who subjected it, in hope [21] that the creation itself will be set free from its bondage to corruption and obtain the freedom of the glory of the children of God.

Truly "He who testifies to these things says, 'Surely I am coming soon.'" And we reply with the apostle John with a loud "Amen. Come, Lord Jesus!" (Rev 22:20).

THE FUNCTION OF SPIRITUAL GIFTS (4:11-12)

Christ directs his church. Aren't you glad for that? He brings us together as a congregation, He brings us together for the purpose of exaltation God and for equipping the saints. Christ does all this as our Head.

The Officers Who Do the Equipping

> **Ephesians 4:11** | And he gave the apostles, the prophets, the evangelists, the shepherds and teachers.

Christ gave leaders to his church. Specifically, he mentions four categories of gifted persons he gives to his church: the apostles, the prophets, the evangelists, and the shepherd-teachers. It's important to

---

[78] Sproul, *Ephesians*, 102.

define and consider each category, since there is much confusion today in the various denominations of the particular nature of each office.

The Apostles

The apostles are first and foremost the Twelve that our Lord chose, minus Judas who was replaced by Matthias. To be clear, Paul is not simply meaning "sent ones" in the general sense. Rather, he is speaking of those select individuals directly appointed and authorized by Jesus Christ to be his immediate representatives on earth. In this sense, he is speaking of "capital A" apostles – the Twelve, Paul himself, Apollos and James, etc.

From our study of Ephesians thus far we understand that the apostles as well as the prophets. Prophets are *foundational gifts* to the Church. The previous mentions of apostles and prophets in 2:20 and 3:5 indicate that "apostles" were the Twelve, and "prophets" were those who preached in association with the apostles (*cf* Acts 11:27ff.; 13:1ff.; 21:4, 9; 1 Cor 14:1). The apostles and the prophets were given to the Church to get her established, but now their role is assumed by the canonical writings of the New Testament. The apostles and prophets with their unique endowments did not extend beyond the apostolic age.[79]

It is important to note that while the formal office of the apostles as foundational gifts of the church has ceased, there are apostolic gifts.

The Prophets

The prophets were also foundational and are no longer are functioning today. They sometimes spoke revelation from God (Acts 11:21–28) and sometimes simply expounded revelation already given (as implied in Acts 13:1, where they are connected with teachers). They always spoke for God but did not always give a newly revealed message from God. The prophets were second to the apostles, and their message was to be judged by that of the apostles (1 Cor 14:37).[80]

While the formal offices of Apostle and Prophet are no longer functioning, all who preach and teach the Word rest on the apostolic and prophetic foundation. The gifts of pastors and evangelists have their full weight on the authority of the apostles and prophets through the Word of God that they gave us. That's why Paul tells all the faithful in

---

[79] Hughes, *Ephesians*, 133.
[80] MacArthur. *Ephesians*, 142.

all the church, even to this day to appreciate the work of those who prophesy.

1 Thessalonians 5:20 | Do not despise prophecies.

Walter Kaiser notes that prophecy can mean either "foretelling" or "forth-telling." The former speaks to the specific function of the prophet who predicted the future activities of God. The latter speaks to ongoing activity of the prophet who spoke as "a preacher of righteousness to his generation and his culture."[81] More than two-thirds of all prophetic activity in the Bible is forth-telling rather than foretelling. The church will only be as strong as its commitment to preach, teach, and obey Scripture. Paul knew that the health of the church would ultimately be determined both by its commitment to preach and by its desire to honor God's Word. The New Testament prophets laid the foundation, but the evangelists and pastor-teachers continue the forth-telling of expositing the Scriptures to the congregations today.

The Evangelists

The work of the evangelist is to preach and explain the good news of salvation in Jesus Christ to those who have not yet believed. He is a proclaimer of salvation by grace through faith in the Son of God.

Philip demonstrates that the evangelist is not a man with ten suits and ten sermons who runs a road show. New Testament evangelists were missionaries and church planters (much like the apostles, but without the title and miraculous gifts), who went where Christ was not named and led people to faith in the Savior. They then taught the new believers the Word, built them up, and moved on to new territory. [82]

The Shepherd-Teachers

Pastors translates *poimēn*, whose normal meaning is shepherd. It emphasizes the care, protection and leadership of the man of God for the flock. Teachers *(didaskaloi)* has to do with the primary function of pastors.

Though teaching can be identified as a ministry on its own (1 Cor 12:28), pastors and teachers are best understood as one office of leadership in the church. Often the word "and" *(kai)* means "that is" or "in particular," making teachers in this context explanatory of pastors.

---

[81] Kaiser, *The Christian and the Old Testament*, 128.
[82] MacArthur. *Ephesians*, 143.

That meaning cannot be conclusively proven in this text, but the text of 1 Timothy 5:17 clearly puts the two functions together when it says: "Let the elders who rule well be considered worthy of double honor, especially those who work hard at preaching and teaching" (lit., "labor to exhaustion in word and teaching"). Those two functions define the teaching shepherd.[83]

The Act of Equipping

> **Ephesians 4:11-12** | And he gave the apostles, the prophets, the evangelists, the shepherds and teachers, **12** to equip the saints for the work of ministry, for building up the body of Christ.

Christ's leaders equip his church for the work of ministry.

The Meaning of Equipping

What does it mean to "equip the saints"? The word "equip" is a word used to describe fisherman getting their nets ready, cleansed, and repaired.[84] Equipping then has to do with the careful and robust application of God's Word and how to live it out in the lives of the saints. God's Word restores you; it cleanses you. When it is applied, it revitalizes you.

The word "equip" was also used of armies, of education, and of child rearing.[85] It is to prepare them, to get them ready for service. My goal each time the Word is opened is to prepare the saints for service to God—in the home, in the workplace, and to our brothers and sisters in Christ.

What does equipping entail? How do pastors equip the saints? In two ways: by teaching and by living out the Word. Pastors (i.e. shepherds) equip the church by teaching how to apply the Word. Teaching can take place through counseling, preaching, teaching, etc. This is both one on one and through expository preaching of the word to the congregation. Shepherds are to be teaching to remind.

---

[83] Ibid.

[84] Sinclair B. Ferguson. *Let's Study Ephesians* (Carlisle, PA: Banner of Truth, 2005), 110.

[85] Walter Bauer and Frederick William Danker. *A Greek-English Lexicon of the New Testament and Other Early Christian Literature* (Third Edition; based on a previous English edition by W.F. Arndt, F.W. Gingrich, and F.W. Danker; University of Chicago Press, 1957, 1979, 2000), 526.

2 Peter 1:12 | I intend always to remind you of these qualities, though you know them and are established in the truth that you have.

Shepherds are to be teaching regularly—in normal and difficult times.

2 Timothy 4:2a | Preach the word; be ready in season, and out of season.

Shepherds are to be teaching to reprove, rebuke, and exhort.

2 Timothy 4:2b | Reprove, rebuke, and exhort, with complete patience and teaching.

The saints need both correction and encouragement. We all stray, and we need to be brought back to the path of God's will. We all need positive, helpful encouragement as to how to apply God's Word to our lives. Pastors equip the church by living out the application of the Word. A pastor is to live out the Word of God in his life.

1 Timothy 4:16 | Keep a close watch on yourself and on the teaching. Persist in this, for by so doing you will save both yourself and your hearers.

The People Who are Equipped

Ephesians 4:12 | To equip the saints for the work of ministry, for building up the body of Christ.

All Christians are equipped so that they might be the ministers of the church. Everyone is expected and encouraged to be involved in active ministry. If you want to be comfortable as a mere spectator, you are not a mature or maturing Christian. The church of Jesus is a place where every member has a ministry of some kind.

Consider who is called to minister – the saints! That's every one of us. All the saints are to be equipped for works of ministry. By the way, a saint is not some Roman Catholic bishop who has been canonized. A saint in the Bible is a simple believer. It merely means "holy one" or "one set apart by God for a special purpose." Paul writes to the saints at Ephesus, and his goal is that the saints should be trained for ministry. Every who is a believer in Christ is a saint.

Since all saints are equipped for the work of ministry, no healthy church can be a church of mere spectators with one minister. A healthy church has as many ministers as there are members! None of us can be spectators. We are all called to build each other up in the faith. We are all clergy. We believe in the priesthood of the believer. That means that there is no separation between clergy and laity. We are all to be priests one to another.

> *1 Peter 2:5, 9* | You yourselves like living stones are being built up as a spiritual house, to be a holy priesthood, to offer spiritual sacrifices acceptable to God through Jesus Christ. ⁹ But you are a chosen race, a royal priesthood, a holy nation, a people for his own possession, that you may proclaim the excellencies of him who called you out of darkness into his marvelous light.

> *Revelation 1:6* | He has made us kings and priests unto God and his Father.

How do we build one another up? First, be *present*. Be present in the congregation at your local church applying the preached Word, getting equipped. God has ordained a way for you to "repair your nets" and to get cleansed by his Word in a corporate setting so that you can be used by him. One way that you undercut the ministry to the Body is by staying home when you have full ability to be fellowshipping with the Body. Is it hard work? Yes! You have to make difficult choices. We are called to "endure hardness, as a good soldier of Jesus Christ" (2 Tim 2:3).

Second, be *pliable*. Be teachable. Jesus said we are to be "teaching them to observe all things whatsoever I have commanded you" (Mt 28:20). You listen to the teaching each time you attend the local church. You are Bereans. You compare the preaching to the Scriptures. You apply it to your life. Then you teach others. Show them how to apply it to their life and their situation. You encourage them from the Word of God. Perhaps you say, but I can't teach anyone! Paul says differently in Romans 15:14, "I myself am satisfied [persuaded] about you, my brothers, that you yourselves are full of goodness, filled with all knowledge and able to instruct one another." The phrase "able to instruct" has been translated "competent to counsel".

Thirdly, be *proactive*. Serve one another. In other words, ministry does not only happen when we meet at this building. We are called to get involved in each other's lives. Don't wait for ministry to happen to you. You are responsible to be the minister. We assemble on Sundays and Wednesdays to get trained to then go out and be intentional and proactive as we minister to one another.

THE PURPOSE FOR SPIRITUAL GIFTS (4:13)

Purpose #1 Involvement

Ephesians 4:13a | Until we all attain to the unity of the faith and of the knowledge of the Son of God.

We are all to be involved in growing the faith of our fellow believers in the local church. The building up of the redeemed involves a twofold ultimate objective, which Paul identifies as "the unity of the faith" and "the knowledge of the Son of God," out of which flow spiritual maturity, sound doctrine, and loving testimony. We are called to have a unity in our faith, where we are all working out in our lives together, joyfully unified in our knowledge of the Son of God in doctrine as well as our dedication to him in our service. Are you involved in your local church?

Unity in Faith, Doctrine

The "faith" is the content of the gospel in its most complete form. We need to clearly understand who Jesus is and what he's done for us. As the church at Corinth so clearly illustrates, disunity in the church comes from doctrinal ignorance and spiritual immaturity.[86] When believers are properly taught, they will have a fuller assurance of their salvation and a deeper joy to serve the Lord. They will not be immature and selfish but involved in Body life with an unselfish attitude, having a clear understanding of their own conversion, based on the Person and work of Christ.

Spiritual gifts when exercised for the glory of the Person of Jesus and his work on the cross breed a unity in the faith. We are all in awe of Christ, and this in turn breeds involvement and care for the congregation. A solid understanding of Christ's humiliation is the greatest encouragement for each part of the Body to work together, in deep humility and love for one another. We are all different. Keeping our eyes on Christ, our exalted Head, keeps us humble, not focused on ourselves but on Christ. Paul alludes to this in 1 Corinthians 12.

1 Corinthians 12:15–22 | If the foot should say, "Because I am not a hand, I do not belong to the body," that would not make it any less a part of the body. [16] And if the ear should say, "Because I am not an eye, I do

---

[86] MacArthur. *Ephesians*, 156.

not belong to the body," that would not make it any less a part of the body. ¹⁷ If the whole body were an eye, where would be the sense of hearing? If the whole body were an ear, where would be the sense of smell? ¹⁸ But as it is, God arranged the members in the body, each one of them, as he chose. ¹⁹ If all were a single member, where would the body be? ²⁰ As it is, there are many parts, yet one body. ²¹ The eye cannot say to the hand, "I have no need of you," nor again the head to the feet, "I have no need of you." ²² On the contrary, the parts of the body that seem to be weaker are indispensable.

We have to work together to attain the unity of faith and doctrine. That means as a result of me daily exercising my spiritual gift, I'm involved in the lives of the local congregation. With this humble unity of the faith, there is a realization that everyone is important. We are all looking out for each other, to makes sure we believe correctly and are trusting Jesus. If we get our eyes off Jesus, disunity follows, and we wrongly depreciate members of Christ's Body. I've seen churches with amazing gifts fall apart because one person with great gifting is exalted above another, and the people with weaker gifts get left behind. Paul tells us how to make sure no one gets left behind, again in 1 Corinthians 12.

1 Corinthians 12:22–25 | The parts of the body that seem to be weaker are indispensable, ²³ and on those parts of the body that we think less honorable we bestow the greater honor, and our unpresentable parts are treated with greater modesty, ²⁴ which our more presentable parts do not require. But God has so composed the body, giving greater honor to the part that lacked it, ²⁵ that there may be no division in the body, but that the members may have the same care for one another.

The visible, outwardly teaching members aren't necessarily the most important ones. Rather, we're to value every believer's role in the local congregation. A believer who says, "I'll only serve if I'm a hand or an eye" is being disobedient to God's Word. That's because we're saved to serve. Everyone benefits. Often times, the believers serving Jesus behind the scenes are like the lungs or heart or brain of the body that you never see, but that you cannot live without.

To recap, Paul says in Ephesians 4:13a, we are first of all growing in the unity of the faith. We are growing in doctrinal solidarity. Oneness in fellowship is impossible unless it is built on the foundation of commonly believed truth. Paul then says we need to go beyond solidarity in doctrine and truth to grow in the unity of knowing Christ in a deeper and more meaningful way. This knowledge of Christ needs to be deeply personal and transformational.

Unity in Knowing Christ

Ephesians 4:13b | Until we all attain to the unity of the faith and of the knowledge of the Son of God.

Being involved in the Body will breed a closer knowledge and personal relationship with Jesus, the Son of God. You will see other believers' walks with Christ, and you will be challenged to know Christ better. This is the specific way the Body is edified by my spiritual gift. They see your relationship with Christ, and they are challenged to grow more in love with Jesus. This is the ultimate good for the Body.

1 Corinthians 12:7 | To each is given the manifestation of the Spirit for the common good.

It is our responsibility to make sure that every brother and sister is growing in their relationship with Christ and growing more deeply in their faith relationship with the Lord. Everyone is responsible for each other. We all need to be involved, using our gifts.

1 Peter 4:10 | As each has received a gift, use it to serve one another, as good stewards of God's varied [multi-colored] grace.

To summarize, I am not legitimately growing unless I am involved in a local church, learning more about doctrine, the person and work of Jesus, and helping others to grow deeper in their walk with Christ. I can have a PhD in theology but be very, very far from true spiritual growth. Spiritual growth is measured by the exercise of my spiritual gift and involvement in the local church. As I grow, I help others to grow in Christ. That begins with a unity in the understanding of the faith, how one is converted by the Person and work of Jesus Christ on the cross. But then we move forward with truly walking with Christ on a moment-by-moment basis. And this walking with Christ produces a mature manhood, what the Bible in other places calls "godliness."

Purpose #2 Maturity

Ephesians 4:13b | Until we all attain to the unity of the faith and of the knowledge of the Son of God, to mature manhood.

Mature manhood in the Christian life is another goal. Peter describes this maturity as "godliness" (2 Pet 1:3-11). It is the idea of godly character based on constantly seeking to please God ("virtue") and learning to do that over and over again ("self-control" and "perseverance"). Maturity is a result of treasuring God's Word in my heart (Psa 119:11) to the point where I don't have to stop and think about the wisest thing to do, but it just comes out of me.

The Beneficiaries of Spiritual Gifts

Paul says the goal is that "we all" come to this place of "mature manhood". That means I am my brother's keeper. I am to be looking for my brothers and sisters in the local congregation to grow into maturity in Christ, conformed to his image (Rom 8:28-29). That means the whole Body benefits when each member exercises the spiritual gifts given by the Lord. I do that by exercising my spiritual gifts in the context of my forever family, the local church. Paul describes this attitude in Romans 1. If you were reading through the New Testament, the first place you would run into the term "spiritual gift" is Romans 1.

The Practice of Spiritual Gifts

Writing to the church at Rome, Paul lays out a clear understanding of spiritual gifts. He takes a personal interest in exercising his gifts in order to help the Roman church grow in their faith.

> *Romans 1:11-12* | I long to see you, that I may impart to you some spiritual gift to strengthen you— ¹² that is, that we may be mutually encouraged by each other's faith, both yours and mine.

It sounds like Paul wants to help them have a gift, but the text actually means that he wants to give them the benefit of his gifts. He wants to impart his spiritual gifts with them. So which spiritual gift do you have, you're wondering? I think it would be fair to say also from this text that you shouldn't bend your mind too much trying to label your spiritual gift before you use it. That is, don't worry about whether you can point to prophecy, or teaching, or wisdom, or knowledge, or healing, or miracles, or mercy, or service, or administration, etc., and say, "That's mine." Instead, the way to think is this: The reason we have spiritual gifts is so that we can strengthen other people's faith; here is someone whose faith is in jeopardy; how can I help him?

The Recognition of Spiritual Gifts

You might say, how do I get going with my spiritual gifts? You don't have to know your spiritual gifts to start growing, but it is something you will discover over time. You ask how?

First, it's discoverable by the Body of Christ. You need mature people in the Body to take note of what you like to do to serve Christ. Several places have Paul (a spiritual father to Timothy) addressing Timothy's gifts.

1 Timothy 4:14 | Do not neglect the gift you have.

2 Timothy 1:6 | Fan into flame the gift of God, which is in you through the laying on of my hands.

This tells us that as mature people in the Body of Christ recognize your gifting, you should stir it up more and more. Let's say you have a desire to teach. You should study and teach more and more and fan it into flame. Perhaps you have gifts of service. You like to fix things. You don't mind cooking. Perhaps there are those who don't mind working in the nursery. Certainly, we don't see "the gift of changing diapers" in the New Testament but serving and the gift of helps and mercy is a spiritual gift. Whatever your gifting is, it will be recognized by more mature Christians in the congregation. They will help you and encourage you to "fan into flame" the gift or gifts that God has given you.

Are you using your spiritual gifts for God? Is God using you to build up the faith of those around you? I want to challenge you to fan the flame of your spiritual gifts. Do everything you can to build up the faith of your brethren. It's not important to name your gift. Be concerned about building up your brothers and sisters' faith. It may be through service or teaching. The focus is not the gift but the glory of Christ.

Purpose #3 Christlikeness

Ephesians 4:13c | ... until we all attain to the unity of the faith and of the knowledge of the Son of God, to mature manhood, to the measure of the stature of the fullness of Christ.

"I want to be like Jesus" should be every Christian's great desire. It's God's desire. God's great purpose for his church is that every believer, without exception, come to be like his Son (Rom 8:29), manifesting the character qualities of the One who is the only measure of the full-grown, perfect, mature man. The church in the world is Jesus

Christ in the world, because the church is now the fullness of his incarnate Body in the world (*cf* 1:23). We are to radiate and reflect Christ's perfections. Christians are therefore called to "walk in the same manner as he walked" (1 Jn 2:6; *cf* Col 4:12), and he walked in complete and continual fellowship with and obedience to his Father. [87]

Consider this: that the measure of your maturity is not your level of Bible knowledge, but how you measure up to Christlikeness. What is your stature, or we might say, how high are you soaring with Christ? And how full is your heart with the fullness of God and Christ? We ought to be "filled with all the fullness of God" (3:19). It is possible here and now. We must be convinced of that.

Conclusion

Some of you might not know about Elon Musk, but he is the founder of PayPal, Tesla Motors, and the SpaceX program. Nasa hired him to bring over half a ton of food and other supplies for the crew aboard the station. The mission is worth 1.6 billion dollars. The first mission by a private company to the International Space Station was aborted before dawn Saturday at Cape Canaveral, Fla., when computers detected an anomaly in one of the rocket's engines and automatically shut down the launch sequence. The countdown for Space Exploration Technologies Corp., or SpaceX, was flawless until about 4:55 a.m. EDT when, at the last second, the rocket engines briefly lit up and then went dark. "Three, two, one, zero and liftoff," announced NASA commentator George Diller before he realized what had happened. "We've had a cutoff. Liftoff did not occur."[88]

More important than the Space Program is God's program for his people: the local church. All the money in the world cannot compare to the worth of one human soul. Are you stewarding your life and spiritual gifts to grow in Christ and to help others to grow? Use your spiritual gift, and you will see how Christ will use you to build his church, and the gates of hell will not prevail against it.

---

[87] MacArthur. *Ephesians*, 157.
[88] Associated Press. (2012, May 19). "SpaceX Rocket Launch Aborted". Retrieved December 29, 2020, from https://www.politico.com/story/2012/05/spacex-rocket-launch-aborted-076513

11 | EPHESIANS 3:14-4:12
THE ABUNDANT CHURCH

That you may be filled with all the fullness of God.
EPHESIANS 3:19

Jesus said, "I will build my church, and the gates of hell shall not prevail against it" (Mt 16:18). He said, "I came that they may have life and have it abundantly" (Jn 10:10). Paul tells us God wants to do "exceeding, abundantly above all that we could ever ask or imagine" (Eph 3:20).

I believe God wants to bring a great, powerful revival to this land, through this church. He's building his church. Yet sometimes we can barely make it through the day. We feel powerless. How can we tap into God's power this morning? The truth is we already have God's power. We have every spiritual blessing in Christ (1:3), but we actually are not often accessing it.

> Key Thought: God wants to give us an abundant church, but we have to overcome our powerlessness before we can have it.

Have you ever felt powerless? I can remember as a child growing up in the winding roads of Louisiana where my most faithful transportation was a Huffy bicycle. I used to go everywhere on that bike. It never failed me... until I was going at top speed at about 15 miles an hour by Michael Barnes' house. Here's the thing – Mike had a big dog. I don't even remember what kind of a dog it was. I just remember one thing about it. It had big teeth. Everything about this dog was big! I couldn't go fast enough. I remember thinking I wanted to grow up. I didn't want to be this dog's meal. Terror raced through my veins as this dog started running next to me and gnawing at my twirling feet that couldn't peddle fast enough! My Huffy bike failed me. Obviously, I survived. I don't remember how I got out of that, but the fact that I'm here today proves I lived through it!

Then came 1987. I begged my mom for a used 1980 C-70 Honda passport moped! She vowed never to get me one of those. It went too fast. But we lived a mile deep into the woods in Louisiana and a moped could be quite helpful. She broke down and got it for me! It wasn't in the greatest shape. It had a part missing from the carburetor, so any time I wanted it to go I had to actually place my hand over the carburetor so that the gas would get suctioned into the engine. I finally rigged the carburetor with a rubber band and a piece of cloth, and I could go anywhere. What's my point? What good is the moped if it has no power? What good is it if it has a broken carburetor and you can't get fuel to the engine?

In the same way, the Christian life is like a car. What good does it do you if you have a beautiful, sophisticated automobile if you don't have the key? No key, no power. Well in the Christian life we have all we need! We've learned about the sufficiency of Jesus Christ, and the believer's resources available in Christ.

WE NEED ENCOURAGEMENT FROM GOD (3:14-19)

We have no power in and of ourselves, so we pray to the Father in heaven, like Paul did, for power.

> **Ephesians 3:14-19** | For this reason I bow my knees before the Father, [15] from whom every family in heaven and on earth is named, [16] that according to the riches of his glory he may grant you to be strengthened with power through his Spirit in your inner being, [17] so that Christ may dwell in your hearts through faith—that you, being rooted and grounded in love, [18] may have strength to comprehend with all the saints what is the breadth and length and height and depth, [19] and to know the love of Christ that surpasses knowledge, that you may be filled with all the fullness of God.

Your View of God

If we are going to see God work among us, we have to get our view of God right. We have a God who loves us so much he sent his Son. He's got his arms outstretched for you. Jesus says, "Come to me!" Look at the Father with arms wide open!

A Loving Heavenly Father

Paul comes to a loving heavenly Father and bows his knees.

Ephesians 3:14 | For this reason I bow my knees before the Father.

We come to a tender, loving, concerned, compassionate, accepting FatherPaul approaches the Father with boldness and confidence, knowing that he is more willing for his children to come to him than they ever are of going to him. He knows that God has been waiting all the while with a Father's heart of love and anticipation.[89]

A Loving Forever Family

Paul comes to a loving heavenly Father and bows his knees

Ephesians 3:14-15 | For this reason I bow my knees before the Father, [15] from whom every family in heaven and on earth is named.

We have a super big family, "from whom every family on heaven and earth is named." We need to remember that a great host of believers has already made it safely to heaven, and when we are all together on the last day, there will be "a great multitude, which no man could number, of all nations, and families, and people, and languages" (Rev 7:9).

It's also a supernatural family! Membership in the family of God does not depend on any earthly relationship, but upon being "born again" (Jn 3:3).

There is a family language: prayer. Paul said, "I bow my knees unto the Father of our Lord Jesus Christ...." (3:14).

There is a family likeness: Christ in us! Every day we should be more and more resembling the Lord Jesus since all who know Christ are "predestinate to be conformed to the image of his Son, that he might be the firstborn among many brethren" (Rom 8:29).

---

[89] MacArthur. *Ephesians*, 101.

There is a family location: heaven and earth. Remember, two places, and only two, contain the family of God. We are the *church militant* on earth, and the *church triumphant* in heaven.

There is a family love: It is an infinite, everlasting love that is poured into your heart by the Holy Spirit. It is so powerful that it banishes all fear and anxiety from your heart (1 Jn 4:18).

So we saw your view of God and the church, and what it ought to be, but let me ask you, what is your experience of God?

Your Experience of God

We need that love relationship with the Triune God, and Paul is about to explain how we get there. I want to get there don't you?

The Infinite Power of the Spirit

Paul knew that God's power had no limit. The supply of power God promises is from the Spirit and it has no end. Paul prays that God would enable them to employ the fullness of that power. Because believers are the habitation of the triune, all-powerful God of the universe, Paul prays that their unlimited energy from Him would be manifested.[90]

> **Ephesians 3:16** | For this reason I bow my knees before the Father...that according to the riches of his glory he may grant you to be strengthened with power through his Spirit in your inner being.

To start with, if you're going to really be effective, and want God's power to be released, you need to have spiritual stamina to be victorious over temptation, to be victorious over the world, the flesh, and the devil. The only way you get there is through Pentecost. You have to put off from you anything that would grieve the Spirit.

Then Paul prays for the Ephesian believers and us to experience Christ's infinite love.

The Infinite Love of Christ

The loving Christ dwells in us.

> **Ephesians 3:17** | That Christ may dwell in your hearts through faith—that you, being rooted and grounded in love.

---

[90] MacArthur. *Ephesians*, 101-102.

God says we ought to be "rooted and grounded" in Christ's love (3:17). The word "dwell" means to make oneself at home. The word is a compound "kata-oikeo" "kata" means "down" and "oikeo" means home. Is Christ "down-home" in your heart? Is he comfortable? Is the Holy Spirit pleased or is he grieved?

There is a book called *My Heart, Christ's Home* by Robert Boyd Munger –perhaps you own it. This is a great book to read to your children. Munger likens the Christian's heart to a house. And the question is, "Is Christ comfortable there?" The heart like a home has a library and then a dining room and then a living room and then a workshop and finally a closet.

The Library – what do you think on? What do you take into your heart? And when the Lord comes into your house, what does he find in the library? What does he find in the control room? You might have a TV in that room. What does he find? Is it trash and triviality, pornography and materialism? Whenever Christ comes in and is comfortable – he renews our mind and comforts our heart with peace. He clears out the garbage books and throws out the trash and replaces it with the Word of God. Truly the blessed man's "delight is in the law of the Lord, and on his law he meditates day and night" (Psa 1:2).

The Dining Room – This is the room of appetites where your desires and appetites are satiated. And Christ wants to know what do you long for? What's on your menu? What do you order? What really satisfies you? The Lord wants to replace all the illegitimate stuff with the will of God so that that alone would satisfy you. We say with David: "Whom have I in heaven but you? And there is nothing on earth that I desire besides you" (Psa 73:25). "The law of your mouth is better to me than thousands of gold and silver pieces" (Psa 119:72).

The Living Room – Your communion with God. The living room is a place of conversation and being together and cultivating relationship. And in this particular story Munger describes how Christ comes into the living room and sits there and sits there and sits there and sits there and nobody ever shows up. What ever happened to prayer? And what ever happened to communion? And what ever happened to fellowship? And what happened to relationship? Do you have a prayer closet? Do you get alone with God?

The Workshop – What are you making? What are you doing with your life? What's your legacy? We've got all these gifts – what are we doing with them? And the answer is most are making toys. And Christ wants to fix it so that you're producing something that has eternal value.

The Closet – In Munger's book he gets through the whole house, but he says there's a terrible stench coming from somewhere. And it's a closet. So the Lord, picking up the scent, goes to the closet and in there is something foul, something dead and it's the place of hidden personal sins. And he throws the door open. And Munger says, "This is too much! I am not going to give him the key."[91] I mean, give me a break. I gave you the library, the dining room, the living room and the workshop and everybody knows in every house if you find the right closet, God only knows what you'll discover in there. God wants your closet. He wants to clean out your personal sins. He wants to sanctify you completely. Listen to the sweet words of our Lord Jesus, "If anyone loves me, he will keep my word, and my Father will love him, and we will come to him and make our home with him" (Jn 14:23).

The Dimensions of Christ's Love

> **Ephesians 3:18-19a** | That you…may have strength to comprehend with all the saints what is the breadth and length and height and depth, [19] and to know the love of Christ that surpasses knowledge.

The Lord wants us to comprehend – to seize upon– to leap and take hold of – to dive for –the love of Christ. Rigorously grasp his love. Do whatever it takes to grasp it. Be greedy for it! But try as you might, you cannot comprehend it. You can't grasp it. It's infinite.

Christ's Love is Wide

It is a love *wide* enough to embrace the world (Jn 3:16). There is no limit to who God will reach. God is not willing that any should perish, but that they should come to repentance.

> *1 Timothy 2:4* | God desires all people to be saved and to come to the knowledge of the truth.

---

[91] Robert Boyd Munger; Andrea Jorgenson. *My Heart Christ's Home: A Story for Old and Young* (Kindle Locations 171-172).

Christ's Love is Long

It is a love *long* enough to last forever. As Ephesians 1:4 says, God's love is so long that it extends to eternity past when he chose us in Christ. From eternity past, God planned to send his Son to save you on that brutal cross. God says:

> Jeremiah 31:3 | I have loved you with an everlasting love.

Before you were formed in your mother's womb, God set his love upon you. It's a love so long it also covers eternity future, "so that in the coming ages he might show the immeasurable riches of his grace in kindness toward us in Christ Jesus" (2:7). As Spurgeon said,

> Christ's love is so long that your old age cannot wear it out, so long your continual tribulation cannot exhaust it, your successive temptations shall not drain it dry; like eternity itself it knows no bounds.[92]

Christ's Love is Deep

It is a love *deep* enough to take Christ to the very depths to reach the lowest sinner.

> Romans 5:6 | For while we were still weak, at the right time Christ died for the ungodly.

Christ took hell for you. Look how low he reached to reach you. When we were dead in our sins God loved us (Eph 2:1-3). He went to the lowest hell for you and freed you from hell's very gates.

Christ's Love is High

It is a love *high* enough to take broken sinners like you and me to heaven. He loves you so much that what he has begun in you he promises to finish (Phil 1:6). He's working everything together for good for you.

> Romans 8:29 | For those whom he foreknew he also predestined to be conformed to the image of his Son.

We've looked at the infinite power of the Spirit, and the infinite love of Christ. Now let's consider the infinite fullness of God.

---

[92] Charles Spurgeon. *Metropolitan Tabernacle Pulpit*, Vol 12, Sermon 707, "Heavenly Geometry" (London: Passmore & Alabaster, 1866), 469.

The Infinite Fullness of God

Ephesians 3:19b | That you may be filled with all the fullness of God.

We are asking that God – the eternal God, the almighty God, the creator God, the sustainer God, the God of the universe, the God who made it all, the God who fills all to fill me? That's incredible. We are that we all are "his body, the fullness of him who fills all in all" (1:23).

The idea is to fill to overflowing, to try to fill a thimble with the ocean. You don't need to wait for this to happen. I had this immediately when I came to know Christ. You already have "all spiritual blessings in Christ" (1:3). The fullness of God in the simplest experience is the awareness of God's presence and love for you.

WE NEED EMPOWERMENT FROM GOD (3:20-21)

When I was just a child, my big brother David planted a little twig in the backyard. Weeks passed, and finally my father noticed it. It was a little tiny tree. He didn't want a tree in our back yard, so each week he mowed it with the lawn mower. My father was persistent. But there was more time my father couldn't mow in Chicago than when he could mow, and my father had to leave the little twig alone. He must have soon given up, because that little twig is a beautiful Maple tree at 5900 Stuart Lane. It's so big you can see it from Google Earth! That little tree was far, far bigger than anything my brother or my father could have imagined. So it is with the plans God has for us.

Ephesians 3:20-21 | Now to him who is able to do far more abundantly than all that we ask or think, according to the power at work within us, [21] to him be glory in the church and in Christ Jesus throughout all generations, forever and ever. Amen.

There may be some chains in your life. There are some impossible situations in your life and perhaps in your heart. Whatever you are praying for, God wants to do far more!

Paul is not sitting in a church service or in a comfortable study. In-stead, the apostle is sitting in a prison in or near the barracks of the Praetorian Guard – the band of elite Roman soldiers assigned to guard the Roman Emperor. Paul may have been in rented quarters at his own expense – chained to Roman soldiers twenty-four hours a day. He is awaiting trial before the Roman officials and has suffered this specific imprisonment for two long years. All Paul can do is sit and wait. The word that describes Paul: *unable*! But Paul doesn't believe that!

An Infinite Power

Ephesians 3:20a | Now to him who is able to do far more abundantly than all that we ask or think.

Essentially, Paul has one message now: God's capacity to answer you infinitely exceeds your ability to ask him! Ask all you want, all you can, everything you can even imagine, and God's capacity to answer you is infinitely greater than you can ask or imagine. God's ability to answer you is far, far above anything you could ever ask or imagine.

Whatever you want to be freed from for Christ and whatever plans you want to accomplish, you are not asking too much, but too little.

This cannot be done with human power. "Not by the might of armies, nor by human power, but by my Spirit says the Lord" (Zech 4:6). We need God's power, as Jesus said, "Without me you can do nothing" (Jn 15:5). "Unless the LORD builds the house, those who build it labor in vain" (Psa 127:1).

He is able to *do*

He is able to do *what we ask*

He is able to do *all* that we ask

He is able to do all that we ask or even *imagine*!

He is able to do *above* all that we ask or imagine!

He is able to do *abundantly* beyond all that we ask or imagine!

He is able to do *exceedingly* abundantly above all that we could ask or think!

He is able to do exceedingly abundantly beyond all that we ask or think, *according to the power working in us*!

There is no exaggeration in this. Human language fails to properly convey the magnitude of God's incredible power. God is sufficient for all you are facing. This verse is testimony of God's abundant sufficiency for everything we are and everything we face.

An Internal Power

Ephesians 4:20b | According to the power at work within us.

We think we need a better spouse or a better job or a better church. That's not the answer. The answer begins with God's work inside of you.

There is a power exploding forth inside of us. It is the same power that raised Jesus from the dead (Rom 8:11). It is the power that comes forth from the Person of the Holy Spirit (1:13-14), who indwells us.

When I was a child of fourteen, I got in trouble with the law, and I was in deep trouble. The judge gave me two options: juvenile detention or a probational work program. One of our kind neighbors stepped up. He was a business owner. He owned a world-renowned propeller shop (Top Gun Prop Shop) near the Louis Armstrong New Orleans International Airport. I was sweeping floors there for $2.65 an hour. I was just glad to get out of trouble. But my expectations of the good Mr. Downs wanted to do for me were low. One day, Mr. Downs' friend pulled up in a restored World War II fighter plane. Mr. Downs asked me, "Do you want a ride?" His pilot took me high into the sky. He asked me, "Do you want to roll"? I had just seen the movie Top Gun, and of course I said, "Yes!" There I was flying upside down, suspended in the air above New Orleans. God's power is like that. It far exceeds our expectations! Over and above and beyond the greatest abundance – this is the power the God has promised you.

WE NEED EFFECTIVENESS FROM GOD (4:11-12)

Now we get to the heart of the message. In Ephesians 4:1-10, we are introduced to our unity in the Spirit and our spiritual gifts. Now this is where the prayer of Paul is answered.

He prays they may know the triune God.
- the infinite power of the Spirit
- the infinite love of Christ
- the infinite fullness of God

Then Paul says that whatever you are asking for, you are asking too little. God wants to do "exceeding, abundantly above" all that you ask or imagine. So how do we get there? We get equipped and involved.

As we consider how to grow in Christ, it is interesting that Paul begins by naming the four teaching gifts to the church: apostles and prophets, which are foundational when it comes to the Word; and then he names the evangelists and teaching pastors / elders, which are functional when it comes to the Word. It is the Word of God that sets people's hearts aright so that they might serve the Lord with gladness.

Paul mentions the apostles and the prophets, which he has already mentioned as foundational offices (2:20). Now he speaks of building the church, like building a building, with pastors and teachers in local churches, and evangelists who are like the missionaries we send out today, planting local churches.

Effective Shepherds

Ephesians 4:11 | And he gave the apostles, the prophets, the evangelists, the shepherds and teachers, [12] to equip the saints...

Paul mentions the apostles and the prophets, which he has already mentioned as foundational offices (2:20). Now he speaks of building the church, like building a building, with pastors and teachers in local churches, and evangelists who are like the missionaries we send out today, planting local churches.

The pastor-shepherds must build up the saints through ministering the Word. The elders are not to do it all. Paul didn't reach all those people in the Ephesian church. He reached a few through the teaching of the Word, but those mature Ephesian believers reached others who in turn reached others.

Effective Saints

Ephesians 4:12a | To equip the saints for the work of ministry, for building up the body of Christ,

The saints are equipped by the word to serve each other. I love to build things. I'm constantly looking, fixing, repairing. I even love to mow my yard. I love to plant flowers. I love to see things being transformed. I have on my wall a picture that Katie made me when she was much younger. It's not the Mona Lisa. But it is a picture of us together when we were in Spain and we built a garage next to our home. Why is this precious? Because Katie had "done what she could".

The saints are called to counsel one another in life-on-life discipleship. We get in each other's lives. We confess our sins constantly to one another. I do that a lot. I'm on the phone every week with some brother in our congregation confessing my sins. You know what God taught me this week? "The opposite of anger or anxiety or despair or pride or foolish thinking is *worship*." A couple in my church told me that. I needed that. Man did I need that. I don't need my wife to change, my church to change, my job to change. I need worship. With that worship, I need to be edifying the saints.

The saints are called to building up the body by evangelism. If you don't evangelize, you will fossilize! A healthy church has about 50% of the people who are solid and grounded and growing, and another 50% that are new and perhaps floundering and just getting introduced to the faith. A healthy church is going to attract all kinds of birds, sometimes strange birds. We regularly have people of all kinds of backgrounds attending and asking questions. Pentecostals, Arminians, Catholics, false converts. They come. We welcome them. We are glad they are there. And slowly, with great love and tenderness, we show them the way of Christ. We patiently help them grow in the Gospel, since some are unfamiliar with even the clear Gospel. We evangelize!

Every believer has to be committed to serve. Imagine if I went to build a house and only built the basement. That would be a disaster. Listen the basement of a house is no good unless the whole house is connected. Or imagine my mother-in-law made a shirt for me but it only had one sleeve, or only one side to it. The shirt is no good unless both sides are sewn together. In the same way, the Body of Christ is severely limited if only one side works. We are to build up the whole Body. We are to do the work of ministry. This is the measure of spiritual maturity.

Conclusion

As we close, let me just say I love Spring! You can see the flowers blooming everywhere! Actually, I love to see all the various colors of the flowers together. The flowers are of every variety of the brilliant colors of the rainbow! God's church is beautiful in that same way. Every one of us is different—with different functions and gifting and abilities, yet we are all one Body.

Fifteen years ago, I was so excited to purchase several beautiful bushes for only ten cents apiece. I was proud of myself for finding such a bargain. I planted them in our back yard in the Spring. They were all barely alive. But I took personal interest and care for those bushes, carefully watering them. By the first year, I was just glad that these bushes even survived and began to blossom. Each year the bushes grew more and more. Today, they are beautifully manicured and look like I paid hundreds of dollars for them.

As much as I wanted those bushes to succeed, I worked on them. I worked so hard. God's working on you too, and he's a perfect Gardener (Jn 15). Keep abiding in Christ and you will be abounding in spiritual fruit. God wants you to succeed more than you want to succeed. He came to give you life and life more abundantly (Jn 10:10).

What do you want to see God do? God wants to do "exceeding, abundantly above all that you could ever ask or think" (Eph 3:20) for your good and his glory! What is your Ephesians 3:20 prayer? Exceeding, abundantly above walk with God? Let do this!

12 | EPHESIANS 4:11-16
ROOTED IN SPIRITUAL MATURITY

We are to grow up in every way into him who is the head, into Christ, from whom the whole body, joined and held together by every joint with which it is equipped, when each part is working properly, makes the body grow so that it builds itself up in love.
Ephesians 4:15-16

Mention the word "perestroika" in Russia today, and you will be greeted with cynicism. The reason is quite obvious. In his book, then Russian President Mikhail Gorbachev made frequent reference to the credibility gap between words and deeds. He insisted that people did not want political slogans that failed to square with reality. "Perestroika" means "the unity of words and deeds," and on that basis Gorbachev attempted to reform the Soviet system. It was a noble aim, but for the Russian people, its failure was painfully evident. The unity between political promises and social reality was a myth; therein, bringing the downfall of Gorbachev's administration.

Ephesians 4:11-16 | And he gave the apostles, the prophets, the evangelists, the shepherds and teachers, [12] to equip the saints for the work of ministry, for building up the body of Christ, [13] until we all attain to the unity of the faith and of the knowledge of the Son of God, to mature manhood, to the measure of the stature of the

> fullness of Christ, **14** so that we may no longer be children, tossed to and fro by the waves and carried about by every wind of doctrine, by human cunning, by craftiness in deceitful schemes. **15** Rather, speaking the truth in love, we are to grow up in every way into him who is the head, into Christ, **16** from whom the whole body, joined and held together by every joint with which it is equipped, when each part is working properly, makes the body grow so that it builds itself up in love.

Every day we watch inconsistency lived out before us on the world's stage. We hear people say one thing; and then, watch people do another thing. All sorts of promises are given, but not many promises are kept. That is how corporate ladders are climbed, positions are gained, and elections are won.

This is not the pathway for the child of God. Spiritual maturity is marked by consistent growth in at least five areas, as our passage in Ephesians 4:11-16 demonstrates.

INDUSTRY: GROWING IN SERVICE (4:11-12A)

As we consider how to grow in Christ, it is interesting that Paul begins by naming the four teaching gifts to the church: apostles and prophets, which are foundational when it comes to the Word; and then he names the evangelists and teaching pastors / elders, which are functional when it comes to the Word. It is the Word of God that sets people's hearts aright so that they might serve the Lord with gladness. It's such a joy to serve the Lord! The Psalmist invites us to praise and serve God. They go together.

> *Psalm 100:1-2* | Make a joyful noise to the LORD, all the earth! ²Serve the LORD with gladness! Come into his presence with singing!

Here we have the blueprint and model of a healthy mature church. True believers crave the meat of Word and the fellowship of the local church body. So here in this passage you've got teaching pastors/elders who are "perfecting the saints" through sound biblical verse by verse teaching, so that they may minister and serve.

Serving Up the Word

> **Ephesians 4:11** | And he gave the apostles, the prophets, the evangelists, the shepherds and teachers, **12** to equip the saints...

A mature church is a church strong in the Word and serving in the world. My goal in every message is to bring God's people to a stronger, healthier relationship with Christ so that they may be used of God to build up their brethren and reach the world.

Paul mentions the apostles and the prophets, which he has already mentioned as foundational offices (2:20). Now he speaks of building the church, like building a building, with pastors and teachers in local churches, and evangelists who are like the missionaries we send out today, planting local churches.

The pastor-shepherds must build up the saints through ministering the Word. The elders are not to do it all. Paul didn't reach all those people in the Ephesian church. He reached a few through the teaching of the Word, but those mature Ephesian believers reached others who in turn reached others. Those who teach are to do so to equip and perfect the saints for the work of ministry. This occurs through the faithful exposition of God's Word.

Building Up the Saints

Ephesians 4:12a | To equip the saints for the work of ministry, for building up the body of Christ,

The saints are equipped by the Word to serve each other. I love to build things. I'm constantly looking, fixing, repairing. I even love to mow my yard. I love to plant flowers. I love to see things being transformed. I have on my wall a picture that Katie made me when she was much younger. It's not the Mona Lisa. But it is a picture of us together when we were in Spain and we built a garage next to our home. Why is this precious? Because Katie had "done what she could". It is a simple expression of pure, innocent love. It's all she had to give me, and she gave all she had. It is precious. That's the worship that is precious to Christ. Our pure, simple extravagant, innocent love for him. The Lord wants us to build. He's not so much concerned about houses and gardens and fences. Those are all fine and fun to build. But God is concerned that we build the lives of men and women, boys and girls.

This is how you know if you are growing in Christ. Are you being equipped to serve the Body of Christ, or are you an onlooker? Immaturity in the Christian life is marked by laziness, being an onlooker, neglect, and even atrophy. Are you building the lives of those in the Body of Christ? Are you doing the hard work of ministry? Are you making sure there are no cracks in the foundation? When I first became a pastor in Chicago, one of our deacons lived in a house across from our church that had a bad foundation. They had to lift up the house and pour a new foundation. It's important to let the Word of God lay the foundation of your life. What joy it is to build on a solid foundation. If we go to church to help us to merely have our "best life now", we are building our house on the sand. But if we go to church to hear the Word of truth taught, to fellowship with true believers, and to do the work of ministry, then we are building our house on the Rock, Christ Jesus.

Maturity in the church means the saints are equipped to do the useful and practical work of ministry. We are not to do that which suits us, but that which we are called to do. We are to do the *work* of the ministry. We are called and equipped to look out for all the saints. We are all responsible for the entire Body of our local congregation.

Imagine if I went to build a house and only built the basement. That would be a disaster. Listen the basement of a house is no good unless the whole house is connected. Or imagine my mother-in-law made a shirt for me but it only had one sleeve, or only one side to it. The shirt is no good unless both sides are sewn together. In the same way, the Body of Christ is severely limited if only one side works. We are to build up the whole Body. We are to do the work of ministry. This is the measure of spiritual maturity.

You know before I was a missionary and a pastor, I was the janitor of my home church on the south side of Chicago. God wanted to test me. God doesn't use you unless you are willing to do anything. I had a college degree in Bible. Yet before I was a missionary, He wanted to test me and see if I could be a good janitor. Listen, God wants you to work hard to build the Body. It's not about doing what you want to do or what you feel you were made to do. It's about serving Christ in whatever way he wants you to. If you are faithful in the little things, God will give you charge over more (Lk 16:10).

UNITY: GROWING IN HUMILITY (4:12B)

Ephesians 4:12b | To equip the saints for the work of ministry, for building up the body of Christ.

In the orchestra, you may have a first seat violin. Even though the violin faithfully leads the violin section, they give way to all the other sections of the orchestra. A good first violin is discreet and precise, only bringing his melody to the forefront at the right time, but then giving way to the other instruments.

You may know of the actor Michael J. Fox. He has Parkinson's disease. How do you know? His body does not move in harmony. Parts of his body move when he doesn't want them to move. He has been very open about how one part of his body will not work in harmony with the other. I would love to take that disease away from him. So it is in the Body of Christ. Unity in the Body means that we are small in our own eyes – that we give way to others and only display ourselves when it edifies the whole Body. Most of the time we are in the background serving the rest of the Body.

Notice it says, "until we all attain to the unity of the faith..." (4:13). Faith is dependence. We are in harmony depending on Christ. We are all small. We are all dependent on one another. Our unity comes out of our weakness! It's good when we realize how weak and small we are. Paul said, "When I am weak, then I am strong" and "when I am weak the power of Christ rests upon me" (2 Cor 12:9-10).

Some of you are looking for the trial to go away. Your goal is to get rid of all trials. The trials aren't going away. If God takes the one you're going through, he'll send you another. He wants you weak. He wants you trusting him. We all come weak and broken and torn – wracked with infirmities. And we say with Paul, "I will glory in my infirmities!" "I will boast in my weakness" (2 Cor 12:9). I will brag about my nothingness and my smallness.

If the measure of spiritual maturity is unity, then immaturity is marked by division, strive, and schism. Spiritual pride is a cheap imitation of spiritual maturity. Actually, spiritual pride is one of the most divisive dangerous qualities of anyone. Search yourself for pride, because it is the foundation of every sin and every form of unbelief.

CONFORMITY: GROWING IN CHRIST'S IMAGE (4:13)

Ephesians 4:13 | Until we all attain to the unity of the faith and of the knowledge of the Son of God, to mature manhood, to the measure of the stature of the fullness of Christ.

Remember we are not what we will be. I remember my kids growing up with a pudgy kid who had so much energy. I wondered what ever became of him. Thanks to Facebook, I've found out that he's now a Marine standing at 6'3" and able to crush me. I could never have guessed that he would grow like that. That pudgy kid had all the DNA to grow to be a fine-tuned athletic machine.

It reminds me of Peter Parker. Remember how Peter Parker became Spiderman? He got bit by a radioactive spider. Understand that the moment he got bit, he had all the power of Spiderman, but not all the skills. He had no idea how to use his powers, but he still had the power. Remember the first time he touched his sink handles? He ripped them off and water spurted everywhere? Remember he got scared and jumped to the ceiling and was stuck there because he didn't know how to release his adhesive hands? He had the power but not the understanding of how to use them.

So it is for every child of God. "His divine power has granted to us all things that pertain to life and godliness" (2 Pet 1:3). Paul has already told us in Ephesians that we are chosen by God and predestined for holiness in Christ.

Ephesians 1:4-5 | He chose us in him before the foundation of the world, that we should be holy and blameless before him. In love ^{5} he predestined us for adoption to himself as sons through Jesus Christ.

Paul's also told us that our inheritance of having Christ in us is predestined so that we might live lives that are "to the praise of his glory."

Ephesians 1:11-12 | In him we have obtained an inheritance, having been predestined according to the purpose of him who works all things according to the counsel of his will, ^{12} so that we who were the first to hope in Christ might be to the praise of his glory.

God has predestined us to grow in conformity to Christ. The test of our maturity is not our Bible knowledge, though that is a wonderful thing. Yet there are many who have preached and taught with amazing gifts about Christ but had no character or holiness. The mark of true believers is a life lived out of a heart conformed to the holiness of Christ.

Our progressive sanctification begins at and flows out of regeneration where we become "partakers of the divine nature" (2 Pet 1:4) in which the very desires of God are put within the believer's heart (*cf* Eze 36:26). This progressive holiness is possible due to our nature being united with the nature of the Holy Spirit.

1 Corinthians 6:17 | But he who is joined to the Lord becomes one spirit with him.

Our present holiness comes out of our union with Christ so that we can "grow in the grace and knowledge of our Lord and Savior Jesus Christ" (2 Pet 3:18). This holiness is progressive, and though the Christian may falter and even for short periods of time fall into deep valleys of sin, the process of sanctification is in no way halted until the day of death or the Second Coming. The Christian should have great assurance that God is going to complete what he started.

> *Philippians 1:6* | And I am sure of this, that he who began a good work in you will bring it to completion at the day of Jesus Christ.

> *1 Thessalonians 5:23-24* | Now may the God of peace himself sanctify you completely, and may your whole spirit and soul and body be kept blameless at the coming of our Lord Jesus Christ. [24] He who calls you is faithful; he will surely do it.

> *Romans 8:29* | For those whom he foreknew he also predestined to be conformed to the image of his Son.

> *Philippians 3:10* | That I may know him and the power of his resurrection, and may share his sufferings, becoming like him in his death.

> *Ephesians 2:10* | For we are his workmanship, created in Christ Jesus for good works, which God prepared beforehand, that we should walk in them.

The test of our maturity is conformity "to the measure of the stature of the fullness of Christ". As C. J. Mahaney has written about this journey into Christlikeness and holiness.

> Sanctification is a process – the process of becoming more like Christ, of growing in holiness. This process begins the instant you are converted and will not end until you meet Jesus face-to-face. Sanctification is about our own choices and behavior. It involves work. Empowered by God's Spirit, we strive. We fight sin. We study Scripture and pray, even when we don't feel like it. We flee temptation. We press on; we run hard in the pursuit of holiness....The power of the gospel conforms us more and more closely, with ever-increasing clarity, to the image of Jesus Christ.[93]

I want to key in on the words that Paul uses in this verse. We are called "to mature manhood, to the measure of the stature of the fullness

---

[93] C.J. Mahaney. *The Cross-Centered Life* (Colorado Springs, CO: Multnomah Books, 2009), 31.

of Christ" (4:13). What is the "measure" and "stature" and "fullness" of Christ? It really is the full and complete heart of Christ. These are words of dimension or capacity. What capacity has God given us? What is he moving us toward? He's moving us to the bigness or stature of Christ. He's moving us to the fullness or greatness of Christ's heart for holiness. He's moving us to the dimension of Christ's realm of glory and communion with God. I know, it all sounds so grand and impossible. It's kind of like Peter Parker pondering what it would be like to have the powers of Spiderman. He didn't know all that he was at first. But he had all that he needed to be Spiderman. It's a silly but helpful analogy for me. So many Christians are living as Peter Parker when they have the power to live the Spiderman life. God has provided every Christian with all the power they need to be like Christ. We simply need to access the power of faith to get there. We will learn that later in this chapter when we look at the "put off" and "put on" principle. Until then, understand, the only reason you are not as holy as God wants you to be is on your part, not on God's. He's given you everything you need in the Holy Spirit.

STABILITY: GROWING IN RESPONSIBILITY (4:14)

What is the difference between an adult and a child? The answer: responsibility. There are a lot of Christians who remain spiritually immature because they refuse to take responsibility for the state of their heart. They blame all their failings on others, just like children. Paul calls us out of this immaturity. He tells us to take responsibility and serve each other. Look at his warning about spiritual immaturity.

> **Ephesians 4:14** | That we may no longer be children, tossed to and fro by the waves and carried about by every wind of doctrine, by human cunning, by craftiness in deceitful schemes.

Paul says: don't be children! Now don't get me wrong, there is a difference between childishness and childlikeness. Now don't get me wrong. Though we are commanded here in this text to "that we may no longer be [immature like] children", the Word of God is filled with admonitions for us to be like children. The New Testament commands childlikeness. But the New Testament forbids childishness. While Paul compares spiritual immaturity to childishness and irresponsibility, childlikeness is actually the secret to rich spiritual growth and responsibility.

We do not expect adults to be kept in the nursery. I'm sure that a baby finds that sucking his thumb is very comforting. But there's something wrong when a thirteen-year-old sucks his thumb. Adults who act like babies are abnormal. There is no place for stunted growth in the Bible. If a baby has his growth stunted and remains a dwarf, something is wrong! Baby Christians are the life of the church when they are first born into God's family. But if you stay a baby Christian, you are a handicap to God's church. Babies are to grow up into the "first principles" of knowing Christ. In school we have reading, writing, and arithmetic. Christian babies also grow by doing the basics. The Christian baby needs Bible reading, praying, and evangelism. Read your Bible, spend lots of time in your prayer closet, and share your faith everywhere you go. You don't need a class for that. It's milk. It's easy. You can do that today.

Some churches are nothing more than nurseries. Instead of everyone finding their place of usefulness, there are fits and tantrums. The pastors don't have time for the meat of the Word because they are too busy changing diapers. Dear saints of God, a pastor's job is not to make you comfortable and happy, but it is to get you off the bottle and out of diapers. It is to get you to take the solid food of God's Word with a deep and satisfying relationship with Christ.

Childlikeness Commended

Childishness is when an adult acts like a child in bad ways and childlikeness is when an adult acts like a child in good ways. Childlikeness is commended in the Scriptures.

Children are commended because of their *faith*.

Jesus says you either have to be a child or be like a child in order to enter the kingdom of heaven.

> *Matthew 18:3* | Jesus said, Truly, I say to you, unless you turn and become like children, you will never enter the kingdom of heaven.

> *Mark 10:15* | Truly I say to you, whoever does not receive the kingdom of God like a child will not enter it at all.

> *Luke 18:16* | Suffer little children to come unto me, and forbid them not: for of such is the kingdom of God.

Children are often gullible, but the positive side is the rich and incredible faith they have. Adults often scoff in their cynicism, but children readily believe that God can do anything.

Children are commended for their amazing *hunger*.

Growing up in childlikeness is commended: it is marked by simplicity, innocence, and a hunger to learn!

1 Peter 2:2 | Like newborn babies, long for the pure milk of the word, so that by it you may grow in respect to salvation.

Psalm 131:2 | Surely I have composed and quieted my soul; like a weaned child rests against his mother, my soul is like a weaned child within me.

Oh, the hunger of a little baby at 2am. He or she cries and cries until mommy comes. The baby cannot be happy until their hunger is satisfied. So it is with a Christian. They hunger day and night for the Word (Psa 1:2).

Children are commended for their *sincerity*.

Children say what's on their mind in unique ways that brings God glory. Because of this, the child is one of God's greatest preachers.

Matthew 21:16 | Out of the mouth of infants and nursing babies you have prepared praise.

1 Corinthians 14:20 | Brethren, do not be children in your thinking; yet in evil be infants, but in your thinking be mature.

Children say the most spontaneous and truthful things. That's what Christians do: they sincerely and worship God. And they are innocent of evil. They don't know the latest Hollywood actors. They are somewhat unfamiliar with all the popular cultural expressions or what's in fashion or out of fashion. They don't know a lot about the world of evil, but they are mature in their character, mainly manifest in their God-centered thinking.

Children are commended because of their healthy *fear*.

When trained well, children manifest an obedience out of love to their parents. They enjoy doing what their father and mother say. They realize they are loved and protected. They live in a reverent fear borne out of love. That's how the Christian act toward their loving heavenly Father.

1 Peter 1:14 | As obedient children, do not be conformed to the passions of your former ignorance.

Ephesians 5:1-2 | Therefore be imitators of God, as beloved children; and walk in love, just as Christ also loved you and gave himself up for us, an offering and a sacrifice to God as a fragrant aroma.

Proverbs 9:10 | The fear of the Lord is the beginning of wisdom.

What joy to imitate the God we love as our Father.

Children are commended because of *humility*.

If I'm in an important meeting, my children know they can call on me anytime with no pride whatsoever. Once I was in speaking with a couple in our church, and I heard from one of my children: "Daddy will you wipe me?" Quite humorous, but what humility to call out for whatever need they have. Remember the words of Jesus about childlike humility.

Matthew 18:4 | Whoever then humbles himself as this child, he is the greatest in the kingdom of heaven.

Childishness Condemned

We need to put away childish things. Childishness is never a good character trait. I fear that some believers, despite their ability to articulate true things about God, are not progressing in Christian maturity. Real gospel growth depends on a right understanding of God, and it manifests itself in the fruit of the Spirit from the heart (Gal 5:22-24). It is possible to be in a church with sound teaching for many years and have stunted growth, though. Don't confuse an ability to expound God's Word with spiritual maturity. Many of the most outwardly godly people have been found out to be fakes, desperately immature spiritually, or worse, completely lost. So let us carefully look at the marks of a spiritually immature person.

Spiritual immaturity is marked by *malnourishment in the heart*.

Consider that there are many Bible-wise Christians that are not Spirit-wise Christians. They are nourished by Bible knowledge but not with the rich doctrine of living in the power of the Spirit. They puff up their mind, but their hearts are largely malnourished. They know the Bible, and in spite of that, they are not marked with the Holy Spirit of God. Instead of joy, you will find that they are easily offended, often angry, quite depressed at times, and if they were honest, they despair and wonder if they will ever have meaningful joy in the Christian life. For many Christians, the Christian life makes them miserable, because they are exhausted, trying to live it out in the flesh. Yet they take comfort in their Bible knowledge. They love the milk of Bible doctrine but choke on the solid food of practicing the Christian life in complete humility and love.

> *1 Corinthians 3:1-3* | But I, brothers, could not address you as spiritual people but as people of the flesh, as infants in Christ. I fed you with milk, not solid food, for you were not ready for it. And even now you are not yet ready, for you are still of the flesh. For while there is jealousy and strife among you, are you not of the flesh and behaving only in a human way?

Paul mentions "jealousy and strife" because the main mark of maturity is not mere outward behavior, but the disposition of the heart. I know very knowledgeable Christians who can teach a Sunday school class but cannot get along with their spouse. There is perpetual strife in the home yet they can a basic systematic theology class for you (ask them, they love to talk about anything related to themselves, what they know). Knowledge puffs up, but love (real spiritual maturity) edifies.

Spiritual immaturity is marked by *inconsistent spiritual growth.*

The author to the Hebrews lamented that after several years of solid biblical teaching, his audience still had not progressed much in their Christian life. He compared the Hebrew people scattered around to spiritual children. They should be maturing, but instead they were childish.

> *Hebrews 5:12-14* | For though by this time you ought to be teachers, you need someone to teach you again the basic principles of the oracles of God. You need milk, not solid food, [13] for everyone who lives on milk is unskilled in the word of righteousness, since he is a child. [14] But solid food is for the mature, for those who have their powers of discernment trained by constant practice to distinguish good from evil.

Paul tied being an infant in Christ with being fleshly. Spiritually immature Christians "ought to be teachers" because they have so much learning, but they don't have the discernment or genuine experience of the Spirit-filled life from the heart to do so. That means you may have the gifting to teach, but you lack the godly character. You can teach about putting away anger beautifully and precisely, but you can't teach about it with any real experience. The immature believer constantly has to learn the basics of Spirit-filled living over and over again. They have to keep being reminded of the "basic principles" of God's Word, but there is no lasting connection. Like an electrical cord with a short in it, some Christians are sometimes on and sometimes off. There's no consistency. One day they are gentle. The next day they are blazing mad. One day they think they are experiencing revival. The next weeks and months they are fighting with their spouse. They cram their heads with knowledge, but it is ineffective because the heart remains small, growth is paralyzed and victory in Spirit-filled living is inconsistent at best. They are not lost, since they want spiritual food, but they can't handle the strong meat of the Christian life. They need "milk, not solid food". They choke on the solid food of living for God from the heart. Spiritual maturity results in peace, kindness, goodness, right living and complete humility. Instead, they use the Bible as a way to pat themselves on the back and have serious struggles loving God and others from their heart. Words of love come easy, but their heart is far away from God at times.

The spiritually immature believer is unskillful in the word of righteousness. He can talk about self-righteousness, that is, the righteousness possible from the power of the flesh. He can talk about a hundred legalistic ways to look holy, but he does not possess holiness in his heart's disposition a lot of the time. Because he or she is a true believer they stumble upon it and are encouraged by the fear of the Lord and the presence of God. He is not gentle or good or kind. He is not chaste and self-controlled. He is impatient and arrogant. They are good at self-righteousness: getting mad at the speck in other's eyes, but they are "unskilled in the word of righteousness"—that is Holy Spirit enabled righteousness. They are blind to the log in their own eye. As a result, there is very inconsistent spiritual growth. Of course, I didn't say no spiritual growth whatsoever. That would be an unbeliever. Every believer is constantly progressing to Christlikeness (Rom 8:29), since they are predestined to do so (Eph 1:4-5).

>Spiritual immaturity is marked by *impulsiveness.*

Writing to the Galatians, he described the impulsivity of the works of the flesh.

Galatians 5:19-21a | Now the works of the flesh are evident: sexual immorality, impurity, sensuality, [20] idolatry, sorcery, enmity, strife, jealousy, fits of anger, rivalries, dissensions, divisions, [21] envy, drunkenness, orgies, and things like these.

This list wasn't meant to be exhaustive, but it gives you a good idea of the kinds of things Paul had in mind. Like a small child who doesn't get his way and throws a fit, the spiritually immature yield to their carnal impulses rather than surrendering them to God and exercising self-control. These fleshly impulses run contrary to our new identity as baptized followers of Jesus. Spiritual infants have a difficult time walking in the Spirit (Gal 5:16), and the fruit of Christian maturity (Gal 5:22-24) is not yet fully formed in them. Let us not keep lamenting spiritual immaturity. Let's press on and be intentional in taking full responsibility for our spiritual growth. Let's move forward, not merely in intellects, but deep down in the disposition of our hearts.

Spiritual Growth Possible

Paul when explaining the ultimate mark of spiritual maturity (agape love) said, he was intentional about manhood and chose to give up his childish ways for maturity.

1 Corinthians 13:11 | When I was a child, I spoke like a child, I thought like a child, I reasoned like a child. When I became a man, I gave up childish ways.

I want you to see Paul's struggle for growth. It's a burden for him. Paul believes that no believer needs to be stuck in spiritual immaturity. He's already told us that every believer is predestined to holiness, i.e. spiritual maturity (Eph 1:4-5). In Ephesians chapters 1-3, Paul laid out who we are in Christ. Then in 4:1, he says "walk worthy." He lays out how, and then he goes as far as he can until he hits the roadblock of spiritual immaturity. He asks as we all are asking: how does a believer get through this roadblock? How do we put away spiritual immaturity? How do we get to real, meaningful spiritual growth in our lives? Paul begins with two deep roots of spiritual immaturity. Listen to the heart of this apostle.

Ephesians 4:14 | That we may no longer be children, tossed to and fro by the waves and carried about by every wind of doctrine, by human cunning, by craftiness in deceitful schemes.

Spiritual growth is marked by *humility*.

Ephesians 4:14a | That we may no longer be children...

How humble of Paul to include himself in this warning. This plural pronoun is shocking to me. Paul knew that he had not arrived, and that in a sense we are all growing until we get to glory. Even after seeing the resurrected Lord and being used as an apostle, he said that he himself had need to avoid spiritual immaturity and to get out of babyhood.

Spiritual growth is marked by *stability*.

Paul turns to the pressing weight on his heart: we are all prone to instability in our lives, the root of which is manipulation by false doctrine. It results in a life being tossed like a rag doll or a wave driven by wind instead of getting hooked to the solid anchor.

Ephesians 4:14b | That we may no longer be children, tossed to and fro by the waves and carried about by every wind of doctrine...

We come to an example from the sea. Spiritually immature believers lack stability because they are like a wave tossed passenger "tossed to and fro" on a ship. It means they lack stability; they are easily led astray. Spiritual children are not established in the truth.

I remember when I lived in Louisiana, I visited a friend off of Lake Ponchatrain. Now the people who live there use a boat to even get to school. One day we traveled around to see friends around the Lake. It was windy, and the waves were higher. That was the first time I was introduced to motion sickness. You get off that boat and you don't know if you are standing on the ceiling or on the floor. Even when you are motionless everything is moving. It's an awful experience. And the Apostle Paul is saying that's the picture of what happens to someone not rooted and established in truth. I want you to be grounded so you can't be tossed about by those waves.

There are many immature believers who are unstable because they are not grounded in the comprehensive, sufficient Word that ought to be exposited word by word, chapter by chapter. So many are looking for the new and the novel. So many are following the culture instead of transforming the culture. That leads to discouraging spiritual instability. There are many unbelievers including the preachers that are involved in this, but there are also some baby Christians. Let us remember Paul's warning to the Galatian church.

Galatians 1:8 | Though we, or an angel from heaven, preach any other gospel unto you than that which we have preached unto you, let him be accursed.

Don't be like a child that is gullible.

Spiritual growth is marked by *discernment*.

Ephesians 4:14c | That we may no longer be children, tossed to and fro by the waves and carried about by every wind of doctrine, by human cunning, by craftiness in deceitful schemes.

Spiritual maturity is evidenced by a deep stability, anchored in Christ. Paul compares living in spiritual immaturity to gambling in a casino. *Kubia* (cunning) is the term from which we get *cube* and was used of dice-playing. Just as today, the dice were often "loaded" or otherwise manipulated by professional gamblers to their own advantage. The term for dice therefore became synonymous with dishonest trickery of any sort.[94]

Spiritual children are easily deceived by false teachers. In other words, children are easily manipulated, like a wave on the sea, like a piece of paper in the wind, it goes on to give an example from the gambling house: spiritually immature people are manipulated "by human cunning, by craftiness in deceitful schemes." The word "schemes" literally means "a cube" and refers to dice. There are those out there that would like to gamble with your soul. Avoid them! Avoid the prosperity TV preachers. I heard of one false teacher that said, "Ye must be born again" refers to reincarnation. I heard Benny Hinn say that there are *nine* members of the Trinity. I heard Robert Schuller say that Paul was wrong to say, "O wretched man that I am". He said if you preach on sin, you'll turn people off. Yet there are some baby Christians following him.

The word "craftiness" is also translated "subtlety" in 2 Corinthians 11:3 (KJV), "The serpent beguiled Eve through his subtilty." There is great deception in these false teachers. They are lost. They are the ones on the day of judgment who will say "Lord, Lord, have we not prophesied in thy name". And Christ will say "Depart from me you workers of lawlessness, I never knew you" (Mt 7:21-23). There are actual believers who follow false teachers. Many false teachers, including Joel Osteen,

---

[94] MacArthur, *Ephesians*, 158.

Robert Schuller, Oral Roberts, Robert Tilton, Benny Hinn, Kenneth Hagin, T.D. Jakes, Beth Moore, and Kenneth Copeland all "have a form of godliness, but they deny the power thereof" (2 Tim 3:5). Those who follow these ministries, if they are believers, are tossed to and fro, here, there, and everywhere because of false doctrine.

Spiritual maturity means instead of being immature like a child and unstable like a wave and having to roll the dice like a casino, you are richly connected in fellowship to godly and growing believers who are committed to living out the Scriptures in love, humility and gentleness. Our eyes have to be on Christ, not on each other. We are not only growing in stability, but as we will see in the next verses, we will be growing in fellowship.

COMMUNITY – GROWING IN FELLOWSHIP (4:15-16)

Ephesians 4:15-16 | Rather, speaking the truth in love, we are to grow up in every way into him who is the head, into Christ, [16] from whom the whole body, joined and held together by every joint with which it is equipped, when each part is working properly, makes the body grow so that it builds itself up in love.

The Balance of Fellowship

Ephesians 4:15a | Rather, speaking the truth in love...

Truth and love are the two balances of the Christian life. We can go to two extremes. We can speak the truth but not in love, in which case we are being *ungracious*. Truth spoken in that spirit often offends and does little good because it alienates the people we are seeking to win. Or we can speak in love and suppress the truth, in which case we are being *unfaithful*. People who do not want to hurt someone's feelings may say nothing and allow a sinful situation to continue. They suffer in silence. True love, however, will always speak at the right time, with the right words, in the right spirit, and using the right approach.[95]

It is the task of Christians to be people of the truth. We are called to search the truth, to understand the truth, to communicate the truth. But it is not simply abstract propositional utterance that we are to make. We are to hold this truth that is precious to them *in love*.[96] Truth

---

[95] J. Phillips, *Ephesians*, Eph 4:15a.
[96] Sproul, *Ephesians*, 107.

preached without a revived heart does damage. We need to "speak the truth in love". This phrase "speaking the truth" is all one word in the Greek New Testament. It is the verb form of the word "truth". It is more than just speaking, but literally "truthing in love".

If all you have is love and tolerance without the truth, you will produce compromise with no moral standard, and you will have a man-centered psychological gospel that really is not good news at all. One person described it as "moral therapeutic deism" that is gutted of real gospel power.

If all you have is truth, you will replace love with a cold, harsh self-righteous pride. You may be wrong at times, but sadly you'll never be in doubt. This will push people away from Christ, because it will be very confusing. Christ in his heart and nature is like God: gentle and lowly in heart. He is mild, meek, and gentle. Truth without love is the opposite of Christ. It may sound right, but it is missing something.

Of course, the emphasis is on speaking the truth, but the idea is to live it out. Christians are to hold forth the truth in order to bring spiritual benefit to others, and they are to do so with a winsomeness that only love can make possible. Then, with a metaphor which is as far as possible removed from that which describes the immature as tossed about like a little boat in a storm, it is said that they will *grow* in stability and spiritual maturity.[97]

John Bunyan said of Christians, "When all their garments are white the world will count them his," and the skeptical German poet Heinrich Heine said to Christians, "You show me your redeemed life and I might be inclined to believe in your Redeemer." The authentic life that speaks the gospel with a spirit of loving sacrifice will be eminently convincing.[98]

The Word of Fellowship

Ephesians 4:15a | Rather, speaking the truth in love...

Without truth found in the forever settled Word of God, there can be no enjoyment of fellowship. You can know the Word without having fellowship, but you cannot have fellowship unless it is founded on the light of the Word of God. Without truth there is no real maturity. "All

---

[97] Foulkes, *Ephesians*, 129.
[98] MacArthur, *Ephesians*, 160.

Scripture is God breathed and is profitable..." that men might be made mature! That's why when Paul went to Ephesus said, "I have not failed to declare unto you the whole counsel of God" (Acts 20:27). As Christians, we are to be people of the truth, which means we are people of the Book. We are to study it day and night and thereby become fruitful and profitable for his Body (Psa 1:1-3).

The Lord of Fellowship

Ephesians 4:15b | ...we are to grow up in every way into him who is the head, into Christ.

From Christ alone, as head, the body derives its whole capacity for growth and activity and its direction as one coordinated, directed entity.[99] Christ is the Lord and Master of every true Christian. We are to be subject to Christ as members of the body are to the head. To grow into his likeness is to be completely subject to his controlling power, obedient to his every thought and expression of will. It is to personify Paul's prayers "For to me, to live is Christ" (Phil 1:21) and "It is no longer I who live, but Christ lives in me" (Gal 2:20).[100]

The Family of Fellowship

Ephesians 4:15b-16 | We are to grow up in every way into him who is the head, into Christ, **16** from whom the whole body, joined and held together by every joint with which it is equipped, when each part is working properly, makes the body grow so that it builds itself up in love.

The Body receives its authority, direction, and power as it grows up in every way into Christ. By living the truth in love, we are called in all things to grow into the likeness and person of Christ, who is the unifying head of the body. This section closes with a metaphorical model of unity. Like the human body, held together by design, the church grows through the coordinated and cooperative work of its many members, who out of love for the whole contribute their individual efforts toward the good of the whole. But the plan and the energy are drawn from the head who watches over and provides for his body. Indeed, our Lord

---

[99] Foulkes, *Ephesians*, 130.
[100] MacArthur, *Ephesians*, 160.

lives his own life out through each of us.[101] We might well say that we are each "Jesus with skin on". But even more than that, in our unity, we are collectively "Jesus with skin on."

Conclusion

In the summer, we will be having a family reunion. It will be interesting to see how we've all changed, especially the children! Children grow in such amazing steady ways. That's what we are called to as Christians. We cannot remain as children, though we must always have the humility and eagerness of a child.

---

[101] Richard J. Erickson, "Ephesians," in *Evangelical Commentary on the Bible*, vol. 3, Baker Reference Library (Grand Rapids, MI: Baker Book House, 1995), 1028.

13 | EPHESIANS 4:17-24
ROOTED IN THE NEW LIFE

To put off your old self, which belongs to your former manner of life and is corrupt through deceitful desires, and to be renewed in the spirit of your minds, and to put on the new self, created after the likeness of God in true righteousness and holiness.
EPHESIANS 4:22-24

I love weddings – but my favorite wedding was my own. My favorite part of the day – the one thing I will never forget – is Jill walking down the aisle. She was radiant with her beautiful white wedding dress. On that wedding day there is a lot of preparation. Not for the guy – on my wedding day I slicked back my hair and put on my tuxedo. It took about 10 minutes. Jill spent an hour with her hairdresser, she spent a year designing the dress and spent hours with all the preparations. Everything had to be perfect.

This is a picture of what we are to be doing as Christ's bride. We are to be readying ourselves that we might be the radiant Bride of Christ – "a glorious church, not having spot, or wrinkle, or any such thing; but that it should be holy and without blemish" (5:27). Sometimes we as Christians do not feel holy and without blemish. That's why the Spirit gives us this passage in Ephesians 4. The first time that I was introduced to these verses I was a brand-new Christian. I had many worldly things clouding my thinking. I was desperate, and the youth pastor pointed me to this principle of mind renewal that has changed my life.

He opened his Bible, and we read the following passage which set me on a freedom giving path of mind renewal.

> **Ephesians 4:17-24** | Now this I say and testify in the Lord, that you must no longer walk as the Gentiles do, in the futility of their minds. **18** They are darkened in their understanding, alienated from the life of God because of the ignorance that is in them, due to their hardness of heart. **19** They have become callous and have given themselves up to sensuality, greedy to practice every kind of impurity. **20** But that is not the way you learned Christ!— **21** assuming that you have heard about him and were taught in him, as the truth is in Jesus, **22** to put off your old self, which belongs to your former manner of life and is corrupt through deceitful desires, **23** and to be renewed in the spirit of your minds, **24** and to put on the new self, created after the likeness of God in true righteousness and holiness.

I came to the conclusion quickly that my life would be one of separation from the world. I would need to withdraw from bad influences and begin to surround myself with godly friends and influences.

THE NEW LIFE IS A LIFE OF SEPARATION (4:17-21)

> **Ephesians 4:17** | Now this I say and testify in the Lord, that you must no longer walk as the Gentiles do, in the futility of their minds.

Have you ever heard of identity theft? More than 16.7 million people had their identity stolen in 2017.[102] This means, somebody who you don't know opens up new accounts in your name and spends your money and your reputation as if they were really you. Identity theft costs $53 billion dollars and 300 million hours in lost time annually for these people. There's another kind of identity theft going on. People who call themselves Christians but still love the world.

> *1 John 2:15-17* | Do not love the world or the things in the world. If anyone loves the world, the love of the Father is not in him. **16** For all that is in the world—the desires of the flesh and the desires of the eyes and pride of life—is not from the Father but is from the world. **17** And the world is passing away along with its desires, but whoever does the will of God abides forever.

---

[102] From Insurance Information Institute. https://www.iii.org/fact-statistic/facts-statistics-identity-theft-and-cybercrime Accessed 25 February 2019.

God told his people of old to be separate from the nations. Peter tells us:

1 Peter 2:9 | But you are a chosen race, a royal priesthood, **a holy nation**, a people for his own possession.

Jeremiah 10:2 | Thus says the LORD: Learn not the way of the heathen.

This is exactly what Paul is saying in Ephesians 4:17, "...you must no longer walk as the Gentiles do". Paul witnesses on the basis of two relationships: himself and the Lord. He's saying – "I want to testify in the Lord – this is God's will. Take this seriously. Whatever you do – don't live like the rest of the world. Separate yourself to God's holy purposes for your life. Be Christlike, which is so different from the world. It's not believers that have gone crazy – it's the world. Stay far away from its ways.

Be Separated from Mindless Living

Ephesians 4:17 | Now this I say and testify in the Lord, that you must no longer walk as the Gentiles do, in the futility of their minds.

The lost have vain, futile, meaningless, purposeless minds. Here we see the contrast between the lost and the saved immediately. The lost have futile, purposeless, empty minds. They want to be "a-mused". They want not to think. They want to forget about life for a while through various mind-numbing activities. The believer, on the other hand, is commanded to think!

Luke 10:27 | Love the Lord your God with all...your mind.

Philippians 4:8 | Finally, brothers, whatever is true, whatever is honorable, whatever is just, whatever is pure, whatever is lovely, whatever is commendable, if there is any excellence, if there is anything worthy of praise, think about these things.

Proverbs 3:5-6 | Trust in the LORD with all your heart, and do not lean on your own understanding. In all your ways acknowledge him, and he will direct your paths.

Everything for the Gentile is here and now. The lost person is trivial and focused on self instead of focusing on God and the eternal. We must always remember that lost people are blind and ignorant of God. They do live with Him in their hearts, and therefore, their minds are futile. We must never, never be influenced by their thinking or way of life. "that you must no longer walk as the Gentiles do, in the futility of their minds" (4:17). The mind drives the life. If the mind is empty, the life will be empty. The lost person can be morally conscientious, but the bedrock philosophies of his life are lies and ignorance and emptiness. This gets down to anthropology, who we really are. What you think upon reveals who you really are. Why is the world so caught up in endless hours of mindless entertainment? Why so many millions of dollars spent on idiotic frivolity? Because of futile mindlessness. The world would have you to stop thinking. John MacArthur said this:

> It's tragic how people will exhaust their money, their bodies, and their minds trying to find meaning in life, only they never find it. Why? Because their thinking is empty and useless, accomplishing nothing.[103]

I read a very wise statement by John Piper about one way we can cut off access to temptation. He says very plainly:

> Turn off the television. It is not necessary for relevance. And it is a deadly place to rest the mind. Its pervasive banality, sexual innuendo, and God-ignoring values have no ennobling effects on the preacher's soul. It kills the spirit. It drives God away. It quenches prayer. It blanks out the Bible. It cheapens the soul. It destroys spiritual power. It defiles almost everything. I have taught and preached for twenty years now and never owned a television. It is unnecessary for most of you, and it is spiritually deadly for all of you.[104]

The world is founded on vanity. It promises meaning and purpose and fulfillment, but it cannot deliver. We cannot trust the outward presentation of this world. There is a trillion-dollar marketing industry that deals in images trying to convince you that the world is full of meaning and significance. Everywhere you look the lost world is plastered on billboards and magazine covers with smiles. They would like you to think they have happy meaningful purposeful lives. The Bible tells a different story. When we look through the lens of Ephesians 4, we find that these people are walking "in the futility of their minds."

---

[103] John MacArthur, "On with the Old, Off with the New, Part 1" study. https://www.gty.org/library/sermons-library/1928/off-with-the-old-on-with-the-new-part-1

[104] "Preaching as Worship: Meditations on Expository Exultation" (*Trinity Journal* 16 [1995]: 29–45), Piper ends with six pointed applications, including this one (p. 44).

Believers instead are to be careful what they set their mind on. This is the mark of every believer.

> *Psalm 1:1-3* | Blessed is the man who walks not in the counsel of the wicked, nor stands in the way of sinners, nor sits in the seat of scoffers; ² but his delight is in the law of the Lord, and on his law he meditates day and night. ³ He is like a tree planted by streams of water that yields its fruit in its season, and its leaf does not wither. In all that he does, he prospers.

All believers have the capacity to think correctly since "we have the mind of Christ" (Phil 4:5). We are commanded to think as Christians (*cf* Phil 4:8). We are told to meditate on God's Word day and night. We are told to love God with all our mind. So when we come right down to it, we realize the battle for the Christian life is in the mind! Be careful what you put your mind on. Be careful to be a good gatekeeper of your soul. Guard your eye-gate. Guard your ear-gate. Guard your heart.

Be Separated from Careless Living

Ephesians 4:18a | They are darkened in their understanding…

To be darkened is to be blinded. It's not a one-time thing and then man gradually comes to his senses. No, this word denotes an ongoing condition or action that, like blindness, man will never naturally come out of. There is a continual, ongoing condition of spiritual darkness. Paul says lost people cannot understand spiritual realities.

> *1 Corinthians 2:14* | The natural person does not accept the things of the Spirit of God, for they are folly [*nonsense/foolishness*] to him, and he is not able to understand them because they [*spiritual things*] are spiritually discerned.

I remember when I first learned I had a genetic eye disease called *keratoconus*. It came on suddenly. Just after I turned thirty, I started having night blindness. I couldn't see the street signs. I couldn't see clearly. I remember before I got it corrected somewhat that I would pull over to the side of the road and actually walk up to the street sign to see it (this was before GPS widely used). I know what you are thinking. That's dangerous! And you are right. But how much *more* dangerous is it to live life in a careless, darkened, blind manner?

In our country a large part of our federal budget is devoted to education. General education and higher education are more widespread now than ever. College graduates number in the hundreds of millions. Our society, like ancient Greece prides itself in its science, technology, literature, art, and other achievements of the mind. Yet our generation is "ever learning but never able to come to the knowledge of the truth" (2 Tim 3:7). We can have great learning, and be completely blinded toward the living God. Paul describes this condition in greater detail in Romans 1:18 and following.

> *Romans 1:18–25* | For the wrath of God is revealed from heaven against all ungodliness and unrighteousness of men, who by their unrighteousness suppress the truth. [19] For what can be known about God is plain to them, because God has shown it to them. [20] For his invisible attributes, namely, his eternal power and divine nature, have been clearly perceived, ever since the creation of the world, in the things that have been made. So they are without excuse. [21] For although they knew God, they did not honor him as God or give thanks to him, but they became futile in their thinking, and their foolish hearts were darkened. [22] Claiming to be wise, they became fools, [23] and exchanged the glory of the immortal God for images resembling mortal man and birds and animals and creeping things. [24] Therefore God gave them up in the lusts of their hearts to impurity, to the dishonoring of their bodies among themselves, [25] because they exchanged the truth about God for a lie and worshiped and served the creature rather than the Creator, who is blessed forever! Amen.

No matter how much education the world has, you cannot trust that they have any meaningful wisdom or discernment for life. They get educated for years in psychology, only to give you labels and excuses for your sin. They will educate you about the harm of smoking or even large soft drinks. Did you hear about this? In New York City, Mayor Bloomberg wants to pass an ordinance outlawing soft drinks above sixteen ounces because obesity is killing the city. They'll outlaw soft drinks. But they won't outlaw abortion! They'll spend millions in education while the majority of time kids are wasting their minds on movies and video games. It is careless to live in darkness. Kids grow up going to church and are able to answer Bible trivia and give the right answers, but do they know Jesus? Or are they darkened in their understanding. One of the first things that a believer experiences at conversion is a correct view of self after having a correct vision of God. Listen to Isaiah:

> *Isaiah 6:4-5* | I saw the Lord high and lifted up...Woe is me for I am undone... or mine eyes have seen the king the Lord of hosts.

A Christian has a clear vision of Christ in everything he or she does. A lost believer is totally careless because of the blindness of their hearts.

Be Separated from Godless Living

Ephesians 4:18b | They are... alienated from the life of God.

Christians are addicted to God. They think of him "all the day long." With the Psalmist they say:

> *Psalm 16:11* | In your presence there is fullness of joy; at your right hand are pleasures forevermore.

A Christian experiences what the Bible calls "the fear of the Lord." It means to invite God into all your thoughts, experiences, and actions. The fear of the Lord is the worship of God in all things. It is to be united with the life of God. Lost people on the other hand, according to Paul (via the Holy Spirit) are "alienated from the life of God." The lost do not fear and worship the Lord in awe and reverence. Paul goes further in Romans 1.

> *Romans 1:28* | They did not like to retain God in their knowledge, God gave them over to a reprobate mind, to do what ought not to be done.

Lost people are quite alive with emotions and even thoughts of God, since they have a conscience. They may even be moved and affected by the Word of God at times. But emotion is a natural event in the heart and life of every person, saved or lost. To be moved by a story is a far cry from repentance and faith. Faith is an entirely different experience. It is to acknowledge and welcome the presence and lordship of God into my heart and life.

In Louisiana, where I lived as a child, they would bury dead people above the ground in a concrete coffin vault. They didn't used to, but because of the water level, the coffins used to creep up out of the ground. The dead were moving in a sense—there is activity. They are being pushed up simply by their environment, but they are not alive. There may be movement, but it's a far cry from a actual life and resurrection. They are quite dead. And it's the same with the spiritually dead. There can be twinges of conscience. A lost person can be deeply moved by the gospel. He can find the fact of Jesus dying on the cross to be emotionally powerful and even make an emotional commitment to Christ. But that is not what saves a person. What is it that saves a person? I'll tell you. It's right here in this verse. It is the "life of God" invading their soul. It is the Spirit of God indwelling a humble, repentant faith-filled sinner. It is a spiritual marriage union with a thrice holy God through faith. It is a spiritual resurrection.

After Pentecost, we have the promise of the very life and presence of God! The Holy Spirit would come upon every one of God's people. We would have the life of God Inside of us! The Spirit comes in according to Ezekiel and says, "I will cause them to walk in my statues and keep my judgments" (*cf* Eze 36:25-27). The signs of life are the life of God in the soul of man!

Be Separated from Heartless Living

Ephesians 4:18-19a | They are darkened in their understanding, alienated from the life of God because of the ignorance that is in them, due to their hardness of heart. **¹⁹** They have become callous...

Their heart of the ungodly is ignorant, blind, and hardened. The Greek word translated "hardness" (*porosis*) refers to a stone harder than marble. It was also a medical term that referred to the callus that forms around a broken bone. The author of Hebrews implores us:

Hebrews 3:15 | Today if you will hear his voice harden not your heart.

Ephesus was the Sodom and Gomorrah of the first century, home to a religion that promoted temple prostitution with young girls, and the most depraved immorality you can imagine. This kind of hardhearted living was what was venerated most in Ephesus. It was a cesspool of rank depravity on every level of society. At the very center of this godless society was the temple of Diana, one of the Seven Wonders of the Ancient World. There was not a more beautiful building in the ancient world. The entire structure was made of pure marble. But this gigantic shrine was not just a center of worship. Underneath its roof, it was more like a small city. The interior of the building occupied an area of almost 100,000 square feet and towered 60 feet high.[105] And yet it was there that Diana was worshipped as the goddess of prosperity and fertility through depraved sensuality and prostitution.

What is harder than the marble of the idol Diana is the temple of the lost person's heart.

> *Ezekiel 36:26–27* | I will give you a new heart, and a new spirit I will put within you. And I will remove the heart of stone from your flesh and give you a heart of flesh. ²⁷ And I will put my Spirit within you, and cause you to walk in my statutes and be careful to obey my judgments.

An unbeliever's life is as hard as the marble of the statue Diana—hard and without feeling toward God. Every time he takes another step of willful rejection, he pours more concrete into his heart. The process is obvious—a man sins and feels guilt and remorse, sometimes very deeply, but tries to deny it.

Then it all went wrong when sin entered the human heart. Paul, in Ephesians 4:17 – 19, offers a not-too-pretty picture of the four chambers of the fallen heart. Relationally we're separated from the life of God, rationally we're darkened in our understanding due to the futility of our thinking, volitionally our hearts are hardened, and emotionally we've lost all feelings and given ourselves over to sensuality. In Ephesians 4:19, Paul chooses a very rare Greek word to describe the emotional condition of the fallen heart. The NIV translates it as "having lost all sensitivity." It means to be "past feeling" or "having ceased to care." Contrast that with God's original design. We now cease to care about our spiritual state and about soothing our soul in our Savior, preferring the pleasure of sin for a season. We cease to care about others and being sensitive to their emotions, preferring instead to use others to meet our every emotional need. We cease to care about experiencing life with depth, preferring shallow and fleeting emotional highs. Paul's word literally means "a-pathos" — without the ability to use our passion as designed by God, without sensitivity to God and others, focused only on ourselves. When we focus our emotions only on ourselves, we become obtuse to emotional messages, we lack emotional intelligence, and we're insensitive and callous to shame. Rather than givers, we're

---

[105] Pliny recorded the length of this new temple at 425 feet and the width at 225 feet. There were 127 columns, 60 feet in height, supported the roof (Pliny the Elder, XXXVI 21).

consumers — taking anything that will make us feel better in the moment.[106]

The more a person tries to eliminate his guilt by rationalization, self-justification, transferring the blame, or by denying sin and eliminating morality, the further away he pushes his guilt until he can't sense it anymore. A Christian on the other hand has the life of God. It's immediately apparent. I used to go places with my lost friends, and I'd get to the door of a movie theater or a bar and I'd have to say, "I can't do this; I'm a Christian." The life of God manifests itself through a believer's life.

Be Separated from Enslaved Living

> **Ephesians 4:19b** | They... have given themselves up to sensuality, greedy to practice every kind of impurity.

Like a slave, the ungodly have given themselves up to their own passions. They cannot control themselves. They are enslaved by the lasciviousness or license of their flesh. The flesh has total power over them so that they obey the powerful desires of the flesh even the uncleanness with greediness. The heart of man is enslaved to sin. Remember the words of Jesus.

> *John 8:34* | Truly, truly, I say to you, everyone who practices sin is a slave to sin.

What is it that is more powerful than the desire for sex and money and impurity? It is the love and intimacy we have with Christ. It is the power that is greater than money. How do we defeat the enslaving idols of the heart? Thomas Chalmers called it "the expulsive power of a new affection." He said,

> The heart is not so constituted, and the only way to dispossess it of an old affection is by the expulsive power of a new one. [107]

The pathway out of any idolatrous affection is to find a greater, more overwhelming affection. Those who know Christ are set free from

---

[106] Robert W. Kellemen. *Gospel-Centered Counseling* (Equipping Biblical Counselors) (Grand Rapids, MI: Zondervan. 2014), 167-168.
[107] Thomas Chalmers. *The Expulsive Power of a New Affection* (Crossway Short Classics) . (Wheaton, IL: Crossway, 2020), 19.

the slavery of sin because we are so satisfied with him, we need nothing else. As Augustine once said:

> You have made us for yourself, O Lord, and our heart is restless until it rests in you.[108]

THE NEW LIFE IS A LIFE OF TRANSFORMATION (4:20-24)

> **Ephesians 4:20-24** | But that is not the way you learned Christ! — [21] assuming that you have heard about him and were taught in him, as the truth is in Jesus, [22] to put off your old self, which belongs to your former manner of life and is corrupt through deceitful desires, [23] and to be renewed in the spirit of your minds, [24] and to put on the new self, created after the likeness of God in true righteousness and holiness.

We are told right off the bat, "don't walk like other Gentiles walk" (4:17). As Christians we are told later in verse 22 to put off corrupt behavior. Instead, we are to put on a new way of thinking and of living.

Be Transformed by the Regenerate Life

The prerequisite for Christian living is regeneration. You did not learn Christ is a direct reference to salvation. To learn Christ is to be saved.

> **Ephesians 4:20-21** | But that is not the way you learned Christ! — [21] assuming that you have heard about him and were taught in him, as the truth is in Jesus.

Paul speaks of a "learning" of Christ, where he divinely teaches the sinner and brings him to the true understanding of the truth by the drawing of the Holy Spirit. To learn of Christ is an invitation to salvation.

> *Matthew 11:29* | Take my yoke upon you and learn of me.

Upon salvation there is a divine transformation of the heart that theologians call regeneration. What is regeneration? A.W. Pink defined the new birth. He said:

> Regeneration consists in a radical change of heart, for there is implanted a new disposition as the foundation of all holy living; the

---

[108] Aurelius Augustine. *Confessions*, (Book 1,1-2,2.5,5: CSEL 33) 1-5.

mind is renovated, the affections elevated, and the will emancipated from the bondage of sin.[109]

Without the new birth, sinners are unable to appreciate and understand the Word of God in any meaningful way.

> *1 Corinthians 3:24* | The natural person does not accept the things of the Spirit of God, for they are folly to him, and he is not able to understand them because they are spiritually discerned.

At the new birth a person becomes "a new creature; the old things passed away; behold, new things have come" (2 Cor 5:17). It is not simply that he receives something new but that he *becomes* someone new. "I have been crucified with Christ," Paul said; "and it is no longer I who live, but Christ lives in me; and the life which I now live in the flesh I live by faith in the Son of God, who loved me, and delivered himself up for me" (Gal 2:20). Biblical terminology, then, does not say that a Christian has two different natures. He has but one nature, the new nature in Christ. The old self dies and the new self lives; they do not coexist. It is not a remaining old nature but the remaining garment of sinful flesh that causes Christians to sin. The Christian is a single new person, a totally new creation, not a spiritual schizophrenic. It is the filthy coat of remaining humanness in which the new creation dwells that continues to hinder and contaminate his living. The believer as a total person is transformed but not yet wholly perfect. He has residing sin but no longer reigning sin (*cf* Rom 6:14). He is no longer the old man corrupted but is now the new man created in righteousness and holiness, awaiting full salvation (*cf* Rom 13:11).[110]

Be Transformed by the Christ-Centered Life

The new life is a Christ-centered life, where we learn to "put on the Lord Jesus Christ" (Rom 13:14) in every area of life.

> **Ephesians 4:20-21** | But that is not the way you learned Christ!— [21] assuming that you have heard about him and were taught in him, as the truth is in Jesus.

The Christian has the mind of Christ (1 Cor. 2:16), and Christ's is the only mind on which he can rely. The obedient, faithful Christian is

---

[109] A.W. Pink. *Studies in the Scriptures, Volume 7* (Lafayette, IN: Sovereign Grace Publishers, 2001), 72.

[110] MacArthur, *Ephesians*, 164.

the one for whom Christ thinks, acts, loves, feels, serves, and lives in every way. [111] In other words—putting on the new man is remembering who you are united to and who lives inside of you.

The Lord himself prays to his Father: "I in them, and you in me, that they may be made perfect in one" (Jn 17:23). Paul speaks of himself and all true Christians: "I am crucified with Christ: nevertheless I live; yet not I, but Christ lives in me" (Gal 2:20). The Christian's focus is now forever indelibly on the indwelling Christ as our great joy and hope of future glory.

Ephesians 3:17-18 | That Christ may dwell in your hearts through faith.

Colossians 1:27 | Christ in you, the hope of glory.

John 15:4 | Abide in me, and I in you. As the branch cannot bear fruit of itself, except it abide in the vine; no more can you, except you abide in me.

What's the basis of this new life? It is the fact that we learn from Jesus himself. He teaches us, and we listen and learn. We are enamored with Jesus Christ, and we change into his image by being taught by him through the ministry of the Holy Spirit applying the Word of God to our heart. We are to put off the old life and put on Jesus by listening to him. How is it that I can actually experience this radical change in my life?

First, understand that outward change is not enough. Many have learned the Bible well without the help of Jesus Christ. Many have changed outwardly without the help of Jesus Christ. Christianity has always been about change at the core of your being—heart change. If your heart is changed, your actions will follow.

Secondly, understand that holiness is possible because of Christ residing in us as our Teacher. He takes up his residence with us not simply to sleep while you sin. He abides in us to work his holiness into this creature that he bought with his own blood. As you grow in your nearness and intimacy with Christ, you will grow in holiness. The daily means of grace are essential for Christian growth: prayer, reading and meditating on the word, applying the word during testing and trials, regular fellowship with other believers through worship services, Sunday school, small groups, and prayer meetings. All of this happens with an intentional awareness of the presence of Christ in all things. If you

---

[111] Ibid., 174.

are saved, I want to comfort you that God is going to make you holy. It may not be happening perfectly at this moment, but it is a promise that all who are called by God to salvation will be "conformed to the image of his dear Son" (Rom 8:28-29).

Thirdly, there must be actual application of the Word of God to the heart and life of the child of God.

Be Transformed by the Crucified Life

The new life is a crucified life. We are called to root out any kind of idolatry or deceptive desire from our lives. How do we do that? Paul tells us simply to put off the old self, be renewed in the spirit of your mind, and put on the new self.

> **Ephesians 4:22** | ...You have heard about him and were taught in him... to put off your old self, which belongs to your former manner of life and is corrupt through deceitful desires.

Identify the Enemy

In learning how to defeat all sin in our lives, the first instruction we receive from the Spirit through Paul is to "put off your old self." The enemy is there named. It's not my circumstances, my health, my lack of finances, or my bad relationships. If you do not begin with taking full responsibility for yourself, you cannot live a transformed life for Christ.

When a crime is committed, the police put out an all-out alert for a criminal. They need a full description if they are going to find him. We look for the desires for the old manner of life. We look for that enemy, and we turn our gaze to a hill, and we see his form. There he is! The enemy is me! We must understand that our greatest battle is against ourselves. John Owen said, "The old man is nailed to the cross, he struggles, strives, and cries out with great strength."[112] Abraham Kuyper said, "God's child remains the old man's grave digger until the hour of his own departure."[113]

In other words, if I want to determine who the enemy is in my life, I need to stop blaming my family, my church, my circumstances, my financial problems, my past, etc. I have to take personal responsibility for my sin and my lack of joy. Until that happens, I cannot change.

---

[112] John Owen. *On the Mortification of Sin in Believers* (Woodstock, Ontario, CA: Devoted Publishing, 2017), 22.

[113] Abraham Kuyper. *The Work of the Holy Spirit* (Grand Rapids, MI: Eerdmans Publishing Co, 1956), 484.

Chase Down the Enemy

We now know that defeating the enemy has nothing to do with changing my circumstances. I need to change myself. So how do I locate and identify the enemy within me so that I can destroy it? It's right there in verse 22—we sniff out the enemy through what the Spirit calls our "deceitful desires".

To put off here has the idea of taking off an old filthy garment or taking out the trash outside the city gates. It means to get it completely out of your life: that means not only your behavior, but especially your heart. So before we can take the trash of our heart out, we have to sniff out where those deceitful desire might be hiding in our hearts!

Now this is where it gets interesting. Without understanding that the victory over sin must come first in your own heart, where the realm of desires are, you cannot be victorious. What are these deceitful desires? What do they look like? Jesus and Paul, in various places, have identified the "works of the flesh." They have put out many categories of how the old self operates (Gal 5:19-21; 1 Cor 3:3; Eph 5:3; Col 3:5; Jas 3:14, 15; Mt 15:18-20).

Theologians, pastors, and Bible teachers have since categorized them to help us grab hold of those toxic desires of our hearts. One attempt at this is a very helpful chart by Dr. Garrett Higbee, that identifies the sin beneath the sin and places these "deceitful desires" into four categories: anger, anxiety, despair, and foolish thinking (dismissing God from our thoughts).

So many Christians deeply desire to have the "perfect peace" and to "be filled with all the fullness of God." But the vast majority of Christians live in defeat, despair, anger, anxiety, and apathy. God doesn't want one ounce of sinful anger or any kind of fear to control us. He doesn't want us to freak out with fear or anger or check out with apathy or defeat, giving into worldly living.

To begin with chasing down sin, you need to do what I like to call "heart homework". You need to look not only at your actions, but at your heart. Are you obeying God from your heart? I don't mean that you have the desire to obey God, but in your heart, from the level of your desires, are you actually obeying and trusting God.

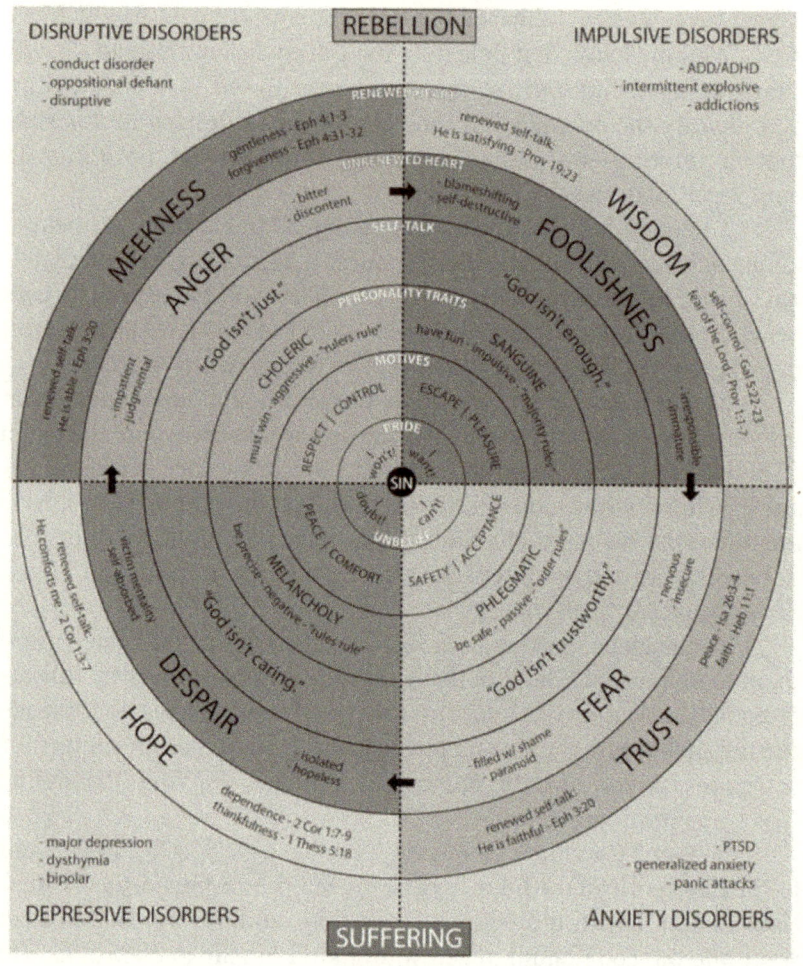

Anger

At the foundation of every sin is unbelief and pride. Begin with the heart-level sin of anger. It's a lack of faith in the justice of God. We feel that we are more righteous or compassionate than God. Look deep in your heart when you are angry and remember the words of James.

James 1:20 | The anger of man does not produce the righteousness of God.

Paul later tells us what to do with anger.

Ephesians 4:31 | Let all bitterness and wrath and anger and clamor and slander be put away from you, along with all malice.

Get rid of all sinful anger from your life. Sniff it out. Hunt it down. Kill it. Take it outside the city gates and burn it in the garbage dump.

Anxiety

What about anxiety? According to the dictionary, anxiety is "a feeling of worry, nervousness, unease, or even terror or fear – typically about an imminent event or something with an uncertain outcome." The Lord teaches us in Matthew 6 that worry is sinful because it is idolatry. "No one can serve two masters" (Mt 6:24). It exchanges a single-hearted devotion to God for the worship of food, clothing, money, or anything else.

Matthew 6:19, 25 | For where your treasure is, there your heart will be also... ^{25} Therefore I tell you, do not be anxious about your life, what you will eat or what you will drink, nor about your body, what you will put on. Is not life more than food, and the body more than clothing?

You need to track down your anxiety and call it what it is: It's idolatry. It's also unbelief and atheism. It displays unbelief in the goodness of God as our Father to care and provide for us (Mt 6:25-34). Jesus basically says, "Pagans worry because they are atheists and don't have anyone to care for them."

Matthew 6:31-33 | Therefore do not be anxious, saying, 'What shall we eat?' or 'What shall we drink?' or 'What shall we wear?' ^{32} For the Gentiles seek after all these things, and your heavenly Father knows that you need them all. ^{33} But seek first the kingdom of God and his righteousness, and all these things will be added to you.

We can rid ourselves of worry if we treasure Christ alone as our Master and enjoy God as our loving Father who promises to bring what he knows is best for me. Being a child of God does not mean we will not have trials. Remember that God will not protect us from anything that makes us more like Christ. That's why anxiety is a theology issue. Do you believe in the goodness of God? If not anxiety will cripple you; it will steal your joy, zap your energy and fill you with terror and dread. If you are worried about your own earthly comfort and security more than your being conformed to Christlikeness, then you will be a worry wart.

Worry is acting like pagan atheists who have no God to care for them. When we worry and forget that God is in control and that he loves us, then we willfully remove ourselves from his embrace, his security, and his comfort. Don't be an "anxiety atheist." Chase down your worry and find out where you are lacking faith in God's goodness and love for you.

Despair

Can depression and despair be sinful? Sometimes, yes. Certainly, there is non-sinful depression that is brought on by a physical illness of some sort. There is also depression of spirit that is the natural outworking of loss and grief. Jesus was a man of sorrows and acquainted with grief, so we are not talking about the normal disappointments of life. Depression is sinful when it turns into despair.

Despair is sinful because it reveals we are fixing our hope on earthly things instead of God, which is idolatry. Whenever we build a house on the sand by trusting in earthly things that fail, anger, anxiety and despair follow. We must place our trust in Christ who is a rock-solid foundation to build on. We must never put our trust in anything that is not guaranteed, so that leaves us with God alone.

We might despair because we want something too much, and it becomes a ruling, inordinate desire (craving, demand, idol) – perhaps even for a good object. We despair when we experience the disappointment or expected disappointment of that ruling desire.

Despair is also sinful because it causes us to dwell in unbelief instead of hoping in God's promises. We begin to tell ourselves: "God doesn't care" instead of hoping and resting in the goodness of God. Chase down your despair, and ask yourself, where am I trusting in earthly things and where do I need to trust in God's good promises?

Foolish Thinking

Foolish thinking and apathy often come when we are tired of the anger, anxiety and despair, and we begin to give up. We just want relief or escape. Or we may just simply not want to care anymore. The biblical definition of foolishness is to dismiss God from your thoughts. Psalm 14:1 gives us a glimpse into a fool's heart. Believers can act like fool-

Even though the pattern of their lives invites God into every moment, if we are honest, we can live as a practical atheist at times.

Psalm 14:1 | The fool has said in his heart, "There is no God."

The fool not thinking in terms of morality, but only satisfying his sinful desires. He doesn't care who he hurts, or what shameful things he does. His only goal is to get some earthly satisfaction.

Proverbs 13:19 | Desire realized is sweet to the soul, but it is an abomination to fools to depart from evil.

Proverbs 10:23 | Doing wickedness is like sport to a fool; and so is wisdom to a man of understanding.

Remember the fool is living in the flesh, and the flesh can never be satisfied.

Proverbs 27:20, NLT | Just as Death and Destruction are never satisfied, so human desire is never satisfied.

The fool is willing to just escape and check out. He doesn't like pain, so he seeks pleasure to dull the pain. Chase down your foolish thinking and see where you are dismissing God from your thoughts and actions.

Be Transformed by the Renewed Life

Ephesians 4:23 | Be renewed in the spirit of your minds.

If you want to see further how to change, there needs to be a humble, teachable spirit of learner. Mind renewal requires an ability to humbly receive and soak in truth. There are many rationalizations we make in order for sin to gain a stronghold in our lives. Let's be practical and consider these four areas of our heart and how we can be "renewed in the spirit of our mind".

Kindness instead of Anger

If you want to fight, then fight for your family, not with them. Pour loads of mercy and meekness upon your family. Righteous anger is always girded up with wisdom and order from above and has a zeal to work toward peace, gentleness, and righteousness (*cf* Jas 3:13-18). Much more could be said, like loving your enemy by being kind to them, praying for them, speaking well of them, and doing good to them (Mt 5:1-12; Lk 6:27-36; Jas 1:19-27; Rom 12:14-21).

If you want to be angry, don't be angry at any person who is made in the image of God. Be angry at Satan. And let vengeance be carried out by God. Paul gives us the exact remedy for sinful anger.

> *Ephesians 4:31-32* | Let all bitterness and wrath and anger and clamor and slander be put away from you, along with all malice. ³² Be kind to one another, tenderhearted, forgiving one another, as God in Christ forgave you.

Instead of anger, be kind! Do kind deeds. Lift your enemy's burdens. That enemy might often be a member of your own family. Kindness literally means to be useful to someone. Then, be tenderhearted. That requires empathy and compassion. Realize that the person who hurts you has their own burdens and problems, and you should be sympathetic toward them. Finally, you need to forgive. Be ready to forgive the person in just the manner that God has forgiven you. Forgiveness is a financial term that means you are willing to cancel their debt and not hold them accountable for what they owe.

Trust instead of Anxiety

Are you trying to get peace apart from God? God commands us not to be anxious or fear, but to fix our minds on him. Be transformed with trust instead of destroyed by anxiety.

> *Philippians 4:6* | Do not be anxious about anything, but in everything by prayer and supplication with thanksgiving let your requests be made known to God.

> *Isaiah 26:3* | You keep him in perfect peace whose mind is stayed on you, because he trusts in you.

> *Isaiah 41:10* | Fear not, for I am with you; be not dismayed, for I am your God; I will strengthen you, I will help you, I will uphold you with my righteous right hand.

Worry is sinful; that's why we are commanded never to worry. Why would anxiety be a sin? Because we become afraid when we magnify anything to be bigger than God. We are called to magnify the Lord.

> *Psalm 34:3* | Oh, magnify the Lord with me, and let us exalt his name together!

Anxiety is idolatry. If you are worried, then what are you making bigger than God in your life. Nothing should control you outside of Jesus Christ. Philippians 4:6-9 tells us to put off worry ("be anxious for nothing") and put on the "PTO" (Pray, Think, Obey) dynamic: *Pray* (4:6, "in everything by prayer"), *think* on what is true and lovely, etc. (4:8, "think on these things"), and *obey* (4:9, "practice these things"). As a result, God promises his peace (4:7, "The peace of God, which surpasses all understanding, will guard your hearts and your minds in Christ Jesus," 4:9, "and the God of peace will be with you"). Chase down that anxiety and replace it with trust. The result of that will be God's perfect peace.

Hope instead of Despair

What are some Scriptures that give hope amid hopelessness based on Christ and his promises?

Psalm 42:5-6 | Why are you cast down, O my soul, and why are you in turmoil within me? Hope in God; for I shall again praise him, my salvation [6] and my God.

Psalm 73:2, 17, 26 | As for me, I almost lost my footing. My feet were slipping, and I was almost gone. [17][I was depressed about the wicked], then I considered their end. [26] My flesh and my heart may fail, but God is the strength of my heart and my portion forever.

2 Peter 1:3 | His divine power has granted to us all things that pertain to life and godliness.

1 Corinthians 10:13 | No temptation has overtaken you that is not common to man. God is faithful, and he will not let you be tempted beyond your ability, but with the temptation he will also provide the way of escape, that you may be able to endure it.

Romans 15:4, 13 | For whatever was written in former days was written for our instruction, that through endurance and through the encouragement of the Scriptures we might have hope. [13] May the God of hope fill you with all joy and peace in believing, so that by the power of the Holy Spirit you may abound in hope.

Lamentations 3:16-18, 21-24 | He has made my teeth grind on gravel, and made me cower in ashes; [17] my soul is bereft of peace; I have forgotten what happiness is; [18] so I say, "My endurance has perished; so has my hope from the Lord."...[21] But this I call to mind, and therefore I have hope: [22] The steadfast love of the Lord never ceases; his mercies never come to an end; ²³ they are new every morning; great is your faithfulness. ²⁴ "The Lord is my portion," says my soul, "therefore I will hope in him."

Chase down your despair, and you will often find you are not trusting God's promises because of your own pain, impatience, and exhaustion. God's promises are there to be medicine to our pain and strength for our soul. Truly we should replace despair with hope and say, "The joy of the Lord is my strength" (Neh 8:10).

Wisdom instead of Foolishness

Replace foolishness with wisdom. Only Jesus Christ can bring a righteous heart. Our righteousness is in him. He "leads us in paths of righteousness for his name's sake" (Psalm 23:3). Righteousness is Christlikeness. The true Christian cannot live comfortably in sin, dismissing God from his thoughts. He can't just escape and check out. He Christ alone can satisfy our desires and give us the expulsive power of a new affection.

> *Philippians 3:8* | Indeed, I count everything as loss because of the surpassing worth of knowing Christ Jesus my Lord. For his sake I have suffered the loss of all things and count them as rubbish, in order that I may gain Christ.

> *Psalm 63:3* | Because your steadfast love is better than life, my lips will praise you.

> *Psalm 16:11* | In your presence there is fullness of joy; at your right hand are pleasures forevermore.

A Christian longs for wisdom and shuns foolishness. True believers are teachable and hungry for solid truth and godly principles from God's Word. On the other hand, a fool will get angry with you if you try to tell them the truth. The truth hurts too much for them to listen to it.

> *Proverbs 23:9* | Do not speak in the hearing of a fool, for he will despise the wisdom of your words.

The fool is not neutral toward wisdom—he hates it. Wisdom is to the fool is what liver is to a lot of people: as freely and frequently as it may be offered to me, I will do everything I can to avoid it.

Wisdom comes from Jesus Christ alone. Wisdom is not intellectual intelligence. Remember we have to be like children to be wise.

Jesus called "uneducated fisherman" to be the greatest in the kingdom. Real wisdom comes from knowing and humbly following Christ.

> *Jeremiah 9:23-24* | Thus says the LORD: "Let not the wise man boast in his wisdom, let not the mighty man boast in his might, let not the rich man boast in his riches, ²⁴ but let him who boasts boast in this, that he understands and knows me, that I am the LORD who practices steadfast love, justice, and righteousness in the earth. For in these things I delight, declares the LORD."

> *Proverbs 1:7* | The fear of the Lord is the beginning of knowledge; fools despise wisdom and instruction.

Chase down those areas of your mind and life that dismiss God from your thinking. Invite God to be a part of every area of your life.

Be Transformed by the Victorious Life

Ephesians 4:24 | And to put on the new self, created after the likeness of God in true righteousness and holiness.

Christ has defeated sin for us and given us the power to "put on the new self" of which he himself is the prototype (Rom 8:28-29). But how do I take hold of that victory and live in the power of Christ, living in the righteous paths of Christlikeness?

Sin is a Defeated Enemy

We have to realize that sin, to be sure, is a defeated enemy. This old self has been dealt a decisive death blow called crucifixion and the result is that I will never return to my old life, enslaved to sin. It's a promise.

> *Romans 6:6* | We know that our old self was crucified with him in order that the body of sin might be brought to nothing, so that we would no longer be enslaved to sin.

> *Galatians 2:20* | I have been crucified with Christ. It is no longer I who live, but Christ who lives in me. And the life I now live in the flesh I live by faith in the Son of God, who loved me and gave himself for me.

Living the victorious life is really an activity of faith in Christ. Christ has defeated sin! Christ lives in me. You will never be what you were! Some remnants of sin may remain in you, but it will not reign in you—it will not rule over you and dominate you. But perhaps this promise is not real to you. You feel defeated, despairing, and undone by sin, kind of like Isaiah who said:

Isaiah 6:5 | Woe is me! For I am lost; for I am a man of unclean lips, and I dwell in the midst of a people of unclean lips; for my eyes have seen the King, the Lord of hosts!

Holiness is a Promised Reality

Through faith, you need to grab hold of Christ, and abide in him. Put on the new life. Be intentional. Start with your heart. Chase down those deceitful desires and find out where you are not trusting God. You have the power, you just need to practice.

Christ made sure that you would have a life of victory over sin. You will never again return to what you were before salvation. Christ promises to hold you tight and bring you with his loving hand through this journey of sanctification.

John 10:28 | I give unto them eternal life; and they shall never perish, neither shall any man pluck them out of my hand.

Jude 24-25 | Now to him who is able to keep you from stumbling and to present you blameless before the presence of his glory with great joy, to the only God, our Savior, through Jesus Christ our Lord, be glory, majesty, dominion, and authority, before all time and now and forever. Amen.

1 Thessalonians 5:23-24 | Now may the God of peace himself sanctify you completely, and may your whole spirit and soul and body be kept blameless at the coming of our Lord Jesus Christ. ²⁴ He who calls you is faithful; he will surely do it.

Hebrews 13:5 | I will never leave you nor forsake you.

Philippians 1:6 | I am sure of this, that he who began a good work in you will bring it to completion at the day of Jesus Christ.

2 Thessalonians 2:13 | God chose you as the firstfruits to be saved, through sanctification by the Spirit and belief in the truth.

Ephesians 2:10 | For we are his workmanship, created in Christ Jesus for good works, which God prepared beforehand, that we should walk in them.

1 Corinthians 1:8-9 | [The Lord] will sustain you to the end, guiltless in the day of our Lord Jesus Christ. God is faithful, by whom you were called into the fellowship of his Son, Jesus Christ our Lord.

Romans 8:29 | For those whom he foreknew he also predestined to be conformed to the image of his Son.

What this means is that Jesus promises to sanctify you and bring you to be "conformed" to his image. Whoever is elected and justified will most definitely be made holy and Christlike in this life. You now have a new calling and promise and power to live the new life.

Conclusion

Once I was driving up the side of Paris Mountain in Greenville, South Carolina. I'm from Chicago, and if you haven't noticed, we don't have many mountains around the Midwest! I was trying to make an important meeting, and the houses were not very well marked. I finally found the house. I couldn't see a driveway, so I thought I'd just drive right up into their yard. I was proceeding just fine until I felt the bottom of my car *slam* against the two-foot drainage ditch that was camouflaged by an equal amount of high grass!

Ever since then, I've tried to be very careful how and where I drive my car! My car was never quite the same after that. You see, wrong pathways have bad consequences. At this moment we are all guiding the vehicle of our life. Every decision you make, every thought you think is taking you somewhere. We need to pay attention. Your steps are taking you somewhere. Your only hope is to have the mind of Christ guiding you on a daily basis. We need to be "renewed in the spirit of our mind." And you know what? When you give your mind and heart over to Christ, you don't need GPS. Jesus becomes your driver! If have Jesus Christ as your driver, then you never have to be lost on the journey of life.

With the Bible, all Christians have a divine GPS to tell us exactly where we should be and where we should go. We must daily *get directions*. Avoid the wrong path. Go down the right path. This daily getting directions in the Christian life is called "renewing your mind." It is a daily connecting to the very person and presence of God. You've got to throw out the old maps of life and follow the new life in Christ.

14 | EPHESIANS 4:25-32
ROOTED IN GODLY COMMUNICATION

Let no corrupting talk come out of your mouths, but only such as is good for building up, as fits the occasion, that it may give grace to those who hear.
EPHESIANS 4:29

The former pastor of College Church in Wheaton, Illinois, Kent Hughes, recounts the power of the tongue in his book *Disciplines of a Godly Man*:

In 1899 four reporters from Denver, Colorado, met by chance on a Saturday night in a Denver railroad station. Al Stevens, Jack Tournay, John Lewis, and Hal Wilshire worked for the four Denver papers: the Post, the Times, the Republican and the Rocky Mountain News. Each had the unenviable task of finding a scoop for the Sunday edition. They hoped to spot a visiting celebrity arriving that evening by train. However, none showed up, so the reporters wondered what on earth they would do. As they discussed options in a nearby saloon, Al suggested they make up a story. The other three laughed - at first. But before long they were all agreed - they would come up with such a whopper that no one would question it and their respective editors would congratulate them on their find. A phony local story would be too obvious, so they decided to write about someplace far away. They agreed on China.

What if we say that some American engineers, on their way to China, told us they are bidding on a major job: the Chinese government is planning to demolish the Great Wall?" Harold was not sure the story would be believable. Why would the Chinese ever tear down the Great Wall of China? "As a sign of international goodwill, to invite foreign trade." By 11 P.M. the four reporters had worked out the details, and the next day all four Denver newspapers carried the story - on the front page.

The Times headline that Sunday read: "Great Chinese Wall Doomed! Peking Seeks World Trade!" Of course, the story was a ridiculous tall tale made up by four opportunistic newsmen in a hotel bar. But amazingly their story was taken seriously and soon ran in newspapers in the Eastern U.S. and even abroad. When the citizens of China heard that the Americans were sending a demolition crew to dismantle the Great Wall, most were indignant, even enraged. Particularly angry were members of a secret society made up of Chinese patriots already against any kind of foreign intervention. Moved to action by the news story, they attacked the foreign embassies in Peking and murdered hundreds of missionaries from abroad. In the next two months twelve thousand troops from six countries, working together, invaded China to protect their countrymen. The bloodshed of that time, born out of a journalistic hoax fabricated in a saloon in Denver, was the time of violence known ever since as the Boxer Rebellion.'

What power the written or spoken word has! Nations have risen, and nations have fallen to the tongue. Lives have been elevated and lives have been cast down by human speech. Goodness has flowed like a sweet river from our mouths, and so has the cesspool. The tiny tongue is a mighty force indeed.[114]

Those who study words tell us that words are important. But one study says how we use those words is even more important. In fact, the researchers concluded that all our communication consists of 7% words, 38% tones, and 55% nonverbal actions. The right words must be spoken at the right time and in the right way.

> *Proverbs 25:11* | A word fitly spoken is like apples of gold in a setting of silver.

Words are powerful! They have the power of life and death.

> *Proverbs 18:21* | Death and life are in the power of the tongue.

---

[114] R. Kent Hughes. *Disciplines of a Godly Man* (Wheaton, IL: Crossway, 1991), 135-136.

Gracious, kind words are unusually powerfully healing! They can actually improve the physical functions of the body.

Proverbs 16:24 | Gracious words are like a honeycomb, sweetness to the soul and health to the body.

Rash words are powerfully destructive. They can feel like a sword or a gunshot going through your chest.

Proverbs 12:18 | There is one whose rash words are like sword thrusts, but the tongue of the wise brings healing.

Self-controlled words are powerfully peace-giving and protective.

Proverbs 15:1 | A soft answer turns away wrath, but a harsh word stirs up anger.

We are told by James, the half-brother of our Lord, that anyone who controls their tongue is a mature Christian.

James 3:2–9 | For we all stumble in many ways. And if anyone does not stumble in what he says, he is a perfect man, able also to bridle his whole body. [3] If we put bits into the mouths of horses so that they obey us, we guide their whole bodies as well. [4] Look at the ships also: though they are so large and are driven by strong winds, they are guided by a very small rudder wherever the will of the pilot directs. [5] So also the tongue is a small member, yet it boasts of great things. How great a forest is set ablaze by such a small fire! [6] And the tongue is a fire, a world of unrighteousness. The tongue is set among our members, staining the whole body, setting on fire the entire course of life, and set on fire by hell. [7] For every kind of beast and bird, of reptile and sea creature, can be tamed and has been tamed by mankind, [8] but no human being can tame the tongue. It is a restless evil, full of deadly poison. [9] With it we bless our Lord and Father, and with it we curse people who are made in the likeness of God.

How then do we transform the tongue? Ephesians 4 gives us our first practical lesson in walking worthy of our calling. It's how our heart is connected to our tongue. Control your heart, and you will control your tongue.

Ephesians 4:25-32 | Therefore, having put away falsehood, let each one of you speak the truth with his neighbor, for we are members one of another. [26] Be angry and do not sin; do not let the sun go down on your anger, [27] and give no opportunity to the devil. [28] Let the thief no longer steal, but rather let him labor, doing honest work with his own hands, so that he may have something to share with anyone in need. ²⁹ Let no corrupting talk come out of your mouths, but only such as is good for building up, as fits the occasion, that it may give grace to those who hear. ³⁰ And do not grieve the Holy Spirit of God, by whom you were sealed for the day of redemption. ³¹ Let all bitterness and wrath and anger and clamor and slander be put away from you, along with all malice. ³² Be kind to one another, tenderhearted, forgiving one another, as God in Christ forgave you.

This passage in Ephesians 4 is a case study in how our heart controls our tongue. Control the heart, and you will control the tongue. Jesus taught us this: your words, whatever they are reveal your heart!

Matthew 12:35 | The good person out of the good treasure of his heart produces good, and the evil person out of his evil treasure produces evil, for out of the abundance of the heart his mouth speaks.

Paul's whole effort in the book of Ephesians is that we would "walk worthy" of our calling. That's the first thing he says at the beginning of this chapter (4:1). He has told them what they were delivered from – and why we used to live like we did. We were hardened against God, darkened and futile in our thinking, separated from God's life, and insensitive to holiness so that we indulged in every kind of sensual vice.[115] By the grace of God we no longer live that way. We put off the old life when we came to know Christ. We were renewed in our heart and mind. Now the new life of Christ following, Christ-imitating begins. Paul begins to lay out for us how we are to do that. The first thing the Spirit has him talk about is what comes out of our mouth.

TRUTHFUL COMMUNICATION (4:25)

Ephesians 4:25 | Therefore, having put away falsehood, let each one of you speak the truth with his neighbor, for we are members one of another.

Christians are truthtellers because they have the Spirit of truth indwelling them. Yet we live in the atmosphere of deceit on this broken planet. Have you ever been lied to? Psalm 116:11 says, "All men *are* liars." The 9th Commandment says, "You shall not bear false witness".

---

[115] Boice, *Ephesians*, 165.

Sadly, we've all broken that commandment because every person on earth has lied at one time or another. We are all guilty, and we all need the Savior.

Lying continues on in various forms in the world. Have you ever studied the pictures of the food at McDonald's or another restaurant? It's never the way it looks in the picture. Who has ever had a bun so perfect and lettuce so crispy? Most of the time the bun is lukewarm, and the lettuce is wilted. It's sleight of hand. One of the first things that Jesus takes care of when he saves us is deception. He changes our hard, deceptive heart.

Hearts that Hate Lies

We as God's people have "put on the new man, which after God is created in righteousness and true holiness" (4:24). He's saying that we have changed in the inner being. Our heart has been transformed. We now have hearts that hate lies.

Ephesians 4:25a | Therefore, having put away falsehood...

"Therefore" Paul says, since you have been renewed in your inner being, in your heart and mind, you now have the inescapable impulse to stop lying and start telling the truth (4:25). Because you are redeemed, the Spirit says you have already put away falsehood, and you've started telling the truth.

The unredeemed heart as the control center of our intellect and emotions, is an organ of deceit. Jeremiah 17:9 says it clearly: "The heart *is* deceitful above all things, and desperately wicked: who can know it?" What we get when we turn to Jesus is a new heart (Eze 36:25-27). We are free from the enslavement of having to tell lies. "So if the Son sets you free, you will be free indeed" (Jn 8:36). Jesus Christ is the "way, the truth, and the life" (Jn 14:6) and because we are followers of him, we are honest, forthright people. Now that we know Christ, Paul assumes that we have already put away this lifestyle of deceit. No longer can we live comfortably in deceit: cheating on our timecard at work, exaggerating reality to make ourselves look good, embellishing arguments when we are angry with 100% words like "never" and "always". None of us is perfect of course, but we can all agree from the heart that deception has absolutely no part of the Christian life. We have hearts that hate lies.

Mouths that Speak Truth

With the indwelling of the Spirit of truth in us, we are compelled continually to tell the truth.

> **Ephesians 4:25b** | Let each one of you speak the truth with his neighbor.

Because we have a new heart, we have the power to bless our neighbors by speaking carefully, gently, and truthfully. We've already been instructed to be "truthing in love" (4:15). It must be assumed that we love our neighbor, and when we speak the truth, we don't just blow up at them and excuse our lack of love on speaking the truth, as so many do to rationalize their sinful communication.

Speaking the truth means that we carefully let due process play out. This is an absolute necessity in our justice system, and it ought to be even more evident in Christ's church. Love teaches us to always think the best. "Love believes all things and hopes all things" (1 Cor 13:7). Matthew tells us for this reason that if we have an offence against our brother, we deal with it immediately, and we go to him and him alone (Mt 5:23-25; *cf* 18:15). If you cannot establish the truth with him alone, then you must take evidence by witnesses.

> *Matthew 18:16* | Every charge must be established by the evidence of two or three witnesses.

A Body that Dwells in Harmony

> **Ephesians 4:25c** | For we are members one of another.

As God's family, living in harmony, we cannot afford to listen to gossip and innuendo. We must hear the evidence from all sides before drawing conclusion. Nothing should be seriously considered unless evidence from both sides is given.

> *Proverbs 18:13, 17* | If one gives an answer before he hears, it is his folly and shame. ¹⁷ The one who states his case first seems right, until the other comes and examines him.

If we do not do what is necessary for fairness and harmony, we will be establishing innuendo and half-truths, which are lies. Lies destroy harmony. Lies push people to live in isolation and fear. We've got to put off falsehood and put on the truth. Our unity depends on it. We've got to live in the truth. Why? Because character assassination hurts the Body of Christ. On the other hand, due process strengthens the whole body.

TRANSFORMED COMMUNICATION (4:28)

Honesty not only flow from the heart to the mouth, but it extends to the life and actions of the transformed child of God.

> **Ephesians 4:28** | Let the thief no longer steal, but rather let him labor, doing honest work with his own hands, so that he may have something to share with anyone in need.

The idea is that when we come to know Christ there is a transformation. If you have been a thief, then you must not simply stop stealing, you must start giving. You must not simply stop bad input into your brain, you must do as Psalm 1:2 says, and "mediate on his Word day and night."

The way you put off the old way of living is by putting on the new way of living. Stop working on the Lord's Day and start attending the gatherings of brothers and sisters. Stop stealing by starting to give. Stop lying by telling the truth. Stop filthy language by studying godly language. Stop being lazy and start serving others. Put the video games down and the remote control down and help others.

TEMPERATE COMMUNICATION (4:26-32)

> **Ephesians 4:26** | Be angry and do not sin; do not let the sun go down on your anger.

This is the kind of anger you and I know so well. We all claim to be expressing "righteous indignation" from time to time, but most of the time what we're really talking about is garden-variety anger: bitterness (grudges), wrath (rage), clamor (tantrums), and evil speaking (a tongue dipped in poison). We all have our weak spots—our "pet peeves" that get inside us and work on our emotions until we're struggling with anger. We have to live in a hurtful world. There is so much to be angry about. So what can we do about it? How can we handle our anger? Let's look at some positive prescriptions.

Don't Curse Your Anger

> **Ephesians 4:26a** | Be angry and do not sin...

So what should we do with the experience of anger? It is something that we all experience, and it is not necessarily sinful, but it is such a powerful experience, and our hearts are so bent toward selfishness, that anger in man is quite often, if not most often sinful. The point of this section is not that we should give full vent to our anger, since this is forbidden by the Lord (Jas 1:19-20; Pro 29:19). It is not even that we should entertain our anger. Indeed, the Spirit culminates the passage by saying that we should "put away all" forms of anger such as "bitterness, rage, shouting," etc. (Eph 4:31-32).

James 1:20 | The anger of man does not produce God's righteousness.

So St. Paul by the Spirit tells us to "be angry" but be sure not to allow that anger to cross the line into sin and selfishness (4:26). It's a seemingly impossible command for broken, self-centered human beings. But we as Christians can, like our Lord, experience anger without sinning. It is quite a difficult undertaking, but it is not only possible but promised if we walk in the power of the Holy Spirit. We know it is possible since Jesus himself was at times deeply angry, for instance, we can remember when he cleaned out the temple from the thieves and money changers (Jn 2:14–15).

God is Angry

As Christians, we need to realize that anger is not in and of itself sinful. Anger is actually a holy and perfect attribute of God—it is part of his justice.

Psalm 7:11, NKJV | God judges the righteous, and God is angry with the wicked every day.

An amazing thing happens with God's anger. It must always be propitiated, satisfied by a righteous requirement that is fair and just. David Powlison speaks of how amazing our God is to divert his anger from us to his beloved Son.... Second, in love, God's anger works to disarm the power of your sin. His hatred of sin is again expressed for your wellbeing. In the present, on an ongoing basis, God deals with indwelling sinfulness. The Holy Spirit pours out God's love in you as a burning fire against evil. He does not destroy you. He destroys sin and makes you new. In steadfast love he remakes us, not by tolerating our sin, but by hating our sin in ways we learn to love![116] Again, listen to Paul: "Be angry and sin not." Don't use your anger to vent for selfish reasons. Use your anger against your sin. That's God's good gift to us.

Jesus is Angry

Jesus was angry at various times when he was on earth. The Bible says that on this day Jesus Christ will come "in flaming fire taking vengeance on them that know not God, and that obey not the gospel of our Lord Jesus Christ" (2 Thess 1:8). The mouths that right now are blaspheming God will be eternally stopped. Every knee will bow, and every tongue will confess that Jesus Christ is Lord (Phil 2:10-11). After Christ comes, we will all face him, and he will be sitting on an awesome radiant throne of judgment, and it says he is the One "from whose face the earth and the heaven fled away" (Rev 20:11). So the triune God has displayed anger since the moment sin entered the world.

God's People are Angry

Of course, since we are made in God's image, anger is also an emotion God has given to all humanity as a tool to maintain a passion for holiness and righteousness. We all have anger in our lives. It is something that exists because things are not right in the universe. Anger simply defined, is taking an emotional stand for one's convictions of right and wrong. It is saying, "I'm against something." Someone has said if you don't experience godly anger for true righteousness, and if you don't have any hatred or anger against sin, how can you know the thrice holy God? The difference with godly anger is that as Christians, our anger drives us to find a righteous solution for the problem we are facing. Godly anger is under God's control. Anger is harnessed by the Christian for righteous purposes. So we run away from inordinate, demanding, selfish anger.

Psalm 37:8 | Refrain from anger, and forsake wrath! Fret not yourself; it tends only to evil.

James 1:19-21 | Know this, my beloved brothers: let every person be quick to hear, slow to speak, slow to anger; [20] for the anger of man does not produce the righteousness of God. [21] Therefore put away all

---

[116] David Powlison. *Good and Angry: Redeeming Anger, Irritation, Complaining, and Bitterness* (Greensboro, NC: New Growth Press, 2016), 126.

filthiness and rampant wickedness and receive with meekness the implanted word, which is able to save your souls.

So much of the wickedness present in the world today is due to unbridled, self-centered anger. Anger that is sin, is anger that is self-defensive and self-serving, that is resentful of what is done against oneself. It is the anger that leads to murder and to God's judgment (Mt 5:21–22). [117] Indeed, John says that anger and hatred is murder in the heart (1 Jn 3:15). Instead, our anger ought to God-centered and even empathetic, as Jesus' anger was when he was grieved that the people were hardened and blinded in their hearts. The man of sorrows is on display here.

> *Mark 3:5* | And he [Jesus] looked around at them with anger, grieved at their hardness of heart, and said to the man, "Stretch out your hand." He stretched it out, and his hand was restored.

Godly anger is also constructive: it works to better the situation and leaves an atmosphere of righteousness and peace behind because it is regulated by God's wisdom (Jas 3:13-18). So how do we get rid of destructive, ungodly anger? Paul answers this question in Ephesians 4:26-32. [118]

Don't Nurse Your Anger

> **Ephesians 4:26b** | Be angry and do not sin; do not let the sun go down on your anger.

Remember that anger is, at some point, a choice. No one can actually "make" us angry. The anger is already there, coming out of our heart. As believers, we have control over the affections and desires of our heart. God promises us that there is always that moment of temptation when the "escape hatch" swings open. In one defining moment, we can choose to put away the impure feelings, as Paul counsels us to do, or we can build a little nest. The moment we take note of an angry impulse and refuse to send it away, we've put the first twig into that nest. And we all know what happens in a nest sooner or later: Something hatches and flies out.

---

[117] MacArthur, *Ephesians*, 185.
[118] Outline (Don't Nurse Your Anger) and some content adapted from David Jeremiah. *Slaying the Giants in Your Life* (Nashville: Thomas Nelson Publisher, 2001), 166-178.

You must not nurse a vengeful grudge in your anger. In fact, God's anger will deliver you from the pain of other people's sins. Because he loves us, the Lord is angry at people who seek to hurt us. In steadfast love, he will deliver us from our enemies. On the last day all causes of pain will be destroyed forever.[119]

The Bible tells us not to let the sun set on our anger. That's simply an eloquent way of saying to clear all your accounts before the day is over and to start each day with clean books. Enforce a twelve-hour limit on feelings of resentment; after that, they should be wiped as clean as God wipes your own sins. After the sun goes down, it's often not a good time to discuss a heavy issue, or really to talk about anything difficult. But even if the sun does go down, don't nurse your anger.

If only it were easy to take this advice. Of all the seven deadly sins, anger is the one that tastes the best. This is the one we actually enjoy; perhaps the word is that we savor our anger. We take it in, welcome it, build the nest—then we begin fantasizing speeches, thinking about how to get even, devising plans of attack. What happens when those fantasies take on a life of their own? They may conceivably become more than fantasies. Think of all the angry speeches you've devised as you lay tossing and turning in bed. What if you really said all the things that passed through your mind? In our flesh, we can enjoy composing those covert, undeliverable speeches; we savor our anger. It's so hard to let go. Clear all accounts when the sun goes down. Realize that if someone owes you, you're probably in debt as well—and be content to break even on the relationship books. We have to remember the Bible tells us to avoid any debt other than the debt of love.

Use your anger to solve problems biblically. Don't blow up! Don't clam up! Don't spiral down! Bridle your anger. Use it to become more productive. Make sure you don't nurse your anger. God's people are not to hold grudges. We are not to hold onto bitterness but put it off. Don't nurse your anger or you a root of bitterness may spring up.

Hebrews 12:15 | See to it that no one fails to obtain the grace of God; that no "root of bitterness" springs up and causes trouble, and by it many become defiled.

---

[119] Powlison, *Good and Angry*, ibid.

Don't Rehearse Your Anger

Ephesians 4:26b-27 | Do not let the sun go down on your anger, ²⁷ and give no opportunity to the devil.

Anger can become malicious and can change into resentment or the holding of a grudge. So Paul gives the practical advice: Do not let the sun go down while you are still angry. What does that figurative expression indicate? To have the sun go down while you are still angry means that you take it to bed with you and the situation is not resolved. The anger is kept inside, and it begins to boil and seethe, perhaps turning into bitterness.

Do you know who loves it when you rehearse your anger? Satan is the accuser of the brethren, so why wouldn't he join in and help you rehearse your bitterness? There's coming a day when that we will be able to rejoice that "the accuser of our brothers has been thrown down, who accuses them day and night before our God" (Rev 12:10). According to Jesus, anger is the first step toward murder (Mt 5:21–26), because anger gives the devil a foothold in our lives, and Satan is a murderer (Jn 8:44).[120] One of the early church fathers, Marius Victorinus (280-363 A.D.), explained how we have the power to stop Satan from doing his work, by controlling our anger.

> The devil can do nothing to us unless we ourselves willingly allow him to do so. This is true in all our acts. Thus, we are masters of our own will.... The devil's opportunity arises from our own vice.[121]

The author of the angry behavior described in Ephesians 4 is unmasked in verse 27. It is the devil. The father of sin is the devil. Sin did not begin on earth; it began in Heaven. Sin did not begin in the human heart but in the soul of Lucifer, the highest anointed cherub in glory. Sin was already active before the fallen Lucifer introduced it into this planet. Satan especially like to reintroduce himself to Christians through anger. Satan hates God and God's people, and when he finds a believer with the sparks of anger in his heart, he fans those sparks, adds

---

[120] Warren W. Wiersbe, *The Bible Exposition Commentary*, vol. 2 (Wheaton, IL: Victor Books, 1996), 41.

[121] Marius Victorinus. *Bibliotheca Scriptorum Graecorum et Romanorum Teubneriana* (Leipzig: Teubner, 1824), 1972:187 [1281A–B].

fuel to the fire, and does a great deal of damage to God's people and God's church.[122]

The devil is not afraid of us personally. Satan is skilled at paralyzing our walk with God, but we can resist him. It's not that we are more powerful than him. Rather, he is desperately afraid of the Holy Spirit who indwells us. Satan never knows when we will enter into all that is available to us—when we will become filled with the Spirit and triumphantly wage battle in his realm. Paul expected that we *will* live triumphant lives. We are not to give place, ground, or opportunity to the devil.[123]

Don't Converse About Your Anger

Ephesians 4:29a | Let no corrupting talk come out of your mouths.

Corrupt Conversation

Corrupt refers to that which is unwholesome or foul and was used of rotten fruit, vegetables, and other spoiled food. Sinful anger has the potential to drive us to a rottenness of spirit and heart which can eventually proceed out of our mouth with the foulest of motives and language. Foul language should never proceed from the mouth of a Christian, because it is totally out of character with his newness of life. Rotten language should be as repulsive to us as a rotten apple or a spoiled piece of meat. Off-color jokes, profanity, dirty stories, vulgarity, double entendre, and every other form of corrupt talk should never cross our lips.[124]

> *Colossians 3:8* | But now you must put them all away: anger, wrath, malice, slander, and obscene talk from your mouth.

Cutting Conversation

Ephesians 4:29a | Let no corrupting talk come out of your mouths...

That word corrupt also carries the idea of cutting—don't let any cutting remark escape you. Many times, we think our words don't cause much damage. We may even tell the person we were "just kidding." Our words are like arrows that pierce, like "sword thrusts" that murder with character assassination (Pro 12:18) that cuts through the soul. The

---

[122] Wiersbe, *Ephesians*, ibid.
[123] Phillips, *Ephesians*, Eph 4:27.
[124] MacArthur, *Ephesians*, 187.

truth is our words can cause a great deal of damage we may not see on the outside. Yet our words may cut much deeper than we meant for them to. It's important that we think before we speak. Once the words are out of our mouth, they cannot be taken back.

Your tongue, in many ways, is like a pair of scissors. With each cutting word, we cut into a person's heart. We can use name calling, lying, slander, gossip, and so many other tools of the tongue. Even the choice to give the cold shoulder, by not saying a word, can be a form of cutting communication. We can say, "I hate you" without saying a word. Consider the damage that can be done with cutting communication. Let's ask God to forgive us for saying mean words to or about others. We can ask God to help us just like David did.

> *Psalm 141:3, NLT* | Take control of what I say, O LORD, and guard my lips.

Constructive Conversation

> **Ephesians 4:29** | Let no corrupting talk come out of your mouths, but only such as is good for building up, as fits the occasion, that it may give grace to those who hear.

Instead of using cutting words, we are to build people up. We are to develop speech that is pure, helpful, and pleasing to God. Paul here mentions three specific characteristics of wholesome speaking: it is edifying, appropriate, and gracious. The words of a Christian are to be good for edification. Our speech should build up by being helpful, constructive, encouraging, instructive, and uplifting. Sometimes, of course, it must be corrective; but that, too, is edifying when done in the right spirit. [125]

> *Proverbs 25:12* | Like an earring of gold and an ornament of fine gold is a wise reprover to a listening ear.

We are to build up a person's faith with our words. We are to converse in such a way that our words become a vehicle and demonstration of the grace of God. I wish it were easy to fix a soul that we have cut into. We can use physical tape to help a person, but a good word can build up and heal the soul. A gracious word is stronger than any

---

[125] Ibid., 188.

adhesive to repair the soul. Speak encouraging and kind and empathetic words: "Good job! I love you. Sorry. I forgive you. I appreciate you."

Don't Worsen Your Anger

Ephesians 4:30a | And do not grieve the Holy Spirit of God.

The worst thing that can happen with anger is that we can grieve the Holy Spirit of God by it. Anger can tempt us to disregard and thereby grieve the Spirit who indwells us. The emotional life of the believer is to be under the sovereignty of God and ruled by the indwelling Holy Spirit of God. We are capable of all different kinds of emotion, including joy, sorrow and bitterness. Some of these emotions are perfectly legitimate and godly. But there are some emotions, that are sinful. Because they are emotions, they seem to rest under our radar. We may know we are not walking rightly with God. We may have the sense that we are grieving the Spirit, but not know why. Search your heart for emotional murder. Confess it and forsake it as the murder that it is. Humble yourself and replace your anger with tenderness that displays meekness, gentleness, and self-control. Do whatever it takes to experience the renewed filling of the Holy Spirit. Don't stop until you are quite sure that you are "filled with all the fullness of God" (Eph 3:19).

Ephesians 4:30 | And do not grieve the Holy Spirit of God, by whom you were sealed for the day of redemption.

Concerning the sealing of the Holy Spirit, Paul is referring to the sealing of ownership (*cf* 1:13-14). I couldn't describe this sealing more beautifully than St. Jerome (347–420 A.D.)

> That we have been "sealed" with the Holy Spirit means that both our spirit and our soul are impressed with God's own seal, signifying that we belong to him. By this we receive in ourselves that image and likeness in which we were created at the outset.... You are sealed so that you may be preserved to the end. You may show that seal on the day of redemption, pure and unblemished and not damaged in any part. You are thereby ready to be counted with those who are redeemed.[126]

---

[126] St. Jerome. J.P. Migne, ed. "Epistle to the Ephesians" in *Patrologia Cursus Completus*. Series Latina. 221 vols. (Paris: Migne, 1844-1864), 2.4.30.

Don't Disperse Your Anger

This is the kind of anger you and I know so well. We all claim to be expressing "righteous indignation" from time to time, but most of the time what we're really talking about is garden-variety anger: bitterness (grudges), wrath (rage), clamor (tantrums), slander (a tongue dipped in poison), and malice (a mean spirit, wishing for evil). We all have our weak spots—our "pet peeves" that get inside us and work on our emotions until we're struggling with anger. We have to live in a hurtful world. There is so much to be angry about. So what can we do about it? How can we handle our anger? Let's look at some positive prescriptions.

> **Ephesians 4:31** | Let all bitterness and wrath and anger and clamor and slander be put away from you, along with all malice.

Here the Spirit through Paul describes the destructive heart disposition of the self-life. If you do not walk in the Spirit, you give yourself over to this foul family of anger. The anger described here is one that is progressive and paralyzing. It is impossible to live the Christian life until it is completely forsaken. "All" bitterness, wrath, anger, etc., must be completely and utterly forsaken. We cannot love God and live with murder in our hearts at the same time. The self-life must be put away, especially in its unseen emotional form. Bitterness and anger, usually over trivial things, can make such havoc of homes, churches, and friendships.

How do we do get rid of it? To begin with, we need to recognize it and take responsibility for it. Chase it down so you can kick it out. Six children of the self-life are named: bitterness, wrath, anger, clamor, slander, and malice. These kinds of expressions just take out your hurt on another person. Don't go near them. The word "all" is mentioned twice for a reason, emphasizing the comprehensive manner in which these sins are to be avoided. Open up the sewer hole of the anger in your heart. Let the Holy Spirit clean you out of "all" of this filthy emotional sewage.

Grudges

> **Ephesians 4:31** | Let all bitterness ... be put away from you.

The first child of the self-life that we all need to get rid of is bitterness. No grudge holding is allowed in the Spirit-filled life. Put off the old self and his bitterness. What is bitterness? Bitterness is "a settled hostility that poisons the whole inner man."[127] It is "a hard-heartedness that harbors resentment about any hurt from the past".[128] Ultimately, bitterness is a poisonous, self-centered disposition of the heart that grieves the Spirit of God and ignores his gentle, dovelike nature. It is one thing to be angry with God's enemies that enslave the people of the earth, as you pray the imprecatory prayers for God to "break their teeth" at the Second Coming, but we must never wish hurt upon a brother or sister in Christ. Neither does our anger want the immediate fulfillment of vengeance. But we give our wrath to the Lord at his second coming.

> *2 Thessalonians 1:7-10* | When the Lord Jesus is revealed from heaven with his mighty angels [8] in flaming fire, inflicting vengeance on those who do not know God and on those who do not obey the gospel of our Lord Jesus. [9] They will suffer the punishment of eternal destruction, away from the presence of the Lord and from the glory of his might, [10] when he comes on that day to be glorified in his saints, and to be marveled at among all who have believed, because our testimony to you was believed.

> *Romans 12:19* | Beloved, never avenge yourselves, but leave it to the wrath of God, for it is written, "Vengeance is mine, I will repay, says the Lord."

You can recognize bitterness when you don't want to get rid of the hurt because it is self-serving and vengeful. The bitter person wants his "pound of flesh." He wants the person who hurt him to pay. The whole world has moved forward, but the bitter person can't get past this *one* thing! A bitter person wants to nurse the hurt and let it fester in their heart and mind. They nurse their hurt and go over it again and again in their heart and mind, thinking of new arguments to throw at the person who hurt them. Again, this goes directly against the merciful grace of the Spirit that dwells within us.

Bitterness will hurt and trouble you while the person that hurt you is often completely unaware. Someone has said: "Bitterness is like drinking poison thinking the other person will die." It will take over your emotions and drain you. It will damage you and others. If you

---

[127] Boice, *Ephesians*, 165.

[128] Andrew T. Lincoln. *Word Biblical Commentary: Ephesians* (Word Books: Dallas, 1990), 308.

nurse bitterness it will spread to others and defile them (Heb 12:15). Get rid of bitterness. As believers we are called to love. We cannot fulfill love for God or love for every single person on this planet with any trace of bitterness in the heart.

Rage

Ephesians 4:31 | Let all ... wrath ... be put away from you.

What is this wrath? It is the Greek word *"thymos"* or something that boils over and then calms down and boils over and calms again! We often speak of it as "rage". It refers to the passion of the moment. It is the "blowing up" of anger. It is like the raging of the sea or the welling up of the volcano. It stirs up anger and burns within. Just when you've calmed down, it comes back. It is fury that is tossed inside the belly. It is translated as both "fury" and "rage". It is said to be a "wild, violent rage deep within...that hasn't yet exploded".[129] Proverbs 10:12 says, "Hatred stirs up strife: but love covers all sins". This wrath is a form of hatred that stirs and stirs inside. This is the opposite of "tenderheartedness". Rage doesn't consider the person, but only wants vengeance. It is not passive. A person of rage can't hold back his anger, but suddenly and sometimes violently lashes out!

This word reminds me of the land mine fields. "Land mines maim or kill approximately 26,000 civilians every year, including... approximately 10,000 children."[130] Land mines do much damage. They blow off people's limbs. There is great physical and emotional pain caused. Most people do not know the land mine is there until they blow up. There is only one answer for land mines, and that is to ban them from being made, and to remove them one at a time. It is the same with this wrath. Get rid of it! Ban it from your soul. You never know when this rage will blow up and destroy people. Throw it away. Disarm yourself. Let it "be put away from you." Throw it far, far away. Put out the fire of rage inside of you as soon as you sense it.

---

[129] P.G. Matthew, *Exposition of Ephesians*, Eph 4:25-32.
[130] Norman Kempster. (2016, January 28). "The Global Land Mine Crisis." Retrieved February 6, 2021, from http://menstuff.org/issues/byissue/minehistory.html#problem.

Anger

Ephesians 4:31 | Let all ... anger ... be put away from you.

Anger is "a settled animosity"[131] toward someone. It is a more internal smoldering, a subtle and deep feeling.[132] Anger has not yet reached the point of rage ("wrath"), but it is working up to it. This often looks like "the cold shoulder." Instead of dealing with the problem with godly zeal, we turn inward and become selfish, cutting off the person that offended us instead of actually dealing carefully and wisely with the problem.

Shouting

Ephesians 4:31 | Let all ... clamor ... be put away from you.

Here is another sin we need to avoid: clamor. It literally means "shouting" or an "outcry" and has the idea of *raising your voice to dominate the conversation*. Stay away from these "loud threatenings".[133] Temper tantrums, of course, are identified with little children. An obstinate child disperses his anger in a number of ways: he squeals, he pounds his fists, he kicks his feet, he rolls on the carpet. He expresses every ounce of the anger and frustration within him. There are some adults who indulge in very adult temper tantrums. They may not roll on the carpet or squeal, but they act out their emotions on their own terms. If you ever needed to wonder if the raising of your voice in threatening anger is a sin, it clearly is according to Holy Scripture. Instead of shouting, we should give a gentle answer.

Proverbs 15:1 | A soft answer turns away wrath, but a harsh word stirs up anger.

Do you ever raise your voice in frustration? Do you shout at your spouse or your children? Do you shout at a friend or a relative to dominate an argument? Even shouting at the TV or another car on the highway may qualify! As Paul says, let this trait "be put away from you" (4:31). Throw this worthless practice into the garbage heap. Get it out

---

[131] P. G. Matthew, *Ephesians*, Eph 4:25-32.
[132] MacArthur, *Ephesians*, 190.
[133] Matthew Henry. *Matthew Henry's Commentary on the Whole Bible: Complete and Unabridged in One Volume*. (Peabody, ME: Hendrickson, 1996), Eph 4:17.

of your life now and forever. Don't resort to raising your voice. Instead speak gently.

Slander

Ephesians 4:31 | Let all ... slander be put away from you.

Slander is the Greek word for blasphemy aimed at mankind (βλασφημια), or injurious speech.[134] It is essentially *misrepresentation* and "false charges...which defame and damage another's reputation".[135] This is a crime in our country. It is called libel. It is to display intentional misrepresentation and disrespect through your words. This sometimes comes through trying to "one-up" someone else in an argument. Some of the more common ways we tend to mischaracterize in the heat of an argument are:

Lethal exaggeration. You know this is going on when someone uses what we call "100% words". Always remember never to use 100% words. Abandon using 100% words such as "you always do that," or, "you never do what I ask you to do."

Name calling. The wife says: "You *never* fill the car with gas". The husband replies: "Well of course I fill up the car most of the time, you liar." Now it is true that his wife is lying, because she is using a lethal exaggeration. But the husband should be displaying a tender heart instead of slandering his wife. By calling each other names we are casting stones while living in glass houses. We must "speak the truth in love". No name calling. Instead of slander, remember these principles from the Bible. First, be slow to speak and slow to anger.

James 1:19-20 | Know this, my beloved brothers: let every person be quick to hear, slow to speak, slow to anger; [20] for the anger of man does not produce the righteousness of God.

Second, never rebuke a person before you fully hear their side.

Proverbs 18:13 | If one gives an answer before he hears, it is his folly and shame.

---

[134] Kenneth S. Wuest. *Wuest's Word Studies from the Greek New Testament : For the English Reader*. (Grand Rapids, MI: Eerdmans, 1997), Eph 4:31.

[135] Merriam-Webster, Inc: *Merriam-Webster's Collegiate Dictionary*. Eleventh ed. (Springfield, MA: Merriam-Webster, Inc., 2003), *slander*.

Here is the three-step process for getting rid of slander and rashly accusing your brother or sister of sin, or slandering them: listen, listen, listen! Only when you have thoroughly listened should you gently, carefully, and kindly respond.

> *Colossians 4:6* | Let your speech always be gracious, seasoned with salt, so that you may know how you ought to answer each person.

Malice

> **Ephesians 4:31** | Let all bitterness and wrath and anger and clamor and slander be put away from you, along with all malice.

Malice is "equivalent to wishing someone evil".[136] This disposition of the heart wishes the worst for the person who they are offended by. Malice, like all anger, is from the family of sin that wants murder. Yet, it's more sophisticated than murder. It is more like wishing that the person was not in existence or not part of your life. It is not appreciating and loving your neighbor. It is an emotional form of hatred. It is part of the old life and should have no part of the believer's life. Put it away.

> *1 John 3:15* | Anyone who hates a brother or sister is a murderer, and you know that no murderer has eternal life residing in him.

Malice behaves with a spirit of meanness, an ugly attitude, and a hateful stance. This nastiness of spirit will lead you to is absolute disrespect and a despising of the person who hurt you, or who you think hurt you. They may not even know about it. In moments of frustration and anger and bitterness, this evil of a malicious heart is often felt. This trait cannot be painted dark enough since it is the attitude of Satan himself. In fact, "malice" is a translation of the Greek word for depravity, a vicious disposition of the heart. This kind of disposition, so contrary to the Spirit of Christ, undermines a person's character, grieves the Holy Spirit, and produces the crop of deadly weeds listed in Ephesians 4:31. These characteristics have no place in the life of a child of the King. They are to be put away. [137]

Sanitize yourself from these six sins that God hates: bitterness (hostility and resentment toward someone), wrath (boiling rage), anger

---

[136] H. D. M. Spence-Jones. *The Pulpit Commentary: Ephesians* (Bellingham, WA: Logos Research Systems, Inc., 2004), 153.

[137] Phillips, *Ephesians*, Eph 4:30.

(holding a grudge; giving the cold shoulder, a settled animosity toward someone; an unforgiving spirit), clamor (raising your voice, loud insults), slander (misrepresentation, one-upping in the argument), and malice (wishing evil toward someone). Let me paraphrase Ephesians 4:31 for you: "Let all manner of bitterness, and rage, and grudges, and raising of your voice, and misrepresentation, be taken off of you and thrown in a garbage heap, with all thoughts of evil towards others." Sanitize yourself from these six evils. These are the filthy rags of the old self. Put them off, and throw them far, far away from you in the garbage heap.

Do Reverse Your Anger

Anger in reverse? What does that mean? We've all done things we've wished we could reverse. We've broken something or said something or done something, and we've wished we could rewind the film of life and reverse the damage. But time is irreversible. The Bible offers an alternative way to reverse things.

> **Ephesians 4:32** | Be kind to one another, tenderhearted, forgiving one another, as God in Christ forgave you.

Christ's selflessness is seen in the believer in three ways: through his kindness, his tenderhearted love, and through his gracious forgiveness.

Kindness

> **Ephesians 4:32a** | Be kind to one another.

When you are wronged, you need to be kind, gentle and good, like God is. The word kind in its ordinary usage in Greek means to be "useful." It means to lift a burden, or to do something helpful for the person that offended you. This is exactly what our Lord Jesus has in mind in Matthew 5.

> *Matthew 5:44-45* | Love your enemies, bless them that curse you, do good to them that hate you, and pray for them which despitefully use you, and persecute you; [45] That ye may be the children of your Father which is in heaven.

What are we to do with people who hurt us? Love them. Bless them. Do good to them. Pray for them. Each time we get evil, we are to return good as Paul said: "Do not be overcome by evil, but overcome evil with good (Rom 12:21). Now this word, "kindness," in our context goes beyond mere human decency and usefulness. This word, *chrēstós*, is the New Testament concept of the Hebrew word *chesed*, God's covenant faithfulness or unrelenting love. This loving kindness is an attribute God possesses and displays to his creation, especially his covenant people (Psa 25:7; 31:19; 65:11), and one Paul desires believers to imitate.[138] Instead of vengeance, we should offer to our enemies what God has offered to us, and to the whole world: "the riches of his kindness ... that leads you to repentance" (Rom 2:4).

Tenderness

Ephesians 4:32 | Be ... tenderhearted.

Tenderhearted has the idea of being compassionate and reflects a feeling deep in the bowels, or stomach, a gnawing psychosomatic pain due to empathy for someone's need.[139] This is basic empathy—thinking of the person before we think of ourselves. We might describe this as "jumping into the other person's casket" of pain and suffering. We realize that people who may hurt us are hurting themselves. This empathy gives us the "good sense" to overlook the offence and minister to the person.

Proverbs 19:11 | Good sense makes one slow to anger, and it is his glory to overlook an offense.

As we approach a person to reconcile with them, we often jump to the forgiveness part. We say: "I forgive you," or "Do you forgive me?" It's almost an impatient attitude to not deal with the problem. But if you want good soil for genuine, heartfelt, sincere forgiveness, you have to first begin with kindness and empathy. Without these two virtues, the third and perhaps most important (forgiveness), doesn't have the good soil to thrive in. Water the soil of your enemy's heart with kindness and empathy and you will see the sprout of forgiveness thriving!

---

[138] Benjamin L. Merkle, "Ephesians," in *Ephesians–Philemon*, ed. Iain M. Duguid, James M. Hamilton Jr., and Jay Sklar, vol. XI, ESV Expository Commentary (Wheaton, IL: Crossway, 2018), 85–86.

[139] MacArthur, *Ephesians*, 190.

Forgiveness

Ephesians 4:32 | Be ... forgiving one another, as God in Christ forgave you.

One of the most terrifying elements of the Lord's Prayer is the petition:

Matthew 6:12, 14-15 | Forgive us our debts, as we forgive our debtors. [14] For if you forgive others their trespasses, your heavenly Father will also forgive you, [15] but if you do not forgive others their trespasses, neither will your Father forgive your trespasses.

Our power and ability to forgive others is a definite mark and evidence of genuine faith in the Lord. If we can't forgive others, how can we profess to know God's forgiveness? As Christians we are forgiven people. We are likewise called to be forgiving people.[140] We should always be ready and willing to hit the reset button over and over again in our relationships.

Forgiveness is a wonderful exercise in the same patience and unrelenting love God displayed for us in Christ. That is the standard of the Christian's forgiveness and nothing less. It seems impossible, but it keeps our forgiveness and patience with other dependent on divine empowerment and grace, for such forgiveness is impossible in our fleshly nature. Yet in the Spirit's power, we have unlimited supplies of compassion, kindness and forgiveness.

Conclusion

What we are talking about is going from a hard, selfish, self-centered heart to a heart of tenderness. This is the pathway to an ongoing state of revival. How do we get there? What I am asking you to do is to lose yourself. Specifically, I am asking you to make a list of any sins that you have not forsaken. By forsaken I mean that you have decided before God that you will never return to that sin. If you cannot make a list in your heart about specific areas of disobedience in your heart, then a holy God will not hear you. You cannot regard iniquity in your heart whatsoever (Psa 66:18). You must look deep into your heart for any known sin (Psa 139:23-24). Does your conscience convict you for anything whatsoever? You must forsake it and do this until you have a clean conscience.

---

[140] Sproul, *Ephesians*, 119–120.

Seek a deep repentance from all sin. Search your heart for all known sin. Has there been bitterness or fury or anger or shouting well up inside of you? Have you been unwilling in your life to give over your pride? Now you must grieve over your sin. Grieve with the Holy Spirit who is grieved in you. Tenderness will come no other way. There must be a wrestling in your spirit, an agonizing of soul for the defilement that you have allowed. You have used many things to numb yourself to the pain of your sin, but let every distraction be cast aside and look at your sin. Look at your pride. Look at your selfish living. Look at the wasted time. Now mourn. Grieve. Let your heart break.

Assuming that you have been born again, that you have a new nature, then by confessing and forsaking your sin, you will begin to *sense a renewed revival and tenderness in your heart.* How do you know if you have a clear conscience a tender heart? How do I know when my heart is no longer hardened? Having a clean conscience is another way of saying, "Keeping your heart pure" or "walking in obedience to God" or "walking by faith". We are called to live with a "broken and contrite heart". This is tenderness.

As your heart breaks and you cry out to God to forgive you, you will *sense the cleansing power of God*. Especially as you confess the forgiveness you have received from Christ before others, the joy will increase. The more you sense your forgiveness, the more whole your spirit will be. You will be filled with the love of God. You will have an overwhelming love for God and joy that you are forgiven.

> Galatians 5:22-23 | The fruit of the Spirit is love, joy, peace, longsuffering, gentleness, goodness, faith, [23] Meekness, temperance: against such there is no law.

These are the evidences of the Spirit, and they are more than emotions. They are affections for God. They are all signs of trust and dependence on God. Every one of these shows an abandon to God.

15 | EPHESIANS 5:1-7
ROOTED IN SEXUAL PURITY

Therefore be imitators of God, as beloved children.
EPHESIANS 5:1

Today we are talking specifically about how we can have victory over sexual sin, and live godly, wholesome and pure lives. This kind of living is the exact opposite of the sinful, selfish, rebellious, greedy, and sensual culture that we live in. How can we avoid the temptation to sexual sin and other life dominating sins?

R. Kent Hughes gives a fantastic illustration in his commentary on the book of Ephesians. He tells of a little boy's mother who had just baked a fresh batch of cookies and placed them in the cookie jar, giving instructions that no one touch them until after dinner. But it was not long until she heard the lid of the jar move, and she called out, "Son, what are you doing?" To which a meek voice called back, "My hand is in the cookie jar resisting temptation!" The fact of the matter is, no one can resist temptation with his hand in the cookie jar. There are open cookie jars all around us. The ever-present cookie jar of our culture is the television, dwelling in the heart of nearly every home in America. Turn it off, and the goodies are present on the internet on your computer and also on your phone. There are cookie jars in an open magazine or a billboard. There are living cookie jars everywhere, inviting passersby to taste their wares. It would be so easy. But when the cookies of sin are removed from the jar, their sweetness is soon revealed to be poison, resulting in misery of the soul. [141]

Keeping one's hand out of the cookie jar is a challenge for all of God's children, and Paul addresses this problem in Ephesians 5. Bear in mind that these verses were addressed to Christians who had come to Christ while living in the notoriously sin city of Ephesus. In that wicked metropolis the dominant religion was the worship of the multi breasted goddess Diana, and ritual prostitution was a way of life. Moreover, there was cultural acceptance of sexual perversion as a valid, and even exalted, way of life. Ephesus is a paradigm of any of the great cities of today's world — from Chicago to San Francisco, New York to LA, Berlin to Madrid, in all of the cities to the farthest reaches of the world, sin is spreading. [142] And we as Christians will stop the spread because the *Holy* Spirit is in our hearts. He will not allow us to be like the world, immersed in pornography and sensuality. Paul calls us to transformed living by realizing four very important things that matter: priorities, people, purity, partnerships.

> **Ephesians 5:1-7** | Therefore be imitators of God, as beloved children. ² And walk in love, as Christ loved us and gave himself up for us, a fragrant offering and sacrifice to God. ³ But sexual immorality and all impurity or covetousness must not even be named among you, as is proper among saints. ⁴ Let there be no filthiness nor foolish talk nor crude joking, which are out of place, but instead let there be thanksgiving. ⁵ For you may be sure of this, that everyone who is sexually immoral or impure, or who is covetous (that is, an idolater), has no inheritance in the kingdom of Christ and God. ⁶ Let no one deceive you with empty words, for because of these things the wrath of God comes upon the sons of disobedience. ⁷ Therefore do not become partners with them.

Sex is a big deal in our culture. The warning Paul gives is to be completely different from the sexualized culture around us and instead reflect the transcendent holiness and purity of God. I've seen so many Christians fall time and time again in the area of sexual sin because they did not take the admonitions seriously that Paul gives in Ephesians 5:1-7. To be sure, this passage is not merely about sexual sin. It's about any life dominating sin. We learn that the Christian's call is to reflect and

---

[141] Hughes, *Ephesians*, 156.
[142] Ibid.

imitate God instead of our depraved culture. No sin should dominate the Christian's life. We are not slaves of Satan for sinning, but slaves of righteousness for God. We should imitate the Lord.

PRIORITIES MATTER: IMITATE GOD (5:1)

Ephesians 5:1 | Therefore be imitators of God, as beloved children.

Our Desire to Imitate God

Paul gives us what has been considered the loftiest command in the Bible. Imitate God! Are you mimicking the beauty of his holiness? They say the highest form of flattery is imitation. The new birth places us in a new family where we are God's beloved children. We all bear the resemblance of our heavenly Father, and our greatest desire is to imitate his heart. The highest compliments I have ever received have been from my children is one of imitation. They'll say, "I want to be just like you when I grow up." As we follow God, our children will want to mirror our tenderness and devotion to God. My daughters, when they were young, would say, "I want to marry someone just like you Daddy!" Wow! Are there any words that are more powerful (and scary) that a father can hear? Just as children in a human family often imitate their parents, so in God's family we are to imitate God. He is our model and prototype. We long to be like him!

Our Endeavor to Imitate God

We are called to be imitators of God as dear children. How is it possible to imitate one who is infinitely above us, the sovereign God of the universe? Certainly, there are some ways we can never be like God. We call these incommunicable attributes. They are what make God to be the transcendent God that he is. God has no beginning – he is eternal. He's all powerful, all knowing, and everywhere present at once. In these ways we cannot imitate God but only submit to him. But there are many attributes that we are to imitate. God calls us to "be holy as I the LORD am holy" (Lev 20:26). He calls us to walk and live in the fruit of the Spirit: to walk in "love, joy, peace, patience, kindness, goodness, faithfulness, gentleness, self-control" (Gal 5:22-23). In fact, 1 Peter tells us that if we are growing in these things, we can "make" our "calling and election sure" (2 Pet 1:10). We can know we are children of God by the priorities of our life. It is our highest desire and endeavor to imitate

God since God put that desire in our hearts. It's our spiritual DNA. Listen to the words of Spurgeon:

> If your life is unholy, then your heart is unchanged, and you are an unsaved person. The Savior will sanctify his people, renew them, give them a hatred of sin, and a love of holiness. The grace that does not make a man better than others is a worthless counterfeit. Christ saves his people, not in their sins, but from their sins. Without holiness, no man shall see the Lord.[143]

O how the child of God seeks after holiness, to be just like God! God is the highest priority of the believer's life. Nothing competes or compares to our devotion to our loving heavenly Father. Priorities matter.

PEOPLE MATTER: LOVE PEOPLE (5:2)

Not only are we to pattern ourselves after God as dear children, but we are to pattern our lives after the love of Christ. Christ showed us that people matter. This is why we must walk in love toward God and others. It's not enough to learn about God and have our own personal walk with Jesus. That's vital, perhaps more than anything. But to be growing and changing in holiness, we have to actually imitate God who sacrificed his Son. There has to be life-on-life discipleship if we are to be holy. We cannot say we love God if we do not love our brother. We demonstrate that we are truly God's children by imitating the sacrifice of the Father, the sanctity of the Spirit, and the suffering of the Son.

> **Ephesians 5:2** | And walk in love, as Christ loved us and gave himself up for us, a fragrant offering and sacrifice to God.

Our Walk of Love

To walk in love is to live the crucified life, since true agape love is to love sacrificially for those who do not deserve it. Our love will be meaningful to others if we can guard our integrity in this cesspool of filth that we live in with all sincerity and purity and faithfulness. Paul later makes the connection of how we are beloved children of God who are to have nothing to do with the sexualized culture all around us. We cannot say we love the Body of Christ if we are also loving the world. No one can serve two masters (Mt 6:24). To be pure, we ought have no

---

[143] Charles Spurgeon. *Evening by Evening* (New Kensington, PA: Whitaker House, 1984), 41.

partnership with the world. When we say no to the world's lies and deceptive delights (like chocolates filled with poop), we are guarding our heart from idolatry which leads to utter misery. We are also protecting the Body of Christ from defilement. It is not loving to compromise my own testimony with any kind of impure thoughts or allowing impure images into my mind, since it will paralyze me spiritually, and hinder my ability to let the Spirit flow through me to others. That's the love we are to walk in. Paul goes on to describe how this love will lead us to have nothing to do with the defiled and sexualized culture of the world, and to live as the sincere, beloved children of God that we are. This indeed is "a fragrant offering and sacrifice to God."

Christ's Demonstration of Love

Walking in love for the believer entails a deep admiration and imitation of Christ, who laid down his life in love for the human race. Indeed, God demonstrated his deep and everlasting love toward us "in that while we were still sinners, Christ died for us (Rom 5:8). Paul calls us to walk in love with God and others, living as a sacrificial lamb for God's glory and for the good of others. He intimates a love toward God that demonstrates a total surrender to him, just as Christ walked in love with his Father, willing to obey the Father in all things, even to go to the cross and give himself up for us according to his Father's plan. He also intimates a total sacrifice for our fellow human beings, for whom Christ died. To live this way is an aromatic, savory offering that smells sweet to God. Paul gave us an entire chapter about how to "walk in love" toward others in 1 Corinthians 13. Love is the fulfillment of the law. As Christians we are called to sacrifice, and to "fill up the sufferings" of Christ, daily laying down our lives, being willing to sacrifice and suffer in Christ's stead (Col 1:24).

Christ lived a life unspotted from the world. He was the perfect unspotted lamb who "gave himself up" for us. The world system is set up for to pamper self and forget others. The Christ life is the opposite. With love and empathy toward sinners, Christ took our hell upon himself, willingly bore the wrath of God on our behalf, and was crushed that he might reconcile us to God. Christ didn't just use words to express his love but jumped into our grave, into our casket, and empathized with sinners as a sympathetic High Priest.

The Pleasing Aroma of Empathy

Our empathy and sacrifice toward the Body smells so good to God. The fragrant offering imagery is helpful to understand how God himself receives our love and worship. The Old Testament sacrificial system is quite fascinating in this regard. A man who had peace with God would bring his best cow or his best lamb and offer it to God for the community. The whole community would smell the savory bar-b-que, and they would come and dine. They would "taste and see" that the Lord is good! They could smell the sacrifice. It was like being invited to a $100 plate dinner for free. That's what Christ did for us. We can lay down our lives in a number of ways, through empathetic listening in our fellowship with one another, humbly washing each other with the Word, and sweetly praying over one another. This is how the Spirit works. The sweet-smelling aroma of our service toward one another when someone is in need or helping a brother or sister or family through generosity and sacrifice is a joy to the Spirit who dwells within us. Is the aroma of empathy toward the Body wafting up to the Father? Are you empathetic like our compassionate High Priest? He jumped into our casket. Before you give a legalistic instruction to your fallen brother or sister, in humility lay your life down for them. Soften their hearts with the empathy of Christ. Give them hope to come out of their casket by pointing them to the transcendent, infinite God who can rescue them. Then in love, pull them out of their idolatry and walk side-by-side with them in holiness, like Faithful walked with Christian in the story of Pilgrim's Progress.

This kind of love is inviting. It is attractive. It's a savory aroma to God and to believers around you. When you believe in someone and care for them, it makes such a difference. Compassion and tenderness are so important. Don't be rude, be gentle. Think the best, hope the best. Paul says that's what love is. If you don't have love, you are like a "resounding gong" or a "noisy cymbal" (1 Cor 13:1-3). People don't care that you know all about God until they know that you care about them.

PURITY MATTERS: AVOID SEXUAL SIN (5:3-4)

> **Ephesians 5:3-4** | But sexual immorality and all impurity or covetousness must not even be named among you, as is proper among saints. ⁴ Let there be no filthiness nor foolish talk nor crude joking, which are out of place, but instead let there be thanksgiving.

Here we are instructed of an absolutely essential mindset that you must master to live a transformed life. It is the mindset of avoiding sexual sin, of purity. The word translated "sexual immorality" is the Greek word *porneia*. It means "any kind of sexual sin whether in thought or deed."[144] One of the ways Paul teaches Christians how to imitate the love of God says very simply: avoid sexual sin. Sexual sin is very different from the love of God. Sexual sin is the epitome of selfishness and a craving to serve self. Sexual sin is a display of the world's self-centered "love" which is merely turning people into objects to be used and abused for one's own satisfaction. It can be as innocent as "loving" someone for how they make *you* feel or what they do for *you*. The Apostle Paul says there's no place for sexual sin in our life, none at all. Such were some of you. You used to be like this, this is in the past, but since you've come to Jesus Christ that's all gone, and now there's no place for that.

> *1 Corinthians 6:9-11* | Or do you not know that the unrighteous will not inherit the kingdom of God? Do not be deceived: neither the sexually immoral, nor idolaters, nor adulterers, nor men who practice homosexuality, [10] nor thieves, nor the greedy, nor drunkards, nor revilers, nor swindlers will inherit the kingdom of God. [11] And such were some of you. But you were washed, you were sanctified, you were justified in the name of the Lord Jesus Christ and by the Spirit of our God.

The Corinthians might have said, "Well sexual activity is just a biological thing. It's no offense against the Lord!" Paul answers such an argument to the Corinthian church in the very next verses.

> *1 Corinthians 6:12-13* | All things are lawful for me, but I will not be dominated by anything. [13] ...The body is not meant for sexual immorality, but for the Lord, and the Lord for the body.

It's not just a biological thing. Your body was not meant for sexual immorality. Your mind was not made to view porn. Your body was made for the Lord. Indeed, the author of Hebrews tells us that a person who persists in sexual immorality will be judged.

---

[144] Johannes P. Louw and Eugene Albert Nida, *Greek-English Lexicon of the New Testament: Based on Semantic Domains* (New York: United Bible Societies, 1996), 770.

Hebrews 13:4, KJV | Marriage is honourable in all, and the bed undefiled: but whoremongers and adulterers God will judge.

Paul says in Eph. 5:5 that this kind of sin should not be once named among us. In other words: there should not even be a hint of sexual sin among any of us, and yet it seems there is far more than a hint among professing Christians.

Statistics clearly prove that pornography addiction has become an enormous problem in America. For instance, according to Dr. Laura Schlessinger, on-line adult entertainment is now a $5-6 billion a year industry. One researcher estimates that 60 million Americans have visited sexually explicit web sites. These figures only represent Internet porn. The numbers involved with pornography as a whole are even greater. "But what does this have to do with the Church?" you ask. Apparently quite a lot. Studies and polls have shown that the percentage of Christian men viewing pornography is the same as that of nonbelievers (33-50%). This could explain the findings of Barna Research, which found that 35% of born-again Christians believe sex outside of marriage is "morally acceptable." The Spirit through Paul says: sexual sin is not acceptable, but it is rotten, selfish, and thoughtless.

Sexual Sin is Rotten

Ephesians 5:3 | But sexual immorality and all impurity ...must not even be named among you, as is proper among saints.

Impurity (*akatharsia*) is a more general term than *porneia*, referring to anything that is unclean and filthy. Jesus used the word to describe the rottenness of decaying bodies in a tomb (Mt 23:27). The other ten times the word is used in the New Testament it is associated with sexual sin. It refers to sinful sexual thoughts, passions, ideas, fantasies, and every other form of sexual corruption.[145] Impurity, or uncleanness has the idea of the rottenness or filthiness of the maggots that eat the corpses. It is used eleven times in the New Testament. Jesus uses it to describe a rotting, stinking corpse. The other ten times, it is used to describe sexual sin. It is to take that which is good and holy, and to rob it and abuse it, and turn it into a rotten thing. Sexual sin is called rottenness because it takes what is good and pure and turns it into rot.

---

[145] MacArthur, *Ephesians*, 200.

Marital intimacy is so precious that those who partake in the sin of *porneia* turn sexual intimacy into rot! It destroys lives. When you are tempted by another person's body, think about that person standing before God. Think about the father and mother of that one. Think about what you are destroying.

> *1 Thessalonians 4:3-8* | For this is the will of God, your sanctification: that you abstain from sexual immorality; ⁴ that each one of you know how to control his own body in holiness and honor, ⁵ not in the passion of lust like the Gentiles who do not know God; ⁶ that no one transgress and wrong his brother in this matter, because the Lord is an avenger in all these things, as we told you beforehand and solemnly warned you. ⁷ For God has not called us for impurity [*akatharsia*], but in holiness. ⁸ Therefore whoever disregards this, disregards not man but God, who gives his Holy Spirit to you.

Sex is designed by God to increase selflessness in marriage. Both married men and women are designed to need sex. A wife, to be intimate, needs her husband to pursue her heart, to cherish her above all women, and to treat her with true, unconditional love. Over time, this builds sexual desire in a wife so that she willingly wants to give herself to her husband. A woman who respects and supports her husband makes the husband want to pursue his wife, first as a dear companion and friend, and then sexually. We will find later in Ephesians (5:25ff) that this is actually a picture of Christ and the church.

Sexual Sin is Selfish

> **Ephesians 5:3** | But sexual immorality and all impurity or covetousness must not even be named among you, as is proper among saints.

Paul speaks of sexual sin as covetousness, which sounds a bit unusual. When you see it as "greedy", it begins to make sense. To catch the force of Paul's words, we need to understand that the word "greed" is sexually freighted in this context. It means greed for someone else's body. Marcus Barth renders it as "insatiability."[146]

It seems that 33-50% of professing Christians, both men and women, think it's ok to struggle with sexual selfishness that leads to pornography or adultery from time to time. The Spirit of God has a

---

[146] Marcus Barth, *Ephesians* (New York: Doubleday, 1974), 561.

different opinion. Through Paul he says: he says: "Let it not be once named among you." There ought not be a hint of the sexual selfishness in the Christian life.

A Testimony of Self-Control

The opposite of sexual selfishness (covetousness) is self-control, and in the Greek mind, it is the ability to say no to self, especially in the area of sexual sin. It is actually found ten times in the New Testament – and it is one of the ninefold fruit of the Spirit in Galatians 5:22-23. The first place we find the preaching of self-control in the New Testament is in Acts 24 where Paul is confronting the Roman proconsul Felix with the gospel. We read:

> Acts 24:25 | For And as he reasoned about righteousness and self-control and the coming judgment, Felix was alarmed and said, "Go away for the present. When I get an opportunity, I will summon you."

Do you know what he was doing? Felix had married Drusilla in an adulterous relationship, and here is Paul in front of Felix, this powerful man, and he says to him, I'd like to give you a sermon Felix. It has to do with the righteousness of sexual self-control as opposed to lack of self-control, which leads to the judgment of God. What he was doing was nailing Felix to the wall on his own relationship to his wife. 1 Corinthians 7:9 says that if a godly man and a woman "cannot exercise self-control, they should marry. For it is better to marry than to burn with passion." In other words, the only legitimate use of intimacy is in marriage.

A Testimony of Appropriateness

Sexual selfishness does not at all align with the Christian faith. It shouldn't be named even once among us—not even a hint—because it's not a proper display of the Christian faith. It's obvious that when we say we have the resurrection power of Jesus, but we have no power to put off sexual selfishness, it does not compute. It's doesn't make sense. God's given us a legitimate way to fulfill those sexual impulses that he gave us for his glory: marriage.

Sexual Sin is Thoughtless

Ephesians 5:4a | Let there be no filthiness nor foolish talk nor crude joking, which are out of place...

People who go after pornography are not at all thinking of others. They are only thinking of themselves. Out of their mouths often come foolish and filthy talk. That which is sacred has become worthless to them, merely an object for their own satisfaction. Thoughtlessness is one of the major strongholds of Satan. Paul gives us three ways to defeat it. We can say no to Satan's grip on us in three ways: No to filthiness; no to foolish talk, and no to crude joking.

No to Thoughtless Filth

Ephesians 5:4a | Let there be no filthiness.

Filthiness is defined as: "obscene, shameful speech involving culturally disapproved themes—vulgar speech, obscene speech, dirty talk."[147] Pornography, and all sexual sin makes God's good gift of sex so defiled in such a thoughtless way. Pornography in particular appears harmless because it seems so nameless. But filthiness is not nameless. You cannot be thoughtless about filthiness if you are a Christian. Attached to every image is a name that God knows, a soul that he cares for, a face that he constructed for his glory, not for a person's sick and sinful fantasy.

One of the great steps forward against sexual sin is to put a name and personality to the face since every person is loved by God and made in his image (Gen 1:26ff). The picture of the sensual woman on a billboard has a mother and father. She's someone's daughter. She may be someone's mama. When you see that, you ought to feel compassion for her and hatred against the devil. "Get her off that billboard" should be your prayer. "Lord save her soul and clothe her not only with clothing, but with righteousness. Every person in the pornographic, filthy images is a person. This is why thoughtless, filthy talk is forbidden for the Christian. It's "out of place" (4:4d). As Christians, we are the ones rescuing people from pornography, not participating in it.

Instead of speaking of the filth of depraved sexual talk, we should exalt sex in the way the Song of Solomon does. The sexual union is

---

[147] Nida, "αἰσχρολογία", *Greek-English Lexicon*, 392.

referred to with exalted, discreet language. Solomon speaks of gardens and leaping gazelles and flowers. All is hidden and discreet and as a result, sex is wonderfully exalted. To bring it out in the open and talk about it in such banal ways is to shame it, make it depraved, and to humiliate the participants in it. There should be no filth by bringing sex outside of the marriage bed.

> Marriage is honourable in all, and the bed undefiled: but whoremongers and adulterers God will judge. —Hebrews 13:4 (KJV)

No to Thoughtless Talk

Ephesians 5:4b | ... nor foolish talk.

To avoid sexual sin, you cannot even put up with what Paul calls foolish, or thoughtless talk about sex. The idea of "foolish talk" is that it is quite literally moronic (from the Greek work *morologia*[148]). This word refers to buffoonery. Even Christians can be guilty using or listening to this silly talk. As Christians we should be sensible, serious, and sincere remembering the words of our Lord.

> Every idle word that men shall speak, they shall give account thereof in the day of judgment. —Matthew 12:36

The word "idle" means careless or thoughtless. It does not mean there is no thinking at all. It means that there is little or no thought for eternity. Every person who has experienced the new birth should be thoughtful when it comes to our conversations, especially about sex. God takes your words seriously. So, should you.

How can we talk moronically about the act that depicts Christ's love for the church? It is sacred. It is exalted. We must not debase sex.

No Thoughtless Joking

Ephesians 5:4c | ... nor crude joking.

We cannot have any part of "crude joking" which is defined as flippant talk or innuendo. The word literally means "to turn something with a quick wit".[149] Be very careful with humor. Our words are not to be flippant but serious, especially when it comes to sacred intimacy reserved for marriage. Even our humor ought to have an edifying

---

[148] Nida, "μωρολογία", *Greek-English Lexicon*, 431.
[149] James Orr, ed. *International Standard Bible Encyclopedia* (1915), *jesting*.

purpose. Let us be clear that humor is a divine gift that can be used to open and refresh the soul, but it ought not be flippant. Be careful of flippant words. The goal of flippant humor is simply a good laugh, not the glory of God. It is hard to go from clowning around to the gospel. We ought to use our humor for the glory of God, not simply for laughter. This is an area that we all struggle in greatly, especially in the lightness of our day and age.

Thoughtlessness is Out of Place

Ephesians 5:4d | Let there be no filthiness nor foolish talk nor crude joking, which are out of place.

Godly sex is sacred. Making it filthy is out of place. Godly sex is serious. Speaking of it thoughtlessly as a Christian is completely out of place. Godly sex is exalted since it is a picture of Christ and the church. Talking about it crudely debases God's good gift, and it is completely out of place for the Christian.

Godly Sex is Celebrated

Ephesians 5:4b | ... instead let there be thanksgiving.

Instead of sexual sin and the rottenness, selfishness, and thoughtlessness that comes with it, there ought to be a celebration of godly sex that elevates it with a spirit of thanksgiving. In Ephesians 5, we may be tempted to see God with a negative view of sex, since he forbids all kinds of sexual immorality. But there is no abstinence needed from the sex he designed. Marital sex was created for the purpose of dealing with mankind's loneliness by mirroring the covenant relationship between Christ and his church (Eph 5:25-33). Orgasm is only the biological part of sex. If biological impulse is ripped away from the beauty of committed marriage, then we vandalize the beauty of sex and place ourselves not much higher than the animal world that lives on raw impulses. Sex becomes a meaningless biological activity if it is ripped away from marriage, using the person for raw impulses alone. Marriage on the other hand is a giving of oneself in covenant faithfulness to another person in unconditional, sacrificial agape love. Sex then becomes elevated to something much more than a biological impulse, but an appropriate expression of empathy and care for a person you have committed not just to have sexual relations with, but to have a friendship like no other friendship, to be young together, grow old together, make mistakes together, clean up messes together. In many marriages this also means raising children together, which brings a whole other level of selflessness. People with healthy marriages testify that sex in marriage is far more satisfying, because it is far more intimate.

Celebrate God's Gift of Sex

Let us celebrate and be thankful for God's gracious gift of sex within marriage. Great sex takes a high level of maturity, of serving another person intentionally, of taking responsibility emotionally and socially to be kind, empathetic and loving. It is to be fully enjoyed in the marriage. It's hard to believe sometimes how richly the Bible celebrates sex. Consider some of the heightened language the Scripture uses to describe the holy delight of marital sex.

> *Proverbs 5:15-20* | Drink water from your own cistern, flowing water from your own well. [16] Should your springs be scattered abroad, streams of water in the streets? [17] Let them be for yourself alone, and not for strangers with you. [18] Let your fountain be blessed, and rejoice in the wife of your youth, [19] a lovely deer, a graceful doe. Let her breasts fill you at all times with delight; be intoxicated always in her love. [20] Why should you be intoxicated, my son, with a forbidden woman and embrace the bosom of an adulteress?

What is King Solomon saying? That the breasts of a wife are intoxicating! He compares it to drinking out of a fresh cistern, with clean water. So refreshing! So strengthening. So clean.

Reject the Enemy's Sex

On the other hand, we might compare selfish sex with pornography or sex outside the marriage covenant to drinking out of a broken cistern. Sexual sin is from Satan. He uses God's good gifts to enslave you and to humiliate you. Consider sinful sex as drinking from a broken cistern.

> *Jeremiah 2:13* | For my people have committed two evils: they have forsaken me, the fountain of living waters, and hewed out cisterns for themselves, broken cisterns that can hold no water.

The filth of sex outside of marriage is like drinking from a broken cistern. When water enters a fresh cistern, the fresh water separates from any impurities and the water can be enjoyed. But a broken cistern is drained of all fresh water, and one is thereby left to drink the dregs of what might flow there like filth and camel dung. Selfish sex hardens the heart to the point where you don't realize you are trying to squeeze sustenance out of camel dung to drink. It defiles you because you have to harden your heart to discard the value of the woman you are stealing from, whether in a photo or a brothel, you are a heartless, selfless, worthless person to do that. It's worse than sucking on camel dung. Instead, drink from God's fountain of living water. Dare to love that special someone enough to marry them. Men, marry that girl before you touch her. Women, don't let him touch you until you are married. Prize the gift of sex and give it to each other on the wedding day.

Of course, there is an entire book of the Bible given the entire marriage relationship, from singleness, to dating, to betrothal, to marriage to growing old together. Listen to the Peasant Princess as she thinks to her wedding day with King Solomon.

Song of Solomon 2:7 | I adjure you, O daughters of Jerusalem, by the gazelles or the does of the field, that you not stir up or awaken love until it pleases.

The love she has for her future husband, she does not want to prostitute and defile it by giving her sexual desires to him before they are covenanted together in holy matrimony. She holds her body, her heart and the electricity of sexual desire very carefully, since it is such a precious gift she wants to give to her husband-to-be. She's got plenty of desire, but she knows she's not married until she's married. She can't let her mind go down that road because she has no appropriate place to fulfill it.

Song of Solomon is much more than a love poem (it is that!), but it is also a wonderful guide to choosing a mate, living well together in marriage, and growing old together. Not only that but it is an incredible metaphor for the relationship between Christ and his bride. It may seem beyond the realm of possibility, especially for singles and newly married people, but God designed the joy of sex to be a faint picture of the intense joy available to us in our walk with Christ.

PARTNERSHIPS MATTER (5:5-7)

Paul makes some shocking statements in this passage: (1) a life of unrepentant sexual immorality will send a person to hell. It's not that it cannot be forgiven but that a hard, unrepentant heart displayed in a life of lose sexual activity is not one that is in any way redeemed. No kingdom citizen could live comfortably in sin for a lifetime. Another shocking statement: no matter how eloquent the words of a professing believer or how sound the theology of said professor of the faith

The Damnation of Immorality

> **Ephesians 5:5** | For you may be sure of this, that everyone who is sexually immoral or impure, or who is covetous (that is, an idolater), has no inheritance in the kingdom of Christ and God.

What does Paul mean? Well, first, consider what this does not mean. Paul doesn't mean that the true believer will never be tempted with sexual sin. It also doesn't mean that the believer will never fail. What it does mean is that those who are damned reveal their own damnation because of their comfort level with sin. They may talk big, have good theology, but big talk is empty and cannot hide the fact that they have "no inheritance in the kingdom of Christ and God."

The Spirit through Paul gives a helpful description about those who may claim Christianity but continue in sin. He later calls them "sons of disobedience" (5:6). The idea is that disobedience dominates their lives. The only way out is to leave that sinful behavior, by repenting from the heart. A true Christian can no longer partner with sexual immorality or any kind of life-dominating sin.

Also, we must not limit damnable living to merely sexual sin. Really, in Paul's lists of categories of sin that keep people out of the kingdom, there are many areas of enslavement to sin. When you have enslaving, life dominating sin, you need total restructuring. Drunkenness, pornography, drug addiction, eating disorders, a pattern of sinful anger, and sexual immorality are just a few examples of what we could call life-dominating sins. They usually affect every area of life. Paul speaks of many of these very problems as sin (1 Cor 6:9, 10; Gal 5:19-21). Throughout the Word of God, they are seen as enslavements that dominate every area of life and cause heartache for the person. Indeed, they bring on the wrath of God (Eph 5:18; 1 Cor 6:12; Deut 21:21; Pro 20:1; 7:6-23; 23:29-35; Isa 5:11, 13, 22; Joel 3:3; 1:5; Amos 6:6; Hosea 4:11).

Life dominating sin of whatever sort will affect every aspect of life: a person's eating habits, home relationships, sleep, job, friends (social life), church attendance and service, emotions (self-pity, anger), economics (finances), health, character and practices (like deceitfulness), marriage and family life. The drunkard, homosexual, drug addict, the abusive bully, are insecure, unhappy people who are destined for hell if they do not repent.

The Deception of Immorality

Let me give you some hope. Sexual sin can be conquered if you are willing to admit the truth to yourself! You must take it seriously. Those who don't do anything about sexual sin die and go to hell because they are lost. I can think of no greater delusion than for someone to think they are a believer and then upon meeting God on Judgment Day to be turned away to enter the flames of destruction. Paul warns us that a person's profession and practice must line up for us to receive their testimony as true.

> **Ephesians 5:6** | Let no one deceive you with empty words, for because of these things the wrath of God comes upon the sons of disobedience.

One of Satan's greatest abilities to deceive is that he can "masquerade as an angel of light" (2 Cor 11:14). He looks good on the outside but is vile on the inside. Timothy McVeigh was a person of great masquerading abilities. McVeigh is known as the most infamous American terrorist in our history. On April 19, 1995 he detonated a homemade truck bomb in front of the Alfred P. Murrah Federal Building in Oklahoma City. The attack killed 168 people and injured over 800 people. What made McVeigh dangerous was that he looked like an ordinary person. He walked away casually from the scene undetected, leaving a bomb that would cause the most amount of damage to the most amount of people. Sexual sin is like the Timothy McVeigh of sins. It looks harmless, but it is cold, calculating, and absolutely deceptive. It will bring such damage into your life. Sexual sin can even damn your very soul.

Don't Be Deceived

The way forward for anyone involved in life dominating sin is to put off the deception that accompanies such sin. Don't be deceived by empty words.

> **Ephesians 5:6** | Let no one deceive you with empty words.

We have to understand the level of deception that was in the atmosphere of the great city of Ephesus. The temple prostitution of

Artemis (Diana) was widespread, not only through Ephesus, but through the entire Roman Empire. We read about Paul in Ephesus in Acts 19.

> *Acts 19:23-27* | About that time there arose no little disturbance concerning the Way. [24] For a man named Demetrius, a silversmith, who made silver shrines of Artemis, brought no little business to the craftsmen. [25] These he gathered together, with the workmen in similar trades, and said, "Men, you know that from this business we have our wealth. [26] And you see and hear that not only in Ephesus but in almost all of Asia this Paul has persuaded and turned away a great many people, saying that gods made with hands are not gods. [27] And there is danger not only that this trade of ours may come into disrepute but also that the temple of the great goddess Artemis may be counted as nothing, and that she may even be deposed from her magnificence, she whom all Asia and the world worship."

Becoming a Christian meant leaving the prostitution cult of Diana that everyone in Ephesus and the world seemed to participate in. Sex was a part of their daily worship that was widespread in the Roman Empire. For instance, one historian writes:

> All kinds of immoralities were associated with the Greco-Roman gods. Not only was prostitution a recognized institution, but through the influence of the fertility cults of Asia Minor, Syria, and Phoenicia it became a part of the religious rites at certain temples. Thus, there were one thousand "sacred prostitutes" at the temple of Aphrodite at Corinth.[150]

The same has been said for the temple of Artemis (Diana) in Ephesus.

> People visited the temple for different reasons: the sailors came because the temple was a brothel, and the grounds were surrounded with palatial outbuildings for temple girls of different prices. Every female devotee of Diana (the Roman name for the goddess Artemis) served two years as a prostitute in the temple precincts with most of her earnings going into the temple treasury. The cult of Artemis taught that by profane intercourse the worshiper insured the increase of financial prosperity.[151]

---

[150] Everett Ferguson, *Backgrounds of Early Christianity* (2d ed.; Grand Rapids: Eerdmans, 1993) 64.

[151] John W. Cowart. *Ephesus: A Wonder of the World* (2005). Accessed 8 February 2021. http://www.cowart.info/Ephesus/ephesus.html

With such a level of sexualization, there can be a deep-seeded pressure to deceive. Some in Ephesus who professed Christ did not want to endure the shame of rejection in walking out of the Diana cult. They was surely pressure to have one foot in the church and the other in the temple of Diana. In Paul's day, there was likely a great blindness to the fact that sexual sin was that bad at all, since it was so deeply imbedded into the culture. Surely Paul is addressing those in who would profess to know Christ while still visiting Diana's temple and participating in the sexual ceremonies.

The point is whether in ancient times or today, a person indwelt with Christ's Spirit would know the shame of sexual sin. Don't be deceived because those who know Christ will be free from sexual sin. They don't merely rely on good theology. Even the best understanding of theology is mere "empty words" if it is not accompanied by the power of a pure life.

Today, the shame of porn and other life dominating sins makes the success of accountability software for phones, computers, and tablets hard to measure. If a person is willing to look at porn, they are willing to lie. The person enslaved to sexual sin has deceived and rationalized sin for so long, he may even believe his own lies. The woman hiding her porn addiction from her husband is so filled with shame, she is likely to keep lying, which may push her to greater and greater enslavement to cover her pain. The only way out for life dominating sin is a divine accountability, which the Old Testament calls "the fear of the Lord." The fear of the Lord is the beginning of wisdom (Pro 1:7) precisely because that fear/worship/reverence is the result of inviting the presence of the Lord into every thought, word and deed. That's an accountability that isn't vulnerable to a software hack!

If straight up deception doesn't work, Satan has another strategy to weaken and defeat Christians and families today. He teaches us to redefine or in some way excuse sin. If he can get you to call sin a sickness, then you don't need to take responsibility for it. There are so many excuses for sin today. The LGBTQ crowd might say: "I was born this way." The under achieving child may say: "I have ADHD." There are many excuses: "My alcoholism is a disease." "My parents abused me." "I'm Irish." Whatever! We cannot defeat sin unless we call sin what it is: sin! Paul speaks of these very problems as sin (1 Cor 6:9-10; Gal 5:19-21).

If you find no power to change in your life, and these sins characterize your life and dominate them, then take the warning seriously: your big theological words may be putting a Band-Aid on a spiritual cancer. You are deceiving yourself and others if you think a child of God can live comfortably in sin. Indeed, the discomfort you feel is just the beginning of God's wrath against you if you don't repent.

The only way to freedom for a child of disobedience is to become a child of God. For the lost person, one or many life dominating sins characterize their life. For the porn addict, sexual sin is his or her life. They can't stop and they don't want to stop. The addict lives for liquor or pot or meth, or what have you. The Christian says, "for me to live is Christ" (Phil 1:21). If you live for sexual pleasure, you cannot have assurance that you have eternal life. Once a person accepts Christ or the believer is reassured of his salvation, he or she can begin to fight.

Tell the Truth

To begin to leave the pathways of sin, you must first admit in your heart that addiction, in whatever form that you are dealing with, has been replacing the true fulfilment in life that only God can give a person through his Son Jesus. Sin is not a disease, but an idolatry of heart. If you can tell yourself the truth and "walk in the light," there is hope (1 Jn 1:7). All true Christians can claim the promise of Romans 6.

> Romans 6:14 | For sin will have no dominion over you, since you are not under law but under grace.

The Deliverance from Immorality

Ephesians 5:7 | Therefore do not become partners with them.

The only way forward is a forsaking of sin by finding a greater joy and satisfaction in Christ. Let me give you some hope. If you partner with God in your sex life, you will avoid so much misery and experience so much happiness. Stop partnering with Satan in your sex life. Stop getting advice from Lucifer for sexual pleasure. God invented sexual pleasure, so you should partner with God and get advice from our good Father. Sexual sin can be conquered and godly sex in marriage should be enjoyed. Selfish sex is satanic sex—it is not meant to help you, but to kill you and make you a miserable slave. You cannot partner with the enemy and expect anything but the mangling of your soul.

I heard the story of a man who was leading a Safari in Kenya in an animal reserve. They were all hundreds of miles from a telephone and many miles even from a main road. The guide is trained to work with lions in the reserve. He's an expert. He knows how to keep his distance. He has several assistants with tranquilizer guns. The people were amazed to see the wild animals. They were a safe distance away, but the guide seemed dangerously close and was in the lion's sights. Suddenly the guide is ripped away from all security and finds himself looking into the mouth of hungry and irritated lion. As his life flashes before his eyes, he realizes he has seconds to live. Suddenly the sound of a gun explodes, and the lion falls over. His life is spared because someone on that safari knew the vicious nature of lions and came prepared.

Now we cannot pull out a gun and shoot Satan, but we can resist him and make him flee from us. Peter tells us:

1 Peter 5:8-9a | Be sober-minded; be watchful. Your adversary the devil prowls around like a roaring lion, seeking someone to devour. Resist him, firm in your faith.

It is possible for a true Christian to become "partners" with the evil one in some life dominating sin, but it is impossible to be happy or comfortable in sin. The true Christian takes a militant stand against any hint of the insatiable impulse for sinful sex. John Owen once said, "You will be killing sin, or else sin will be killing you."[152] God has given us victory and freedom from life dominating sins. John tells us: "Greater is he that is in you than he that is in the world" (1 Jn 4:4). Jesus said, "Anyone who sins is a slave to sin" (Jn 8:34). If you are miserable in the shackles of sin, come to Jesus afresh and anew.

Find Jesus as a Refuge

To those who are enslaved in the bondage of sin Jesus says, "Come unto me all who are weary and heavy laden, and I will give you rest" (Mt 11:28). There is a rest for the person enslaved to sexual sin. There is a place of freedom and enjoyment of Christ that releases us and expels the power of sexual sin through a new and more powerful affection. There is a sweetness in Christ is far better than anything sex or anything else in this world can offer. "But how? How can I have this freedom?" you ask. We get a clear answer in the rest of the chapter, but

---

[152] Owen. *Mortification of Sin*, 154.

the first answer is that without partnership with God in salvation through a new heart, there is no hope for release from sexual slavery. Those without Christ await a Christless eternity, no matter how much they promise they know him. God may be revealing your sexual sin to help you see how lost you may be. If you are dealing with sexual sin, as a Christian, you can reconnect with God in a powerful way that will deliver you. If you are lost, you will find yourself powerless to leave your sexual sin behind.

Flee Sexual Temptation

What should you do when you encounter temptation? Remember Joseph? He was tempted by Mrs. Potiphar. What should you do when you encounter temptation? Run! Do as Joseph did and get out of the situation. Have nothing to do with it. God always gives us a way of escape.

> *1 Corinthians 10:13-14* | No temptation has overtaken you that is not common to man. God is faithful, and he will not let you be tempted beyond your ability, but with the temptation he will also provide the way of escape, that you may be able to endure it. ¹⁴ Therefore, my beloved, flee from idolatry.

We are to flee idolatry of any kind. Idolatry is another word for the wrong kind of heart worship. John Calvin said, "The heart is an idol making factory." [153] Anything that takes the place of God is an idol. The moment you take a good blessing from God, like sex, money, food, friendship, and start demanding it and needing it like a savior, you have begun to worship idols.

It's no surprise that God's good gift of sex can be easily turned into an idol. The Bible warns us quite often to avoid making sex an idol. Sexual sin will not make us happy, but miserable.

> *Proverbs 6:26-29, NKJV* | For by means of a harlot a man is reduced to a crust of bread; and an adulteress will prey upon his precious life. ²⁷Can a man take fire to his bosom, and his clothes not be burned? ²⁸Can one walk on hot coals, and his feet not be seared? ²⁹ So is he who goes in to his neighbor's wife; whoever touches her shall not be innocent.

---

[153] John Calvin, *Institutes of the Christian Religion*, Ch XI, Para 8.

Proverbs 6:32-33, NKJV | Whoever commits adultery with a woman lacks understanding; He who does so destroys his own soul. [33] Wounds and dishonor he will get, and his reproach will not be wiped away.

Have no partnership with these sins! Don't put yourself in places where you are tempted.

Forsake Life Dominating Sin

I believe Paul is expanding on what Jesus said. Jesus tells us we have to radically amputate sin in every part of our lives.

Matthew 5:27-30 | You have heard that it was said, 'You shall not commit adultery.' [28] But I say to you that everyone who looks at a woman with lustful intent has already committed adultery with her in his heart. [29] If your right eye causes you to sin, tear it out and throw it away. For it is better that you lose one of your members than that your whole body be thrown into hell. [30] And if your right hand causes you to sin, cut it off and throw it away. For it is better that you lose one of your members than that your whole body go into hell.

Job 31:1, NKJV | I have made a covenant with my eyes; Why then should I look upon a young woman?

Forsake sexual sin and glorify God with your body in godly marital sex. Use your body as the temple of the Holy Spirit that it is.

1 Corinthians 6:18–20 | Flee from sexual immorality. Every other sin a person commits is outside the body, but the sexually immoral person sins against his own body. [19] Or do you not know that your body is a temple of the Holy Spirit within you, whom you have from God? You are not your own, [20] for you were bought with a price. So, glorify God in your body.

Pleasure is part of sin's seductiveness and addictiveness. Sin is seductive because it offers temporal pleasure over which I have some control. Eve, when she sinned in the garden, not only wanted what was good, pleasing, and desirable, she also wanted the godlike status of being able to satisfy herself, of being her own self-sufficient source of pleasure. Pleasure's temporal, finite nature makes it addictive. Consider

Jeremiah 2:23-24 | How can you say, 'I am not unclean, I have not gone after the Baals'? Look at your way in the valley; know what you have done—a restless young camel running here and there, [24] a wild donkey used to the wilderness, in her heat sniffing the wind! Who can restrain her lust? None who seek her need weary themselves; in her month they will find her.

Jeremiah compares giving in to sinful seduction to an animal in heat. Once we start down the path of finite pleasure, we feel a sense of urgency, an immediate. If you wish to seek the food of this world, then you will consume it until it gushes from your nostrils (Num 11:18 – 20). If you wish to separate yourself from the spiritual umbilical cord that connects you to God, then you will enslave yourself to endless addictive cycles to fill your God-vacuum. [154]

Find Ultimate Satisfaction in Christ Alone

Sexual sin can be conquered because the love of Christ is more powerful than sexual sin. What is it that is more powerful than the desire for sex and money and impurity? It is the love and intimacy we have with Christ. It is the power that is greater than sex. How do we defeat the enslaving idols of the heart? Thomas Chalmers called it "the expulsive power of a new affection." He said:

> The heart is not so constituted, and the only way to dispossess it of an old affection is by the expulsive power of a new one. [155]

The pathway out of any idolatrous affection is to find a greater, more overwhelming affection. Those who know Christ are set free from the slavery of sin because we are so satisfied with him, we need nothing else. The true Christian cannot live comfortably in sin, dismissing God from his thoughts. He can't just escape and check out. He Christ alone can satisfy our desires and give us the expulsive power of a new affection.

> *Philippians 3:8* | Indeed, I count everything as loss because of the surpassing worth of knowing Christ Jesus my Lord. For his sake I have suffered the loss of all things and count them as rubbish, in order that I may gain Christ.

> *Psalm 63:3* | Because your steadfast love is better than life, my lips will praise you.

---

[154] Robert Kelleman. *Gospel-Centered Counseling: How Christ Changes Lives* (Grand Rapids, MI: Zondervan, 2014), 147-148.
[155] Chalmers. *Expulsive Power,* 19.

Psalm 16:11 | In your presence there is fullness of joy; at your right hand are pleasures forevermore.

Find your rest and satisfaction in Christ alone. As Augustine once said:

> You have made us for yourself, O Lord, and our heart is restless until it rests in you.[156]

Conclusion

If you read this and fear that you may not be born again, take heart. The fact that you fear might mean that you truly do know Christ. You have a tender heart, and that is a wonderful evidence of the Spirit. This is not the time to gain assurance. This is the time to repent and turn back to Christ. "Therefore, as you received Christ Jesus the Lord, so walk in him" (Col 2:6).

Make a purity commitment with your parents or with a trusted friend if you are a single adult. A purity commitment might look something like this:

- Commitment #1: I commit to reserve my purity for the person God wants me to marry. I commit not to give my body in any way to anyone except to the person I have committed my life to on the day of holy matrimony.

- Commitment #2: I commit to refuse to participate in conversations that promote or joke about immorality. If I do speak in this way, I will confess to those I was conversing with that I sinned.

- Commitment #3: For men and women: I commit to wear modest clothing that in no way promotes sensuality. I will "occasionally" ask a godly believer if my clothing is too revealing (too tight, too short, etc.).

- Commitment #4: I commit to confess each time I view pornography or have any sexual contact with an accountability partner to who will help me keep this covenant. I commit to register with the technology of choice that

---

[156] Aurelius Augustine. *Confessions*, (Book 1,1-2,2.5,5: CSEL 33) 1-5.

promotes the wisdom and safety of accountability whether or not I struggle with pornography.

There is hope! God promises to conform all of His children into the image of his dear Son, Jesus Christ (Rom 8:28-29). We must take every provision to avoid sexual immorality of any kind. It ought not once be named among us. The fight is real against sexual sin. You may be discouraged at times. You may fall and fail, but the righteous will keep getting up and moving forward. Consider God's promises.

Proverbs 24:16 | The righteous falls seven times and rises again, but the wicked stumble in times of calamity.

1 Thessalonians 5:24 (KJV) | Faithful is he that calls you, who also will do it.

Philippians 2:12-13 | Work out your own salvation with fear and trembling, [13] for it is God who works in you, both to will and to work for his good pleasure.

16 | EPHESIANS 5:8-21
ROOTED IN THE SPIRIT'S FILLING

Do not get drunk with wine, for that is debauchery, but be filled with the Spirit.
EPHESIANS 5:18

What would happen if you pull into a gas station and fill your car up with diesel? I even saw a gas station that had kerosene. That could have some devastating effects on a car. In order to benefit from the diesel, you have to have a diesel engine. In the same way, there is only one way to live the Christian life: in the power of the Spirit. The arm of the flesh will fail you. Paul says in another place:

Galatians 5:16 | Walk in the Spirit, and you will not gratify the desires of the flesh.

It is that very truth that Paul is giving in this passage. He says later in Ephesians 5:18, "...do not get drunk with wine, for that is debauchery, but be filled with the Spirit." As Christians, we to be continually filled with the Holy Spirit. What does that look like? Paul paints it for us here in Ephesians 5.

Ephesians 5:8-21 | For at one time you were darkness, but now you are light in the Lord. Walk as children of light [9] (for the fruit of light is found in all that is good and right and true), [10] and try to discern what is pleasing to the Lord. [11] Take no part in the unfruitful works of darkness, but instead expose them. ¹² For it is shameful even to speak of the things that they do in secret. ¹³ But when anything is exposed by the light, it becomes visible, ¹⁴ for anything that becomes visible is light. Therefore it says, "Awake, O sleeper, and arise from the dead, and Christ will shine on you." ¹⁵ Look carefully then how you walk, not as unwise but as wise, ¹⁶ making the best use of the time, because the days are evil. ¹⁷ Therefore do not be foolish, but understand what the will of the Lord is. ¹⁸ And do not get drunk with wine, for that is debauchery, but be filled with the Spirit, ¹⁹ addressing one another in psalms and hymns and spiritual songs, singing and making melody to the Lord with your heart, ²⁰ giving thanks always and for everything to God the Father in the name of our Lord Jesus Christ, ²¹ submitting to one another out of reverence for Christ.

THE REGENERATION OF THE SPIRIT (5:8-10)

Ephesians 5:8 | For at one time you were darkness, but now you are light in the Lord. Walk as children of light.

The image here is of a completely new nature: we were not just in darkness, but we were darkness. Now, because of the regenerating work of the Holy Spirit (Eze 36:25-27), we are now light in the Lord. There has been a conversion. Now we have the new ability to actually walk as children of the light.

During the Feast of Tabernacles there was a great ceremony called the "Illumination of the temple" which involved the ritual lighting of four golden oil-fed lamps in the Court of Women. These lamps were huge menorahs, like candelabras that were seventy-five feet high. They were lighted in the temple at night to remind the people of the pillar of fire that had guided Israel in their wilderness journey and God's Shekinah glory that once filled the temple. All night long the light shone their brilliance; it is said, illuminating the entire city. During this ceremony the priests and Levite's would use their own worn-out clothing for wicks. In celebration and anticipation, the holiest of Israel's men danced and sang psalms of joy and praise, before the Lord. This festival was a reminder that God had promised to send a light, the true Light, to a sin-darkened world. [157]

---

[157] Mitch and Zhava Galser, *The Fall Feasts of Israel* (Moody Bible Institute: Chicago, 1987).

Imagine that you are in ancient Jerusalem during the Feast of Tabernacles. Visualize seeing these massive menorahs giving a tremendous amount of light. Now imagine the impact of the words said by Jesus in the temple courtyard when he announced:

> John 8:12 | I am the light of the world. Whoever follows me will never walk in darkness, but will have the light of life.

The light that Jesus promises is not the light of the pillar of fire. That pillar just represented the true fire, the Shekinah glory, the very presence of God. If we follow Jesus, He promises that we will have the light of life, which is the Holy Spirit. This is exactly what Paul was saying in Ephesians 5:8.

In Conversion We Have A New Nature

> **Ephesians 5:8** | For at one time you were darkness, but now you are light in the Lord. Walk as children of light.

The premise of "walking as children of light" is the fact that darkness has been turned to light. Darkness is referring to the unregenerate state. We were at one time lost, unregenerate, darkness. But now you are light; now you are saved. It's a radical nature change. Paul is using the metaphor of creation, calling light out of the darkness, to illustrate the miracle of regeneration. There's been a fundamental change in nature. Think of the Genesis account. Man's fallen nature is akin to the earth that was "without form and void" with "darkness covering the face of the deep." But what did God say? "Let there be light!" (Gen. 1:1-3). Suddenly, order came out of chaos. Light came out of darkness. That's a powerful picture of what God has done in our soul when we came to know Jesus. He changed the very nature of our heart in regeneration. In regeneration, we get the nature of our Father. Biblical counselor Robert Kelleman describes it beautifully.

> Like Father, like son. We are born again of incorruptible seed. Born from above to reflect the image of our Creator. We are reborn with a new nature, a new heart — new soul, mind, will, and emotions — reborn with a renewed ability to relate (to God, others, and our self), think, choose, and feel in Christlike ways. God creates a new heart within us — new capacities, disposition, inclinations, purity. The old dies. The new lives. We are not only sons and daughters

(reconciliation); in Christ we are saints. This is the amazing grace of regeneration. [158]

Paul refers to this very thing when describing the radical change that happens to a believer when they are born again.

2 Corinthians 4:6 | God, who said, "Let light shine out of darkness," has shone in our hearts to give the light of the knowledge of the glory of God in the face of Jesus Christ.

When God created man, he formed him in his own image and after his own likeness. In man's fall into sin, the moral image of God in man became corrupted and distorted. Our mind which had been illumined by divine truth became spiritually blind. We became "darkness". It is not that we were merely in spiritual darkness. Our very nature was spiritual blind, dark, depraved, fallen. Our main problem is not that we are in and among dark and sinful influences. It is not our sinful environment. It is not our friends or our family or the movies we watch. Without Christ we can do *nothing*. He alone can bring our dark hearts to being hearts that glow with the light of his presence. Jeremiah, the prophet of old said:

Jeremiah 17:9 | The heart is deceitful above all things, and desperately wicked: who can know it?

Sinners are blinded by their own sinful heart, the very nature that informs their will. Most don't even seek a change. Various warnings are given throughout the Word of God unveiling the depraved nature of the lost person.

Romans 3:10-12 | None is righteous, no, not one; [11] no one understands; no one seeks for God. [12] All have turned aside; together they have become worthless; no one does good, not even one.

Job 14:4 | Who can bring a clean thing out of an unclean? not one.

Jeremiah 13:23 | Can the Ethiopian change his skin, or the leopard his spots? then may ye also do good, that are accustomed to do evil.

1 Corinthians 2:14 | The natural person does not accept the things of the Spirit of God, for they are folly [*irrational*] to him, and he is not able to understand them because they are spiritually discerned.

---

[158] Kelleman. *Gospel-Centered Counseling,* 188.

Paul says without Christ we are "darkness". Before salvation, we were living in the realm of darkness where the god of this world, Satan, had blinded our eyes. But look at our present light. Christ has "delivered us from the power of darkness, and hath translated us into the kingdom of his dear Son" (Col 1:13). We are now "light in the Lord". We now have the power to say *no* to sin and *yes* to God. You have the power to follow God. You have the power as he says in verse 1, to "be imitators of God as dear children". You now have the nature to do what is right. You can say with Paul, "I can do *all* things through Christ who strengthens me" (Phil 4:13). Whatever his will is you have the power to do it. In conversion we are given a new nature. And out of that new nature comes a new behavior.

In Conversion We Have a New Behavior

Ephesians 5:8b-9 | Walk as children of light [9] (for the fruit of light is found in all that is good and right and true).

Wherever there is a true nature change (light) there is always fruit that is attached to the tree. Wherever there is the root of something, there will be fruit. God says you cannot separate salvation from godly living. James says, "faith without works is dead" (Jas 2:26).

Throughout the Bible we find that the fruit of faith is a godly life. Godly living does not save us – rather it is the evidence that we are saved. Motion does not make a car a car. It is simply a car doing what a car does. Jesus says, "You will recognize [true and false converts] by their fruits" (Mt 7:16). "A good tree does not bring forth corrupt fruit, neither does a corrupt tree bring forth good fruit" (Mt 7:18). John reminds us:

> *1 John 3:6, 10* | No one who abides in him keeps on sinning; no one who keeps on sinning has either seen him or known him.... [10] By this it is evident who are the children of God, and who are the children of the devil: whoever does not practice righteousness is not of God, nor is the one who does not love his brother.

From this passage, I want you to see the impossible command: to "walk as children of light" (5:8b). We who were so long used to walking in darkness are now able to walk that shines with the pure light of God. God has imprinted his likeness in the heart of every true believer and re-created our inner being into the "new self, created after the likeness of God in true righteousness and holiness" (4:24). In that transformation, God put within our nature the capacity to desire true righteousness and holiness. As a bird loves to fly like the mother and father bird that birthed him, so a Christian loves to imitate his heavenly Father. A true child of God finds it pure joy and pleasure to imitate God. Why? Because he has been given the capacity to imitate God. It is now his nature.

A Christian is designed to live for Christ. A fish is designed to swim. Birds are designed to fly. Worms are designed to crawl. Christians were designed to live in conformity to Jesus Christ. When you take the bird out of the sky and swim the bird, you kill the bird. When you take the dog off the leash and drop him from the sky, you kill the dog. When you take the fish out of the water and walk the fish, you kill the fish. So, the first humans, Adam and Eve, when they departed from the design of their Maker, they destroyed themselves (and all after them). Christians, through the new birth, are redeemed and redesigned with a new nature that soars above the sinful world in the righteousness of Christ.

And so as dear children, we want to imitate God. As newborn babies, we desire the "sincere milk of the word". We sincerely want it, and we sincerely hold to it. Godly behavior that imitates the Father flows from a transformed heart. And that brings a desire to please the Lord in all things.

In Conversion We Have a New Master

Ephesians 5:10 | And try to discern what is pleasing to the Lord.

Being regenerated, you have a decision. You can live like a sinner — your past identity under Satan — or you can live as a saint — your new identity in Christ. Sin has already lost. Christ defeated it. He's your Master now, not sin. More than that, he's your Victor now. He fought the battle, conquered sin, crucified your old nature, and implanted a new, potent nature within you. In your deepest being you now want to reject life dominating sin, and you have the power to do so.

What does Paul mean when he says true children of light discern what is acceptable or pleasing to the Lord? The word proving means to put on trial, to examine, or to try by fire.[159] In the Greek translation of

---

[159] Spiros Zodhiates. *The Complete Word Study Dictionary: New Testament* (Chattanooga, TN: AMG Publishers, 1993), G1381.

the Old Testament (the Septuagint), we find the same word in Proverbs 17:3, "The refining pot is for silver, and the furnace for gold: but the LORD tries the hearts." We ought to examine everything in life to see if it is pleasing to the Lord. The pathway to true happiness is to live out of our new, regenerated heart. They sincerely want to please the Lord.

Children of light don't have to fake their Christian life. They deeply desire to please the Lord. That reminds me of a story from ancient history. In the ancient world, dishonest pottery dealers filled cracks in their inferior products with wax before glazing and painting them, making worthless pots difficult to distinguish from expensive ones. The only way to avoid being defrauded was to hold the pot to the sun, making the wax-filled cracks obvious. Dealers marked their fine pottery that could withstand 'sun testing' as *sin cera*— "without wax." Those who know Christ "walk as children of light" (5:8). They sincerely desire to do "what is pleasing to the Lord" (5:10).

2 Corinthians 5:9 | We make it our aim to please him.

1 Corinthians 10:31 | Whether you eat or drink, or whatever you do, do all to the glory of God.

The word "glory" means "to give the right opinion of." We need to give the right opinion of God as His ambassadors and representatives in all that we do. Every moment we have a choice to make to please God or please ourselves. Can you say in your heart of hearts that you have no other ambition than to please the Lord?

THE ROADBLOCKS TO SPIRIT FILLING (5:11-17)

Ephesians 5:11-17 | Take no part in the unfruitful works of darkness, but instead expose them. ¹² For it is shameful even to speak of the things that they do in secret. ¹³ But when anything is exposed by the light, it becomes visible, ¹⁴ for anything that becomes visible is light. Therefore it says, "Awake, O sleeper, and arise from the dead, and Christ will shine on you." ¹⁵ Look carefully then how you walk, not as unwise but as wise, ¹⁶ making the best use of the time, because the days are evil. ¹⁷ Therefore do not be foolish, but understand what the will of the Lord is.

Worldliness

The child of light should not become involved in evil even by association. We cannot witness to the world if we do not go out into the world; and we cannot go far into the world before coming in contact with all sorts of wickedness. But we are never to identify with that wickedness or give it opportunity to take hold in our own life. To compromise God's standards is to weaken our witness as well as our character. No act of unrighteousness is permissible.[160]

Avoid the Darkness

Ephesians 5:11a | Take no part in the unfruitful works of darkness.

Avoid the works of darkness. They are unfruitful. Christians are to live lives that are separated from the world. They are pilgrims and foreigners in a strange land. As David says often in the Psalms, "I am a pilgrim and a stranger on this earth" (Psa 39:12; Heb 11:13). This world is not my home, I'm just a passin' through!

We dare not take part in the ways of the enemy. You may recognize the name Benedict Arnold. He was a hero on the American side in the revolutionary war until he became a traitor and switched to the British side. We cannot be a traitor to the cause of Christ. We should have nothing to do with the enemy.

Let's be clear what this verse does not mean. We are not to become isolationists. We cannot do that as Christians. We are called to reach the world, not to cut ourselves off from it entirely. We are called to influence the world and to transform it from the inside out.

Avoiding the darkness does not mean that we become preservationists. Godliness is not found in one culture or time period. We are to redeem the culture we are in. "To the weak I became weak, that I might win the weak. I have become all things to all people, that by all means I might save some" (1 Cor 9:22). We have to reach people in their own culture and language, not just export a cultural Christianity that we are comfortable with.

What avoiding the darkness does mean is that we can have no part with sinful activity. We are not even to have contact at all with a fellow believer who is openly sinning. "I wrote you in my letter not to associate with immoral people," Paul said to the Corinthians. "I did not at all mean with the immoral people of this world, or with the covetous and swindlers, or with idolaters; for then you would have to go out of the world. But actually, I wrote to you not to associate with any so-called

---

[160] MacArthur, *Ephesians*, 211.

brother if he should be an immoral person, or covetous, or an idolater, or a reviler, or a drunkard, or a swindler—not even to eat with such a one" (1 Cor 5:9–11; *cf* 2 Thess 3:6, 14).[161]

In order to affect change in this world, we must first protect our life from evil. How effective can a general be if he is cohorting with the enemy? We cannot compromise in our Christian walk. We must maintain holiness and discipline in our life if we are going to be effective. God will not use a dirty vessel.

Expose the Darkness

Ephesians 5:11 | Take no part in the unfruitful works of darkness, but instead expose them.

Compromise with sin is a compromise of your power in Christ to affect the world! Are you affecting the world, or is the world affecting you? How do we have influence on a godless world? Why, it is so simple a child can understand it—they sing about it. "This little light of mine, I'm gonna let it shine."

Matthew 5:16 | Let your light shine before others, so that they may see your good works and give glory to your Father who is in heaven.

Everything ought to be different: what you watch on media and television, how you drive, what spouse you are looking for, how you treat your spouse, your language, your thought life, etc. We should shine and expose the works of darkness. As you live in the light, the light from your life has an amazing effect: it exposes the unfruitful works of darkness.

The effects of darkness and light are antithetical. From the perspective of the sciences, disease flourishes in the dark, and total darkness brings death to earth's fauna and flora. Similarly, spiritual darkness brings sterility — "fruitless deeds," as Paul calls them in verse 11. The popular songs of darkness promise great things but give only barrenness — the "apples of Sodom" as some have called it.[162]

To ignore evil is to encourage it; to keep quiet about it is to help promote it. The verb here translated expose can also carry the idea of

---

[161] Ibid.
[162] Hughes, *Ephesians*, 166.

reproof, correction, punishment, or discipline. We are to confront sin with intolerance. [163]

Silence the Darkness

> **Ephesians 5:12** | For it is shameful even to speak of the things that they do in secret.

Don't even speak of them! We must not be tricked into partaking in darkness by talking about the things that the wicked do in secret. We must not expose ourselves to them. Darkness shelters evil and helps it fester. "Night has no shame." The leaven of sin silently swells in the darkness until the whole life is infected. [164] Start talking about the darkness and examining it, and you will see how Satan tricks you and pushes you into the pool of depravity, into the deep end of the devil's disgusting way of living. People through curiosity have often put their toe in the water only to find themselves swimming in the deep end of the filth of depravity. Don't even speak about these things.

Sleepiness

> **Ephesians 5:13-14** | But when anything is exposed by the light, it becomes visible, **14** for anything that becomes visible is light. Therefore it says, "Awake, O sleeper, and arise from the dead, and Christ will shine on you."

If Satan can keep Christians asleep, he will keep his hold on this world. The moment Christians wake up, they start shining the light everywhere, and people start waking up. Once a Christian awakens, he begins to admonish those who might try to speak of those things that should remain hidden. An awakened life illumines evil to show its consequences. That's why those in darkness are sometimes uncomfortable around Christians.

Light Exposes Sinners

What happens when Christians wake up out of their sleepy slumber? Sinners become arrested when they see their sin visible. Suddenly when a sinner is drawn to Christ, his sins become visible, and almost unbearable. Spurgeon said, for the one converted, "Sin is like a nest of vipers slithering upon you that you despise and want to take off of

---

[163] MacArthur., 212.
[164] Hughes, *Ephesians*, 166.

you!"[165] The light exposes. This is a sure sign of the conviction of the Holy Spirit. Light is that which makes things manifest, that which shows them to be as they actually are. When sin is revealed, it loses its "hiddenness" and is seen for the ugliness it is.[166] What changed Saul of Tarsus? He saw the Lord! What changed Isaiah? "My eyes have seen the King the Lord of hosts" (Isa 6:5).

Light Transforms Sinners

Ephesians 5:14a | For anything that becomes visible is light.

Now Paul gives us a hope for evangelism. Our life and testimony of light not only exposes sin but can also transform the sinner (2 Cor 4:6). Some inevitably come out of the darkness and respond favorably to the light, and they themselves become light: "for anything that becomes visible is light" (5:14). Those who accept the process of reproof and exposure can repent, put their faith in Christ, and become light in the Lord.[167]

Wake Up to the Light!

Paul quotes an ancient text based on Isaiah 60:1-2 likely paraphrased for a hymn of the ancient Church.

Ephesians 5:14b | Therefore it says, "Awake, O sleeper, and arise from the dead, and Christ will shine on you."

If the light of Christ and the gospel is so powerful, why would we as Christians want to remain asleep? We need to see Jesus. We need to wake up. Wake up, sleepy head! Wake up and the light of Christ will shine on you and through you. Get up, get out of bed. Stop being so comfortable in this world. Wake up! Using Isaiah 60:1-2 in ancient hymn form, we see three lines. The first, "Sleeper awake!" is a call for Christians to wake up from their spiritual slumber. Although some view this line as a reference to conversion, it is better to see it as an exhortation to disobedient or wayward believers. The second line, "Arise from the dead" is a reawakening of faith in Christ, arise from sleepy, sinful practices, and awake anew and afresh in Christ's resurrection power. Believers have died to sin and therefore must not let sin enslave them

---

[165] Charles Haddon Spurgeon. *New Park Street Pulpit, Vol 2.* "Turn or Burn" preached December 7, 1856.

[166] MacArthur, 213.

[167] Merkle, "Ephesians," 92.

(Rom 6:11–13). The third line, "Christ will shine on you" is a promise given to those who obey by putting away sin and following the example of Christ. They will awake with resurrection power that shines on them and empowers, guides, sustains, and directs them in their discipleship journey.[168] Such things are so lofty, that talking about them is not enough. Paul, as it were, lifts his voice and sings the ancient hymn!

Wasting Time

> **Ephesians 5:15-17** | Look carefully then how you walk, not as unwise but as wise, **16** making the best use of the time, because the days are evil. **17** Therefore do not be foolish, but understand what the will of the Lord is.

Paul warns us to avoid the unfruitful use of our time. Don't be idle! Our time is not our own. It is a stewardship from God. Therefore, we are called not to use our time for our own comfort, but to please God with it. Our time is perfectly measured. Everyone gets 24 hours in a day. Busy people are not given a special button they can push to get 28 hours. If you find out where that button is, please inform me. Unfortunately, no such button exists. Therefore, a wise person knows we have very little time in this life, and our time must be invested wisely. He remembers the words of James who said, "Life is like a vapor that appears for a little while and then vanishes away." Time is a precious commodity that is quickly passing away.

A Serious Walk

> **Ephesians 5:15** | Look carefully then how you walk, not as unwise but as wise.

In order to make the best use of the time, we need to walk carefully and circumspectly. I've never lived on a farm. But I've visited them. And I can tell you, when you are on a farm you want to walk carefully and circumspectly. You've got to watch where you are stepping! You can't just run through a field on a farm where cows roam. They leave behind these cow patties that aren't pleasant when you step in them. You have to look carefully, keeping a close eye on where you are stepping so you can get to your destination unhindered.

---

[168] Ibid.

In the same way, as believers, we are to watch where we are stepping, not as unwise, but as wise. In other words, we are to live like the people we *are*. In Christ we *are* one, we *are* separated, we *are* love, we *are* light, and we *are* wise—and how we walk and live should correspond to what we are. At salvation every believer has been made wise.[169] Paul wrote to Timothy:

> 2 Timothy 3:15 | You have known the sacred writings which are able to give you the wisdom that leads to salvation through faith which is in Christ Jesus.

Let's be wise and watch where we are stepping as Christians. Let's be friends with sinners, but not act like sinners. Let's be the light, and not put our light under the bushel of compromise or worldliness or sleepy Christianity. Let's shine as lights and walk as wise people.

A Superb Walk

Ephesians 5:16a | Making the best use of the time.

Time is a non-renewable resource. In other words, you live in this moment once, and once it passes away, it is gone forever.

> James 4:14, NKJV | For what is your life? It is even a vapor that appears for a little time and then vanishes away.

That's why Paul says we are to make the very best use of our time. Use it wisely. We are not just to wake up and wonder what we are going to do. We need to be driven by Scriptural priorities.

Redeeming the Mundane Time. Life may be mundane, but we are to redeem your time from the mundane. We spend many hours in getting ready for the day, driving to and from work, down time at work, break time, or doing mundane tasks around the house. Many of the things we do are automatic functions that require no thinking. How can you redeem that time?

If you are driving, turn off your radio. Instead, get an interesting audio book—it could be theological, historical, scientific, whatever. Expand your heart and mind. You can also use an mp3 player in your car for this. Use the mundane time for praying for people. Use the book Operation World. Each day a different country is listed with its needs.

---

[169] MacArthur, 218.

Learn about the countries of the world so that you can have more compassion in prayer and pray for

Redeem the Downtime. Sometimes we have downtime. Don't just let it fly by. The difference between those who change the world and those who are changed and compromised by the world is what you do with your down time. Take time at each time of the day to intentionally meditate on a passage of Scripture. Learn a verse during your morning devotions and bring your mind back to it during your downtime. Instead of surfing the web, checking out Facebook, watching television or media, binge watching Netflix and Prime, etc., do something fun with your family. Read a missionary biography together.

Redeem the Home Time. Husbands, we have a tendency to think that time spent at home is a waste of time. We would never say it, but most men are goal oriented. We like to see big projects accomplished. Most of the time there are no great mountains to scale at home. I have cheated my family out of time so that I can get more projects done at work. What I've realized is that God will bless me with efficient use of my time if I put priorities first. We've got to spend quality time with our family. As I said time is a non-renewable resource. Use it wisely.

Let me also make an application for parents and children. Be careful of time wasters for our children such as video games and films (even though they are good films). As parents we are stewards of our children's time as well. Instead, spend time with your children. Memorize Bible verses together. Play a family game together. Have a family night at home. It doesn't have to cost anything. Time with your family is a non-renewable resource.

Redeem the Crunch Time. Sometimes we find life to be unrelenting, and we feel crushed under the weight of it. It's easy to put things off instead of getting them done. We have to have biblical priorities. We are called not just in getting things done, but in getting the right things done. That means getting done what God wants done and what glorifies him most, no matter what I feel like. The Scottish preacher Alexander MacLaren (1826–1910) put it this way:

> No unwelcome tasks become any the less unwelcome by putting them off till tomorrow. It is only when they are behind us and done, that we begin to find that there is a sweetness to be tasted afterwards, and that the remembrance of unwelcome duties unhesitatingly done is welcome and pleasant. Accomplished, they are full of blessing, and there is a smile on their faces as they leave us. Undone, they stand

threatening and disturbing our tranquility, and hindering our communion with God. If there be lying before you any bit of work from which you shrink, go straight up to it, and do it at once. The only way to get rid of it is to do it.[170]

Our time is perfectly measured. Everyone gets 24 hours in a day. Busy people are not given a special button they can push to get 28 hours. If you find out where that button is, please inform me. Unfortunately, no such button exists. Therefore, a wise person knows we have very little time in this life, and our time must be invested wisely. He remembers the words of Job who said, "My life passes more swiftly than a runner. It flees away without a glimpse of happiness. It disappears like a swift papyrus boat, like an eagle swooping down on its prey" (Job 9:25-26, NLT). Time is a precious commodity that is quickly passing away. Time is a non-renewable resource. In other words, you live in this moment once, and once it passes away, it is gone forever. Use it wisely.

Ephesians 5:16b | Making the best use of the time, because the days are evil.

The days are evil. They are pregnant with things that will fill your time with waste, worldliness, and rob you of your tie. Instead of living without planning, we are to live every moment of time to the fullest. Paul says:

Colossians 3:23 | Whatever you do, work heartily, as for the Lord and not for men.

Young Jonathan Edwards made a series of resolutions one year early on in his life. One of those resolutions reads this way:

Resolved: Never to lose one moment of time, but to improve it in the most profitable way I possibly can.[171]

The missionary-martyr Jim Elliot said in his college days at Wheaton College in Illinois:

---

[170] Alexander MacLaren. *Record of Christian Work* (Moody: East Northfield, Mass, 1910), 338.
[171] Jonathan Edwards. *Works, Volume 1* (Converse: New York, 1829), 68.

Wherever you are, be all there. Live to the hilt any situation you believe to be the will of God.[172]

A Saintly Walk

Ephesians 5:17a | Therefore do not be foolish.

We come to another important principle: don't be foolish in your walk. Foolishness is living life as if there is no God. We need to redeem the time with a wise, God-focused life. We are called to forsake foolish thinking, which biblically is a dismissal of the Lord from our thoughts. The fool says in his heart, "There is no God" (Psa 14:1). The fool is a practical atheist, living as if God doesn't exist or as if God is far away. For the Christian, this couldn't be farther from the truth. We are the temple of the Holy Spirit. God is with us and will never leave us. And yet, sin can blind us in a moment of anger or anxiety or despair, and we dismiss God from our thinking.

Remember the fool is living in the flesh, and the flesh can never be satisfied.

Proverbs 27:20, NLT | Just as Death and Destruction are never satisfied, so human desire is never satisfied.

The fool is willing to just escape and check out. He doesn't like pain, so he seeks pleasure to dull the pain. Christ alone can satisfy our desires.

Philippians 3:8 | Indeed, I count everything as loss because of the surpassing worth of knowing Christ Jesus my Lord. For his sake I have suffered the loss of all things and count them as rubbish, in order that I may gain Christ.

Psalm 63:3 | Because your steadfast love is better than life, my lips will praise you.

A fool will make dumb choices over and over again. He doesn't think about the bad consequences of his choices. He is willing to waste away and die as a result of their choices, only thinking about the next thrill. He has no wisdom or sense. He's numbed and paralyzed his understanding.

---

[172] Jim Elliot in Kenneth Boa's book *Conformed to His Image: Biblical and Practical Approaches to Spiritual Formation* (Zondervan: Grand Rapids, 2001), 269.

A Satisfying Walk

Ephesians 5:17 | Therefore do not be foolish, but understand what the will of the Lord is.

When we understand God's will, we won't have to be foolish. We will be wise and we will be satisfied and most happy carrying out his will. God's will is not for us to be comfortable in this world, but we will be most happy when know his will and pursue it.

How do we find God's will? Begin with prayer which a total submission to doing the will of God. James said that if we lack wisdom, we are to "ask of God, who gives to all men generously and without reproach, and it will be given to him" (Jas 1:5). Then, seek the kingdom, his church, his Word, seek his face in prayer, seek the fellowship of believers, the joy of the Holy Spirit, and all things that display Jesus as King and Lord. If you do that, all the things we seek, like clothing, how to spend our time, what to eat, what to do, and how to walk wisely in this life will all be added unto you (Mt 6:33). When you live this way, you will have perfect peace, tranquil trust, jubilant joy, and wise walking! You will have God's shalom upon you and all around you. There is no happier life when you understand what the will of the Lord is!

False Worship

Ephesians 5:18a | And do not get drunk with wine, for that is debauchery.

Now Paul's not just picking on the sin of drunkenness. This could be applied to any sinful thing that controls a person and leads them to excess. Every time you turn to an idol instead of Christ, you are wasting your life. Paul is getting at the idea of being filled with anything rather than being filled with the Spirit. He's aiming at false worship.

Of course, it is never the Lord's will for a Christian to be drunk. This especially needed to be said in Ephesus, which was the heart of Greek culture and a wine country where overindulgence was common. The wine-god Bacchus dominated many lives and even enslaved some in the Church — just as it does today.[173]

Obviously, no one who has a lifestyle of drunkenness will enter into the kingdom of heaven. Paul gives a comparison and a contrast with

---

[173] Hughes, *Ephesians*, 172.

wine. Indulgence with alcohol will lead you to debauchery, which literally means "to waste your life" or to be "unsalvageable". It is the very word used of the prodigal son when it says he "wasted his substance with riotous living" (Lk 15:13). Don't yield yourself to this substance that will control you. Of course, this could be said of anything we turn to in order to numb the pain. People turn to all kinds of things to escape the brokenness of this life including co-dependent relationships, materialism, pornography, substance abuse, sex, smokes, you name it, the stress of this life will always lead a person to unraveling. Only the Spirit of God can fill us and give us true satisfaction in our lives.

What is needed is the flood of the Spirit. Jesus told the Samaritan woman, "... whoever drinks the water I give him will never thirst. Indeed, the water I give him will become in him a spring of water welling up to eternal life" (Jn 4:14).[174] Jesus will satisfy us as the Spirit floods our soul with Living Water!

THE REALITY OF SPIRIT FILLING (5:18-21)

Now Paul begins to talk about what life is like for a person that is not at all controlled by this world. He's not drunk with wine or controlled by anything else in this world. Here the reality of Spirit filling is explained.

> **Ephesians 5:18-21** | And do not get drunk with wine, for that is debauchery, but be filled with the Spirit, [19] addressing one another in psalms and hymns and spiritual songs, singing and making melody to the Lord with your heart, [20] giving thanks always and for everything to God the Father in the name of our Lord Jesus Christ, [21] submitting to one another out of reverence for Christ.

What Spirit Filling is Not

There are many ideas of what Spirit filling might be. This concise, straightforward command is loaded with significance for you if you're a believer. However, that significance is often misunderstood, misapplied, or missed altogether. To begin with, many Christians are unclear about what the verse does not mean. Once you discard the incorrect meanings you can then focus on what Paul is really saying.

---

[174] Ibid., 174

Not a Lack of Self-Control

First, the Spirit's filling is not where you lose control, but where the Spirit controls you. So many people look at the filling of the Spirit almost as a holy zap, where it is a mystical happening. It is sometimes confused with a sudden emotion. So many unholy things have been done in the name of the filling of the Holy Spirit. We think of what has been called "the Toronto blessing" and there, people are acting drunk and laughing uncontrollably – calling this a work of the Spirit. People's hearts are twisted, and most people involved in this kind of thing are naïve and confused or even deceptive.

Not Stoic Resolve

Second, being filled with the Spirit is not the notion at the other extreme—simply stoically trying to do what God wants us to do, with the Holy Spirit's blessing but basically in our own power. It is not an act of the flesh which has God's approval. Christianity never urges us to "white knuckle" our sanctification. It has to be in the power of the Spirit.

Not a Second Blessing

Jesus said, "And I will ask the Father, and he will give you another Helper, that He may be with you forever; that is the Spirit of truth, whom the world cannot receive, because it does not behold him or know him, but you know him because he abides with you, and will be in you" (Jn 14:16–17). The Holy Spirit is permanently indwelling all believers upon conversion.[175] Regeneration and indwelling is a one-time act where the believer is baptized in the Spirit, but the filling of the Spirit is a moment by moment surrender to God.

There is such a thing as "Second Blessing" theology that teaches that a person is first saved when he puts his faith in Christ, and then later receives the Holy Spirit's baptism. While we appreciate certainly for a continual filling of the Holy Spirit, we must understand that each believer receives the Spirit at conversion. Holy Spirit baptism is not an extra experience you need to seek; it is something you have from the moment you are saved. This baptism is a theological reality, an act by which Jesus Christ through the agency of the Spirit places you into the Body of Christ (1 Cor 12:13; *cf* Jn 7:37 -39).

---

[175] MacArthur, 246.

An understanding of the Greek for "be filled," *plerousthe*, quite clearly reveals the correct meaning of Paul's command in Ephesians 5:18. A literal translation of the verb would read something like "be being kept filled." The idea is one of keeping yourself constantly filled, as you yield moment by moment to the leading of the Spirit. It fits perfectly with the process of walking by the Spirit.

An accurate rendering of the Greek verb also destroys the widespread old time Wesleyan and modern Charismatic notion that being filled is a one-time emotional experience you initiate, which instantly places you into some inner circle of spiritual maturity.

It's not a second blessing, but a moment by moment blessing we seek where the Spirit takes full control of us. It's a daily yielding, not a second blessing, if you will, but a second, a third, a twentieth, and a thousandth. Each moment we are to be yielding to the Spirit's control.

Not Receiving More of the Spirit

Being filled with the Spirit does not describe a process of progressively receiving him by degrees or in doses. Every Christian not only possesses the Holy Spirit but possesses him in his fullness. God does not parcel out the Spirit, as if he could somehow be divided into various segments or parts. "He gives the Spirit without measure," Jesus said (Jn 3:34).

What Spirit-filling Is

Ephesians 5:18-21 | And do not get drunk with wine, for that is debauchery, but be filled with the Spirit, [19] addressing one another in psalms and hymns and spiritual songs, singing and making melody to the Lord with your heart, [20] giving thanks always and for everything to God the Father in the name of our Lord Jesus Christ, [21] submitting to one another out of reverence for Christ.

Separation from Sin

Ephesians 5:18a | And do not get drunk with wine, for that is debauchery.

Spirit filling is a decision to be controlled by God's Spirit rather than sin. You will always be a slave to something. You are either a slave to God or slave to sin (Jn 8:34; Rom 6:13). A choice to be filled with the Spirit is a choice to be done with all sin. If you are toying with the world you are not filled with the Spirit. Spirit-filled Christians are done looking to the world for satisfaction. They don't turn to idols. They have nothing to do with the unfruitful works of darkness. They want the Spirit to control every part of their heart and life. The Spirit brings a filling that overflows the human soul. It's not just a filling to capacity, but beyond capacity. It's also important to note that when a person is "drunk with wine" it leads to debauchery, doing things that they would never do while sober. In a sanctified way, when the believer is filled with the Spirit, he or she does so much more than they could ever do normally.

The Saturation of the Spirit

Ephesians 5:18b | And do not get drunk with wine... but be filled with the Spirit.

The word "filled" means, "completeness or filling beyond capacity." In context, it is a filling with the Trinity. Believers are to be filled *by* Christ (4:10, "he ascended that he might fill all things"), *by means of* the Spirit (5:18), *with* all of the fullness of God (3:19).[176] "Be being filled", to be technical, is present tense, imperative, passive. This could be literally translated, "Be being filled." It has the connotation of a continuous replenishment, an ongoing and repeated filling. The Spirit-filled life does not rest on yesterday or look to tomorrow but is a moment by moment surrender in the present.

When we use the word fill in English, we normally think of something being placed into a container such as milk being poured to the brim of a glass, water being run into a bathtub, or gasoline being pumped into a gas tank. But none of those examples conveys precisely the meaning of to fill or be filled as does the Greek *pleroo*, a form of which is used in Ephesians 5:18.

Pleroo has three shades of meaning that are helpful in illustrating the scriptural meaning of Spirit-filled. The first carries the idea of *pressure*. It is used to describe wind billowing the sails on a ship, providing the impetus to move the vessel across the water. In the spiritual realm, this concept depicts the Holy Spirit providing the thrust to move the believer down the pathway of obedience. A Spirit-filled Christian isn't motivated by his own desires or will to progress. Instead, he allows the

---

[176] Biblical Studies Press, *The NET Bible First Edition Notes* (Biblical Studies Press, 2006), Eph 5:18.

Holy Spirit to carry him in the proper directions. Another helpful example of this first meaning is a small stick floating in a stream. Most of us have tossed a stick into a creek and then run downstream to see the twig come floating by, propelled only by the force of the water. To be filled with the Spirit means to be carried along by the gracious pressure of the Holy Spirit.

Pleroo can also convey the idea of *permeation*. The well-known pain reliever Alka Seltzer illustrates this principle quite effectively. When you drop one or two tablets into a glass of water, they instantly begin to fizzle and dissolve. Soon the tablets are transformed into clear bubbles throughout the glass, and the water is permeated with the distinct flavor of the Alka Seltzer. In a similar sense, God wants the Holy Spirit to permeate and flavor our lives so when we're around others they will know for certain we possess the pervasive savor of the Spirit.

There is a third meaning of *pleroo*, actually the primary one in the New Testament, which conveys the sense of domination or total control. It's not the vessel being filled, but overflowing, being completely dominated by the flow of water, being carried away, if you will, by a flood, or an ocean.

Spirit filling, in one sense, is a passive idea. Paul says to "be filled," which implies the believer's yielding to the Spirit. We do not fill ourselves, but we yield and surrender to the Spirit who fills us. The work of the Holy Spirit in us and on our behalf, can be appropriated only as he fills us. Paul tells us in Galatians: "Walk by the Spirit, and you will not gratify the desires of the flesh. 25 If we live by the Spirit, let us also keep in step with the Spirit" (Gal 5:16, 25). We see this is a moment-by-moment choice to yield to the Spirit and walk in step with him. This, of course, is not an option for the Christian. We are predestined for holiness (Eph 1:3-4; Rom 8:28-29; Eph 2:10). Those who know Christ will listen and obey him because they have been granted a new nature with the Spirit who causes them to walk in God's statures and moves upon them to carry out his will (Eze 36:25-27). True believers will hear the imperative of this command to "be filled." To not yield to the Spirit is disobedience and foolishness. To yield, for the Christian, is pure joy.

What Spirit-filling Produces

For the God of the universe to fill us is to satisfy us with an infinite blessing and fullness. As a result of this filling a number of things happen for the believer.

Scripture Saturated Speaking

Ephesians 5:19a | Be filled with the Spirit, addressing one another in psalms.

Scripture saturated speaking flows out of the fellowship of Christians when they gather. On one hand, Paul writes about "addressing one another," as opposed to singing and making music, which appear in the next sentence. This led John Stott to call what is involved here fellowship. On the other hand, the sentence does speak of "psalms, hymns and spiritual songs" which sounds like worship. Probably the right view is a combination of the two. It is fellowship, but not that of the coffee hour. It is that deeper, closer communion Christians have when they worship God together.[177]

Singing in the Spirit

When the Spirit fills the believer, there is not only the addressing one another, but also an abundance of singing with one another. This has nothing to do with sheer ability or talent. This has to do with intangible joy.

Ephesians 5:18-19 | Be filled with the Spirit, ¹⁹ addressing one another in psalms and hymns and spiritual songs, singing and making melody to the Lord with your heart.

When you are obeying the Spirit, you are going to be totally given over to God's control, and no matter what is happening, you can sing of God's person. The Psalms, hymns, and spiritual songs are God-centered. We are filled with joy that God is in control, such joy that it moves us to singing! There is singing because there is a joyfulness about God's control. Someone has said, "Things learned in song are remembered long." Martin Luther said:

> Let God speak directly to his people through the Scriptures, and let his people respond with grateful songs of praise.[178]

Luther wanted the whole world to remember Psalm 46. Do you know Psalm 46? You do if you've ever sung, "A Mighty Fortress is Our God." It is important that we sing at church and in the home. Singing

---

[177] Boice, *Ephesians*, 188-189.
[178] Martin Luther in Keith and Kristyn Getty, *Sing!* (Nashville, TN: B&H Publishing Group, 2017), 17.

will aid your families Scripture memory. James tells us that Christians who are cheerful should sing praise to God.

James 5:13 | Is anyone among you suffering? Let him pray. Is anyone cheerful? Let him sing praise.

A Christian sings in private. The Spirit-filled Christian, regardless of his musical ability, will find himself filled with such joy that he or she will burst out with praises in song to God. Paul says you as a Christian will be at times "singing and making melody to the Lord with your heart" (5:19b). Sometimes it's with a worship song on Christian radio. Sometimes the most unmusical people will sing and make up songs to the Lord out of sheer joy. Sometimes a song can be in the heart without a word being said.

A Christian sing corporately. Paul says you will sing both "to yourselves" and "to the Lord." A Spirit-filled Christian finds intense joy in corporate worship. A person who is Spirit-filled is not focused on the musicians or even his fellow believers, but on the Person of God and his truth. When the beauty of God fills the heart, mere spoken words are not enough. God is worthy of our songs of praise and adoration.

Sincere Thankfulness

Ephesians 5:20 | Giving thanks always and for everything to God the Father in the name of our Lord Jesus Christ.

A Christian is sincerely thankful for God's sovereign control and guidance. There is a trust that is displayed with gratitude. A complaining heart is not filled with the Spirit. Choose to be filled with the Spirit by having a thankful Spirit, knowing God is in control of all things.

What is it that we complain about? Perhaps the list includes dirty diapers, layoffs, stubborn spouses, harsh bosses, lazy co-workers, difficult neighbors, crazy drivers, discouraging sickness, your own never-ending tiredness, and insanely frigid weather (if you live where we do near Chicago). Do you complain about these things? You cannot complain and be filled with the Spirit at the same time. Choose to be filled with the Spirit by having a thankful Spirit. That does not mean you are thankful because of all things, but in and through all things you can be thankful that God is conforming you to Jesus Christ. We don't thank God for the painful hit of the chisel, but on what God is doing in us through chisel. It is these trials and difficulties that we should "count all joy" that test your love and stretch your dependence on God's Spirit, conforming you to Christ (Jas 1:2-3, Rom 8:28-29).

Submission to One Another

Ephesians 5:21 | Submitting to one another out of reverence for Christ.

The filling and control of the Holy Spirit will lead us to a spirit of humility. We will desire to seek the welfare of others before our own and to be mutually submissive. The rest of the book discusses how this submission works out. In the rest of chapter 5 and through 6:9, Paul expands on the principle of believers' submission as it controls the relationship of husbands and wives, children and parents, and slaves and masters.[179]

Every one of us has authority over us. All authority on earth is broken, but it is ordained by God in spite of the brokenness. In Romans 13, Paul speaks of government, saying "the powers that be are ordained by God" (Rom 13:1). We all ought to submit with reverence for Christ: children submit to parents, wife submit to husband, husband submit to Christ, all people submit to authority, Christians submit to elders, all of us submit to Christ, and all of us submit one another because of Christ. Christ submits to God, and God submits to no one.

Choose to be filled with the Spirit in your submission to all those in authority over you. Joyfully submit to your supervisors and bosses. Joyfully submit in your family relationships. Wives submit to husbands. Husbands, submit to God by loving your wife, learning her, and leading her in humility and gentleness. Spirit-filled and Spirit-led children submit to their parents.

That brings me to an important point. There is no such thing as the stage of "teenage rebellion". That idea was invented to excuse irresponsible parents. Teenagers who love God will rarely give their parents trouble, much less rebel. In fact, they are often the most fervent people God uses. Think of those who died young in Christ's service: Perpetua (d. 203 A.D., age 21), David Brainerd (d. 1749, age 29), Jim Elliot (d. 1956, age 28). All these served God from a young age and gave their life for Christ. And of course, there are many Scriptural examples of those who served God from their youth: Joseph, Daniel and his friends (Shadrach, Meshach, and Abednego), David, Josiah, and many others.

---

[179] MacArthur, 269.

Study of the Word

This last one we get from the parallel passage in Colossians 3:16. Paul wrote this while he was under house arrest in Rome. Instead of saying "be filled with the Spirit" he wrote a parallel idea. He said:

> *Colossians 3:16* | Let the word of Christ dwell in you richly in all wisdom; teaching and admonishing one another in psalms and hymns and spiritual songs, singing with grace in your hearts to the Lord.

Being filled with the Spirit is the same as "letting the word of Christ dwell in us" in a rich and profound way (*cf* Psa 1:2).

Conclusion

Being filled with the Spirit is vital to understanding the rest of this letter from Paul. He goes on to speak of godly living in the home, relationships between husband and wife and children, and even slaves. He then speaks of our battle in spiritual warfare.

One of my favorite cars was my beloved 1998 dark green Ford Taurus. That car was special because it was a gift to my wife and when we would come home for visits from Spain. Once we moved back, we added a lot more miles on it. I drove it until it couldn't drive any more. I knew it was the end when the transmission gave out. The job of a car's transmission is to make sure that the right amount of power goes to your wheels to drive at a given speed. Cars don't move very well when the gears are paralyzed. Without the Spirit of God in the Christian's life, a person cannot live the abundant life. Before we had the Spirit, we were dead in our sins. The Spirit quickens us and empowers the Christian for full and abundant living. We need to "be being filled" with the Spirit.

17 | EPHESIANS 5:22-24
GOD'S DESIGN FOR WIVES

Wives, submit to your own husbands, as to the Lord.
EPHESIANS 5:22

I heard about an older couple sitting by the fire side. With his arm around his sweetheart, he turned to his wife and said, "After fifty years I've found you tried and true."

His wife was hard of hearing, so she said, "What?"

He repeated, "After fifty years I've found you tried and true."

She replied, "After fifty years I'm tired of you too!"

Ladies, I hope after fifty years you are not tired of your husband! I want to show you the secret to his heart today and the secret to a very happy marriage. The secret to a happy and lasting marriage is for you and your husband to live according to God's design. God has a created order that allows all things to function according to His perfect plan.

Do you ever have conversations with your children, and you are happy and surprised they have a good understanding of something? Many years ago I was talking to my daughter Katie, when she was just a little girl, and I told her wasn't it wonderful to know the Lord and how she will probably one day raise her family in godliness. Her response was delightful. She said, "Isn't my husband going to raise our family?" I told her "Yes, but you are going to be his helper." I was so happy that she understood that. I can't remember ever teaching her, except she's seen it lived out in our home.

The last two chapters of Ephesians is all about Spirit filled living. We could entitle this study "Spirit-Filled Wives" or "Spirit-Filled Families." A Spirit filled family begins with a husband who loves his wife and a wife who is submitted to her husband in surrender to God.

> **Ephesians 5:22-24** | Wives, submit to your own husbands, as to the Lord. [23] For the husband is the head of the wife even as Christ is the head of the church, his body, and is himself its Savior. [24] Now as the church submits to Christ, so also wives should submit in everything to their husbands.

This passage is about married women, but it is vital to everyone here in the Body of Christ today. To those who are single or widowed, these verses are important for you as well. You may get married one day, and you need to pay attention very carefully. Every one of us came from homes and some of them were very dysfunctional. We all need to get a biblical perspective on the home. We are looking at what submission looks like in the family.

THE BEAUTY OF GOD'S DESIGN FOR THE WIFE (5:22-24)

> **Ephesians 5:22** | Wives, submit to your own husbands, as to the Lord.

The Wife is Prized

The word "submit" is Greek military term meaning to arrange troop divisions in a military fashion under the command of a leader. God is our general! We are all to serve where God has put us. Ranks in an army must function together. Without that you have disarray.

To understand when this order was established, please turn back to Genesis 2:18 where the whole foundation is laid for a woman's place in the home. We read that in God's perfect creation there was something "not good." Let's see what that is: "And the LORD God said, It is not good that the man should be alone; I will make him an help fit for him." God made the woman a helper suitable for the man. Married ladies here today, you are designed to be your husband's helper. This is the order God established at the creation of the world.

Without order there is no worth. Imagine I were to show you the car I just purchased. My little Honda Fit. And the engine was strapped into my young son Evan's car seat. And you lifted up the hood and there was Evan playing in the engine compartment. That would be cute, but you would not be very impressed with the way I rearranged my new car! Or imagine you are looking for a new house to put your family in. You walk in, and the toilet and shower are in the living room. It might be convenient, but it devalues the house! You go to the bedroom and next to the hamper with dirty clothes is the dinner table. I think you might lose your appetite! You look in the bathroom and there is a greasy stove next to a sink where a man is shaving. You are either in Alice and Wonderland, or things are quite out of order. When things are out of order, they lose their dignity and value. I say that to make the point that a woman is to be prized. There is a difference between masculinity and femininity. The order is that man is the head, and the wife is to be supportive and submissive.

The Wife is Protected

A woman is to be prized and protected. She is the fragile vase as 1 Peter 3:7 says. She is special. She is so important that she is to be prized. She should be given an environment that she can flourish and grow in. She is not meant to lead. A man is made to protect that which is precious. A wife, in God's order is to be protected.

> **Ephesians 5:22-23** | Wives, submit to your own husbands, as to the Lord. [23] For the husband is the head of the wife even as Christ is the head of the church, his body, and is himself its Savior.

So, man is the head – the head designates authority. Now the sad thing in our culture is that headship has come to be known as a dictatorship, but it is not. It is important that we understand what submission does not mean. Our culture is quite confused when defining submission, because they view it as subservient, but it is not. In fact God's order for the home give a woman the most honor (1 Pet 3:7).

Not Inferiority

First, submission does not mean that a wife is in any way inferior to her husband.

> *Galatians 3:28-29* | There is neither Jew nor Greek, there is neither bond nor free, there is neither male nor female: for you are all one in Christ Jesus. [29] And if you are Christ's, then are you Abraham's seed, and heirs according to the promise.

When it comes to our standing before God, there is no distinction between male and female. We're all equally created in the image of God, equally fallen and in need of salvation. Submission isn't a matter of who is smarter or the most deserving. Submission in marriage is simply another reflection of the beautiful pattern of roles seen in the Trinity. The Son has submitted to the Father through all eternity, fulfilling his will, seeking to please him.[180]

Not Supporting Sin

Secondly, submission does not mean you give into the sinful demands of your husband. No matter what authority has been given to a person by God, no one has the authority to make you compromise your conscience. When the religious leaders told the apostles to stop preaching in the name of Jesus, they replied "We ought to obey God rather than men" (Acts 5:29). If your husband asks you to lie or sin in any way, you should kindly refuse.

Not Universal Agreement

Thirdly, submission does not mean always agreeing with everything your husband does. All human authorities make mistakes. Sometimes we husbands think we are making fantastic decisions, and they turn out to be disastrous. You are allowed to respectfully give counsel to your husband. You are his helper. He needs your help. If after you've clearly given your perspective and prayerfully presented your point of view, your husband continues on a course that you disagree with, but which isn't sinful, you are obligated to support and obey him.[181] In the meantime, you can pray for your husband to make wise decisions, and to help you to trust in the sovereign plan of God.

Not Taking Christ's Place

Finally, submission does not mean that your husband takes the place of Christ. You are to submit to him as unto the Lord, but only the Lord is going to satisfy your longings. Your husband is going to fail. I didn't have to tell you that he has already failed you miserably. Wives, the sooner you realize that the deepest longings of your heart can only be satisfied by God, the happier you will be.

---

[180] Elyse Fitzpatrick. *Helper by Design* (Chicago: Moody Publishers, 2003), 147.

[181] Ibid., 149.

The Wife is Pictured

Ephesians 5:24 | Now as the church submits to Christ, so also wives should submit in everything to their husbands.

Marriage is an earthly institution. "In the resurrection they neither marry, nor are given in marriage, but are as the angels of God in heaven" (Mt 22:30). Why is that? Because our temporary marriages are a type and picture of our marriage to Christ. Marriage on earth points to our eternal marriage to our Bridegroom, Jesus Christ. Paul says, "This is a great profound mystery: but I speak concerning Christ and the church" (Eph 5:32).

A wife is to respect her husband at all times even if he doesn't deserve respect at the moment. This is God's Law. It is his command. God's been making happy marriages for a long time. He's the wisest Being in the universe. He makes no mistakes. The only way your family is going to have God's blessing is if you follow God's pattern. If you decide not to, you are going to severely mess up your life and the lives of your children if you have any. Determine right now to follow God's pattern and demonstrate the picture of Christ and the church.

Pictured in the Trinity

The example for submission is within the Trinity. The members of the Godhead practice submission to one another. The members of the Trinity are co-equal in power and glory, yet the submits to do the Father's will. The Spirit speaks not of himself but of Christ. The word most often used in the New Testament for submission or subjection is a military term that indicates proper placement and rank. It means, "to arrange under, to subordinate, to subject oneself, to obey, to submit to one's control, to yield to one's admonishment or advice."[182]

Submission flows out of your submission to the Lord. On your own you will not be able to submit to your husband's leadership. We see in Genesis 3, that following the Fall, the woman's desire has been to get out of God's created order and take the leadership of the home. God says to Eve: "Your desire shall be to your husband, and he shall rule over you" (Gen 3:16). The idea here is that "Eve's desire will be to dominate her husband," but her place is under the rule of her husband. It was not difficult before the Fall for Eve to submit to her husband. In

---

[182] Nida, *Greek-English Lexicon*, 467.

fact, it was delightful. But after the Fall, we all have self-will and pride and a deceitful heart. Our pride is always going to tell us that our way is best. We have a built- in tendency to distrust authority. But let me repeat, godly submission flows out of a wife's submission to the Lord Jesus Christ. She needs God's strength and grace to trust her husband. Submitting to her husband is submitting to God's created order.

Established at Creation

We need to understand also that submission was established at creation. The woman's place of submission is not a result of the fall but was part of God's divine plan from the beginning.

> *Genesis 2:18* | Then the LORD God said, "It is not good that the man should be alone; I will make him a helper fit for him."

This occurred sometime before the Fall. To depart from God's created order is to depart from God. This was the order before the Fall. "For Adam was first formed, then Eve" (1 Tim 2:13). The wife's purpose in life is to help the man. She is to help her husband achieve his goals. She is to mold the children. She is to be a keeper at home. Based on that order of creation, submission is embracing the mission and vision of your husband. As we said, the word "submit" in our text is a military term used for troop alignment. Soldiers are to carry out the commands of their generals. The general is Jesus. A wife is to follow her husband as her husband follows Christ (1 Cor 11:1).

Wife, do you know your husband's calling? Are you looking out for his interests? Are you helping him or opposing him? Above all, submission is a spiritual issue. It is not simply outwardly embracing your husband's goals and vision, but it is a real submission to the Lord.

THE BATTLE FOR GOD'S DESIGN FOR THE WIFE

A husband is to provide places of safety, so his wife can flourish. Sadly, husbands don't always do that. It's hard to submit when your husband at times is selfish. Sometimes submission can be a battle.

The Struggle of Worthiness

Ephesians 5:22 | Wives, submit to your own husbands, as to the Lord.

Submission is not based on a husband's worthiness. He will never be worthy. Godly submission flows out of a wife's submission to the Lord Jesus Christ. A wife's life must be anchored to the sovereignty of

God. She must trust that God has put them together in marriage, and that the Lord is going to guide her husband. She needs God's strength and grace to trust her husband's leadership. A wife's submission to her husband is ultimately submitting to God and his created order.

Christian men and women struggle with fulfilling their God given roles. Often men do not want to lead, or if they do, they may lead with a heavy hand. Women often do not want to follow, or if they do, they do it with resentment or fear and not joy. Most marriages begin with amazing bliss, but then the honeymoon is quickly over. The man thinks his wife is now going to be his servant. The wife thinks the man is going to forever be Prince Charming. What a wake-up call. Many marriages very quickly descend into nitpicking, unhappiness, a lack of forgiveness, and even deep bitterness at times. Finally, there can be an ongoing anger or rage which leads people to want to end the marriage.

The Battle of Fatherlessness

Over 50% of people in America to seek to end the marriage. Those that divorce think ending their marriage will end the nightmare. A very sad problem when God's plan for marriage is not followed is the children do not have a father in the home. Understand that once a marriage ends, the real nightmare begins, especially for the children. USA Today reported, "The United States has the weakest families in the Western world because we have the highest divorce rate and the highest rate of solo parenting".[183] I want to speak of this firsthand, because I was raised by a single mother. If I had not come to know Christ, I would have been a cause for the crime statistics to go up. I speak from personal experience that without a father in the home, mom goes to work, and children are often left on their own. "A child left to himself brings his mother to shame" (Pro 29:15). Fatherlessness is the greatest weapon Satan has to destroy a nation. If you want to destroy a nation, take the fathers away, and you will destroy the family unit.

Fatherless children are causing many of the out-of-wedlock births in our country. There is a rise in alcoholism, drug use, vandalism, and theft. My friends and I were the vandals that most people are afraid of. When I see vandalism and things defaced, it is a familiar sight. My

---

[183] Sharon Jayson. "Divorce Declining, But So is Marriage" USA Today. Published July 18, 2005. Accessed 25 February 2021. http://www.usatoday.com/news/nation/2005-07-18-cohabit-divorce_x.htm

friends and I would do the same thing to vacant houses when we were children. Most of my friends were from single parent homes, and none of us had a mom who loved the Lord. So, we lived a very sad existence bringing our mothers to shame.

One of my heroes is a dear spiritual mother in the faith, Jane Harding. Jane was married to a man that was good friends with the infamous Teamsters' boss, Jimmy Hoffa, before he disappeared. Jane's husband was a lost sinner. He was unfaithful. He was not always kind to her. He struggled with alcohol. He was so busy with work that he wasn't always home. It's not always possible to stay with a man like that, but Jane was determined not to break up the marriage. As long as she and her children were safe, she wanted her boys to have a father in the home. Was it hard? Yes. One of her son's became a pastor and was one of the men of God who pointed me to Christ when I was young. How does a wife submit to a man like that? She didn't think of her husband's worthiness, because he wasn't worthy to have such a godly wife. She always thought of her submission as following the Lord. Her husband brought her great sadness, but she never lost her joy or determination because her eyes were not on her husband, but on the Lord.

The Unseen Battle

Paul later will tell us where the real battle in the home is: in the unseen realm.

> *Ephesians 6:12* | For we do not wrestle against flesh and blood, but against the rulers, against the authorities, against the cosmic powers over this present darkness, against the spiritual forces of evil in the heavenly places.

Our enemy is another sphere that we cannot physically see. It is not that people are our problem. Wife, you ought not see the cause of your warfare as your husband or children. Our great concern is not with the hurt or harm people can do to us. We must see beyond them to the cause. Our concern is not with people or politics, or political parties, or the physical wars raging across the world. As followers of Jesus Christ, our primary concern is that there is something behind all that we see with our eyes. The unseen authorities of the underworld are fighting against us. We out never to fight against our spouse, but for our spouse. We are in the battle together. You cannot stay standing against the devil without the strength of the Lord. You must take every precaution. You must put on the "whole armor of God" (6:11). Without it you cannot stand against the wiles of the devil. Walk in the Spirit in those gospel shoes. Put on the breastplate of Christ's righteousness, the helmet of your assurance of salvation, the belt of truth found, wrapping yourself in God's Word, guarding yourself with the shield of faith, and above all, take up that greatest weapon, the sword of the Spirit, using the Word of God offensively.

THE BLESSING OF GOD'S DESIGN FOR THE WIFE

Without loving husbands and Spirit-filled submitted wives, the fabric of the family in our country will fall apart. We see the devastation in our country before our very eyes. There has been a 1000% increase in unmarried couples living with one another since 1970 to today. Only one in four households in America have both a married husband and wife in the home. The very hinge of our society is the mother in the home bearing and raising the children and being a help to her husband. Today, we have rejected that as a society. Couples are divorcing at a rapid rate. Some are not getting married at all. We cannot do this without horrific consequences to families and children. Bitter children can easily turn into burdens on society: vandals, gang bangers, fornicators, and thieves. Without the mother keeping the home, there is chaos in society. The wife can have a major impact on changing the world as she upholds God's order of creation in her home. Think of the acronym: H.O.M.E. She is the helper, organizer, molder, and evangelist in the home. That's how a wife can change the world.

The Helper of the Home

She is to submit to her husband and make his breadwinning a success. She is a helper fitted for her husband (Gen 2:18). Eve was made to help and compliment Adam. She is not to be the head of the home. She's got an even more important job than being the head of the home. She is to be the heart and help of the home.

The Organizer of the Home

It takes work, but there is blessing to having a commitment to being a godly wife and mother. She is the organizer of the home. She is to guide the home. Look at Titus 2:3-5, "Older women likewise are to be reverent in behavior, not slanderers or slaves to much wine. They are to teach what is good, 4 and so train the young women to love their husbands and children, 5 to be self-controlled, pure, working at home, kind, and submissive to their own husbands, that the word of God may not be reviled". It is a full-time job to raise a child. It takes all the influence you have. There is no substitute for spending time with your child. You are responsible to organize your child's life according to godliness. You will give an account.

The Molder of the Home

A wife is to bear children if she is able. This is one of the most important jobs in the world. Paul says to Timothy, "So I would have younger widows marry, bear children, manage their households, and give the adversary no occasion for slander" (1 Tim 5:14). Every moment Mom is molding her children. Everything you do is being observed by innocent eyes, taking in their Mama's heart in the home.

We often don't realize the power of simply living for the Lord in front of our children. They are watching us. They are listening. They're not taking notes literally, but they are taking note of every action, and every moment they are applying it to their own hearts. Every decision we make, we are helping form our children to either excuse their behavior because of their parents or making the hard choice to do right since they saw Mom and Dad do right. Molding takes place every moment you are with your children, so make sure you are living for Christ. Talk about your failures with them so they know that even when you sin, you have an Advocate with the Father. They don't need you to be perfect, but they do need you to be humble.

The Evangelist of the Home

Paul says to his spiritual son in the faith: "I am reminded of your sincere faith, a faith that dwelt first in your grandmother Lois and your mother Eunice and now, I am sure, dwells in you as well" (2 Tim 1:5–6). The real key to Timothy's faith was not just missionary Paul. It was missionary Grandma and missionary Mom. The greatest mission field in all the world is not the distant lands of the world. The greatest mission field is your home. The faith of a mother is one of God's greatest weapons against the enemy. A mother's faith covers a child and guides them for a lifetime. You may be a wife without children, but we all have spiritual children that we are called to influence.

I think of the testimony of Jill's family. She is the twelfth generation in her family to accept Christ as Savior. Twelve generations back, her ancestors were Anabaptists. They were actually from a royal family in Switzerland. Three brothers had to flee because of persecution of their faith in Christ. Where would Jill and I be without Jill's faithful mother and father? What about her faithful grandmother and grandfather? What about all those godly mothers and fathers before that? Each generation took it upon themselves to evangelize the next generation. That's the secret to changing the world. That's why the greatest mission field in all the world is the family.

Conclusion

Married ladies, God's way is the best way. His order is the only order. Yield to your husband's headship. Cheer him on. In doing so you are preaching the gospel and showing your submission to the lordship of Christ. Your most influential place on earth is in the home. You are there to be a molder of children. You have the most important job in the world.

18 | EPHESIANS 5:25-33
GOD'S DESIGN FOR HUSBANDS

Husbands, love your wives, as Christ loved the church and gave himself up for her, that he might sanctify her, having cleansed her by the washing of water with the word, so that he might present the church to himself in splendor, without spot or wrinkle or any such thing, that she might be holy and without blemish

EPHESIANS 5:25-27

Husbands, love your wives! So, says the apostle in verse 25. Then he says in verse 32, "This mystery is profound, and I am saying that it refers to Christ and the church." So, this is a message more about worship than it is about wives.

What we are going to find today is that men who don't love their wives have a worship problem, they don't have a wife problem. Husband, how much do you love your dear wife? A husband was watching a football game one night, and his wife stepped in front of the TV and posed a question: Do you love me more than football? To which he replied, "Step aside woman, I can't see the screen." She again asked him if he loved her more than football to which he replied again, "Out of the way." She asked him a third time the same question. He saw her persistence and thought for a minute and said, "I love you more than hockey."

This may be funny, but it is sad. This is really more common than not. Married women are lonely and wish their husbands would just talk to them. Men like this are selfish. They are to prize and protect and provide for the wife. Married men don't love their wives as they ought because they may struggle with a number of things: trusting God and others (so we manipulate and control to hide our insecurity), being selfless (we are only concerned about ourselves), taking responsibility (we can be immature), or asking for forgiveness and admitting we are wrong (we are prideful and even arrogant).

How can you as a married man be the godly husband God wants you to be? I know the married ladies will be paying attention, but the single ladies need to be paying attention too, because they need to know what to be careful to stay away from a selfish, carnal man. A self-centered man will bring you more sorrow than you know. Single men need to pay attention too. You may have the gift of singleness now, but any day God could give you the gift of marriage. Godly husbands are called to be godly leaders, godly lovers, and godly learners.

HUSBANDS SHOULD BE LEADERS (5:22-25)

The husband is the head of the woman. he is her leader.

Ephesians 5:22-25 | Wives, submit to your own husbands, as to the Lord. [23] For the husband is the head of the wife even as Christ is the head of the church, his body, and is himself its Savior. [24] Now as the church submits to Christ, so also wives should submit in everything to their husbands. [25] Husbands, love your wives, as Christ loved the church and gave himself up for her.

What is biblical headship? The text here indicate that headship is an expression of agape love, a love that is willing to sacrifice everything for the well-being of another. Immediately we see that there is confusion about headship. Ask the average man what headship means to them, and he will suggest words like: power, authority, control, or leadership. The Bible uses a different word to describe headship: love. You will exercise your leadership, authority, etc., through your love. Strip authority of love and you have a monstrosity. Raw power is tyranny.

Not Superior Leadership

Ephesians 5:23 | The husband is the head of the wife even as Christ is the head of the church, his body, and is himself its Savior.

To be the "head" of the home is not a relationship of superiority. It is actually using your position to love, build, and nurture a relationship of deep sacrifice with your wife. As husbands, we are to lower ourselves as Jesus did. He came in the form of a servant to lay his life down for us (Phil 2:7-8). Husbands demonstrate their headship by sacrificing themselves for the wife. With that in mind, notice our text does not say "Husbands rule over your wives, command them, demonstrate your authority over them and command them around." It says, "Husbands, love your wives, as Christ loved the church and gave himself up for her." Give yourself up for your wife. Christ is the head of the Church, and as such, he leads her, protects here, and puts all things under his feet, under his authority to do good to her.

> *Ephesians 1:22-23* | And he put all things under his feet and gave him as head over all things to the church, [23] which is his body, the fullness of him who fills all in all.

Christ is the head for the sake of the church. Whatever he does, he does for the sake of his bride. He has her best interests in view.

Not Selfish Leadership

The command for a husband to lead is not to exercise his authority by demanding submission, but the command is to love your wives, "as Christ loved the church and gave himself up for her." This is not an authority that says, "Serve me, meet my needs, fulfill my selfish and petty desires." Rather, this is an authority and a leadership that is sacrificial for the purpose of benefiting your wife.

Servant Leadership

Remember James and John wanted to be leaders, and so they asked if they could sit on either side of our Lord Jesus when he comes into his kingdom. But Jesus said, true godly leadership is exercised by the humble. We are to use our leadership to serve as Jesus did.

> *Matthew 20:25-28* | But Jesus called them to him and said, "You know that the rulers of the Gentiles lord it over them, and their great ones exercise authority over them. [26] It shall not be so among you. But whoever would be great among you must be your servant, [27] and whoever would be first among you must be your slave, [28] even as the Son of Man came not to be served but to serve, and to give his life as a ransom for many.

Serve means to "minister to the needs of others". You are most like Christ when you are serving others, i.e., your wife. Leadership means facing the hard problems and taking the burden off of those who are following you. A deserter runs away from problems. The godly husband serves his wife. He doesn't run and hide behind the TV, work, etc. When a problem sticks its head up, the husband is there to serve. He moves in patiently and meets the conflict head on. He is willing to get his hands dirty in the process of finding solutions, knowing that every problem has a biblical solution. His attitude is "my wife's problem is my problem."

Leadership is not a shield or a sword; it's not a club to beat people with. It's a towel and basin to serve, meet needs and get my hands dirty with the things of life that really matter.

> *John 13:1–5* | Now before the Feast of the Passover, when Jesus knew that his hour had come to depart out of this world to the Father, having loved his own who were in the world, he loved them to the end. ² During supper, when the devil had already put it into the heart of Judas Iscariot, Simon's son, to betray him, ³ Jesus, knowing that the Father had given all things into his hands, and that he had come from God and was going back to God, ⁴ rose from supper. He laid aside his outer garments, and taking a towel, tied it around his waist. ⁵ Then he poured water into a basin and began to wash the disciples' feet and to wipe them with the towel that was wrapped around him.

Spiritual Leadership

> **Ephesians 5:26** | Husbands, love your wives... that he might sanctify her, having cleansed her by the washing of water with the word.

A godly husband is a spiritual teacher. He is growing himself spiritually, and he should lead by his hunger of the Word. He is someone who can teach because he is someone to emulate. His character is innocent and blameless. Deuteronomy 6 says the godly husband is to lead his family by teaching them the Word of God. Are you a student of the Word? Are you a leader? Teach your wife with all humility.

> *1 Corinthians 14:35* | If there is anything they desire to learn, let them ask their husbands at home. For it is shameful for a woman to speak in church.

Husbands should provide an inviting environment for their wives to ask questions. This is not a teacher-student relationship. A wife is a co-heir of the grace of life (1 Pet 3:7). This is not a time to talk down to her. This is a time to jointly study the Word together and enrich each other. This passage implies that the has such a close relationship with the wife that she wouldn't humiliate him in a church meeting (like a small group gathering) or we might even say today, on social media. It is the husband's responsibility to provide a sweet atmosphere of the Word in the home where Christ is sanctifying both the wife (and the husband) "by the washing of water with the Word."

Husbands with children are also to be teaching their children. "Fathers, do not provoke your children to anger, but bring them up in the discipline and instruction of the Lord" (6:4). In fact, Paul is likely thinking of Deuteronomy 6, where we are called to teach our children through all the menial activities of life. We are called to teach our children diligently.

> *Deuteronomy 6:5-7* | You shall love the Lord your God with all your heart and with all your soul and with all your might. [6] And these words that I command you today shall be on your heart. [7] You shall teach them diligently to your children, and shall talk of them when you sit in your house, and when you walk by the way, and when you lie down, and when you rise.

HUSBANDS SHOULD BE LOVERS (5:25-33)

> **Ephesians 5:25-33** | Husbands, love your wives, as Christ loved the church and gave himself up for her, [26] that he might sanctify her, having cleansed her by the washing of water with the word, [27] so that he might present the church to himself in splendor, without spot or wrinkle or any such thing, that she might be holy and without blemish. [28] In the same way husbands should love their wives as their own bodies. He who loves his wife loves himself. [29] For no one ever hated his own flesh, but nourishes and cherishes it, just as Christ does the church, [30] because we are members of his body. [31] "Therefore a man shall leave his father and mother and hold fast to his wife, and the two shall become one flesh." [32] This mystery is profound, and I am saying that it refers to Christ and the church. [33] However, let each one of you love his wife as himself, and let the wife see that she respects her husband.

What is agape love? First let us look at what it is not.

Husbands Lack Agape Love

Ephesians 5:25 | Husbands, love your wives, as Christ loved the church and gave himself up for her.

What an impossible command! In and of themselves, husbands have no true agape love. That's because agape love goes far beyond mere human love. Agape love is not mere *emotion*. Love, as God defines it, is not primarily an emotion. The world says, "when the feeling stops, the love is over." Love is not a tingly sensation. Love is not sentimentalism. Love has nothing to do with how you feel. God so loved the world that he gave his only Son. He didn't look at the world and say, "I just can't resist them; I've got to get them in heaven. They're terrific." There wasn't one thing in us that was deserving. We were enemies; we hated God; we were sinful and vile, but God loved us anyway. And he loved us so much, he gave himself.

Agape love is not mere *appreciation*. It is not just saying nice words to someone. "Faithful are the wounds of a friend; profuse are the kisses of an enemy" (Pro 27:6). Love is more than empty words. Love is action. Love is an act of your will that chooses the best for the other person. We can say all kinds of nice things to a person and it not help them. Sometimes love is saying very hard words to a person.

Agape love is not *admiration*. It is not simply liking or being fond of someone. Agape love goes far beyond admiration. It sacrifices for those that are not admirable.

Husbands Need God's Love

Ephesians 5:25 | Husbands, love your wives, as Christ loved the church and gave himself up for her.

No husband will ever find the kind of love Christ demonstrated inside himself. For a godly husband to love his wife, he must obtain a God-sized love, since he so loved the world that he sacrificed his Son for his Son's bride, the church. We read in our Bible that "God is love" (1 Jn 4:16). Jesus is the exact imprint of God's love. The only way for a husband to have the capacity for God-sized love for his wife is to become conformed to the imprint of Christ (Rom 8:29).

God's Love is Self-Sacrificing

By looking at the cross we can say that agape love is a voluntary abandonment of self-preservation for the good of another. Consider 1 John 4:16: "So we have come to know and to believe the love that God has for us. God is love, and whoever abides in love abides in God, and God abides in him." Agape love is a God-centered, sacrificial love. Understand the Bible makes a shocking statement like: "God is agape – sacrificial love." Take that in. He is sacrificial love. Husbands use your position of authority to sacrifice your life for your wife.

You cannot truly love your wife as you ought without being born again into this love. This kind of selfless love is impossible to know simply through human nature. You must have the divine nature dwelling in you. We must "become partakers of the divine nature" (2 Pet 1:4). God must dwell in you. This is the only way to experience God-centered love. The most striking description of self-sacrificing love is from 1 Corinthians 13.

> *1 Corinthians 13:4-8a* | Love is patient and kind; love does not envy or boast; it is not arrogant [5] or rude. It does not insist on its own way; it is not irritable or resentful; [6] it does not rejoice at wrongdoing, but rejoices with the truth. [7] Love bears all things, believes all things, hopes all things, endures all things. [8] Love never ends.

Paul here gives a pretty exhaustive understanding of what agape love is, what it is not, and how it acts. Let's apply it to the husband.

What agape love is...

- Love is *patient*. A loving husband gives his wife time to grow.
- Love is *kind*. A loving husband helps his wife to grow by bearing her burdens, carrying deeply about her, and pointing her to Christ.

What agape love is not...

- Love is not *jealous*. A loving husband isn't envious over his wife's position, place or gifts, nor over how she uses her time.
- Love is not *boastful* or *arrogant*. A loving husband doesn't use inflated words or have an inflated view of self.
- Love is not *rude*. A loving husband does not act unfittingly but tries to lovingly "fit" with his wife in their marriage union.
- Love is not *selfish*. A loving husband lays aside his "rights" for the good of his wife. He refuses to insist on his own way.

- Love is not *irritable*. A loving husband is not put off by the hang ups of his wife as she grows.
- Love is not *resentful*. A loving husband forgives and keeps no record of his wife's wrongs.
- Love *does not rejoice in wrongdoing*. A loving husband does not parade his wife's failures in front of her or others.
- Love *rejoices in spiritual growth*. A loving husband rejoices when his wife walks in the truth.

What agape love always does...

- Love *always protects*. A loving husband bears or covers the reputation of his wife with care. He never airs dirty laundry but lauds her and lifts her reputation up.
- Love *always believes the best*. A loving husband trusts and gives the benefit of the doubt to his wife, always thinking the best of her.
- Love is *always optimistic*. A loving husband sees God's work in his wife and is excited and hopeful to see what God is going to do next.
- Love *always perseveres*. A loving husband goes beyond normal limits and boundaries for his wife in all her imperfections and failings. He perseveres and endures, never leaving her behind.
- Love *always produces eternal fruit*. The consequences of a husband's love to his wife will never fail and never end. We will carry this kind of agape love into the eternal state. When everything else in this life crumbles and passes away, love remains.

God's Love is Self-Originating

Agape love is different than mere human love. When a young man reveals his heart with a passionate declaration, "I love you!" at least in part he means that he finds the woman he loves lovely. At least some of his love is elicited by the object of that love. But God loves what is unlovely.[184] The distinction of God's love for us is that his love is "self-originating."[185] When God's love transforms a believer, we are given the ability to love in some manner as God loves. No longer is love dependent on the object of love. It is now self-originating. In other words,

---

[184] D.A. Carson, *Showing the Spirit: A Theological Exposition of 1 Corinthians 12-14* (Grand Rapids: Baker Books, 1997), 65.

[185] James Brennan, "The Exegesis of 1 Corinthians 13," *Irish Theological Quarterly* 21 (1954): 270-78 as quoted in Carson, *Showing the Spirit*, 65.

God's Spirit in your heart is where God's love for your spouse now starts. I love the words of A.B. Simpson.

> Let us but feel that He has His heart set upon us, that He is watching us from those heavens with tender interest, that He is following us day by day as a mother follows her babe in his first attempt to walk alone, that He has set His love upon us, and in spite of ourselves is working out for us His higher will and blessing, as far as we will let Him – and then nothing can discourage us."[186]

A husband's love should reflect the self-originating love of God, that our love would not depend on our wife's worthiness, but on her worth in God's eyes, as God's beloved daughter.

God's Love is Unexpected

God's love is so amazing because it is unexpected. We have no problem understanding God's judgment because we are very clearly all guilty. God's love for guilty sinners amazes us. Understand the Bible makes a shocking statement like: "God is agape".

> 1 John 4:16 | So we have come to know and to believe the love that God has for us. God is love, and whoever abides in love abides in God, and God abides in him.

God's Love is Voluntary

Agape love is a voluntary act of the will, a choice. "God so loved the world that he gave his only Son…" (Jn 3:16). I've heard men say about their wife "I just don't love her anymore". Well, then choose to love her. You've stopped abandoning yourself for the good of your wife. Start anew right now. We can measure our love for our wives by an objective standard. We are loving them only as we are conformed to the image of Jesus Christ and are laying down our lives for our wives.

Husbands Should Act Out God's Love

We read in our Bible that "God is love" (1 Jn 4:16). Jesus is the exact imprint of God's love.

---

[186] A. B. Simpson, as quoted in *Once-A-Day: Walk with Jesus* (Nashville: Zondervan, 2012), 65.

The Wife Should be Prized

A loving husband sacrifices to the extent where the wife feels prized. Your wife should feel that she is special and worthy of attention.

> **Ephesians 5:25** | Husbands, love your wives, as Christ loved the church and gave himself up for her.

Christ loved his bride so much that he laid down his life for her. That means if a husband is imitating Christ, he will prize his wife. "Who can find a virtuous woman? for her price is far above rubies" (Pro 31:10). The loving husband prizes his wife above every other relationship in his life. He treats her as special. Ask her: Do I clearly show you that you are the most important person in my life? How does she know she is the number one priority in your life? How does she know she is special? Do you put her first above: job, parents, children, toys, hobbies?

Your wife should know she is significant! She is important. How do we know that we are significant to Christ? He gave his life or us! Your wife will know this by you sacrificing for her. This is the essence of love. She is valuable to you because of who she is, your wife, not because of what she does - your laundry, meals, clean, etc. Is she as valuable as (based on how you treat her): your job, your new car, your hobbies, your computer, your vacation time, your sports, you getting your own way? Do you abuse your wife emotionally? This can happen by saying hurtful things, sarcasm about her looks, weight, insensitivity to her tears, or criticizing her publicly. I challenge you to ask your wife today, "Do you see me making you the #1 priority in my life, second only to Jesus Christ?" Does your wife feel significant because of your love?

The Wife Should be Cleansed

> **Ephesians 5:26-27** | That he might sanctify her, having cleansed her by the washing of water with the word, ²⁷ so that he might present the church to himself in splendor, without spot or wrinkle or any such thing, that she might be holy and without blemish.

Jesus promises to sanctify us with his truth, and his Word is truth (Jn 17:17).

The Wife Should be Protected

Ephesians 5:28-29 | In the same way husbands should love their wives as their own bodies. He who loves his wife loves himself. ²⁹ For no one ever hated his own flesh, but nourishes and cherishes it, just as Christ does the church.

Protected Socially

The idea of protection shows up in several concepts in these verses. First, a godly husband will provide social stability and companionship. A Christlike husband will not neglect his wife *socially*. The husband provides social stability and being present and investing himself in his wife and his home. She should know the loving and protecting presence of her husband in every realm of domestic life. He should invest in her socially. D. Martyn Lloyd-Jones noticed this was one way men were not loving their wives as their own body. He said:

> It is lamentable that a man should get married and then proceed to neglect his wife. In other words, here is a man who has married, but who in essential matters goes on living as if he were still a bachelor. He is still living his own detached life. He still spends his time with his men friends. I could elaborate on this very easily, but the facts are so familiar that it is unnecessary. But I have a feeling that I detect a tendency even in Christian circles, and even in evangelical circles, to forget this particular point. A married man must no longer act as if he were a single man; his wife should be involved in everything.[187]

Some men enjoy taking their wife on a date night. Some just enjoy quiet dinners at home. Husband, when you are home, be all there. Leave work at work. Invest socially in your wife. Ask about her day. Listen to her. Don't be wandering to the news on your cell phone. Don't be answering calls and texts and emails. Be sure to focus on her. Don't just mumble at her. Look her in the eyes. Allow yourself to laugh with her. Make good memories together.

Protected Physically

Second, a husband will provide physical safety for his wife. He will protect his wife by guarding her and making sure she feels safe. We are to protect our wives physically. That entails providing a safe home. It may mean learning how to handle a weapon to protect your wife and children. It means when the snow starts falling or the grass needs

---

[187] Lloyd-Jones, *Ephesians 5*, 217.

cutting or there is a repair emergency, that these things fall on the husband's shoulders. He's the man. He protects her and uses his strength to provide a safe and thriving environment for her to live.

Protected Emotionally

Another way to protect your wife is with *emotional* stability. A Christlike husband is a moderate man, a man who is not given to anger, anxiety or despair. He is a man who doesn't check out and escape when things are emotionally tense. He doesn't blow up in anger, neither does he clam up or give the cold shoulder when he is hurt by his wife. He instead loves his wife as he loves himself. He gives himself the benefit of the doubt; so should he do with his wife. He should think the best of her and her motives. He should believe her and entrust his heart to her. A godly man has emotional integrity. He doesn't get his emotional needs met by another woman or by letting off steam with his friends as a primary way of relief. No, he entrusts himself and his emotions to his dearest friend on the earth, his beloved wife. She's not fully able to bear everything. No one is. Only the Lord can fully bear our deepest and most crushing emotions. But she is there to her husband's helper with her warm embrace, her listening ear, and her gentle encouraging glance. By being "fully there" with your wife, you are protecting her emotionally.

Paul uses the word "cherish" for this idea in verse 29, "For no one ever hated his own flesh, but nourishes and cherishes it, just as Christ does the church." Cherish means to put a guard around. Like when you injure your arm, you rub your arm. Or when you hit your thumb with a hammer, you feel the pain, and you do all you can to relieve it. You guard yourself from any further pain. We are to protect our wives emotionally. Put a guard around your wife. Make sure she is rested. You rest your body if it is hurting. You do everything you need to so that your body might thrive in the most optimal way. Do you do that for your wife? Do you know when she is hurting? Do you protect her emotionally?

Provide emotional stability to your wife by listening to her. Don't compare her to your mom or other women – make her feel that she is just right for you. Get excited about what she loves. Often, men expect their wives to always follow them to the game, concert, or rodeo. Ask God to give you a liking for what she likes.

The Wife Should be Provided For

Ephesians 5:29 | For no one ever hated his own flesh, but nourishes and cherishes it, just as Christ does the church.

The idea of nourishment is seen in a husband's commitment to provide for his wife in a number of ways.

Financial Provision

First, there is provision *financially*. A man should not even be considering marriage if he doesn't have an income sufficient to provide for his wife. A husband is to be the provider of the home. Paul says very bluntly:

> *1 Timothy 5:8* | If anyone does not provide for his relatives, and especially for members of his household, he has denied the faith and is worse than an unbeliever.

A man who does not neglect himself, but cares for himself, will take care of his finances so that he can live without the harassment and worries that debt brings. Are you making sure the finances are where they need to be? This is one of those crushing things. Finances are your responsibility. Make sure that you are careful to love your wife by putting the burden on yourself – finding ways to live within your means, save money, and provide a sense of financial well-being in the home.

I've seen men claim to be the most pious and spiritual men, even great leaders of the church, who do not adequately provide for their wife and children. I am not speaking of poverty for being poor is no sin. I am speaking of destitution. There are some misguided Christian men who think there is something spiritual and good to neglect adequate provisions for the home, as long as they are "doing the work of the Lord." This idea is upside down. Evangelism is absolutely necessary, but a man who doesn't care for his life is not living out the love of Christ in the most basic, elementary way. A man should be weary of himself in evangelism or teaching who doesn't first display the gospel at home.

Social Provision

Second, a husband should provide for his wife in the *social* realm. He makes sure he is home and engaged with his family. He comes home from work in order to work some more. He doesn't shut down and veg when he walks through the door. He listens and doesn't berate his wife for her weaknesses. He doesn't put her down for wanting to talk after a long day with the children. No husband can be the savior for his wife. The Savior is Jesus. If we are sure we are nourished by Jesus, a husband and wife will be truly satisfied. The swiftest way to misery is to have Jesus-like expectations of your wife. The godly husband is patient with his wife's needs. He points her very gently and lovingly to Jesus. He's socially generous with his wife and children.

Spiritual Provision

A man is the pastor of his home. He is to provide everything his wife and their children need to be able to meet and fellowship with Christ. There is a rhythm to spiritual provision. The godly husband provides a pattern for worship *within the home*. He makes sure prayer is offered at mealtimes. He leads in family devotions. He takes the lead in catechizing his children (we use the 52-week *New City catechism*). He prays over his wife before she nods off to sleep. If they are blessed with children, he evangelizes them. He instructs and corrects them. He encourages his wife in the ways of the Lord.

Just as Christ nourishes our souls with his living water, we should also nourish and cleanse our wives with the Word of God. Your wife needs you to love her by the bread of life. Are you helping her grow spiritually? A loving husband will set a consistent example of self-control as he walks in the Word. Are you walking in a way that points your life to Jesus? Your dear wife is a weak sinner and needs your daily encouragement and nourishment from the Word. That doesn't mean that you preach at her or "shove it down her throat" with pharisaical demands. It does mean gentle encouragement that is Scripture saturated and inviting.

The loving husband provides a pattern for times for worship *with the congregation*. He is to be sure he is not working on the Lord's day, unless there is an emergency, or the man is doing an essential service, like an on call medical doctor (where people's lives are at risk). So many men fail to provide a rhythm of spiritual activity for the home. The neighbors should be able to know the rhythm as well as anyone. Sunday morning, they see the family vehicle is gone. Wednesday night prayer, they see your family is at church again.

The loving husband is sure to provide the means of grace ever and always to his wife and if they are so blessed, to his children. Prayer, the Word, and fellowship with the saints. He involves his wife in ministry, gently noting her personality, gifts and disposition. Perhaps she is one who serves behind the scenes. Perhaps she teaches women and children. Whatever her gifting, he encourages it.

The Wife Should be Cherished

Ephesians 5:29-30 | For no one ever hated his own flesh, but nourishes and cherishes it, just as Christ does the church, **30** because we are members of his body.

A wife needs to be cherished. [188] How much is a wife and mother worth? Wives, especially those with children, have a very difficult and often stressful job. MSN Money once reported from a 2012 study that based on the job responsibilities of a wife and mother, their annual salary would be $96,000.[189] My wife, at times, will not ask for help so it's important for me to discern, pray, and analyze what my wife's needs are. Because we have five young children, we set up a system where someone in our family watches our children for one morning a week so that my wife can have time to shop and even swim.

One of the easiest ways for me to discover the difference between loving and cherishing was to compare the famous biblical chapter on love (1 Cor 13) with the Song of Solomon, a book devoted to cherishing. Consider these comparisons:

Love is about being gracious and selfless. "Love is patient and kind" (1 Cor 13:4). Cherishing is about being enthusiastic and enthralled. "How much better is your love than wine, and the fragrance of your oils than any spice" (Song 4:10).

Love tends to be quiet and understated. "Love does not envy or boast" (1 Cor 13:4). Cherishing boasts boldly and loudly. "My beloved is radiant and ruddy, distinguished among ten thousand" (Song 5:10).

Love thinks about others with selflessness. "Love is not arrogant or rude. It does not insist on its own way" (1 Cor 13:4-5). Cherish thinks about its beloved with praise. "Your voice is sweet, and your face is lovely" (Song 2:14).

Love doesn't want the worst for someone. "Love does not rejoice at wrongdoing" (1 Cor 13:6). Cherishing celebrates the best in someone.

---

[188] The section on "Cherishing" adapted from Gary Thomas. "What Cherishing Your Spouse Really Means" September 11, 2018. Focus on the Family.

[189] MSN Money. "How much is a homemaker worth?" (Jan 18, 2012). Archived.

"Behold, you are beautiful, my love; behold, you are beautiful" (Song 1:15).

Love puts up with a lot. "Love hopes all things, endures all things" (1 Cor 13:7). Cherishing enjoys a lot. "His mouth is most sweet, and he is altogether desirable" (Song 5:16).

Men, our wives want more than simply to be loved. They want to hear, "You have captivated my heart, my sister, my bride; you have captivated my heart with one glance of your eyes" (Song 4:9).

Love and cherishing complement each other. Without the bedrock force of love, cherishing won't last. It'll be a sentimental ideal that is lost in the real world. Without cherishing, love feels like a duty more than a delight.

The Wife Should be Pictured

A man and his wife picture Christ and the church in a number of ways. He has a new household, a new oneness, and a new mystery.

A New Household

Ephesians 5:31a | Therefore a man shall leave his father and mother and hold fast to his wife.

It's important to leave father and mother and cleave to your new marriage. God has created a new household. It is not healthy to share everything with mom and dad anymore, especially dirty laundry. I'm not talking about clothing.

One of the greatest barriers to successful marriage is the failure of one or both partners to leave father and mother. In marriage, a new family is begun and the relationships of the former families are to be severed as far as authority and responsibilities are concerned. Parents are always to be loved and cared for, but they are no longer to control the lives of their children once they are married. The idea of "cleave" literally means to be glued or cemented together. Husbands and wives are to leave their parents and to cleave to, be cemented to, each other. They break one set of ties as they establish the other, and the second is more binding and permanent than the first.[190]

Establishing a new household means that you provide emotional stability to your wife by spending time with your wife. It requires you spend a lot of quality time together. You are to leave father and mother

---

[190] MacArthur, *Ephesians*, 302.

and cleave to your wife. Have no other female friends. Your wife as well well want to unload her heart and burdens to you. She may have a very close bond with her mother, but there are now healthy boundaries since a new household is established.

A New Oneness

Ephesians 5:31b | And the two shall become one flesh.

It matters how you display oneness in your marriage. Most of the time that means you should have financial unity. No longer is there her bank account and my bank account (unless you have agreed for organizational reasons). You should both have access to any monies accrued. You should do everything together: sleep together, eat together, fight together (hopefully not with each other), make up together. Every husband and wife should seek to serve in their local churches. Families that serve together and pray together stay together. When two are one the way God intended it, there will be harmony, romance, togetherness, and connection.

A New Mystery

Ephesians 5:32 | This mystery is profound, and I am saying that it refers to Christ and the church.

This is a study not about your wife, but about your worship. Marriage is a mystery! I think everyone would say Amen to that! But what does Paul mean? In the Bible, the term "mystery" means "a hidden reality that is now revealed". In other words, it is a picture of Christ and the church, but it was not revealed until Christ came to earth. It wouldn't have made sense. Unknown to the people of the Old Testament (it was a 'mystery'), marriage was designed by God from the beginning to be a picture of the believer's union with Christ. Back when God was planning what marriage would be like, he planned it for this great purpose: it would give a beautiful earthly picture of the relationship that would someday come about between Christ and his church".[191]

---

[191] George Knight III, "Husbands and Wives as Analogues of Christ and the Church" in *Recovering Biblical Manhood and Womanhood: A Response to Evangelical Feminism,* edited by John Piper and Wayne Grudem (Wheaton, IL: Crossway Books, 1991), 175-76.

Paul's teaching on marriage, like the Lord's teaching in Mark 10:2–12, is based on Genesis 2:23–24. Marriage was God's idea. Its purpose was to make paradise complete—to bring Heaven down to earth. In instituting marriage, God had eternity's values in view and the ultimate reality of Christ and his church in mind.[192]

A New Culture

Ephesians 5:33 | However, let each one of you love his wife as himself, and let the wife see that she respects her husband.

Love and respect is not the way of the world, but it is required of every loving husband and submissive wife. This is the culture of Jesus!

HUSBANDS SHOULD BE LEARNERS

The only way a family can function to please God with unity, purpose and direction is for all members to understand and work at fulfilling their God-given roles. Oneness (unity) will only be achieved as each know, accept, and work hard at fulfilling their varying, but complementary roles. 1 Peter 3 has the secret of how to grow in your marriage.

> *1 Peter 3:7* | Likewise, husbands, live with your wives in an understanding way, showing honor to the woman as the weaker vessel, since they are heirs with you of the grace of life, so that your prayers may not be hindered.

God calls the husband to understand his wife. Few motives in human experience are as powerful as the yearning to be understood. Being listened to means that we are taken seriously, that our ideas and feelings are recognized, and, ultimately, that what we have to say matters."[193] Unless the husband is a mind reader, the only way he can understand his wife is by listening to her express her heart to him.

Three ways for the husband to learn his wife are listed in this verse: attention, gentleness, and honor.

Attention

You are to learn about your wife. Find out what hurts her and protect her from it. Have lots of conversations with her. Get to know her.

---

[192] Phillips, *Ephesians*, Eph 5:31–32.
[193] Michael P. Nichols, *The Lost Art of Listening, Second Edition: How Learning to Listen Can Improve Relationships* (New York: Guilford Publications, 2009), 9.

You are the initiator. God stated this principle in the form of a command. The husband is to show his wife attention. The command to "live with your wives in an understanding way" implies more than sharing the same address. Peter reinforces God's original plan for marriage which states: "the two shall become one flesh" (Gen 2:24). Therefore, the husband living with his wife in an understanding, listening way fulfills, in part, the one flesh relationship. The husband who views this as optional demonstrates he doesn't want to show his wife attention. He has some serious growing up to do. The word "understanding" means a knowledge based on personal experience. That is, because of interaction with them, and heartfelt listening to them, you understand or know them. Our culture says, "You just can't understand a woman." But God says to the husbands, you must understand your wife and you must learn to "live with them in an understanding way." Jay Adams writes:

> To be understanding, he must try to enter into her situation and see as much as he can what she is facing from the woman's viewpoint. That is difficult to do, but that is what it means to be understanding of another person: to try to get into her shoes.[194]

Gentleness

You are to treat your wife as a weaker vessel or a "fragile vase". This means you show honor. She is a precious treasure. She is a fragile vase. She is emotionally more sensitive than you for the most part. Protect her! Do not tear her down. You can win the argument and destroy your wife! Don't do it. In other words, husbands, treat with respect and sensitivity this fragile creature God has made, called woman. She is not fragile only because you are physically stronger, but because you can crush her spirit with brutish words and actions of disrespect.

Honor

She is an expensive, fragile vase. She needs to know she is prized. The responsibility here is on the husband to give the honor to his wife. Therefore, a husband cannot use the excuse that "she doesn't deserve it." The husband must give honor to his wife by being a learner regardless of his wife's imperfections. When a husband knows his wife, treats

---

[194] Jay Adams, *Christian Living in the Home* (Phillipsburg, NJ: Presbyterian and Reformed Publishing, 1972), 97.

her with respect, loves her, provides for her, as the marriage covenant requires, he then honors her.

A clear warning is sounded at the end of this Scripture. You want God to listen to your prayers? Then take heed to this command. A husband's prayer life is affected by the kind of learner he is. In other words, marriage is a measure of your walk with God. If a couple is not right with each other, they are not right with God. Consider some implications to a husband's marriage and family if his prayer life is being hindered by his disobedience to 1 Peter 3:7. According to Psalm 66:18, what are the results of harboring unconfessed sin in our hearts? David says: "If I regard wickedness in my heart, the Lord will not hear."

"Hindered" is in the present tense and passive. Failure to give due honor to the wife will result in the cutting off of the efficacy of prayer. In other words, a couple that is not in matrimonial harmony will find it difficult to pray together and for one another. A couple's domestic relationship has a profound impact on their spiritual fellowship with God. Our relationship with God can never be right if our relationships with our fellow man are wrong.

Your wife wants a husband who will call her during the day, listen to her, take her advice, and see her as your very best friend. She wants to be "number one" in your life. More importantly, God requires that we as men care for our wives as a precious, fragile vase.

Ways for a Husband to Honor His Wife

Husbands, here are some ways you can honor your wife.

1. *Be sensitive to her needs.* If you ask what it is she needs, then listen carefully, she will reveal her needs to you. Then ask God to help you meet as many of those needs as you can.

2. *Let your actions, as well as your words, show her respect.* Don't sit in front of the TV while she washes the dishes, picks up after the kids and gets them to bed. She's more than mommy, maid, cook and nurse - she's your fragile vase, remember?

3. *Pay attention to her when she talks with you.* Put down the paper, look her in the eyes, and respond in more than monosyllables.

4. *Do not speak harshly to her and never tear her down, especially in public.* You can deeply wound her spirit by a harsh, discounting word. It's bad enough when you do this in private, but it's devastating when done in public. Remember, a wounded heart finds it hard to give love.

5. *Accept her feelings.* You may not understand them, but you must respect them as real and viable. Never tell her, "There's no reason to feel that way, Honey." The worst thing to tell a hurting wife whose emotions are out of control is: "control yourself!" Instead care for her as a priceless, fragile vase.

6. *Do not compare her unfavorably to someone else and never try to change her.* When you criticize, you are saying, I don't like you the way you are. Be different or I won't love you. On the other hand, if you show her you love and accept her just the way she is, she may change simply because she doesn't feel pressured to do so. Regardless, you must commit yourself to allowing her to be all that she can be, not all you want her to be.

7. *Never do anything to betray her trust.* Unfaithfulness is the ultimate dishonor to your wife. Before God, commit yourself to be a faithful husband. Accept her for who she is and love her as the woman God made for you and planned to be your wife before the world began.

Conclusion

It is vital that you work on your marriage if you have that gift. Why? Paul concludes helping us remember the glorious relationship that marriage pictures.

Ephesians 5:32-33 | This mystery is profound, and I am saying that it refers to Christ and the church. ³³ However, let each one of you love his wife as himself, and let the wife see that she respects her husband."

Marriage pictures Christ and the church in a number of marvelous ways. There is *anticipation*. Courtship and engagement pictures the fact that we anticipate Christ's soon return, when we will experience our eternal wedding day. There is *passion*. We love our Bridegroom. We sacrifice for him as he has sacrificed for us. There is *purity*. We are pure and faithful to Christ as we wait for his return. There is *provision*. We can expect Christ to nourish and provide for us while we wait. There is *protection*. We can live under the protection of Christ. There is *completion*: Christ completes us. There is *procreation*. In Christ we bear fruit. Marriage is a picture of Christ and the church, therefore "let each one of you love his wife as himself, and let the wife see that she respects her husband" (6:33). What a joy and delight to participate in such a marvelous mystery and to know my love in marriage points to Christ and his beloved Bride, the Church.

19 | EPHESIANS 6:1-4
ROOTED IN LOVE POWERED PARENTING

Children, obey your parents in the Lord, for this is right.
EPHESIANS 6:1

Someone said, "It is not enough to raise your kids in church; you must raise them in Christ!"[195] It takes the love of God to raise children. We are going to see that in Ephesians 6. I must know the love of Christ before I can show that love to my children. It's kind of like allowance. You've got to have income before you can give your children allowance. In the same way you must have the inflow of God's love before you can flood it in your child's direction.

The greatest mission field in this world today is the family – our children! We must give them first priority. We have eighteen years of planting and watering and seeing spiritual fruit come from them. We must make the children that God gives us a major priority in our lives so that we can lead them to Christ. The responsibility to demonstrate the love of God to the child is given to the parents, and specifically to the father. Remember the words of Jesus in Matthew 19:14, "Let the little children come to me and do not hinder them, for to such belongs

---

[195] Tom and Chaundel Holladay. *Love-Powered Parenting: Loving Your Kids the Way Jesus Loves You* (Grand Rapids, MI: Zondervan, 2012), 172.

the kingdom of heaven." How God loves us as his dear children. So, we should be instruments of his love to our children!

I read about one pastor, who thought he had it all together before he and his wife had any children. Before they had children, he boldly preached on "How to Raise Your Children." After they became parents, the message became "Some Suggestions to Parents"— and with two more children, it changed to "Feeble Hints to Fellow Strugglers."[196]

What would you say is the goal of parenting? As parents we are representing our loving heavenly Father to our children. That's a lofty goal. That's a daunting task! Just as God intends marriage to be a reflection of his relationship with the church, the way we raise our children ought to be a reflection of the relationship our heavenly Father has with us. Our heavenly Father, Almighty God, has a perfect relationship with us. He is a perfect, loving Father. God loves his children, all true believers in Christ with a perfect, everlasting love!

Our love toward God is never perfect. We sin in thought, word, and deed. As Christians, if we are honest, we are all disobedient children of our heavenly Father. No matter how much we want to be perfect we mess royally, mess up so often! Our completed perfection has to wait until we get to heaven. We will never while on this earth be a perfect reflection of God's love. However, that doesn't mean we shouldn't seek to emulate his example of love to his dear children. I believe Ephesians 6:1-4 is really a command for fathers to be like our heavenly Father.

> **Ephesians 6:1-4** | Children, obey your parents in the Lord, for this is right. ²"Honor your father and mother" (this is the first commandment with a promise), ³"that it may go well with you and that you may live long in the land." ⁴Fathers, do not provoke your children to anger, but bring them up in the discipline and instruction of the Lord.

What are the two greatest commandments? Love God and love people. This passage tells us how to love the most important people in your life if you are a parent. Love your children. The exposition of this passage is fairly simple. Paul directly addresses two people in the home: children and fathers. He says the same thing in Colossians 3.

---

[196] Charlie Shedd. *Promises to Peter* (Waco, TX.: Word, 1970), 7.

Colossians 3:20-21 | Children, obey your parents in everything, for this pleases the Lord. ²¹ Fathers, do not provoke your children, lest they become discouraged.

THE CHILD'S RESPONSIBILITY (6:1-3)

Children are a gift from the Lord. Children (*tekna*) does not refer particularly to young children but to all offspring. Sons and daughters still under their parents' roof are to obey and honor them.[197] William Barclay notes that under the Roman law of *patria potestas* ("the father's power") a father had incredible authority.

> A Roman father had absolute power over his family. He could sell them as slaves; he could make them work in his fields, even in chains; he could take the law into his own hands, for law was in his own hands, and he could punish as he liked; he could even inflict the death penalty on his child. Further, the power of the Roman father extended over the child's whole life, so long as the father lived. A Roman son never came of age."[198]

A Child's Obedience

Ephesians 6:1 | Children, obey your parents in the Lord, for this is right.

It is precisely because children are not born in a neutral state (Eph 2:1-3, Rom 3, Gal 5:19-21), but in rebellion to God, that the gospel must be at the forefront of discipline. Children are to obey their parents because God has commanded them to do so. One of the means, if not the primary means, that God uses to draw children to himself is this confrontation that occurs when children are called to obey God.

A simple definition of obedience is "living under and submitting to God's authority." So when the earthly Jewish rulers told Peter to stop preaching the gospel, he still kept an obedient heart and said, "We ought to obey God rather than men" (Acts 5:29).

There should be an obedience that children are to give to parents. This has nothing to do with the parents' worthiness. They are not worthy. But they are to do this because God is worthy, and he has outlined this in his law. Respect for parents is of such grave importance to God that Moses commanded, "He who strikes his father or his mother shall surely be put to death," and "He who curses his father or his mother

---

[197] MacArthur, *Ephesians*, 311.
[198] Barclay, *Ephesians*, 208.

shall surely be put to death" (Exo 21:15, 17; *cf* Lev 20:9). Either to physically or verbally abuse a parent was a capital offense in ancient Israel.[199]

Cuteness, of course, is *not* obedience. The Bible commands children to obey their parents. It does not command them to be their friend. Certainly, we are to be loving, gentle and nurturing, but we are the guardians of their souls. Some parents are tempted to be overly soft on their children. Others are too harsh. Some parents would say they have a soft spot in their heart for their child. Two-year-old little Johnny is called to come to the mother or father. Johnny doesn't whine or fuss, he simple furrows his eyebrows together and sticks his little lip out. And what do these new parents say? "Aw, look at little Johnny, isn't that little lip sooooo cute!" Parents, what is cute at two is not cute at twelve or twenty-two! That little lip is an outward sign of an inward condition of selfishness and rebellion. By doting over their seemingly "cute" rebellion, you are teaching your child to disobey you. This may seem harmless now but remember the eternal law of the harvest: "What ever you sow, you will also reap" (Gal 6:7) and in another place, "If you sow to the wind, you will reap the whirlwind" (Hos 8:7). You are planting seeds in your child that will one day cause them to break your heart and bring your children shame. You must not look upon your children simply as "cute", but as the greatest mission field in all the world! When Jesus lifted up his eyes upon Jerusalem, he wept. He was moved with compassion on them. He saw them without guidance—as sheep with no shepherd.

Another warning is to follow through on helping your children obey. The third time is not obedience. You might say, "Johnny, don't make me count to three!" or, "If I have to tell you *one* more time, you're really going to get it!" Whether it is one more time or a third time, what you are teaching your child is that it is not necessary to obey the first time. Let me give you the Biblical pattern for obedience. A child should obey *immediately, sweetly, and completely*.

- *Immediately*—he is to come right away.
- *Completely*—he is to do exactly what you say, not halfway!
- *Sweetly* (with a happy attitude)—he is not to complain or make an excuse or challenge.

---

[199] MacArthur, *Ephesians*, 312.

This is the pattern not only for our child's obedience. It's the pattern for anyone's obedience. That's how we should all obey the Lord.

A Child's Attitude

Ephesians 6:1 | Children, obey your parents in the Lord, for this is right.

We should expand on the sweetness of the attitude in obedience. A child should always obey their parents "in the Lord." Obedience is always based on the worthiness of God, not the parents. The Lord is worthy of a good attitude in the heart from both the parents and the child. Surely a little child can learn that a good attitude is the best attitude. Honoring and obeying parents is clearly a good thing, and it is good when a child comes to realize that his world operates according to God's direction—and that things will go well for him when he embraces that standard. Yet the job of the Christian parent is not done at that point. The absolute necessity of coming to faith in Christ must always be stressed. The commands of God show us our inability to obey in our own strength. Only the power of the gospel can motivate children (and parents) to obedience from a heart of love. And the only way to have true joy in obedience is to know the love of Christ, and to see that obedience is the fruit of faith in Christ. A child shouldn't obey just for life to be better (even though it will go better). A child's obedience should flow out of the love and joy that comes from trusting in Christ as Savior.

A Child's Life

Ephesians 6:2-3 | "Honor your father and mother" (this is the first commandment with a promise), ³"that it may go well with you and that you may live long in the land."

Paul now quotes the fifth commandment, the first of the ten to have a promise, or warning with it. Paul's point is that the immediate wellbeing of children is tied to their obedience not only to mother and father, but to all authority. For example, a young child who constantly defies his parents places himself in physical and spiritual danger. He may place himself physically in harm's way simply by ignoring parental direction that is designed to protect him. Since God is the one who sets up all authorities on earth (Col 1:15-20), submitting to authority is the path of wisdom and safety for a child. And if a child does not learn to submit to authority on a domestic level, how can he or she do well in civil society? The point is that if your child does not learn from mother and father, bad consequences will happen outside the home, in school with teachers, at work with bosses. He won't do well if he can't follow his teacher's instructions or his boss's instructions. And sadly, if he still won't listen, then the police, the courts, and the prison system will have to teach him. He may not live very long on the earth.

Have you known someone on the job that just could not get along with the boss? What is their life like? Not very pleasant is it? God has set these things in place. The parent-child relationship is so important that it affects your relationship with everyone else.

This is so foundational that you must get a hold of this. Children will not do well in the earth, they will not function well in the society, they will not make a good transition from dependence to independence unless they learn the meaning of authority and unless they learn to honor those they should honor.

THE FATHER'S RESPONSIBILITY (6:4)

The Negative Command

Ephesians 6:4a | Fathers, do not provoke your children to anger.

A Command for Fathers

Paul addresses fathers because it is the primary responsibility in a two-parent home for the father to lead in the area of child rearing. The Heidelberg Catechism, question 31, applies our union with Christ to his three offices as prophet, priest and king. [200]

As *prophet*, it is the father's responsibility to teach the Word of God in the home, with passion and interest in ways that are helpful to children, sometimes even play acting out scenes of the Bible. Other times, reading through in a child's translation or paraphrase they can understand. Fathers are mainly to teach the basics for young children: the attributes of God, the Lord's prayer, the ten commandments. We also use the 52-week New City catechism. As they get older you can guide them as they read through the Bible themselves, talk over the sermons at mealtimes and walks, and spend quality time with them answering their questions (Deut 6:4-7). Most importantly, as prophet, we

---

[200] Joel R. Beeke, "How Should Men Lead Their Families?" Booklet. Reformation Heritage Books.

are to point our children to Christ and familiarize them with the impossibility of keeping the law in our own power, the desperate need for cleansing from sin, and the joy of being adopted by our Abba, Father.

As *priest*, I am first to sacrifice myself for my wife and for my children. Also as priest, I am to intercede for my children and teach them to intercede for themselves. We should be seeing answers to prayer on a continual basis. They should see me in my priestly role, joyfully hearing from God both personally and on behalf of our family. There should be many priestly sacrifices of praise and thanksgiving to the Lord.

As *king*, I am to defend my children. I am to trust in Christ my Divine Warrior (Rev 19:11-16). I am the gatekeeper of my home. I am to fight a spiritual war with divine weapons, not weapons of the flesh (2 Cor 10:4–5). Fathers must fight this battle with the kingly authority entrusted to them to defend their precious ones. I have to defend them against unwise electronic media, unhelpful or worldly friendships, unwise romantic relationships and regulating relationships with members of the opposite sex. I'm also there to help defend my child against unjust authorities. Joel Beeke asks:

> Are you willing to go to bat for your child if his schoolteacher or coach requires him to do something that violates his conscience? King Lemuel's mother told him, "Open thy mouth for the dumb in the cause of all such as are appointed to destruction. Open thy mouth, judge righteously, and plead the cause of the poor and needy" (Prov. 31:8–9). If that applies to kings and their subjects, how much more should fathers speak up for their children? I am not offering an excuse for public temper tantrums or political manipulation. But a father should stand up for his children against powerful and intimidating figures with fearless, respectful integrity. He must also teach them to stand up for themselves against such injustice. [201]

As king a father should not only defend but discipline his children. If children are disciplined, even corporeally, when they are young, they often will remember very little of the need for this kind of correction. Discipline should only be administered after loving and kind instruction. I often use the ten commandments. Will often say, "Which of the commandments did you break?" It could be coveting. It could be dishonoring mother and father. I ask them if they've mainly disobeyed me or God, and they will reply: "I've disobeyed God." Then I will tell them,

---

[201] Beeke, ibid.

"I am a sinner too, and I am so grateful and unworthy to be your parent." We have a sweet time so that the heart is already changed before any consequence is given. In times that this change of heart does not happen in the child, I am still sweet with them, but allow them to have the help of correction to bring the change in their heart. Afterward is the best time to lovingly continue their instruction. The Puritans would say: "The wax is most moldable when it is soft." I use that time to mold my child's heart so that we don't have to correct very often.

A Command for Gentleness

Fathers should be gentle, not harsh. In being harsh, he may harden his child's heart. A father should be very careful of his authority. Most fathers, especially new fathers, don't understand the power of their position. A father may be, in his own mind, giving a simple command to a child, but he must always be gentle and kind, because a father can easily break a child's spirit. Don't break their heart.

To provoke to anger suggests a repeated, ongoing pattern of treatment that gradually builds up a deep-seated anger and resentment that boils over in outward hostility.[202] This is often the case with children, even in Christian homes. We wonder why when the child comes of age, he flees from Christ. There are many reasons for this but could one reason be the stubbornness or insensitivity of the father. Christian fathers don't realize that their zeal for Christ can come across at times as controlling or as angry.

How often I used to do this when my children were smaller. I could be capricious and impulsive instead of thoughtful and careful in correcting my children. It's easy to provoke them and exasperate when there is no foundation of love. When a father is not gentle and kind and not displaying the love of our heavenly Father, the children become afraid and eventually discouraged and even bitter. Immature fathers can be impatient, overbearing, irritated, rude, selfish, loud, harsh, and difficult. All of that drives our children away from God. We can say we love God all day long, but how do we express his tender love to our children?

---

[202] Ibid., 317.

The Positive Command

Ephesians 6:4b | Bring them up in the discipline and instruction of the Lord.

Instead of neglecting kindness and provoking our children to anger, we should be nurturing them with the tenderness of discipline and the admonishment of instruction.

Tenderness: Love them!

Ephesians 6:4b | Bring them up...

John Calvin translates "bring them up" with the words, "let them be kindly cherished," and then goes on to emphasize that the overall idea is gentleness and friendliness.[203] Love your children. Guide them. I think of God's description of how he brought up Israel in the book of Hosea.

> *Hosea 11:1-4* | When Israel was a child, I loved him, and out of Egypt I called my son.... it was I who taught Ephraim to walk; I took them up by their arms... I led them with cords of kindness, with the bands of love.

Oh, that we would have that kind of tenderness and bands of love.

Discipline: Live for Christ with them!

Ephesians 6:4b | Bring them up in the discipline ... of the Lord.

Think of the word "discipline" as discipling. Look at how Jesus taught his disciples with a gentleness and a tender care for their souls. Oh, how he loved them! That's the attitude we should have toward our children. The full expanse of the word "disciple" has to do with training. This brings to mind the discipleship mentality of Deuteronomy 6.

> *Deuteronomy 6:6-7* | These words that I command you today shall be on your heart. ⁷ You shall teach them diligently to your children, and shall talk of them when you sit in your house, and when you walk by the way, and when you lie down, and when you rise.

---

[203] *Calvin's Commentaries: The Epistles of Paul the Apostle to the Galatians, Ephesians, Philippians and Colossians*, trans. T. H. L Parker (Grand Rapids, MI: Eerdmans, 1974), p. 213.[203]

A father, if he is bringing up his children can say to them, "Be imitators of me, as I am of Christ" (1 Cor 11:1). So we should be living out our faith with our children. This means with tender care, we should bring our children into our prayer room, into our time with God. They should know the squeeze of our hand in prayer, the tear of the Spirit that runs down our face. They should be compelled to pray by the Spirit through the Word because of the earnest atmosphere of the home.

Instruction: Counsel them!

Ephesians 6:4b | Bring them up in ... instruction of the Lord.

The word "instruction" comes from the Greek noun *nouthesia*. The word is translated "to counsel, admonish, correct, mildly rebuke, or instruct," "to provide instruction as to correct behavior and belief."[204]

Counsel with the Tenderness

In the New Testament, this word is almost always accompanied with tenderness and tears. Paul uses this word in two key places. First, we hear Paul address the Ephesian believers.

Acts 20:31 | Therefore be alert, remembering that for three years I did not cease night or day to admonish every one with tears.

He's reaching the heart of the Ephesians. Consider as well how tenderly Paul admonishes the Corinthians.

1 Corinthians 4:14 | I do not write these things to make you ashamed, but to admonish you as my beloved children.

The best way to admonish your children as a father is to first empathize with your child if they have sinned and need correction. We are all sinners. We should never have a holier-than-thou attitude, but "jump into the casket" of our child's sin. "Oh wretched man (or child) that I am! Who will deliver me?" (Rom 7:24). Our goal is not mere outward obedience, which any child of hell can do. Our goal is to reach the heart, so that the child can obey God out of love and joy. My admonishment is always gospel centered. If the child is not yet a Christian, I will encourage them that their only hope for real joyful obedience is by knowing Christ. If they already know Christ, I will encourage them that

---

[204] Nida, *Greek-English Lexicon*, 414.

their sins can never affect their position in Christ, only their relationship with him, and that when they confess and forsake their sins, their relationship with God will be restored (1 Jn 1:9-2:3; Pro 28:13).

Counsel with the Word

To bring our children up in the instruction (counsel) of the Lord is essentially counseling our children by applying the Word of God to their lives. It means to counsel the heart with the aim of thereby changing the behavior. The result is that your child learns not only to hear the Word only, but to actually walk in the Word from a joyful heart (Jas 1:22-25). The instruction of the father brings truth to bear on the life of his beloved child. If we want our children to obey the Lord, then they must see their parents following the Lord.

OUR HEAVENLY FATHER'S LOVE

Let's consider how to reflect the love of our heavenly Father to our children. Does God want us to obey as his children? Absolutely. But what always ought to be the motivation of obedience? Love. "If you love me, you will keep my commandments" (Jn 14:15). If you want the joy and power to raise your children for Christ, you have experienced the Father's love: how rich and how deep, how wide and how high is the love of Christ. Without the constant flow of the Father's love in our hearts, we cannot gently and lovingly bring our children up in the Lord. Without God's love overflowing, we are weak, discouraged, and even embittered parents.

We may want to teach our children something – how to cook or sew or take care of a pet, but we cannot teach them if we don't already have the knowledge ourselves. We can learn it together with them, but we have to be willing to obtain that knowledge if we are going to pass it on. So, it is with God's agape love. We cannot pass on that God-like love unless we personally possess it and are possessed by it ourselves. Isn't it wonderful to know the unconditional, undying love of your heavenly Father?

That reminds me of one time when we were in a restaurant called *Steak and Shake*, and Evan got his leg caught between the spokes of a chair. The fear that was upon his face was awful. As a tender father, I gently calmed him and carefully loosed him from the chair. I could have lectured him, but instead I dealt with him in compassion and mercy. I didn't shame him, but I held him and loved him, and he felt the tender mercies of me and I hope of our heavenly Father.

There have been many times when my children have defied me. When my children disobey me or Jill, I may have to chasten them, but it is only with an attitude of tender mercies. This is how we "bring them up" and nurture them in Christ. Jesus teaches us in Luke 6:36, "Be merciful, even as your Father is merciful."

The Father's love is also expressed in his grace toward us. Look at how deep his grace is. If we are moved by God's mercy toward us, which is God not giving us the punishment we deserve, then we ought to be all the more moved by God's grace. Grace is God giving us his favor and goodness that we don't deserve.

Someone has defined agape love as "God's unconditional, radical, sacrificial commitment to our well-being." God freely gives us his love unconditionally, all the while knowing that we will at times abuse it, disregard it, and take advantage of it. We will sin against it. We will fail to express thanks for it. He will never stop displaying his love toward us in giving us his Holy Spirit and the benefits of his Son. God's love is unconditional. He is not capricious. To be capricious is to change on a dime, to be led by a whim. God's love is not fleeting and contingent on changing things. His love is unconditional and therefore never changes. God's love for you existed before you existed. Jeremiah 31:3, "I have loved you with an everlasting love; therefore, I have continued my faithfulness to you."

I asked Jill's mom one day if she had any advice in parenting. She said the first is "Do unto others as you would have them do to you." Treat your children how you would want to be treated. And the second is, if you are doing that, "Obey me". This is how God is to us. Children are to obey in an environment of love. We do not let them act always according to their whims. "The Lord disciplines the one he loves, and chastises every son whom he receives" (Heb 12:6).

Conclusion

What discipline in the lives of our children does is that it provides a wonderful fence, so we can love and care for our children. A fence is a wonderful invention, for it keeps the danger out, and it keeps the blessing in. It is a boundary to keep the harm away and to provide safety to those within. When we start going too far away from God and move past his "fences", he sends chastening trials to bring us back into his fence, which we can imagine as his arms. He always chastens us in love. He is patient and kind even in his discipline, because his discipline is like putting the fence a little higher so we are not so "prone to wander" as the old hymn says. God's tender mercies never fail even in discipline. His motive of discipline is to draw us near to himself. It is to give us a warning not to leave his loving arms. So, our discipline ought to be toward our children.

Parents, provide your children an environment that reflects God's relationship with us. If we want to see the Father's love for us, look to the Cross. How amazing is it that our great God would give his only Son to make a wretch his treasure! What undying love! What honored children we are!

20 | EPHESIANS 6:5-9
ROOTED IN WORKING FOR JESUS

> *Bondservants, obey your earthly masters with fear and trembling, with a sincere heart, as you would Christ.*
> EPHESIANS 6:5

I remember living in Spain, and I would ask my neighbor: "How was work?" "What?" he asked in unbelief. Work is work." I understood. He had a great job, but he put up with it. He lived for vacation. He lived for the weekend. God has given us a completely different mindset with the Christian work ethic. Our nation is founded on the work ethic. What is the secret? Christians turn their work into worship for God. It becomes pleasurable even in the worst working conditions.

We have much opportunity to turn our work into worship, because in our lives we are going to work a lot. It is estimated that a person will spend about 100,000 hours at employment in his lifetime, and that's only a 43-hour work week. Most of us work plenty more than that. But just on a 43-hour work week, that would be like working without stopping for over 11 years! But brothers and sisters, this is not primarily a message about work but about worship. It is a message about how our hearts are changed by the power of Christ, and we have a new Master and a new mandate, and a new motivation.

Work occupies a lot of our life. Some might make the great mistake of separating their work from their worship of God. The study before us is about how everything we do, especially our work, is our worship to God. In other words, worship is not just on Sundays and Wednesdays, but it is us valuing and honoring and adoring God every minute of every day. We serve Jesus Christ at church, at home, at work, and at play. Everything we do is worship. Paul comes to a place in Ephesians where he addresses slaves and household servants. He wants to show them how they can glorify God in their work. Let's listen to what Paul says.

Ephesians 6:5-9 | Bondservants, obey your earthly masters with fear and trembling, with a sincere heart, as you would Christ, **6** not by the way of eye-service, as people-pleasers, but as bondservants of Christ, doing the will of God from the heart, **7** rendering service with a good will as to the Lord and not to man, **8** knowing that whatever good anyone does, this he will receive back from the Lord, whether he is a bondservant or is free. **9** Masters, do the same to them, and stop your threatening, knowing that he who is both their Master.

Paul's theme is that Christians are to live honorably in all circumstances. This is particularly difficult for slaves in the ancient world, who have no rights.

Our modern western context is so vastly different than the apostles' day. When our children are young, we wonder, what will they be when they grow up? We dream about it. In modern America, it's usually whatever vocation the child chooses. But in our passage, Peter addresses slaves – household servants – some of whom, at the time, did not have a choice regarding their state in life. Some were born into slavery. Many were forced into it by defeat of war or because of massive debt. Others were criminals and mandated into it as a punishment.[205] Paul's point is that Christians are not governed or mastered by their constantly shifting and sometimes unjust or unfair circumstances. Christians are counter-cultural salt and light who are called to honor God in all circumstances. Christians know God is sovereign, kind and

---

[205] Gavin Kendall, Gary Wickham. *Understanding Culture* (London: Sage Publications, 2001), 109.

powerful in leading his people – including those who happen to be slaves – to be light to a very dark world.

It has been estimated that up to thirty million out of sixty million people were slaves of some sort in ancient Rome,[206] though the majority were hired servants. Only around twelve million (one-fifth of the Roman empire) were in servitude without pay.[207] That means that up to one-half of the entire society was enslaved or in servitude to the other half. In fact, many of the churches that Paul planted throughout the Roman Empire were made up of a large majority of slaves. In looking at Paul's address to slaves of the first century, we have to be careful not to pour in our modern experience of slavery. Wayne Grudem points out that the horrible degradation of slaves in 19th-century America gives the word 'slave' a far worse connotation than is accurate for most of the society to which Peter was writing.[208] "Most persons in slavery were treated well; they had been born in the house of their owner and they had been trained to perform important domestic, industrial, business, or public tasks."[209] Some slaves were actual educators "where they brought their specialist knowledge of such topics as philosophy and medicine to the Roman world."[210] By the time of the Christian era, sweeping changes had been introduced which radically improved the treatment of slaves. Slaves under Roman law in the first century could generally count on eventually being set free. Very few ever reached old age as slaves. Slave owners were releasing slaves at such a rate that Augustus Caesar introduced legal restrictions to curb the trend. Almost

---

[206] According to MacArthur (*Slave*, p. 25), the actual number of unpaid slaves was around twelve million, though it would be up to thirty million if one would include all kinds of slaves, from hired domestic servants, to those who had sold themselves into slavery to pay off debt, to those who were enslaved through war, and even to those who were born into slavery.

[207] Murray J. Harris, *Slave of Christ* (Downers Grove, IL: InterVarsity Press, 1999), 34. According to the International Standard Bible Encyclopedia, "In the larger cities, such as Rome, Corinth, Ephesus, and Antioch, as many as one-third of the population were legally slaves and another one-third had been slaves earlier in life" (Scott Bartchy, "Servant; Slave," in Geoffrey W. Bromiley, ed., ISBE, vol. 4 [Grand Rapids: Eerdmans, 1988], 420).

[208] Wayne Grudem. *1 Peter: An Introduction and Commentary, Vol 17* (Downers Grove, IL: InterVarsity Press, 1988), 131.

[209] Scott Bartchy. *Mallon Chresai: First-century Slavery and the Interpretation of 1 Corinthians 7:21*, SBL Dissertation Series 11 (Missoula, MT: SBL, 1971), 174.

[210] Mark Cartwright. Ancient History Encyclopedia, "Slavery in the Roman World." West Sussex, UK: AHE, 2013.

fifty percent of slaves were freed before the age of thirty.[211] In the Roman Empire a person might become a slave if he had a great amount debt, so he would sell himself into slavery to pay the debt. Most slaves though came from the territories Rome conquered, through defeat in war. A person might be a doctor, a teacher, or a merchant, and suddenly, if Rome conquered his land, he could be a slave.

Slavery often gave the person a somewhat safe place to exist in the Roman Empire. You would have food, clothing, a warm bed. Slaves could own property and, in some cases, even own other slaves. It is true that when a person became a slave, he would lose all of his rights. However, there were laws passed in the days of the apostles that allowed for slaves to purchase themselves out of slavery and become citizens (1 Cor 7:21).[212] The only ones that could never become free were slaves that became criminals. They were branded, and as such, they could never attain freedom.[213] According to R. K. Hughes:

> Being a slave did not indicate one's social class. Slaves regularly were accorded the social status of their owners. Regarding outward appearance, it was usually impossible to distinguish a slave from free persons. A slave could be a custodian, a salesman, or a CEO. Many slaves lived separately from their owners. In fact, selling oneself into slavery was commonly used as a means of obtaining Roman citizenship and gaining an entrance into society. If you worked hard, there was a possibility of adoption into the family by the time you were 30, which meant the coveted Roman citizenship. Shockingly, Roman slavery in the first century was far more humane and civilized than the American/African slavery practiced in this country much later.[214]

Paul taught something amazing in his writings. It is especially seen here: he elevated all people. The ground is level at the cross. There is no male or female superiority. No difference between Jews or Gentiles. No superiority between slaves and free people. I love that fact that in the early church, there were congregations where the gifting of the Spirit was such that a slave was the pastor over his master where he was a congregant. That is the beauty of the ground being level at the

---

[211] Hughes, *Ephesians*, 206.
[212] John F. MacArthur. *Slave: The Hidden Truth About Your Identity in Christ* (Nashville: Thomas Nelson, 2012), 188.
[213] Brian K. Harvey. *Daily Life in Ancient Rome: A Sourcebook* (Indianapolis, IN: Focus, 2016), 99.
[214] Hughes. *Ephesians*, 206.

cross. We are all equally deserving of hell, and all equally in desperate need for a Savior. It is only Jesus Christ that can take these distinctions and erase them by the Cross. Slaves, which were despised in Roman society are now made equal to their masters. And masters are brought down to be slaves of Jesus Christ.

With that in mind, let's consider Paul's advice to slaves and apply it to our own lives. We all are in the workplace, but how can we turn our work into worship?

FOCUS ON OUR ULTIMATE MASTER (6:5)

Ephesians 6:5 | Bondservants, obey your earthly masters with fear and trembling, with a sincere heart, as you would Christ.

Worshipping while we work is made possible by a focus on our New Master while we work. Jesus Christ is now LORD. I am not my own master. I can't just do what I want any more. I have to listen to what Christ says. And basically, he says how you treat your boss reveals what you think of Me! Therefore, worshipping Christ begins with your attitude at work. It is now one of sincere submission to the will of God. We should submit to the authority of our employer as if they were Christ. Christ has put us where we are, and we ought to fulfill his will right where we are.

Obeying our Master

Ephesians 6:5 | Bondservants, obey your earthly masters... as you would Christ.

Paul's point in this passage is that no matter who you work for, you should work for them as if they are God the Son. Your employer ought to think, "my employee must think I'm God" because of his hard work and faithfulness. In other words, your work is not just work; it is worship. Don't let your work hours be fruitless, dry, barely bearable endurance. Your work ought to demonstrate your love and dedication to God. How can we do that?

Remember you must have undergone a spiritual transformation. If you've been born again, everything about you changes, especially your work. Paul describes this transformation here. He says, if you are a Christian, then no matter who you work for you are not truly serving them, but Jesus Christ if you are a Christian. This transforms everything about us. It transforms our attitude. Paul says it again in Titus 2.

> *Titus 2:9–10* | Bondservants are to be submissive to their own masters in everything; they are to be well-pleasing, not argumentative, not pilfering, but showing all good faith, so that in everything they may adorn the doctrine of God our Savior.

We need to paint an accurate picture of Christ with our work. Does your life "adorn" the gospel of Jesus Christ? Yes, we have human bosses and overseers. But ultimately, the Christian is working for God. He is the one to whom we are responsible for the work we do. And we should work with excellence, knowing that it will please him if we do. Seeing God as our boss allows us to trust him with whatever happens that day: "Lord, I give you this day and trust you for what you have planned. I thank you that I have you as a boss whom I can trust without reservation." Would that make a difference in how you approach your job? As Paul called himself a "bondservant of Christ" (Rom 1:1), so are we all. When someone asks us, "What do you do?" We ought to be able to answer, "I serve Christ as a (fill in the type of work you do). Seeing our jobs that way will provide the motivation we need to work with excellence.

As long as your employer is not telling you to do something that is sinful, you ought to consider it to be the will of God for your life and obey it. Paul starts with the same word that he uses for children to parents: "obey!" Carry out your boss's wishes as if he were Christ. That means you have a "can do" attitude. That means no griping and complaining. If your boss has a certain goal for the day, obey what he says—your boss's goal is God's will for you. Don't do something else and make an excuse why it's not done. It is because of this fact that Christians ought to be the best workers in the world!

Worshipping our Master

> **Ephesians 6:5** | Bondservants, obey your earthly masters with fear and trembling, with a sincere heart, as you would Christ.

Fear and trembling? That's an evidence of worship. We don't worship our boss, but he might think we are! Obviously, there is something greater going on here than just work. You are a light in a dark city. You are reflecting Jesus Christ in you while you work. This is about glorifying Christ and evangelizing your workplace by demonstrating how a Spirit-filled person works. In other words, where you work and what you do for work is not nearly as important as how you work. So how do we turn our workplace into a worship time for Christ? Paul tells us very clearly: "Bondservants, obey your earthly masters with fear and trembling, with a sincere heart, as you would Christ" (6:5).

Even when jobs or coworkers are hard to like, we are to work as though God is our boss. That means doing tasks with joy, a servant's attitude, respect for others, diligence, and obedience to those in authority. Imagine what the workplace could be if all believers approached their jobs this way. Worship Christ while you work. Your employer may not deserve your wholehearted obedience, but Christ does.

> *Colossians 3:23* | Whatever you do, work heartily, as for the Lord and not for men.

A born-again person is gripped by the fear of the Lord, the very presence of God, and it affects his work ethic. There is carefulness about a Christian's work. If Christ is present with you while you are working, watching over you, you will have a deep carefulness about your work. You will care about what you are doing. It's important because it is for Christ. Let me mention one more thing. Some young Christians are idealistic. They think that if they could only be in ministry then all would be well. The truth is that every job we do is ministry. We are doing it for the Lord!

Loyal to our Master

> **Ephesians 6:5** | Bondservants, obey your earthly masters with fear and trembling, with a sincere heart, as you would Christ.

We are to *work with a sincere heart*. There is a sincere loyalty to Christ, no matter how unworthy our earthly masters may be. We can work with sincere joy because our Master's blessing is upon our work. The sincerity in work mentioned here means to have your heart "single, not having an ulterior or double motive, but an attitude of simplicity, purity, sincerity, and faithfulness."[215] We might not always be able to trust that our earthly employers have our best in mind, but we know in

---

[215] Zodhiates, *Word Study Dictionary*, "sincere".

sincerity that our heavenly Master does all things for his glory and our good.

Work is therefore a blessing and can be sincerely invested in for Christ. We have to remember that work is not a consequence of the curse of sin. Work is not a curse, but a blessing! God created work before the fall of mankind into sin. Our work is actually worship to God! Again, this was before the fall of mankind into sin.

> *Genesis 2:15* | The LORD God took the man and put him in the garden of Eden to work it and keep it.

> *Psalm 100:2* | Serve the LORD with gladness! Come into his presence with singing!

When you read about Joseph in the book of Genesis, you see his sincere loyalty to the Lord. We see Joseph's master was not Potiphar or the prison warden or Pharaoh. Joseph's Master was the Lord. Joseph put the Lord first in his work. He turned his work into worship. Is the Lord with you in your work as he was with Joseph?

At work your loyalties ought not to be divided. You ought to have your heart's focus set on doing what your boss says as if it were Christ giving you orders. There ought to be a sincere zeal about what you are doing because you are doing it for Christ. Whether you manufacture widgets, sweep floors, or manage a team of people—the joy is not in making money or in simply getting the job done, but in serving Christ! Paul says—take is so seriously, that you are totally focused on doing it. Keep your mind on it. Keep focused.

FOCUS ON OUR ULTIMATE MISSION (6:6-7)

Perhaps you have a mission statement at your job. Most mission statements say something like this: "The mission of our company is to please the customer by making widgets."

A Mission to Please God

The mission statement of every Christian is similar: our mission is to "please God" in all that we do!

> **Ephesians 6:6** | Not by the way of eye-service, as people-pleasers, but as bondservants of Christ, doing the will of God from the heart.

Our ultimate mission is to carry out the will of God and please him. The first question of the Westminster catechism is "What is the chief end of man?" What is it? "Man's chief end is to glorify God and to enjoy him forever." Our work should glorify God. This is what Paul says in verses 6-8. We are not at work to make ourselves look good to the boss. We work hard so that we might give the right opinion of Jesus Christ.

Our mission is to carry out the will of God. Jesus said in John 8:29, speaking of the Father, "He who sent me is with me. He has not left me alone, for I always do the things that are pleasing to him." Christ obeyed the Father in all things. In Mark 6:3, they asked of Christ, "Is this not the carpenter?" Christ spent 30 years in utter obscurity and many of those years, he spent working hard as a carpenter. He worked as a carpenter, but his ultimate mission was to do the will of his Father. That's our mission! A godly work ethic brings glory to God! We need to be faithful in how we work. In fact, God commands us to work quietly and faithfully.

> *Colossians 3:23* | Aspire to live quietly, and to mind your own affairs, and to work with your hands, as we instructed you, [12] so that you may walk properly before outsiders and be dependent on no one.

A Mission to Serve God

> **Ephesians 6:6a** | Not by the way of eye-service, as people-pleasers, but as bondservants of Christ.

The Christian's mission is to work for God all the time. Wherever a Christian is, his God is with him. We are indwelt by the Holy Spirit. Do you work harder when the boss is watching? Then you are working for the wrong boss. King Jesus is always watching. He never leaves us or forsakes us. You are not at work to please yourself, but to please God and to do his will! We ought to work with the awareness of our Master's presence always. Solomon says that work will never satisfy you. I know you believe me, but let's listen to Solomon. Work without Christ at the center is meaningless.

> *Ecclesiastes 2:11* | Then I considered all that my hands had done and the toil I had expended in doing it, and behold, all was vanity and a striving after wind, and there was nothing to be gained under the sun.

A Mission to be Satisfied by God

Ephesians 6:6b-7 | Doing the will of God from the heart, [7] rendering service with a good will as to the Lord and not to man.

Work is a great blessing. It's not a blessing in and of itself. People who treat work as the end and goal of living are actually unsatisfied and miserable. God alone satisfies. People who work for God can do so "from the heart" as they "do the will of God." Now they can work for God anywhere and do anything because they are working for God "with a good will as to the Lord and not to man." Their goal is not to lift man up or a certain company up. Their goal is to work in such a way that lifts God up. That's where true satisfaction is found. Work is merely a means of how God provides for us. But work is not meant to be a savior. We cannot love money. Work should not be worshipped. It is meant to be used in worship to God. If your job is the center of your life you will be miserable. Can I be happy if I make the goal of my life work? Will work make me happy? Will job security and a dream job make me happy? Work can never satisfy the soul of man fully. It is a gift, but it ought not be a god to us. Remember the wise words of our Lord.

Mark 8:36–37 | For what does it profit a man to gain the whole world and forfeit his soul? [37] For what can a man give in return for his soul?

Work will not ultimately satisfy you if that is what you are living for. You were not made for your job. You were made to glorify God.

FOCUS ON OUR ULTIMATE MOTIVATION (6:8-9)

Motivated by More than a Paycheck

We do not work primarily for a reward on earth. Our reward is that Christ will be pleased with us at His coming. That ought to motivate and drive everything that we do. back from the Lord, whether he is a bondservant or is free."

Ephesians 6:8 | Knowing that whatever good anyone does, this he will receive back from the Lord, whether he is a bondservant or is free.

No longer is our mandate to please ourselves or to please the boss or to bring home a check. Our mandate is to do the will of God – to bring glory and honor to Him! We no longer do our best work just when the boss is looking. Our mandate is to do the will of God all the time. You are to Please God. That's what ought to motivate you while you work. If you are born again, no longer is your motive money when you go to work. It's not a paycheck.

> *Proverbs 15:3* | The eyes of the LORD are in every place, keeping watch on the evil and the good.

Motivated by Our Mutual Master

Worshipping while we work is made possible by a focus on new motivation looking for the moment of Christ's return. We are slaves of Christ. In the Roman Empire whether a Christian was free or a slave, they had one Master.

> **Ephesians 6:9** | Masters, do the same to them, and stop your threatening, knowing that he who is both their Master.

At the moment of Christ's return there will no longer be any earthly positions in the Body of Christ. The cultural divisions that carry such weight on earth will be done away with forever.

In Christ there is a unity and an equality. Roman masters if they were believers, were to treat slaves as people, not as property. If they were both saved, they were brothers. If they were not, they were to be evangelized. Probably many Christians who owned slaves set them free. Regardless, there was an equality that comes forth loud and clear in this verse that is revolutionary. Paul says in verse 9, "Masters, do the same to them, and stop your threatening, knowing that he who is both their Master and yours is in heaven, and that there is no partiality with him".

At Christ's coming, all the earthly distinctions that we've held to will be done away with. There were great class distinctions in society. Paul in our passage in Ephesians levels all class distinctions and brings everyone level before the cross. We all know about Jews and Gentiles. They hated each other when they were lost, but when they were saved, God united them in one Body. All distinctions were gone. Even though we weight for the kingdom to come, the kingdom has already begun in a very real sense. We are one in Christ our King. Ethnic distinctions are done away with in Christ. Our ethnic distinctions become a picture of the beauty of our Creator God who brings a unity to our diversity. We all have different family and ethnic backgrounds. We have cultural differences. And that is a beautiful thing. God makes each of us unique to display His glory. But He brings our diversity together into one Body to glorify Him in unity! So, Paul can say in 1 Corinthians 12:

> *1 Corinthians 12:13* | ...by one Spirit are we all baptized into one body, whether we be Jews or Gentiles, whether we be bond or free; and have been all made to drink into one Spirit.

There were the male and female roles in Roman society. Women had almost no rights in Roman society. She could not own property. She could not vote or go into politics. But those distinctions and privileges are done away with in Christ. Men are no greater than women in God's universe. We may have different roles, but are all equally worthy of hell, and we should all be equally amazed that God could save a wretch like you or me. And of course, there were the divisions of slaves and free people in the culture. In normal society all these distinctions divided people.

But as Christianity swept through the Roman empire, these divisions were erased in the church. The distinctions remained in society, but under the cross, those who were not esteemed were now esteemed. Christianity had the effect of bringing dignity and worth to every individual, making the ground level at the cross.

Paul says in Galatians 3:26-29 that we are all brothers and sisters in Christ if we have been born again. Listen to these astounding words and remember the day in which they were written:

> *Galatians 3:26-29* | For in Christ Jesus you are all sons of God, through faith. [27] For as many of you as were baptized into Christ have put on Christ. [28] There is neither Jew nor Greek, there is neither slave nor free, there is no male and female, for you are all one in Christ Jesus. [29] And if you are Christ's, then you are Abraham's offspring, heirs according to promise.

Conclusion

May God make us all servants of Christ, turning our work into worship of Christ. Focus on your Master, Jesus Christ. Focus on his mission: do the will of God, please him, not men. And finally, focus on the moment of his coming. He could come at any moment. Are you serving him faithfully and waiting for his return at every moment? I trust you are!

21 | EPHESIANS 6:10-13
ROOTED IN SPIRITUAL WARFARE

Finally, be strong in the Lord and in the strength of his might.
EPHESIANS 6:10

Paul is on his final application for how to "walk worthy" in the Lord (4:1). He's told us how to walk worthy in the new life, in marriage, with children, and then in our work environment. Now he turns the corner from our Jerusalem and Judea and Samaria, and he tells us how to walk worthy in the world. The world is a great war zone.

> **Ephesians 6:10-13** | Finally, be strong in the Lord and in the strength of his might. [11] Put on the whole armor of God, that you may be able to stand against the schemes of the devil. [12] For we do not wrestle against flesh and blood, but against the rulers, against the authorities, against the cosmic powers over this present darkness, against the spiritual forces of evil in the heavenly places. [13] Therefore take up the whole armor of God, that you may be able to withstand in the evil day, and having done all, to stand firm.

The Christian life is a great battle. This life is nonstop warfare. The struggle is real. It is personal. It is spiritual. We must be on our guard. This is the greatest battle you will ever fight, and God is fighting for us.

OUR STRENGTH (6:10)

We feel so weak, getting his from every side at times, and we all know it. We are at war. In fact, we are engaged right now in the mother of all battles. No war in history can compare with the battle you and I are fighting. It can be the cause of either your greatest joy as a Christian or your deepest pain. We feel so weak so often, but our struggle on this earth is a blessing in disguise. Struggle and affliction are necessary in God's plan. Pain and struggle must run their course in order for proper growth to occur.

The Significance of Strength

Ephesians 6:10a | Finally, be strong.

Some Christians are unaware of the power they have to live the Christian life. Many are emotional casualties of spiritual warfare. They are discouraged, depressed, downtrodden, and defeated. Others are angry and anxious. Others still are trying escape through foolish thinking and unwise behavior, trying to cut the battle short. But we can't get away from the command. *Be strong in the Lord and in the strength of his might*. We need strength.

I learned of the man who found a cocoon of the emperor butterfly. He took it home to watch it develop. One day a small opening appeared. He observed the caterpillar struggling for several hours to pass its body past a certain point – a very small opening. Finally, this well-intentioned observer concluded there must be something wrong. So, he took a pair of scissors, and snipped the remaining top of the cocoon. The moth emerged of course very easily. The body was large and swollen, it's wings small and shriveled. He expected in a few hours that the wings would spread out in natural beauty, but they didn't. Instead of having the natural ability to fly, the moth crawled around dragging around shriveled wings and a swollen body – without the ability to fly.

Only later did the man understand that the constricting cocoon and the struggle was necessary to pass through, because the struggling through that constricting hole was God's way of passing fluid from the body into the wings – that the wings might be large and developed and the caterpillar be transformed into a butterfly able to fly with ease.

God wants you to live a transformed life, and that only comes through struggle, pain, and difficulty. If we cut it off, we will be walking around with swollen fleshly habits in our life with shrunken spiritual wings, and no power to fly.

God allows us in this spiritual battle, not to cut the pressure short, but to allow us to learn how to depend on the strength of the Lord. Basic to the effective Christian life is preparation. The untrained believer becomes the defeated believer who seeks to serve the Lord in his own wisdom and power. The strength of the Christian life is dependence on God, being strong in the Lord, and in the strength of his might. Any other strength proves to be powerless. [216] How do we get this strength?

The Source of Strength

> **Ephesians 6:10** | Finally, be strong in the Lord and in the strength of his might.

Our strength has a divine location: *in the Lord*. Lack of victory in the spiritual battle reflects a lack of understanding of our divine resources. Every Christian has problems, but it's the inability to move beyond the problem, the inability to get past the failure, that keeps us in spiritual defeat. Victory is found in dependence on God, so Satan's plan is to detach us from dependence on God.

This says the battle is the Lord's, not ours. God is the mighty divine warrior. God supplies the strength, not us. Our job is to "dress for success" by putting on the armor God supplies. "Be strong in the Lord!" It's the same battle cry that God gives to the Prophets such as Isaiah 42 and Hosea 11. The Old Testament frequently portrays God as a great warrior who gives the mighty war cry.

> *Isaiah 42:13, NIV* | The LORD will march out like a champion, like a warrior he will stir up his zeal; with a shout he will raise the battle cry and will triumph over his enemies.

We see this warrior God calling his people from east to west to return. And he leads his people with the roar of a lion. Our God is like a mighty Aslan leading us into battle.

> *Hosea 11:10* | They shall go after the LORD; he will roar like a lion; when he roars, his children shall come trembling.

This is the constant picture of the Old Testament, and it is the very theme that Paul picks up. Our Lion, our mighty Warrior roars, and we

---

[216] MacArthur. *Ephesians,* 337.

need to come trembling. He alone is the source of our strength. Paul says to the Ephesians, where Timothy would be the pastor:

> 2 Timothy 1:7 | God has not given us a spirit of fear but of power and love and of a disciplined mind.

Let's determine not to walk in our own strength, but to "be strong in the Lord and in the strength of his might" (6:10).

OUR WEAPONRY (6:11)

> Ephesians 6:11 | Put on the whole armor of God, that you may be able to stand against the schemes of the devil.

Paul ends his letter to the Ephesians with a call to battle and a provision of weaponry. What? I thought Jesus was supposed to bring me peace. Wait a minute. I became a Christian for God to heal me. What's this about fighting? That's right. God has called you to fight. He's issued us all we need in order to fight. Nothing is lacking. That's why he calls it "the full armor of God."

The Description of Our Armor

> Ephesians 6:11a | Put on the whole armor of God.

Our armor is described as being a supernatural armor. Indeed, it is called "God's armor." How amazing. This is comforting since the location of the war we are fighting is in the unseen realm. Since there is an invisible war going on, we need the appropriate armor. Jesus said, "I came not to bring peace but a sword" (Mt 10:34). God has called you to fight against his enemies, but his greatest enemies are unseen. Indeed, Christ came to "destroy the works of the devil" who functions in an invisible realm (1 Jn 3:8). Indeed, "For the weapons of our warfare are not carnal but mighty in God for pulling down strongholds" (2 Cor 10:4). Our weapons are not in the carnal realm we can see, but in an invisible realm where our mighty God dwells!

The reason you and I need God's supernatural armor is that we are fighting a spiritual enemy (6:12). The strategies we are seeking to defeat are from the devil. It's hard enough to fight an enemy you can see. It's much harder to fight someone you can't see. That is exactly the kind of enemy we face. Spiritual warfare is that conflict being waged in the invisible, spiritual realm that is being manifest in the visible, physical realm. In other words, spiritual warfare is a battle between invisible, angelic forces that affects you and me. The cause of the war is something you and I can't see. But the effects are very visible in the realm we live in every day. Some Christians been wounded morally in the battle. They cannot control their passions, or they make poor moral choices.

The Depiction of Our Armor

Ephesians 6:11b | ... the whole armor of God.

Paul uses the metaphor of a soldier to describe how the Christian is to fight the enemy. Since the war is unseen, it is vital for us to put on the armor God provides for us. The charge to put on the "whole armor of God" is both a command and a promise, the promise being that if we will really put on the full armor of God, we will stand and be victorious.

Paul was probably chained to a Roman soldier when he penned the words of Ephesians, and looking at the soldier's armor, he was inspired by the Holy Spirit to see in it the analogy of God's spiritual provision for our battle with Satan and his angels. He was also certainly alluding to the picture of God's armor throughout the Old Testament. First he certainly thought of God's very armor displayed in Isaiah.

> *Isaiah 59:17* | He put on righteousness as a breastplate, and a helmet of salvation on his head; he put on garments of vengeance for clothing, and wrapped himself in zeal as a cloak.

> *Isaiah 11:5* | Righteousness shall be the belt of his waist, and faithfulness the belt of his loins.

Perhaps the apostle's mind went from the song of Moses ("The LORD is a warrior; the LORD is his name," Exo 15:3) to the Lord's promise to drive out the Canaanites (Deut 7:1-2), to the Captain of the Lord's armies appearing to Joshua (Josh 5:13-15). In so many ways we see that Paul had a lot of images for the Christian's warfare to draw from as he was led by the Holy Spirit to write about this spiritual armor.[217]

Those who have traveled through Tolkien's most imaginative Middle Earth perhaps remember that Bilbo Baggins passed on to his

---

[217] For an excellent study on God as Warrior, see Tremper Longman. *God Is a Warrior* (Studies in Old Testament Biblical Theology Series) (Grand Rapids, MI: Zondervan Academic, 2010), 22.

successor, Frodo, a finely wrought coat of delicately woven mail which was secretly made under the mountains by dwarves and was virtually impenetrable, thus saving their Hobbit skins on several occasions. But here with Paul, in the context of ultimate spiritual reality, we are offered real armor wrought on the anvils of Heaven which will protect us in real war if we will but wear it. [218]

The Demand for Our Armor

> **Ephesians 6:11c** | That you may be able to stand against the schemes of the devil.

There is great demand for the amor in the Christian life since it is the only way to achieve victory. Standing is vital when you are fighting in war. We cannot fall back, and we cannot retreat. Paul tells us here that our goal is to stand firm. That means we are to hold the ground Jesus has already won for us. Jesus has already invaded Satan's domain and won back all the territory Adam lost. Our job is to hold the ground Jesus has won, not to fight to win. We are fighting *from* a position of victory, not *for* victory. We need an armor that will allow us to live a consistent, forward moving Christian life. Paul says we need a kind of armor that will help us "be able to stand against the schemes of the devil" (6:11b).

The Design of Our Armor

> **Ephesians 6:11d** | ... the schemes of the devil.

Our armor is designed by God himself with the intention to stop and stand against and move past the "schemes of the devil." Now the devil is the most psychopathic mastermind that exists in the universe. The human race is totally depraved, meaning every part of man's nature is touch by the brokenness of sin and the fall. We are not as depraved and evil as we could be. But in the totality of our being we are touched by sin. Our intellect, emotions, and body is suffering the effects of the fall. From the top of our head to the sole of our foot, inside and out, we are "dead in sin" (Eph 2:1-3) and "weak" to come to Christ (Rom 5:6). But the devil is more than totally depraved. He is utterly depraved. He is as evil as any being could be. If humanity were utterly depraved,

---

[218] Hughes, *Ephesians*, 221-224.

the human race would be out of existence by lunch time since we would quickly put one another to death. Human beings are not utterly depraved. But Satan is. If he could, he would wipe out the human race in a moment. Thankfully he is limited in what he can do by our loving God. Satan's greatest offensive weapon is unbelief, and that is the motivation behind every one of his schemes. So the armor that God gives is one that is woven in faith by grace in Christ. We might better understand the putting on of the armor with a simple command Paul gives in another epistle: "put on the Lord Jesus Christ" (Rom 13:14). The onlyway any of us can stand against the schemes of the devil is if another fights for us. Indeed, our greatest defense is to put on our Lord.

OUR ENEMY (6:12)

Satan's aim is to rip Christians off their feet unexpectedly. He wants them to be down and grovel. There is an enemy always attacking you. He never stops. You must not rest for a moment. It's a tricky war because it's invisible.

> **Ephesians 6:12** | For we do not wrestle against flesh and blood, but against the rulers, against the authorities, against the cosmic powers over this present darkness, against the spiritual forces of evil in the heavenly places.

You must be aware that you are always at war though you cannot see it. That mentality makes you more awake and aware of constant attack. As Ed Welch said:

> There is something about war that sharpens the senses. You hear a twig snap or the rustling of leaves and you are in attack mode. Someone coughs and you are ready to pull the trigger. Even after days of little or no sleep, war keeps us vigilant.[219]

Satan has no compassion for anyone. He is utterly depraved. He wants to kill and destroy. We have to be careful as believers not to be fooled by him. Paul says, "We would not be outwitted by Satan; for we are not ignorant of his designs" (2 Cor 2:11).

---

[219] Ed Welch in John Piper, *When I Don't Desire God: How to Fight for Joy* (Wheaton, IL: Crossway Books, 2004), 102.

The Enemy's Position: Unseen

Ephesians 6:12a | For we do not wrestle against flesh and blood.

Satan is puppeteering the masses. Our enemy is not those who break our hearts, inflict spiritual and emotional pain upon us. Those who attack us spiritually are just the pawns of Satan. "We do not wrestle against flesh and blood." Then who do we wrestle against? Paul describes them as satanic rulers and authorities. Our enemy sends in his best thugs. They are the enemy, not our dear family and not even any other human being. Our enemy is puppeteering men and women in the great unseen battle. The difficulty is that we have an invisible war. We can't see him, but we see his evil presence everywhere. The difficulty of this war cannot be overstated. Without the armor of God, it is like we are fighting against an invisible army. As Calvin said:

> Paul intimates that our difficulties are far greater than if we had to fight against men. Where we resist human strength, there is a visible war: sword is opposed to sword, man contends with man, force is met by force, and skill by skill; but here the case is very different, for our enemies are such as no human power can withstand. We cannot even see them. [220]

The battle is for souls. The strong man has his goods. Understand that when man fell into sin, all mankind became the slave of Satan. Mark 3:27 gives a story about Christ conquering the devil and says that Christ would enter into the strong man's house (in other words, the devil's world) and take the spoil of his goods (which in this parable are the people of the world). Of course, Christ says before he can enter the strong man's house, he has to first bind the "strong man." Christ does that at the cross!

The Enemy's Princes: Regional Rulers

Ephesians 6:12b | For we ... wrestle against the rulers.

This is literally talking about evil angels who have governing power over certain areas of the earth. They are princes or governors or rulers. We learn from Daniel 10 that Satan places spirit princes over various

---

[220] John Calvin. *Calvin's Commentaries: The Epistles of Paul the Apostle to the Galatians, Ephesians, Philippians and Colossians*, Volume II, trans. T. H. L. Parker (Grand Rapids, MI: Eerdmans, 1974), 218.

kingdoms of men on earth. We read of "the prince of Grecia" and also of "the prince of Persia." The prince of Persia alone was powerful enough to hinder the herald angel and keep him from fulfilling his commission for three weeks. Such crowned dignities of Satan wield enormous power, but they are defeated foes for the Christian. We wrestle against them in prayer and Christian service. They strongly resent any challenge to their terrible hold on the kingdoms of men.[221] We read in the Gospels that certain demonic spirits have dominion over certain parts of the earth. It is only where human beings give them dominion.

We can imagine the demons have guilds and expertise in various forms of deception and destruction. What works in the Middle East is different than what works in China or the United States. But these are sophisticated rulers and governors who have doctorates in deception. They know how to deceive people and keep them in bondage.

How did Satan get his power and position of authority in the unseen realm over mankind? God did not give Satan dominion over the earth. God gave man that authority, but Adam yielded that authority to Satan in the fall. Remember that Adam and Eve had dominion over the earth, but the moment they bought into Satan's lie, they became his slaves. Jesus said, "You are of your father the devil, and the lusts of your father you will do" (Jn 8:44). It is said of all the lost:

> 2 Timothy 2:25-26 | God may perhaps grant them repentance leading to a knowledge of the truth, [26] and they may come to their senses and escape from the snare of the devil, after being captured by him to do his will.

We must always remember as believers that Satan has no power over us. James says, "Resist the devil and he will flee from you" (Jas 4:7).

Where did this all begin? How did evil angels become evil in the first place? We have the whole story of Satan's rebellion in apocalyptic narrative recorded in the book of Revelation.

> Revelation 12:7-12 | Now war arose in heaven, Michael and his angels fighting against the dragon. And the dragon and his angels fought back, [8] but he was defeated, and there was no longer any place for

---

[221] John Phillips, *Exploring Ephesians & Philippians: An Expository Commentary*, The John Phillips Commentary Series (Kregel Publications; WORDsearch Corp., 2009), Eph 6:12b.

them in heaven. ⁹ And the great dragon was thrown down, that ancient serpent, who is called the devil and Satan, the deceiver of the whole world—he was thrown down to the earth, and his angels were thrown down with him. ¹⁰ And I heard a loud voice in heaven, saying, "Now the salvation and the power and the kingdom of our God and the authority of his Christ have come, for the accuser of our brothers has been thrown down, who accuses them day and night before our God. ¹¹ And they have conquered him by the blood of the Lamb and by the word of their testimony, for they loved not their lives even unto death. ¹² Therefore, rejoice, O heavens and you who dwell in them! But woe to you, O earth and sea, for the devil has come down to you in great wrath, because he knows that his time is short!"

Jesus said, "I saw Satan fall like lightening from heaven" (Lk 10:18). Many of those who rebelled against God in the beginning are now chained up awaiting destruction. Jude 1:6 speaks of some of the "angels who did not stay within their own position of authority, but left their proper dwelling, he has kept in eternal chains under gloomy darkness until the judgment of the great day." But there are myriads of these wicked army of Satan roaming around free, tempting and harassing and harming God's saints.

> *1 Peter 5:8* | Be sober-minded; be watchful. Your adversary the devil prowls around like a roaring lion, seeking someone to devour.

Of course, Satan was stripped of his power through the Cross. Jesus Christ puts down the reign of terror through his Cross.

> *Colossians 2:13–15* | And you, who were dead in your trespasses and the uncircumcision of your flesh, God made alive together with him, having forgiven us all our trespasses, ¹⁴ by canceling the record of debt that stood against us with its legal demands. This he set aside, nailing it to the cross. ¹⁵ He disarmed the rulers and authorities and put them to open shame, by triumphing over them in him.

He is called the "god of this world" (2 Cor 4:4) not because he created it, because he has no power to do that. He is given this description because he has enslaved the people of this world.

The Enemy's Power: Decision Makers

Ephesians 6:12c | For we ... wrestle against... the authorities.

When Paul tells us who our actual wrestling match is against, he uses an interesting term: authorities, or literally, "decision makers."

The Greek word translated "powers" is *exousia*. It is the usual word for delegated authority, for the liberty and right to exert power.[222] All the human race has delegated him complete authority by joining forces with him in their sin. Adam was the first to cede authority from God to Satan over his life, and we have all followed suit.

Satan is called "the prince of the power of the air" (Eph 2:2). This speaks of Satan's kingdom being this world. The devil and his angels set the trends and fashions in this world system. People, because of sin, have given themselves to this ruthless evil spirit. Satan has the authority in this world to set what is popular and not. This word "denotes the power which decides."[223] Though Satan decides what is done in the realm of wickedness, he can only decide for those who cede authority to him. One early church father put it this way.

> Marius Victorinus | The devil can do nothing to us unless we ourselves willingly allow him to do so. This is true in all our acts. Thus we are masters of our own will.... The devil's opportunity arises from our own vice. (280-363 A.D.) [224]

Satan is stronger than any one of us. Satan's power is beyond human. Satan is an angel, a spirit being. Satan does not have the limitations of flesh and blood. You and I cannot compete with the devil in our own strength. We can't outsmart the master deceiver. This is why we must "be strong in the Lord, and in the power of his might" (6:10). Satan also has great power because of his vast experience. He has untold years of experience at being the devil. He is called in Revelation 12:9, "the great dragon... that old serpent, called the Devil, and Satan, which deceives the whole world." You are not the first human being he has come up against. He deceived the first man and woman in the garden, and he's since deceived every human being that has ever walked the planet except one, Jesus Christ. Satan has been against much smarter

---

[222] John Phillips, *Exploring Ephesians & Philippians: An Expository Commentary*, The John Phillips Commentary Series (Kregel Publications; WORDsearch Corp., 2009), Eph 6:12c.

[223] *Theological dictionary of the New Testament*. 1964-c1976. Vols. 5-9 edited by Gerhard Friedrich. Vol. 10 compiled by Ronald Pitkin. (G. Kittel, G. W. Bromiley & G. Friedrich, Ed.) (electronic ed.) (2:566). Grand Rapids, MI: Eerdmans.

[224] Marius Victorinus. *Bibliotheca scriptorum Graecorum et Romanorum Teubneriana* (Leipzig: Teubner, 1824), 1972:187 [1281A–B].

and stronger people than you and me, and he has won. Thankfully, Satan is not stronger than God. He is a limited, created, finite being.

1 John 4:4 | Greater is he that is in you, than he that is in the world.

Hebrews 2:14 | Christ came to destroy him that had the power of death, that is, the devil.

Colossians 2:15 | Christ by his cross spoiled principalities and powers, he made a shew of them openly, triumphing over them in it.

1 John 3:8 | For this purpose the Son of God was manifested, that he might destroy the works of the devil.

Satan has no power over the believer whatsoever unless the believer yields to Satan. He was defeated at the cross, and he has no power whatsoever over you as a believer.

James 4:7 | Submit yourselves therefore to God. Resist the devil, and he will flee from you.

The Enemy's Planning: Cosmic Powers

Ephesians 6:12d | For we ... wrestle against... the cosmic powers over this present darkness.

Literally, these are the "cosmic administrators of darkness." They plan what is going to distract man's attention from God. The devil's plans have an ultimate goal: keep the entire cosmos in darkness.

2 Corinthians 4:4 | In their case the god of this world has blinded the minds of the unbelievers, to keep them from seeing the light of the gospel of the glory of Christ, who is the image of God.

John 5:19b | The whole world lies in the power of the evil one.

Perhaps one order of evil angels administrates the deceptions of false religion. Another order administrates addictions to substances. Another order administrates the media and other worldly distractions, another the various idols of materialism, etc. The wicked one and his demons administrate the fads, fashions, and distractions of this world. They are the planners of the vanity fair. That is why as believers, we must not allow ourselves to be forged into the mold of the enemy.

Romans 12:2 | Do not be conformed to this world, but be transformed by the renewal of your mind, that by testing you may discern what is the will of God, what is good and acceptable and perfect.

The Enemy's Plentitude: Evil Armies

Ephesians 6:12e | For we ... wrestle against... the spiritual forces of evil in the heavenly places.

These hordes of demons are a great army. Paul calls them "spiritual forces of evil." We don't know how many demons there are, but likely far more than the human race. There are so many that they are arranged as army units, forces of evil. We have the Air Force and the Delta Force. This is the Evil Force. The goal of demons is to organize for evil.

The Enemy's Policy: Evil

Ephesians 6:12e | For we ... wrestle against... the spiritual forces of evil in the heavenly places.

Satan and his armies are experts in evil. They have one main priority: to spread evil of any kind. They want to deceive and destroy Christians to render them paralyzed and ineffective. He follows no rules of engagement. He is utterly depraved. Satan and his demons will stop at nothing. These are wicked spirits whose main desire is to transgress God's ways and to bring disorder and destructible to the human race. Satan already guides the minds of lost people, but he loves to take the reins of the minds and emotions of God's people. Christians can say "for me to live is Christ" (Phil 1:21), but these demons can say "for me to live is to oppose Christ." Their hearts are filled with pure wickedness.

The tactics of Satan and his demons are to use lies (Jn 8:44), deception (Rev 12:9), murder (Psa 106:37; Jn 8:44), and every other kind of destructive activity to attempt to cause people to turn away from God and destroy themselves. Demons will try every tactic to blind people to the gospel (2 Cor 4:4) and keep them in bondage to things that hinder them from coming to God (Gal 4:8). They will also try to use temptation, doubt, guilt, fear, confusion, sickness, envy, pride, slander, or any other means possible to hinder a Christian's witness and usefulness.[225]

---

[225] Wayne A. Grudem, *Systematic Theology: An Introduction to Biblical Doctrine* (Leicester, England; Grand Rapids, MI: Inter-Varsity Press; Zondervan Pub. House, 2004), 415.

These armies of evil beings are organized against both Christians to paralyze them and make them ineffective, and against non-believers who are in the devil's chains of slavery.

Satan's strategy is always to use deception. Satan is the "father of lies" (Jn 8:44). The reason Satan has turned to deception is that he cannot outwit God. Satan tried to overcome God in heaven, and that gamble failed. Satan's power will never be a match for God's. Satan transforms himself into "an angel of light" (2 Cor 11:14). He looks like one of the good guys.

The Enemy's Place: The Spiritual Realm

Ephesians 6:12e | For we ... wrestle against... the spiritual forces of evil in the heavenly places.

These hordes of evil angels operate "in the heavenly places" of the unseen realm. Heavenly does not intimate anything holy, but merely unseen. The New Testament brings us behind the scenes into this unseen realm, and how some of the angels fell and became evil through their rebellion against God. Peter accounts:

2 Peter 2:4 | God did not spare angels when they sinned, but cast them into hell and committed them to chains of gloomy darkness to be kept until the judgment.

Jude 6 | The angels who did not stay within their own position of authority, but left their proper dwelling, he has kept in eternal chains under gloomy darkness until the judgment of the great day.

The emphasis is on the fact that they are removed from the glory of God's presence and their activity is restricted. They are on a leash, with eternal chains. But their activity is active.

1 Peter 5:8 | Be sober-minded; be watchful. Your adversary the devil prowls around like a roaring lion, seeking someone to devour.

Because the devil works in the unseen realm, a lot of his activity is in the mind. We have to "put on the whole armor of God" through prayer and learning how to use the Word, walking by faith with God, and then we will "be able to stand against the schemes of the devil" (Eph 6:11b).

Satan is like the spiritual mafia. Do you know where the mafia headquarters is? Do you know what street? Of course not. Do you know who they are as you walk past them on the street? No. Why? Because they are undercover. They don't want to be found out. They look like everyone else. They have what looks like legitimate businesses, but they are just fronts! So it is with Satan. He has a deceptive front. He transforms himself into an angel of light. Deception is his trade. Satan heads the spiritual mafia that controls people and even nations. People wonder how a nation can produce a Stalin or a Hitler. The explanation is the massive work and deception of Satan. That's how powerful he is. Satan is so experienced at deception that Revelation 20:8 says one day he will deceive all the nations of the entire world!

The Enemy's Panic: Time is Short

We don't read about it here in Ephesians, but the apostle John tells us in Revelation that the devil is in a panic.

> *Revelation 12:12* | Woe to you, O earth and sea, for the devil has come down to you in great wrath, because he knows that his time is short!

Satan is a defeated foe! He has no power over the child of God. Because of the Cross our accuser in cast down. As Revelation 12:10 says, "And I heard a loud voice saying in heaven, Now is come salvation, and strength, and the kingdom of our God, and the power of his Christ: for the accuser of our brethren is cast down, which accused them before our God day and night." Satan is doomed. He may harass you; he may accuse you; he may try to overpower you. But you must understand, if you know Christ, he can never defeat you. In fact, he is an enemy that is already defeated!

OUR VICTORY (6:13)

> **Ephesians 6:13** | Therefore take up the whole armor of God, that you may be able to withstand in the evil day, and having done all, to stand firm.

The Protection for Our Victory

> **Ephesians 6:13a** | Therefore take up the whole armor of God.

Christ is the Victor who provides us his armor. The only way we can stand in our victory, is to put on the whole armor of God that our Lord provides. Jesus is the Lion of the tribe of Judah, the King of all kings and Lord of all lords. He is the Captain of the Lord of Hosts that gave

Joshua his victory (Josh 5:13-15). He's the One who wrestled with Jacob (Gen 32:22-32). He cannot lose because the victory is already won. All we need to do is take up the armor and put on the Lord Jesus Christ. When David tried on Saul's armor, it didn't fit. But Christ's armor fits us perfectly. We must have a wartime mentality. God gives no deferments or exemptions. His people are at war and will continue to be at war until he returns and takes charge of earth. But even the most willing and eager soldier of Christ is helpless without the armor God provides every Christian. That is Paul's point here: take up the full armor of God. Victory is assured. We will look in the next chapter of how the armor relates to the gospel. Here's a preview. The belt of truth is the gospel of Christ from beginning to end, found throughout the Word of God. The breastplate of righteousness is the righteousness of Christ. The shoes for your feet are given to stand firm and ready to proclaim the gospel of peace. The shield of faith is the ability to apply the Word of God as a shield to your life, extinguishing all the flaming darts of the evil one. The helmet of salvation is the assurance of the faith we hold to. The sword of the Spirit is the word of God, by which we wield God's promises for our own lives. Take up this armor, and you are guaranteed victory.

The Peril in Our Victory

Ephesians 6:13b | That you may be able to withstand in the evil day.

We live in the evil day. Carnal weapons won't work. We need our armor because "the evil day" is upon us (6:13). One translation calls it the time "when things are at their worst" (NEB). It's the time when all the underworld breaks loose and comes against you.

As Christians, we often think our struggle is against flesh and blood, against the people we see and know. As a result, we have temporary solutions for our problems. There's a pill, a program, a plan for everything. But the church of God does not cure her ills with earthly remedies in the evil day. The church is a Spirit-filled living organism. We fight not against flesh and blood but against demonic powers. We need to know who we are fighting against. That's why we take up God's divine, omnipotent armor. We can withstand easily with the Lord fighting for us. Though the day may be evil, his light and life can bring the city of God to earth. We can rejoice as we stand firm on Mount Zion.

The Promise of Victory

Ephesians 6:13c | And having done all, to stand firm.

Don't just resist and withstand but conquer and take ground. Stand firm in Christ and see how he moves forward against the gates of hell! Christ has all power. Why would you want to be strong in anything else? "We don't negotiate with terrorists". This has been the policy of our country since its inception. We don't talk about compromise with the enemy. The only way we talk with the enemy is on terms of surrender. The devil knows he is defeated, so when you are standing firm, resisting the devil, he has to "flee from you" (Jas 4:7). Look at these promises of victory.

1 John 4:4, KJV | Greater is he that is in you, than he that is in the world.

John 15:5 | Without me you can do nothing.

Romans 8:32 | He who did not spare his own Son but gave him up for us all, how will he not also with him graciously give us all things?

Philippians 4:13 | I can do all things through him who strengthens me.

Romans 8:31 | If God is for us, who can be against us?

When Martin Luther stood before the Diet of Worms he was accused of heresy. After being condemned for declaring that men are saved by faith alone in Christ alone, he declared, "My conscience is captive to the word of God.... Here I stand, I cannot do otherwise."[226] Every believer who is faithful to God's Word cannot do otherwise than stand firm.

Conclusion

Jim Elliot died preaching the gospel to those who put him to death. The Huaorani Indians who killed him, said at the death of the five missionaries, the curtains were thrown back and they saw a host of angels and heard singing. The natives told Steve Saint (son of Nate Saint, friend and fellow missionary with Jim Elliot) something else that happened the day those missionaries died:

---

[226] Martin Luther in Eric Metaxas. *Martin Luther The Man who Rediscovered God and Changed the World* (New York: Penguin Random House, 2017), 216-218.

Dawa, one of the three women told me that after the killing she saw outsiders above the trees, singing. She didn't know what this kind of music was until she later heard records of Aunt Rachel's and became familiar with the sound of a choir. Mincaye and Kimo confirmed that they heard the singing and saw what Dawa seems to describe as angels along the ridge above Palm Beach. Dyuwi verified hearing the strange music, though he describes what he saw more like lights, moving around and shining, a sky full of jungle beetles similar to fireflies with a light that is brighter and doesn't blink. Apparently, all the participants saw this bright multitude in the sky and felt they should be scared, because they knew it was something supernatural.[227]

How did those five missionaries get to that place of such courage and boldness? How were they as young men able to go to war against the unseen enemy and win? They understood that they had to release their grasp on all things temporal. Each of the five missionaries who died, as well as their killers, witnessed the unseen war with physical angels singing from the thrones of authority they were given by the Lord. Who won that day? It wasn't the cosmic wicked ones. Though these missionaries died, there truly was something to sing about. Those missionaries had already given up their lives that others might live. We all know the story of how the missionary women went in after their husbands died. They evangelized this tribe, and a great majority placed their faith in Christ. Heaven wins! Angels sing! The victory of the unseen war has already been decided. Jesus triumphs. His people win. One of the five missionaries, Jim Elliot knew this. He knew that to take up the armor, he had to put away the things of this world. Listen to his prayer.

> Father, let me be weak that I might release my clutch on everything temporal. My life, my reputation, my possessions, Lord, let me lose the tension of a grasping hand. Even, Father, would I leave the love of fondling-how oft I have released grasp only to obtain what I prize by "harmless longing," the fondling touch. Rather, open my hand to receive the nail of Calvary—as Christ was opened—that I, releasing all, might be released, unleashed from all that binds me here. He thought

---

[227] Steve Saint, "Did They Have To Die?", *Christianity Today*, September 16, 1996.

heaven—yea, equality with God- not a thing to be clutched at all—so let me release my grasp. [228]

Let go of all that is earthly. You cannot wield the weapons God has for you unless your hands and heart are free from the things of this earth. Open up the war chest. Take out God's armor. Be strong in his strength. See beyond the shadows, the darkness and the evil. Move forward toward the light of Christ who leads us in the battle! All life is war. From the cradle to the grave, we fight. Before the new birth, we were held captive by the devil. Now we must "stand against the schemes of the devil". Though Christ has delivered the death blow to the powers of darkness, they are not yet fully destroyed. At the end of Paul's life, he said "I have fought a good fight." As long as we live on this broken earth, we too must have a wartime mentality.

---

[228] Jim Elliot in Elizabeth Elliot. *Shadow of the Almighty* (Peabody, MA: Hendrickson Publishers, 2008), 74.

22 | EPHESIANS 6:14-17

ROOTED IN GOD'S ARMOR

Put on the whole armor of God, that you may be able to stand against the schemes of the devil.
EPHESIANS 6:11

One night I was at our church building quite late at night. Someone had donated several hundred books to my library, and I lost track of time. It must have been 11:30 at night. All the sudden the fire alarm goes off. I call the fire department which tells me to call 911. So, I get ready to call 911—so far about three and a half minutes have passed, and in front of me are two fire trucks and eight firemen decked out head to toe in full fire gear! They come running toward the building with pickaxes ready to tear down the front door. I'm glad I was there. I find it fascinating that in our towns throughout our nation with only a moment's notice, firemen can be on the scene in a moment! They are our heroes. We also as God's soldiers ought to always have our spiritual war gear on! We hear about it in Ephesians 6.

This is not a physical war with traditional weapons of warfare like guns, tanks, missiles, and bombs. This is a spiritual warfare that is being waged in every town, city, state, country and continent on earth for the heart of men, women and children. Eternal destiny is at stake. Eternal rewards are at stake. This is like no war that people have ever seen, and it is as real as any battle waged throughout the pages of history. God has given us a war chest and provided armor and weaponry in it.

When Yahweh put on his armor in the Old Testament, it looked exactly like the armor Paul describes. Yahweh "put on righteousness as a breastplate, and a helmet of salvation on his head; he put on garments of vengeance for clothing and wrapped himself in zeal as a cloak" (Isa 59:17). Then it says he put on a belt of truth. He said, "Righteousness shall be the belt of his waist, and faithfulness the belt of his loins" (Isa 11:5). But when Yahweh became flesh, he was defenseless on purpose. He was nailed to a cross for the sins of the world. Now we know that Christ could never stay in the grave. He's the ultimate Warrior who conquered death. You don't want to meet him when he returns. The apostle John got a glimpse of him in the great book of the Apocalypse. He saw what Jesus Christ our Warrior looks like in his glorified armor. Listen to John testify.

> *Revelation 1:12-17* | I turned to see the voice that was speaking to me, and on turning I saw seven golden lampstands, [13] and in the midst of the lampstands one like a son of man, clothed with a long robe and with a golden sash around his chest. [14] The hairs of his head were white, like white wool, like snow. His eyes were like a flame of fire, [15] his feet were like burnished bronze, refined in a furnace, and his voice was like the roar of many waters. [16] In his right hand he held seven stars, from his mouth came a sharp two-edged sword, and his face was like the sun shining in full strength. [17] When I saw him, I fell at his feet as though dead. But he laid his right hand on me, saying, "Fear not, I am the first and the last.

Look at our Lord brandish his weapon. He is all glorious, yet he still chooses to use a sword: one that proceeds from his mouth, the two-edged sword, which is the Word of God. The same sword that Jesus will use to slay the unbelieving nations, is the same sword we believers have to bring the nations to Jesus. We can cut people in their hearts, as those who came to the Lord at Pentecost ("when they heard this they were cut to the heart," Acts 2:37).

> **Ephesians 6:14-17** | Stand therefore, having fastened on the belt of truth, and having put on the breastplate of righteousness, [15] and, as shoes for your feet, having put on the readiness given by the gospel of peace. [16] In all circumstances take up the shield of faith, with which you can extinguish all the flaming darts

of the evil one; **17** and take the helmet of salvation, and the sword of the Spirit, which is the word of God.

The first three pieces of armor—girdle, breastplate, and shoes (6:14–15)—were for long-range preparation and protection and were never taken off on the battlefield. The shield, helmet, and sword, on the other hand, were kept in readiness for use when actual fighting began, hence the verbs taking up and take.

THE BELT OF TRUTH (6:14)

The first piece of God's divine armor he gives us is the belt of truth.

Ephesians 6:14a | Stand therefore, having fastened on the belt of truth.

In the Old Testament God wears this belt (Isa 11:5; 59:17). The first thing the soldier always did when he was getting ready to meet the enemy, was to gather all his clothing together and fix it firmly in position by means of this tight band or belt which then held all his clothing in position. You will find that this very picture frequently used in the Scriptures. We see this illustrated spiritually by Peter when he says:

Romans 6:14 | Therefore gird up the loins of your mind. —1 Peter 1:13, NKJV

The Belt's Freedom

Honestly, if you lost your belt, you lost the battle. You didn't have time to gather your garment. You had to have your hands free to fight. The soldier needed something to gather his tunic so that he could be unencumbered and free to fight. The belt keeps the soldier from snags.

There was a real need for the war belt in ancient times. For instance, these soldiers wore a long tunic that flowed down to the ground. The tunic was an outer garment that served as his primary clothing. It was usually made of a large square piece of material with holes cut out for the arms and head. Ordinarily it flowed down to the ground. But when it came time to fight, the soldier would pick up his tunic and tuck it into his belt for mobility in battle. The battle that every Christian has is in the mind. In many ways, this belt of truth affects the eyes since the truth crystalizes our worldview, how we see the world. James Montgomery Boice, former pastor of Fourth Presbyterian

Church in Philadelphia alludes to this as he explains what the belt of truth is all about.

> It is dangerous to rush into battle without having the great doctrines of the faith fixed firmly in our understanding... In Christianity truth comes first, then action follows. Without truth, without sound doctrine, without the knowledge of who God is, who we are, what we have become in Christ, and what we have been called to do... we will be vulnerable to Satan's onslaughts and schemes.[229]

The Belt's Fastening

The Word of God is utilized in two weapons – the belt of truth and the sword of the Spirit. The belt of God's Word fastened to the believer's mind provides an inward transformation, readiness, and clear vision for battle through the Word of God, and the sword is an outward advancement of the Word of God. You cannot wield the Sword of the Spirit if you are not wearing your belt of truth! Our Lord tells us how we need to be dressed for battle. "Stay dressed for action and keep your lamps burning" or as the KJV says, "Let your loins be girded about, and your lights burning" (Lk 12:35). What was he saying? Stay focused. Be ready for action!

How then do we fasten the belt of truth to our lives? By utterly surrendering to the revelation of God in his Word. We either take everything the Word of God and surrender every inch of us to it, or we have no authority at all. David tells us that we hide God's Word in our hearts so that we stay far away from sin and focused on our victory.

Psalm 119:11, NKJV | Your word have I hid in mine heart, that I might not sin against you.

Paul later tells Timothy that we as soldiers cannot be entangled with the pursuits of this life.

2 Timothy 2:4 | No soldier gets entangled in civilian pursuits, since his aim is to please the one who enlisted him.

Take a break from media. You may not have time for your Bible because when you are down and discouraged you go to media instead of God. Most of what is on TV is geared to deceive you. The world's media is filled with the deceptions of the wicked on. Turn off the TV and radio for a while and instead be "looking unto Jesus the Author and

---

[229] Boice, *Ephesians*, 244-245.

Finisher of our faith" (Heb 12:1-2). Sadly, many Christians are confused and snagged by looking unto the media. You cannot gird up the loins of your mind through the true "Bible belt" unless you turn off the world's spicket of worthless things. Turn off the filth and silly and vain things from going into your mind. Remove distractions, search your heart for idols. These are perhaps gifts from God but can overtake your life if you put God in their place. It could be sports, family, job. All good things, but remember that anything can be an idol if you let it take the place of God. What is it that controls you if it is not Christ? As the hymn writer said, "Break down every idol, cast out every foe".

The Belt's Function

The belt of truth functions as night vision goggles. No matter what happens around the soldier, he can see what others can't. The belt clears the limbs from getting tripped up. That's what the Bible does for the mind. It clears us from getting tripped up with anger, anxiety, despair and foolish, worldly thinking. With the belt of truth, we can take down "strongholds, casting down arguments and every high thing that exalts itself against the knowledge of God, bringing every thought into captivity to the obedience of Christ" (2 Cor 10:4-5). The one who wears the belt of truth is never confused about the chaos around him. That Word of God, the belt of truth gives him clarity to see reality when all around him is pitch black evil and darkness. Be saturated in the light of the Word of God. With the belt of truth, we pray, celebrating that God's Word gives light.

> *Psalm 119:105* | Your word is a lamp to my feet and a light to my path.

Would you trust a soldier without his gun belt? Would you trust a doctor if he hadn't gone to medical school? Would you trust a driver if this was his first time in the driver's seat? Would you rely on a driver if he was under the influence of alcohol? Certainly not. The belt of truth is far more crucial than any earthly preparation or sophisticated weaponry. It straightens out our vision so we can see the battle correctly. Wear the belt of truth. The blessed man's "delight is in the law of the LORD; and in his law he meditates day and night." This blessed man is truly prosperous and fruitful. He is "like a tree planted by the rivers of water, that brings forth his fruit in his season; his leaf also shall not wither; and whatever he does prospers" (Psa 1:2-3). If you put on the belt of truth, you are guaranteed victory. What are you doing to put on the belt of truth? Commit to reading the Bible this year. Are you reading it regularly, daily? Are you saturated in it? Are you hungry for it?

THE BREASTPLATE OF RIGHTEOUSNESS (6:14)

Ephesians 6:14b | Stand therefore... having put on the breastplate of righteousness.

The Breastplate's Forger

If God "put on righteousness as a breastplate" (Isa 59:17), then so should we. This is a breastplate that God himself made. Specifically, it's forged through the life of Christ. His righteous deeds guard us and protect our most vulnerable part: our heart. What is this righteousness? It is the righteousness of Christ. It's his integrity, his perfection, his wisdom for life. We don't have this on our own. Salvation can never be through our own works of righteousness. Without the breastplate, we are completely unprotected from the dragon, who is the accuser of Christ's church. He slithers around whispering all our sins to us. We are sinners in need of Christ's righteousness.

> *Titus 3:5-7, KJV* | Not by works of righteousness which we have done, but according to his mercy he saved us, by the washing of regeneration, and renewing of the Holy Ghost; [6] Which he shed on us abundantly through Jesus Christ our Savior; [7] That being justified by his grace, we should be made heirs according to the hope of eternal life.

If you are in Christ, God sees you through your robe of adoption – there is no stain, no spot in you. He says: "You are my child! You know me! I know you! To me you are only holy!" The Lord of righteousness forged the breastplate by his own perfect life, which he lived for you. Put it on! That breastplate is like the clean clothing given to Joshua, the high priest in the days of the return from exile.

> *Zechariah 3:3-4* | Now Joshua was standing before the angel, clothed with filthy garments. [4] And the angel said to those who were standing before him, "Remove the filthy garments from him." And to him he said, "Behold, I have taken your iniquity away from you, and I will clothe you with pure vestments."

This breastplate reminds me of how Adam fled naked from the sight of the Lord, clothed only in his flimsy fig leaf, but God killed an animal and clothed him with a garment that cleansed and covered the nakedness of sin (Gen 3:7-8). It reminds me of the words in Isaiah's prophecy.

> *Isaiah 1:18* | Come now, let us reason together, says the Lord: though your sins are like scarlet, they shall be as white as snow; though they are red like crimson, they shall become like wool.

The Breastplate's Function

Righteousness means being made right. Christ's righteousness gives us right standing with God. We could never protect ourselves from Satan's arrows without this breastplate. Notice the armor is not our own, but God's. Paul said he did not have his "own righteousness, but the righteousness of God which is by faith" (Phil 3:9). So, what is this righteousness? Since it is not our own righteousness, which is filthy rags, then it is an infinitely perfect righteousness. It is "the righteousness of God which is by faith". To be justified is to have this righteousness. To be justified means to be "declared righteous" not based on my works but based on the work of Christ in my place. According to Isaiah, that's something to sing about!

> *Isaiah 61:10* | I will greatly rejoice in the LORD, my soul shall be joyful in my God; for he has clothed me with the garments of salvation, he has covered me with the robe of righteousness.

The Breastplate's Form

With God's breastplate, we are formed into Christ's image, and we give fame and honor and glory to God. Our heart beats with the heart of God. God leads us by his Holy Spirit into the "pathways of righteousness for his name's sake" (Psa 23:3). We are God's masterpiece, formed and predestined to walk in righteousness and holiness (Eph 1:4; 2:10).

Paul knew the armor well, being chained for years to a Roman soldier day and night. A Roman soldier would never go to battle without his breastplate. He would be too vulnerable. It would be like a soldier today on the front lines without a bulletproof vest. So, the breastplate covers the most important part of the body. It guards our heart. Even though Satan is a defeated foe, we need to watch our heart.

> *Proverbs 4:23* | Keep your heart with all diligence; for out of it is the fountain of life.

Daily, the Christian feels his vulnerability, and throws himself upon the righteousness of Christ. Daily, we depend on the cleansing of the word. Daily, we are empowered by the Spirit's limitless strength and the limitless love of Christ.

As believers in Christ, we are not only given the righteousness of Christ, but we are being conformed to his righteous likeness and image (Rom 8:29). Daily, the force of God's blade is cutting off the dead parts of our life so that we can grow and bear fruit.

> *John 15:2* | Every branch that does bear fruit he prunes, that it may bear more fruit.

Christ has hoisted this piece of armor upon you, and it can never be taken away from you. It is the righteousness of Christ. We didn't make this armor, Christ himself did. When we wear this, God leads us to fruitful, righteous lives, with a clean conscience and a heart of integrity. When we are actively walking with the breastplate of Christ's righteousness, it's noticeable. People give glory to God as they see the "oaks of righteousness" that God planted.

> *Isaiah 63:3* | They will be called oaks of righteousness, a planting of the LORD for the display of his splendor.

The Breastplate's Pharmacy

Every believer should live in the assurance of victory. We will never be what we once were. We can never go back to that sinful lifestyle. The Christian can no longer live comfortably in sin.

What happens when Satan's fiery dart gets under your armor? Whenever we allow any fiery dart of sin or doubt to get below the armor of righteousness, even then God has healing powers. He tells us to use the 1 John 1:9 medicine of confession and forsaking of our sins.

> *1 John 1:9* | If we confess our sins, he is faithful and just to forgive us our sins and to cleanse us from all unrighteousness.

> *Proverbs 28:13* | Whoever conceals his transgressions will not prosper, but he who confesses and forsakes them will obtain mercy.

> *Proverbs 24:16a* | For though the righteous fall seven times, they rise again.

What glory that we can confess our sins, and God is faithful to forgive. That means he will forgive you 100% of the time. He's also just to forgive. That means if God didn't forgive you, because of the blood of Christ, he would be unrighteous. He has bound himself to his promise to forgive every child of God.

The Breastplate's Faith

The breastplate is the assurance that I am righteous in Christ. This breastplate is often not entirely fastened when the believer comes into the family of God. But the truth is that at the moment of salvation, I am totally righteous in Christ before God. What Paul is getting at is the internal battle that we face. There is a battle in the inner man, the inner most being. The frontal attack of the enemy is going to come always on whether you truly are saved or not. The devil will insinuate that you must work for your salvation. He accuses the brethren. When we consider the breastplate of righteousness, we always remember we can never have perfect faith or perfect repentance on earth. We are not saved by perfect faith or perfect repentance but looking to the blood of Christ with the simplest and feeblest of faith, like the grain of a mustard seed. It is amazing that with that meager faith, we are transferred into God's kingdom, and given this glorious breastplate of righteousness, forged by the very life and death of Christ.

THE BOOTS OF PEACE (6:15)

The boots of peace represent the aggressive, forward moving, posture and attitude of victory that Christ has gained for us. Today we have shoes for every conceivable type of activity. We have dress shoes, work shoes, leisure shoes. In athletics there are special shoes for every sport, sometimes several types for a given sport. A tennis player might wear one type of shoe on a concrete court, another kind on clay, and still another on grass. Likewise, football and baseball players wear different shoes to play on different surfaces. A soldier's shoes are more important even than an athlete's, because his very life could depend on them. As he marches on rough, hot roads, climbs over jagged rocks, tramples over thorns, and wades through streambeds of jagged stones, his feet need much protection. A soldier whose feet are blistered, cut, or swollen cannot fight well and often is not even be able to stand up—a perilous situation in battle. Without his boots, a soldier cannot very well handle his sword or shield and cannot advance rapidly or even retreat.[230]

Ephesians 6:15 | Stand therefore... and, as shoes for your feet, having put on the readiness given by the gospel of peace.

Galatians 6:14 | But far be it from me to boast except in the cross of our Lord Jesus Christ, by which the world has been crucified to me, and I to the world.

The Boots' Praise
Paul gets the idea from Isaiah 52

Isaiah 52:7 | How beautiful upon the mountains are the feet of him who brings good news, who publishes peace, who brings good news of happiness, who publishes salvation, who says to Zion, "Your God reigns."

Here we announce, "God is the victor!" We have an evangelistic heart that proclaims the glory of the gospel to the worst of sinners. Jesus doesn't call those who think they are righteous to repent (Lk 5:32). They are so blind that there is no hope for them in their self-righteous pride. It's those who know they are sinners who have hope with God. There is an army of evangelists who proclaim the good news. We say: God's in control. He reigns. He's done it all from beginning to end to obtain your salvation. That's good news. Christ said, "It is finished." And then he died. There was nothing more to do. He paid it all. His resurrection shows that his payment was accepted by the Father and death was conquered.

The Boots' Posture
The boots give us the spiritual swagger of heart because the Lord has made you ready through his own blood. Our swagger comes from the victory of Christ, not our own boasting, which would be foolish. You cannot play football very well in dress shoes. The bottoms are too slick. You'd be sliding all over. What you need is cleats. A soldier does not go out to war in tennis shoes, but in combat boots! And so, we as Christians must always be prepared, alert, awakened, and ready for battle. When all the powers of earth and hell come against your soul, you take that boot of peace and hit them square in the teeth! You see, in order to

---

[230] MacArthur, *Ephesians*, 354.

have peace, you have to go to war! You have to have a posture of victory! Have you ever seen a champion in a posture of despair and defeat? No, his feet are firmly established for victory, and he's not moving.

The Boots' Peace

The boots are ones which take us places that need God's peace and reconciliation. We must be prepared each day to share the gospel of peace with a lost world. The most victorious Christian is a witnessing Christian.[231] Earlier in Ephesians, Paul had said that Jesus is our peace (2:14). So we're still talking about getting dressed up in Jesus. The "gospel of peace," the good news of Jesus Christ, not only brings us truth and righteousness, but it also brings us the peace of God because we have peace with God. As we take steps in life, the good news of our relationship with God will confirm our steps with rest in the soul.

The Boots' Preparation

The word "readiness" has the general meaning of being prepared. In Titus 3:1 Paul uses the term to exhort believers "*to be ready* for every good deed." A good pair of boots allows the soldier to be ready to march, climb, fight, or do whatever else is necessary. Christ demands the same readiness of his people.[232]

The Boots' Position

We must develop a spiritual swagger as a soldier in the absolute confidence and trust of our God that with a holy certainty when we stand up for his holy purpose and cause, he will stand up and fight for us. We are unstoppable, we are unconquerable, and we are untouchable for he is unstoppable, unconquerable, and untouchable. We have grown up with a version of Christianity that cowers before giants of fear, anxiety, worry, sin, circumstance and worldly pressures. We need the swagger of David who proclaimed:

> *Psalm 3:6, NKJV* | I will not be afraid of ten thousands of people that have set themselves against me round about.

Do you have the aggressive, forward moving, posture of victory?

---

[231] Wiersbe, *The Bible Exposition Commentary*, vol. 2, 58.
[232] MacArthur, *Ephesians*, 354.

THE SHIELD OF FAITH (6:16)

Ephesians 6:16 | In all circumstances take up the shield of faith, with which you can extinguish all the flaming darts of the evil one.

A Shield of Togetherness

With the shield of faith, we have the confidence that God wins. The shield was large, usually about four feet by two feet, made of wood, and covered with tough leather. As the soldier held it before him, it protected him from spears, arrows, and "fiery darts." The edges of these shields were so constructed that an entire line of soldiers could interlock shields and march into the enemy like a solid wall. Roman soldiers lined up side by side in close formation with their shields together, and all of them were covered as they advanced. This suggests that we Christians are not in the battle alone.

A Shield of Trust

This is not just any shield. God himself is our shield. When you stand behind this shield, trusting God completely, you become untouchable.

> *Psalm 3:3* | But you, O LORD, are a shield about me, my glory, and the lifter of my head.

> *Psalm 18:2* | The LORD is my rock and my fortress and my deliverer, my God, my rock, in whom I take refuge, my shield, and the horn of my salvation, my stronghold.

Our faith cannot be based on emotion. The "faith" mentioned here is not saving faith, but rather living faith, a trust in the promises and the power of God.[233] Our faith cannot be based on the testimonies of others who have been delivered. It can't be clichés or things you've heard repeated over and over again. We have to have a trust in the promises of God – that his very voice speaks to you. His voice in your heart engenders confidence. You must lay hold on God's own claims of who he is. He's your shield and your defender.

When John Paton (b.1824, missionary to the New Hebrides Islands of the South Pacific) was translating the Bible for a South Seas island tribe, he discovered that they had no word for trust or faith. One day a

---

[233] Wiersbe, *The Bible Exposition Commentary*, vol. 2, 58.

native who had been running hard came into the missionary's house, flopped himself in a large chair and said, "It's good to rest my whole weight on this chair." "That's it," said Paton. "I'll translate faith as 'resting one's whole weight on God.' "[234]

A Shield of Testing

The arrows that Satan throws at us are "fiery". We've seen the movies that picture what ancient war was like. Satan has poison and fire on the tips of all his arrows. If you start following Christ, you will be persecuted.

> 2 Timothy 3:12 | Indeed, all who desire to live a godly life in Christ Jesus will be persecuted.
>
> John 15:18 | If the world hates you, know that it has hated me before it hated you.

From the moment we follow our Lord by faith, we will be tested in all kinds of ways, and sometimes God even allows "a messenger of Satan" to harass us, so that we might remain humble (2 Cor 12:7). But even if we are not directly afflicted, his darts will constantly barrage us.

In New Testament times the tips of arrows would often be wrapped in pieces of cloth that had been soaked in pitch. Just before the arrow was shot, the tip would be lighted, and the flaming missile would be shot at the enemy troops. The pitch burned fiercely, and on impact it would spatter burning bits for several feet, igniting anything flammable it touched. In addition to piercing their bodies, it could inflict serious burns on enemy soldiers and destroy their clothing and gear. The most reliable protection against such flaming missiles was the shield, whose covering of metal or leather soaked in water would either deflect or extinguish them. The spiritual flaming missiles against which believers need protection would seem primarily to be temptations. Satan continually bombards God's children with temptations to immorality, hatred, envy, anger, covetousness, pride, doubt, fear, despair, distrust, and every other sin.

The only way to extinguish Satan's flaming missiles of temptation to doubt God is to *believe* God, taking up the shield of faith.[235] "Every

---

[234] MacArthur, *Ephesians*, 358.
[235] Ibid., 358-359.

word of God is tested," the writer of Proverbs tells us. "He is a shield to those who take refuge in him" (Pro 30:5). David reminds us:

> *Psalm 18:30* | The word of the LORD is tried; he is a shield to all who take refuge in him.
>
> *1 John 5:4* | This is the victory that has overcome the world—our faith.

A Shield of Triumph

The evil one's flaming arrows will be extinguished by believing the promises of God. This is how we resist the devil, and he has no choice but to flee. The evil one refers to the devil, whose supernaturally evil schemes we are to stand firm against and "to resist in the evil day" with the armor God supplies (6:11-13). Paul here again emphasizes that our struggle is against *personal* forces of evil—not simply against bad philosophies or wrong ideas, as liberal theologians and preachers have long maintained. Our battle is not against abstract evil influences but the personal evil one and his hordes of personal demons.

THE HELMET OF SALVATION (6:17)

Ephesians 6:17a | And take the helmet of salvation.

The helmet is not the cocky attitude of a highly trained CIA operative-but a humble swagger that comes from confidence in God's invincibility, his guaranteed victory, his assured triumph or what's known in Scripture simply as "rejoicing in your salvation." We know who is the ultimate Champion: Jesus Christ. It's the confidence of the twice-born. And when you wear this attitude (this helmet) then you carry the boast and confidence of the ultimate David, Jesus Christ. In him, you truly are undefeatable.

This joy is not from anything on this earth, but in God alone. One day God will wipe away all tears, and he will be our God and we shall be his people. This is the helmet Paul speaks of in Ephesians 6, and it will protect you during all the disappointing circumstances of life.

We're talking about the confidence in a full final, total salvation when we will be glorified, and you will never sin again. You need to put on this helmet each day. In other words, you need to constantly be encouraging yourself that this life is only temporary. The pain, the disappointment, and the trouble are not what you were created for. Put on the helmet of hope, that one day you will never sin again, and you will dwell in Christ's presence forever. That's where our joy for living comes from.

The fact that the helmet is related to salvation indicates that Satan's blows are directed at the believer's security and assurance in Christ. The two dangerous edges of Satan's spiritual broadsword are discouragement and doubt. To discourage us he points to our failures, our sins, our unresolved problems, our poor health, or to whatever else seems negative in our lives in order to make us lose confidence in the love and care of our heavenly Father.[236]

The helmet is a constant reminder of the deliverance that God gives us. In the end, we have won the war against Satan. What the helmet was to the Roman soldier, salvation is to the Christian soldier. There can be no victory unless the mind is protected with God's Word.

> *Romans 8:6, NKJV* | For to be carnally minded is death, but to be spiritually minded is life and peace.

A significant battlefield for Christians is in the area of our minds. We must be careful to protect ourselves from wrong or improper thought patterns and be transformed by the renewing of our minds (Rom 12:2). Every thought can be brought captive to the obedience of Jesus Christ (2 Cor 10:4-5). The Roman helmet also protected the jawbone, with armor extending down to the chin. We must control our tongues and speak words that glorify God (Eph 4:29; Jas 3:1-12), stating that we have overcome the darkness and that no weapon formed against us shall prosper.

THE SWORD OF THE SPIRIT (6:17)

Ephesians 17b | And take ... the sword of the Spirit, which is the word of God.

A Specific Sword

The sword to which Paul refers here is the shorter sword, which varied in length from six to eighteen inches. It was the common sword carried by Roman foot soldiers and was the principal weapon in hand-to-hand combat. Carried in a sheath or scabbard attached to their belts, it was always at hand and ready for use. It was the sword carried by the soldiers who came to arrest Jesus in the Garden (Mt 26:47), wielded by

---

[236] MacArthur, *Ephesians*, 360.

Peter when he cut off the ear of the high priest's slave (Mt 26:51), and used by Herod's executioners to put James to death (Acts 12:2). The term Paul uses here for word is not *logos*, which refers to general statements or messages, but is *rhēma*, which refers to individual words or particular statements. The apostle is therefore not talking here about general knowledge of Scripture but is emphasizing again the precision that comes by knowledge and understanding of specific truths. Like Jesus did in the wilderness, we need to use specific scriptural truths to counter specific satanic falsehoods. [237]

This is the most audacious element of heavenly war. This is not the sword of the flesh. It's not Goliath's sword of natural power, but God's sword of the Spirit. It's impossible to escape. Nothing in this entire universe can defend against its striking blow. It cracks the pale of darkness, ushers light into the caverns of illusion and forces all lies to stand naked before the bar of truth. The precious sword makes its bearer unstoppable. It's designed for taking territory-for rescuing the imprisoned, for freeing the oppressed, and for extending the borders of the kingdom.

The emphasis of the present passage is on how believers are to use the sword of the Spirit. It is not a physical weapon designed by human minds or forged by human hands (as noted in 2 Cor. 10:3–5) but the perfect spiritual weapon of divine origin and power. Like the shield of faith and the helmet of salvation, it is always to be at hand, ready to be taken up (vv. 16*a* and 17*a*) and used when a battle begins.

A Scripture Sword

Paul explicitly states that the sword of the Spirit is Scripture, the word of God. The Scottish pastor and writer Thomas Guthrie said,

> The Bible is an armory of heavenly weapons, a laboratory of infallible medicines, a mine of exhaustless wealth. It is a guidebook for every road, a chart for every sea, a medicine for every malady, and a balm for every wound. Rob us of our Bible and our sky has lost its sun. [238]

Of the divine authorship of Scripture John Wesley said,

> The Bible must have been written by God or good men or bad men or good angels or bad angels. But bad men and bad angels would not

---

[237] Ibid., 368.
[238] Thomas Guthrie. *The Way to Life: Sermons by Thomas Guthrie* (New York: Robert Carter & Brothers Publishers, 1876), 91.

write it because it condemns bad men and bad angels. And good men and good angels would not deceive by lying about its authority and claiming that God wrote it. And so the Bible must have been written as it claims to have been written—by God who by His Holy Spirit inspired men to record His words using the human instrument to communicate His truth. [239]

The sword of the Spirit is also an offensive weapon, capable of inflicting blows as well as deflecting those of the enemy.

Hebrews 4:12-13 | For the word of God is living and active, sharper than any two-edged sword, piercing to the division of soul and of spirit, of joints and of marrow, and discerning the thoughts and intentions of the heart. [13] And no creature is hidden from his sight, but all are naked and exposed to the eyes of him to whom we must give account.

A material sword pierces the body, but the Word of God pierces the heart. The more you use a physical sword, the duller it becomes; but using God's Word only makes it sharper in our lives. A physical sword requires the hand of a soldier, but the sword of the Spirit has its own power, for it is "living and powerful" (Heb. 4:12). The Spirit wrote the Word, and the Spirit wields the Word as we take it by faith and use it. A physical sword wounds to hurt and kill, while the sword of the Spirit wounds to heal and give life. But when we use the sword against Satan, we are out to deal him a blow that will cripple him and keep him from hindering God's work.[240]

A Two-Sided Sword

This sword is double-sided. One side defeats the devil. The other side cuts men's hearts so that they come to know Jesus. One brings destruction to the kingdom of darkness, the other delivers people into the kingdom of light.

It's not the Bible lying on your coffee table that makes the enemy flee, but the trained mind filled with the knowledge of truth, activated by the power of the Holy Spirit and exercised in an appropriate situation. It's similar to what Jesus said in the Gospel of John.

---

[239] John Wesley. *The Arminian Magazine: Consisting of Extracts and Originals on Universal Redemption*, vol. 13 (London: New Chapel, 1790), 34.

[240] Wiersbe, *The Bible Exposition Commentary*, vol. 2, 59.

John 6:63 | The words that I speak unto you, they are spirit, and they are life.

The sword is only useful if you keep it sharp. Keep your knowledge of God's Word sharp by constantly reading it, meditating on it, and speaking his promises. Satan loves to keep us out of the Word. To make Scripture reading and meditation a priority, we need to think of it as more important than our daily food.

Conclusion

Let's turn to Revelation and see who wins.

Revelation 19:11-21 | Then I saw heaven opened, and behold, a white horse! The one sitting on it is called Faithful and True, and in righteousness he judges and makes war. [12] His eyes are like a flame of fire, and on his head are many diadems, and he has a name written that no one knows but himself. [13] He is clothed in a robe dipped in blood, and the name by which he is called is The Word of God. [14] And the armies of heaven, arrayed in fine linen, white and pure, were following him on white horses. [15] From his mouth comes a sharp sword with which to strike down the nations, and he will rule them with a rod of iron. He will tread the winepress of the fury of the wrath of God the Almighty. [16] On his robe and on his thigh he has a name written, King of kings and Lord of lords. [17] Then I saw an angel standing in the sun, and with a loud voice he called to all the birds that fly directly overhead, "Come, gather for the great supper of God, [18] to eat the flesh of kings, the flesh of captains, the flesh of mighty men, the flesh of horses and their riders, and the flesh of all men, both free and slave, both small and great." [19] And I saw the beast and the kings of the earth with their armies gathered to make war against him who was sitting on the horse and against his army. [20] And the beast was captured, and with it the false prophet who in its presence had done the signs by which he deceived those who had received the mark of the beast and those who worshiped its image. These two were thrown alive into the lake of fire that burns with sulfur. [21] And the rest were slain by the sword that came from the mouth of him who was sitting on the horse, and all the birds were gorged with their flesh.

Some of you know my family's heritage is from Scotland. My oldest son learned how to play the bag pipes and toured with a bagpipe band for four years. His great grandfather came from Scotland after fighting for his country in the First World War. He enlisted when he was only 14 years old. He had some fight in him, though he was just a boy. World War I was an awful conflict. Hundreds of soldiers would be encamped in ditches. Rain, cold, and hunger could not stop them. Their motto was "for the Crown of Scotland!" They would think of their homeland and their families and they would clothe themselves in loyalty for the crown of Scotland! My grandfather was a prisoner of war for a time. He had so much fighting experience before he came to America on a boat to Ellis Island in 1925, and he had only a quarter century under his belt. Why did he fight so valiantly? He fought for his homeland. That's why we fight as Christians. This battle is only temporary. And we know that we are fighting from a standpoint of victory. We want to see so many come out of the Land of Darkness and the City of Destruction to the Celestial City where Christ reigns.

Dear brothers and sisters be strong in the Lord! The ancient war cry of Israel is our war cry! Only be strong and courageous, for the battle is the Lord's!

23 | EPHESIANS 6:18-24
ROOTED IN BLESSING

Peace be to the brothers, and love with faith, from God the Father and the Lord Jesus Christ. Grace be with all who love our Lord Jesus Christ with love incorruptible.

EPHESIANS 6:23-24

The apostle Paul is now at the very end of his letter to his beloved Ephesian church. He wants to leave them with how very blessed they are. He's already told them they are "blessed with all spiritual blessings in Christ" at the very beginning of his letter (1:3), and it is appropriate that he describes a few of these blessings as he closes. He begins by letting them know the great blessing of prayer. He then rejoices over the blessings of preaching and pastors. Then he closes like the a great fireworks display and leaves them with the blessing of being blessed by God with peace, love, faith, and grace.

Ephesians 6:18-24 | Praying at all times in the Spirit, with all prayer and supplication. To that end, keep alert with all perseverance, making supplication for all the saints, [19] and also for me, that words may be given to me in opening my mouth boldly to proclaim the mystery of the gospel, [20] for which I am an ambassador in chains, that I may declare it boldly, as I ought to speak. [21] So that you also may know how I am and what I am doing, Tychicus the beloved brother and faithful minister in the Lord will tell you everything. ²² I have sent him to you for this very purpose, that you may know how we are, and that he may encourage your hearts. ²³ Peace be to the brothers, and love with faith, from God the Father and the Lord Jesus Christ. ²⁴ Grace be with all who love our Lord Jesus Christ with love incorruptible.

THE BLESSING OF PRAYER (6:18)

When the Wright brothers invented the first fixed wing airplane on December 17, 1903, it changed the nature and future of warfare. No longer was hand to hand combat the only way to fight. Today, a company of soldiers only needs to communicate with the Air Force in order to win the victory. With prayer, every Christian has a heavenly "Air Force"! In modern warfare, there is always a soldier who watches the battle and gives the coordinates of the enemy to the fighter jets in the air. If taking out the enemy from the ground is not possible, then the fighter jets are called in.

After giving all the spiritual armor for the Christian, which is our security in Christ and in the gospel, the apostle Paul says that we must call in the heavenly Air Force through prayer. Listen to the words of the Apostle Paul.

> **Ephesians 6:18** | Praying at all times in the Spirit, with all prayer and supplication. To that end, keep alert with all perseverance, making supplication for all the saints.

All lasting fruit in the Christian life comes through cooperation and surrender to God in prayer. Martin Luther is quoted as saying, "I have so much to do today that I must spend the first three hours in prayer." Robert Murray McCheyne said, "A man is what he is when he is on his knees, and nothing more."[241] John Wesley rightly said, "God does nothing but by answered prayer, and everything with it."[242]

What does it mean to pray? The word "praying" gives prominence to the devotional side of wrestling with God. No wonder Satan feels threatened whenever a believer prays. This "praying" is not the weak and stammering of the believer, nor the wandering and inadequate

---

[241] Robert Murray McCheyne. *Memoir and Remains of Robert Murray McCheyne* (Dundee, Scotland: William Middleton Publishing, 1855), 406.

[242] John Wesley. *The Works of John Wesley: Volume 11: Thoughts, Addresses, Prayers, Letters* (Grand Rapids, MI: 1872), 437.

prayer he makes. The fact that a child of God is appealing to the almighty Father is what causes Satan to fear. Living the Christian life without prayer is like a soldier going into battlefield blindfolded and sleepwalking with no armor. It's a sure death sentence. Paul tells us how we can stay alert through prayer.

Stay Alert with Practical Prayer

Ephesians 6:18a | Praying at all times.

We are to pray at all times – literally "in all seasons" or for "every occasion." We are to pray in the Spirit. Prayer is to be Spirit directed. We are to pray with all prayer and supplication. That is all kinds of prayer. Specifically, he speaks of supplication, which is a "heart cry" or an "unburdening of the heart for a deep need" and a plea for God's supply. Paul and Jesus both teach us that our prayers should be continual.

1 Thessalonians 5:17 | Pray without ceasing.

Luke 18:1 | Jesus said, "Men ought always to pray and not to faint."

Pray at all times. You cannot afford not to pray.

Stay Alert with Powerful Prayer

Ephesians 6:18b | Praying... in the Spirit.

The Christian stays alert by keeping in step with the Spirit. The Spirit always uses the Word, so a prayerful Christian is a Word-centered Christian. We are not walking forward in our own wisdom, but we are sensitive to the Spirit of God who is leading us. Because the Spirit is leading, anything is possible in prayer. Don't close your eyes to what God can do through discouragement, anxiety, anger or despair. Keep your eyes open as a warrior intercessor because prayer is powerful! Prayer is how God changes the impossible! Prayer is how God takes what is naturally impossible and makes it possible!

Stay Alert with Persevering Prayer

Ephesians 6:18c | To that end, keep alert with all perseverance.

We are to have persevering prayer. Keep alert in prayer. There are many roadblocks to prayer. Laziness can be a big problem. We have to persevere through the weakness of our bodies and remember the words of our Lord Jesus: "Watch and pray so that you will not fall into temptation. The spirit is willing, but the flesh is weak" (Mt 26:41). We learn to persevere by receiving answers to prayer, but our motive must be correct. "When you ask, you do not receive, because you ask with wrong motives" (Jas 3:4). Our motive should be God's glory. Sometimes we pray: "Lord change this person" because we want a more comfortable life. Many prayers can come out of a desire to live on Easy Street. We have to have selfless, others-edifying, God-glorifying motives. Another reason we don't get answered prayer is because of sin in our lives. Remember the words of Isaiah.

> *Isaiah 59:1-2* | Surely the arm of the Lord is not too short to save, nor his ear too dull to hear. ² But your iniquities have separated you from your God; your sins have hidden his face from you, so that he will not hear.

If you are not seeing answered prayer, keep alert to sin in your life. Your iniquities can never condemn you as a child of God (Rom 8:1), but it will hurt your relationship with the Father. Another roadblock that keeps us from staying alert in prayer with all perseverance is an unforgiving spirit. If you find yourself unable to hear God, or get through to God in prayer, you need to search your heart for any bitterness or grudges you may have and leave your gift at the altar, so to speak, and as soon as possible, reconcile with your brother or sister (Mt 4:24; Mk 11:24). Even the wrong treatment of our mate can hinder our prayers (1 Pet 3:7). A further killer to persevering prayer is stinginess in giving.

> *Proverbs 21:13* | Whoever closes his ear to the cry of the poor will himself call out and not be answered.

Ask the Holy Spirit to just search you, not because he's down on you, but so he can get the kink out, so the love and the power of God can really flow into your life.

Stay Alert with Plentiful Prayer

Ephesians 6:18d | Making supplication for all the saints.

The word "supplication" intimates that God will indeed supply what we earnestly and sincerely ask if it is according to God's will. Whatever you are praying for, remember God wants to do "exceeding, abundantly above all that you could ever ask or imagine" (Eph 3:19).

We are to pray for this incredible of grace to be poured out on all the saints. A saint is a "holy one" or "one who is separated from the world for God's purposes." God wants to answer your prayers with plentiful answers that fill up the storehouses of the hearts of all God's people.

THE BLESSING OF PREACHING (6:19-20)

After the blessing of prayer, Paul asks them to pray for his preaching. Though he is making this request chained to a Roman soldier, he still considers himself to have an active ministry of preaching.

> **Ephesians 6:19-20** | And also for me, that words may be given to me in opening my mouth boldly to proclaim the mystery of the gospel, [20] for which I am an ambassador in chains, that I may declare it boldly, as I ought to speak.

Prayer is that which changes everything. Paul closes his whole exhortation with a request. Pray for me! Paul was only a man. All pastors and preachers are only men. Without your prayers, they will falter.

Open Door for Proclamation

Paul needs prayer so that he can open his mouth boldly and preach the gospel. It's amazing what God can do when people are praying for the preacher.

Five young college students were spending a Sunday in London, so they went to hear the famed C.H. Spurgeon preach. While waiting for the doors to open, the students were greeted by a man who asked, "Gentlemen, let me show you around. Would you like to see the heating plant of this church?" They were not particularly interested, for it was a hot day in July. But they didn't want to offend the stranger, so they consented. The young men were taken down a stairway, a door was quietly opened, and their guide whispered, "This is our heating plant." Surprised, the students saw 700 people bowed in prayer, seeking a blessing on the service that was soon to begin in the auditorium above. Softly closing the door, the gentleman then introduced himself. It was none other than Charles Spurgeon.[243]

William Booth, founder of the salvation army was used mightily by the Lord. There are a few recordings left from him from about a

---

[243] As quoted in *Our Daily Bread*, April 24, 2006.

hundred years ago. One is very eloquent, powerful preaching. Another is him preaching, struggling, and you hear him shout, as he was known to do, "Pray!" Who was he talking to? He was talking to the people we might say are "under the stage". He would have people praying for him during the services. Are you a warrior intercessor? Do you pray for the Word as it is preached? Do you believe that so much of what God does, he does in answer to the prayers of his saints?

Open Door for a Prisoner

When Paul wrote these words, he was a prisoner. He was "an ambassador in chains." But he does not pray to be released from prison. He would go from house arrest, and later he would be put under the streets of Rome in the Mamertine Prison. But he does not ask them to pray for his healing. What does he ask for? Does he say his ministry is over? No! He prays for fearless proclamation! Even when he asks for prayer for himself, he is God-centered and others-focused.

Paul was not an orator. Paul prays for "utterance" that he might open his mouth boldly. Paul was not an orator. The Corinthian church taunted him because of it. They said, "his presence is weak and his speech contemptible". We forget that Paul was not a good natural speaker. It is important to observe that we have a man here who was a witness of the resurrected Christ on the Damascus road, yet he is just as weak as any of us. He needs prayer. He requests prayer. Pray for me. Pray as I preach, that I might bring the conviction of the Holy Spirit. Pray that I will have boldness in declaring the Word of God.

Pray for fearless proclamation! Paul asks specifically that God would give him the ability to speak "boldly" –that is freely, frankly, holding nothing back. Not covering anything because it might be offensive. We need to pray for preachers today that they would not be influenced by what comes in during the offering. We need to pray that preachers will not be people pleasers. Paul was ridiculed and considered himself a "fool for Christ" because of it.

THE BLESSING OF PASTORS (6:21-22)

Paul tells them that with the letter of Ephesians that he's just completed, he's also sending his dear friend and fellow pastor, Tychicus. This man is described in many places, but above all things, he was an itinerate pastor, willing to go anywhere to shepherd God's people.

Ephesians 6:21-22 | So that you also may know how I am and what I am doing, Tychicus the beloved brother and faithful minister in the Lord will tell you everything. ²² I have sent him to you for this very purpose, that you may know how we are, and that he may encourage your hearts.

Pastor Tychicus

Paul concludes his letter by letting the dear saints at Ephesus know how he is doing, entrusting his ministry to his dear co-laborer in ministry, Pastor Tychicus. This shepherd of shepherds is to transpose and deliver this letter to the Ephesian church. Tychicus is mentioned in the companion letter to the Colossians. He was a native of Asia Minor (Acts 20:4) and possibly of Ephesus. He and Onesimus carried the Epistle to the Ephesians, the Epistle to the Colossians, and possibly a letter to the Laodiceans (Col 4:16) to the churches of Asia. Tychicus was one of the men chosen to accompany Paul when he took a financial gift from the Gentile churches to Jerusalem. On occasion Paul used Tychicus as a messenger (2 Tim 4:12; Titus 3:12).[244]

An Invested Brother

Ephesians 6:21a | So that you also may know how I am and what I am doing, Tychicus... will tell you everything.

Tychicus, being a very close companion of Paul, is mentioned five times in the New Testament and is closely aligned with Paul's missionary journeys (Acts 20:4; Eph 6:21–22; Col 4:7; Titus 3:12; 2 Tim 4:12). He's deeply invested in the church planting ministry of the apostle Paul in Asia Minor. We can imagine

He's a man who is always ready and willing to go anywhere and do anything for the kingdom. Paul trusts Tychicus to tell the Ephesian church how he is and what he is doing. Tychicus is so invested that he can tell the Ephesian congregation with firsthand knowledge "everything" that God is doing in and through Paul's ministry. The ironic thing is that a lot of what he's going to tell them is how God's work is not bound by Paul's chains. God is working mightily despite Paul's imprisonment.

Tychicus would bring information about Paul's health, for instance. Paul was not a well man. He had not completely recovered from

---

[244] Phillips, *Ephesians*, Eph 6:21a.

the ill-treatment and maulings he had suffered in championing the cause of Christ.

There would also be information about Paul's finances. Paul had no regular income as far as we know. He lived by faith. God's people helped him. Although Paul never mentioned his financial needs, he did say on one occasion that he had learned how to have plenty and how to do without.

The Christians at Ephesus were probably wondering whether Paul had prospects of a speedy or late trial. Tychicus would be able to bring the saints up to date on the details of Paul's approaching legal battle. The mills of justice were evidently moving slowly.

Tychicus would also report on Paul's psychological condition. In Scripture Paul nearly always appears as a victorious Christian, on top of his circumstances. But 2 Corinthians implies that he experienced great suffering from satanic harassment too. This brought Paul to a state of humility and not worry, anxiety or despair. His suffering actually expanded his heart and mind to remain humble so that he could receive more revelation about the beauty of Christ and the expansion of God's kingdom.

There would also be stories about soldiers won to Christ, news of Paul's latest Epistles, a description of the house where Paul lived, the remarkable account of a vital Christian ministry being carried on despite chains, tales of visitors coming to Rome from all over the world. Tychicus would have to relay all this information. It would be grist for the mill of prayer.[245]

A Beloved Brother

Ephesians 6:21b | Tychicus the beloved brother.

I love what Paul calls Tychicus—"the beloved brother." He was sent to encourage the hearts of the Ephesian church because he had endeared himself to Paul and likely any Christians he came into contact with. This was the reputation of Tychicus's character. Anyone who is filled with the kind of self-sacrificing agape love of God is going to beloved by all.

The family of God makes brothers and sisters of all who love the Lord. Some become beloved brothers, often nearer to us than our

---

[245] Ibid.

natural siblings. Tychicus had the privilege of being a beloved brother to the great apostle Paul. Ministry can be messy, and a deep love is needed in order to not get discouraged. To be a functioning member in those messy situations, you must be able to endear yourself to the members of your local church by opening your lives together. You must take each brother or sister where they are. You must not judge their spiritual life just because they are not exactly where you are. Love them.

A Faithful Brother

Ephesians 6:21c | So that you also may know how I am and what I am doing, Tychicus the ... faithful minister in the Lord.

Tychicus was also a faithful minister. The word translated "minister" in Ephesians 6:21, *diakonos*, means "an active servant." Tychicus was willing to devote himself to the service of God; he was a helper to Paul and an active worker for the cause of Christ. Paul had chains on his arms; Tychicus had them on his heart. His sole ambition was to be useful in relieving Paul's restrictions and furthering the kingdom of God. People like Tychicus are invaluable in the Lord's work.[246]

Tychicus, as a faithful servant was worthy of Paul's trust and confidence. Faithful men are not perfect men, but are consistently growing in Christ from the heart, exhibiting the fruit of the Spirit. Tychicus was entrusted to transcribe this letter while Paul dictated to him, and he is going to deliver it to the Ephesian congregation on behalf of Paul. Tychicus at one time was a pagan, but now he is chosen and favored by God to work with Paul.

Tychicus was very likely a native of Ephesus. He might have been one of those who gathered to hear Paul in the meeting hall at the school of Tyrannus in Ephesus (Acts 19:9). During that time, it seems that Tychicus lived up to his name. He was served God faithfully, and it became apparent to Paul. God's grace was so obvious in the life of Tychicus, that when Paul left to finish his third missionary journey after founding the Ephesian church and to go to Jerusalem with an offering from the churches of Asia Minor, he chose Tychicus to go with him.

---

[246] Ibid.

Pastor Paul

Ephesians 6:22 | I have sent him to you for this very purpose, that you may know how we are, and that he may encourage your hearts.

Paul is in prison, but he has a pastoral concern the church far away in Ephesus. He wants to encourage his brothers and sisters there. Paul was locked up, but it didn't stop him from pouring out his heart to God and to the churches. He wanted the precious Ephesians to know how he was. He is likely under house arrest in Rome around 60 to 62 AD. Soon after this Paul would be back again, this time in the Mamertine prison, on his final imprisonment, which was a road to glory.

Paul's great struggle as he ends the book of Ephesians is that he cannot greet the sweet church at Ephesus in person. Timothy is a pastor at Ephesus, but we find that when Timothy leaves to assist Paul, Tychicus on various occasions fills in for Timothy. Tychicus also apparently replaced Titus for a time, so that Titus could come and comfort the apostle Paul. Here we see a model of shared leadership. Tychicus does the same thing for Timothy at the church of Ephesus (2 Tim 4:12).

What a heart Paul had for the Ephesians. He not only teaches them with this letter, but while he is suffering in jail, he is busy to recruit and enlist others to care for the spiritual well-being of the Ephesian congregation. Paul doesn't do this for monetary gain or for temporary fame. He does it for God's glory and the Ephesians' good. He's not a hireling pastor but one that is willing to lay down his life for the sheep.

THE BLESSING OF BLESSINGS (6:23-24)

Paul closes with a fourfold benediction. The word "benediction" refers to speaking the blessing of God over someone. A benediction is not for imploring the blessing of God, but rather celebrating it since we already have it. He gives reminds them of God's blessing upon them that they should receive with open palms. God wants to bless his children more than we want to be blessed.

What has God blessed all Christians with? Paul celebrates God's blessing on the Ephesian Christians (and us) in four ways: *Peace*—our reconciliation with Christ. *Faith*—our trust in Christ. *Love*—our affection from Christ. *Grace*—our favor in Christ. Open your palms because God wants to give you "exceeding, abundantly above all that you could ask or think" (Eph 3:19). Listen to Paul's blessing upon the Ephesian church.

> **Ephesians 6:23-24** | Peace be to the brothers, and love with faith, from God the Father and the Lord Jesus Christ. ²⁴ Grace be with all who love our Lord Jesus Christ with love incorruptible.

Peace

> **Ephesians 6:23a** | Peace be to the brothers.

Christians above all have the blessing of peace upon them because Christ has reconciled us to the Father by his blood.

The Peace of God's Control

Paul reminds us that nothing ultimately bad can happen to us since we have the blessing of God's peace upon us. We are reconciled with God, and we have God's shalom, his well-being upon us with all the brothers and sisters in Christ. No matter what happens, we can be assured that all that is happening for our good and God's glory, so that we can receive the fullness of God's blessing for us in Christ (Eph 1:3, 11; Rom 8:28-29). The essential experience of peace is knowing that God is in absolute control of my life to do me good and to conform me to Christlikeness. Remember God will not protect me from anything that will make me more like Christ. God's peace is not a utopia. It is not the removal of hardship or trial (Jas 1:2-3). It is knowing he is with me through the hardship and is using it to make me mature in Christ.

The Peace of God's Presence

Peace means that we have God's comforting presence with us at all times. We can say, "My beloved is mine, and I am his" (Song 2:16). He leads us to paths of righteousness for his name's sake" (Psa 23:3). We are always to walk in God's shalom. The warmth of our Father's face is always shining upon us. That means no anxiety, anger, or despair should characterize the Christian.

The Peace of God's Reconciliation

We may be at war in this world, but we are at peace with our dear God and all his people. That doesn't mean we are exact replicas of each other or that we agree on everything. But it does mean we are perfectly unified in Christ because of our union with him. Our peace comes from our reconciliation with Jesus. We say with Aaron and all the Levitical priests, as true priests of the Lord Jesus:

> *Numbers 6:24-26* | The LORD bless you and keep you; ²⁵ the LORD make his face to shine upon you and be gracious to you; ²⁶ the LORD lift up his countenance upon you and give you peace.

The wall of hostility has been torn down in the church. Those who were once enemies are now brothers and sisters in Christ. This is because those who were far off are now brought near. What peace! What reconciliation.

Love

> **Ephesians 6:23b** | Love ... from God the Father and the Lord Jesus Christ.

We as Christians, have the blessing of God's infinite everlasting love upon us. This is God's *agape*, self-originating and self-sacrificing love for the betterment of another. The is the primary mark and identifier of every Christian (Jn 13:34-35; 1 Jn 5:2). The perfect love of God perfects the child of God and guards him or her from fear, which it always casts away (1 Jn 4:18). Love never fails and never ends; it is the perfection of character that we know now but will know without interruption for eternity (1 Cor 13:8a). When everything else passes away, God's love of us and through us remains. It remains because it is God's everlasting love to us. Try to comprehend that God has loved us for all eternity (Jer 31:3). This is what the entire book of Ephesians is headed toward and rightfully ends with (6:24).

Tychicus is one who can express God's love to the Ephesian church from Paul. Paul did not forget for a moment the tender love of so many in the Ephesian church. He remembered his last farewell to the Ephesian elders at Miletus when "they all wept sore, and fell on Paul's neck, and kissed him, sorrowing most of all for the words which he spake, that they should see his face no more" (Acts 20:37–38). Tychicus would bring them comforting news because Paul was optimistic about the outcome of his impending trial.

> *1 John 4:19, KJV* | We love him, because he first loved us.

This love is a Trinitarian love, found in the Father and his Son, our Lord Jesus Christ. In Father and Son, original love is known, and

"God's love has been poured into our hearts through the Holy Spirit who has been given to us" (Rom 5:5).

Faith

Ephesians 6:23c | Love with faith, from God the Father and the Lord Jesus Christ.

Another blessing is recounted: the faith to embrace the love of God. It's hard to receive the infinite goodness of God as those who have been rescued from the pit of sin. We feel so unworthy. That's why Paul reminds us that the agape love of God must always be accompanied by faith, the trust that God really does love us. We can entrust our whole selves to such a God of love. Christian love is always motivated by a trust in the love of tender Father in heaven. We trust all he is doing to transform us into the image of Christ. We put our full weight on the finished work of Christ, the gentle guidance of the Spirit, all to the ultimate glory of the Father of our Lord. Do you want to increase your faith? Dare to believe that God loves you infinitely based on nothing in you. Let his love lead you to greater faith and greater faithfulness.

Grace

Ephesians 6:24a | Grace be with all.

The final blessing is recounted: the blessing that makes eGrace is God's unmerited favor and unlimited power. Paul was a prisoner of Rome, yet he was richer than the emperor because he was lavished with God's grace. No matter what our circumstances may be, in Jesus Christ we are "blessed with all spiritual blessings."

Conclusion

Ephesians 6:24 | Grace be with all who love our Lord Jesus Christ with love incorruptible.

There is an incorruptible love that is poured into our hearts by the Spirit. The grace he pours into our heart enables us "to grasp how wide and long and high and deep is the love of Christ, and to know this love that surpasses knowledge—that we may be filled to the measure of all the fullness of God" (Eph 3:18-19).

The word translated "sincerity" in Ephesians 6:24 literally means "without corruption." Our love should be incorruptible. It should be a an unfading love that takes on the nature of immortality (*cf* 1 Cor 15:42). There are many things that can bring corruption into my love for Jesus. There are many competing loves that contend with my love for Jesus. The love of sex, the love of money, the love of reputation, the love of success, the love of respect, the love of comfort, the love of knowledge, the love of possessions. The list of competing loves that could corrupt my love for Jesus is endless. What is it right now that is competing with your love for Jesus? With his final word, Paul leaves us face to face with our Lord Jesus Christ, contemplating a love relationship that reaches into eternity.[247]

Hence the final words of Ephesians caps off its central message: that in Christ Jesus and through the redemptive grace of the triune God, believers experience now the inauguration of the new creation and will dwell with our Lord in unified peace in new, incorruptible resurrection existence. As our risen Messianic King dwells in incorruptibility now as first fruits, so shall all his people live together with him in incorruptible glory forevermore.

---

[247] Ibid.

SELECTED BIBLIOGRAPHY

In order of appearance in the commentary

COMMENTARIES

James Montgomery Boice, *Ephesians: An Expositional Commentary* (Grand Rapids, MI: Ministry Resources Library, 1988).

D. Martyn Lloyd-Jones. *God's Ultimate Purpose: An Exposition of Ephesians 1* (Grand Rapids, MI: Baker Books, 1978).

John F. MacArthur Jr., *Ephesians*, MacArthur New Testament Commentary (Chicago: Moody Press, 1986).

Bryan Chapell, *Ephesians* (Phillipsburg, NJ: P & R Publishers, 2009).

R. C. Sproul, *The Purpose of God: Ephesians* (Scotland: Christian Focus Publications, 1994).

John H. Sailhamer, Tremper Longman, and David E. Garland, *The Expositor's Bible Commentary* (Grand Rapids, MI: Zondervan, 2017).

R. Kent Hughes, *Ephesians: The Mystery of the Body of Christ*, Preaching the Word (Wheaton, IL: Crossway Books, 1990).

S. Lewis Johnson. *Discovering Romans: Spiritual Revival for the Soul* (Nashville: Zondervan).

D.A Carson, *New Bible Commentary: 21st Century Edition* (4th ed.) (Leicester, England; Downers Grove, Ill., USA: Inter-Varsity Press, 1994).

Charles Hodge, *An Exposition of Ephesians* (Wilmington, DE: Associated Publishers and Authors Inc., 1972).

John Phillips, *Exploring Ephesians & Philippians: An Expository Commentary*, The John Phillips Commentary Series (Kregel Publications; WORDsearch Corp., 2009).

John Stott. *The Message of Ephesians: God's New Society,* (Downers Grove, IL: InterVarsity Press, 2014).

N.T. Wright, *Paul for Everyone: The Prison Letters: Ephesians, Philippians, Colossians, and Philemon* (London: Society for Promoting Christian Knowledge, 2004)..

William Barclay, *The Letters to the Galatians and Ephesians* (Philadelphia: Westminster Press, 1958)..

Francis Foulkes, *Ephesians: An Introduction and Commentary*, vol. 10, Tyndale New Testament Commentaries (Downers Grove, IL: InterVarsity Press, 1989).

Sinclair B. Ferguson. *Let's Study Ephesians* (Carlisle, PA: Banner of Truth, 2005).

Richard J. Erickson, "Ephesians," in *Evangelical Commentary on the Bible*, vol. 3, Baker Reference Library (Grand Rapids, MI: Baker Book House, 1995).

A.W. Pink. *Studies in the Scriptures, Volume 7* (Lafayette, IN: Sovereign Grace Publishers, 2001).

Warren W. Wiersbe, *The Bible Exposition Commentary*, vol. 2 (Wheaton, IL: Victor Books, 1996).

St. Jerome. J.P. Migne, ed. "Epistle to the Ephesians" in *Patrologia Cursus Completus*. Series Latina. 221 vols. (Paris: Migne, 1844-1864).

Andrew T. Lincoln. *Word Biblical Commentary: Ephesians* (Word Books: Dallas, 1990).

H. D. M. Spence-Jones. *The Pulpit Commentary: Ephesians* (Bellingham, WA: Logos Research Systems, Inc., 2004).Benjamin L. Merkle, "Ephesians," in *Ephesians–Philemon*, ed. Iain M. Duguid, James M. Hamilton Jr., and Jay Sklar, vol. XI, ESV Expository Commentary (Wheaton, IL: Crossway, 2018).

Marcus Barth, *Ephesians* (New York: Doubleday, 1974).

Wayne Grudem. *1 Peter: An Introduction and Commentary, Vol 17* (Downers Grove, IL: InterVarsity Press, 1988).

John Phillips, *Exploring Ephesians & Philippians: An Expository Commentary*, The John Phillips Commentary Series (Kregel Publications; WORDsearch Corp., 2009).

SERMONS

Charles H. Spurgeon. "Adoption," Sermon delivered on Sunday evening February 10, 1861.

Charles Spurgeon. *Metropolitan Tabernacle Pulpit*, Vol 12, Sermon 707, "Heavenly Geometry" (London: Passmore & Alabaster, 1866).

Charles Spurgeon. *Metropolitan Tabernacle Pulpit*, Vol 29, Sermon 1755, "The Top of the Ladder" (London: Passmore & Alabaster, 1882).

Charles Haddon Spurgeon. *New Park Street Pulpit, Vol 2*. "Turn or Burn" preached December 7, 1856.

John MacArthur, "On with the Old, Off with the New, Part 1" study. https://www.gty.org/library/sermons-library/1928/off-with-the-old-on-with-the-new-part-1

Thomas Guthrie. *The Way to Life: Sermons by Thomas Guthrie* (New York: Robert Carter & Brothers Publishers, 1876).

ANCIENT SOURCES

Augustine of Hippo, "A Treatise on the Merits and Forgiveness of Sins, and on the Baptism of Infants," in *Saint Augustin: Anti-Pelagian Writings*, ed. Philip Schaff, trans. Peter Holmes, vol. 5, A Select Library of the Nicene and Post-Nicene Fathers of the Christian Church, First Series (New York: Christian Literature Company, 1887).

Aurelius Augustine. *Confessions*, (Book 1,1-2,2.5,5: CSEL 33).

Martin Luther. *What Luther Says: An Anthology* (St. Louis, MO: Concordia Publishing House, 1959).

Matthew Henry. *Matthew Henry's Commentary on the Whole Bible: Complete and Unabridged in One Volume*. (Peabody, ME: Hendrickson, 1996).

John Newton. *The Christian Spectator*, vol 3 (New Haven, CT: S. Converse, 1821).

John Calvin, *Institutes of the Christian Religion*.

John Calvin. *Calvin's Commentaries: The Epistles of Paul the Apostle to the Galatians, Ephesians, Philippians and Colossians*, Volume II, trans. T. H. L. Parker (Grand Rapids, MI: Eerdmans, 1974).

John Calvin. *Sermons on Ephesians* (Banner of Truth: Carlisle, PA, 1973).

Jonathan Edwards. *The Works of Jonathan Edwards, Volume 1*, ed. Edward Hickman (Edinburgh: The Banner of Truth Trust, 1974).

Jonathan Edwards. "An Essay on the Trinity," in Treatise on Grace and Other Posthumously Published Writings, ed. Paul Helm (Cambridge, UK: Clarke, 1971).

John Wesley. *The Works of John Wesley: Volume 11: Thoughts, Addresses, Prayers, Letters* (Grand Rapids, MI: 1872).

John Wesley. T*he Arminian Magazine: Consisting of Extracts and Originals on Universal Redemption*, vol. 13 (London: New Chapel, 1790).

Richard Sibbes. *The Bruised Reed and Smoking Flax* (London: Gooch Booksellers, 1630).

John Bunyan. *The Works of John Bunyan, Volume 1* (London: Blackie and Son, 1866).

J. C. Ryle (1816-1900). *A Call to Prayer—with Study Guide* (Pensacola, FL: Chapel Library).

John Owen. *On the Mortification of Sin in Believers* (Woodstock, Ontario, CA: Devoted Publishing, 2017).

Robert Murray McCheyne. *Memoir and Remains of Robert Murray McCheyne* (Dundee, Scotland: William Middleton Publishing, 1855).

BIOGRAPHICAL

Lyle Dorsett. *A Passion for God: The Spiritual Journey of A. W. Tozer* (Chicago: Moody, 2008).

Roberts Liardon. *God's Generals Dwight L. Moody* (New Kensington, PA: Whitaker House, 2008).

Iain Murray. *D. Martyn Lloyd-Jones: The First Forty Years, 1899-1939* (Carlyle, PA: Banner of Truth, 1982).

Eric Metaxas. *Martin Luther The Man who Rediscovered God and Changed the World* (New York: Penguin Random House, 2017).

DICTIONARIES

Theological dictionary of the New Testament. 1964-c1976. Vols. 5-9 edited by Gerhard Friedrich. Vol. 10 compiled by Ronald Pitkin.

(G. Kittel, G. W. Bromiley & G. Friedrich, Ed.) (electronic ed.) (2:566). Grand Rapids, MI: Eerdmans.

Walter A. Elwell and Barry J. Beitzel, "Eschatology," *Baker Encyclopedia of the Bible* (Grand Rapids, MI: Baker Book House, 1988).

Grant R. Osborne, "Baptism," *Baker Encyclopedia of the Bible* (Grand Rapids, MI: Baker Book House, 1988).

Paul J. Achtemeier, "Providence", Harper & Row and Society of Biblical Literature, *Harper's Bible Dictionary* (San Francisco: Harper & Row, 1985).

Kenneth S. Wuest. *Wuest's Word Studies from the Greek New Testament : For the English Reader*. (Grand Rapids, MI: Eerdmans, 1997).

Walter A. Elwell and Barry J. Beitzel, "Redeemer, Redemption," *Baker Encyclopedia of the Bible* (Grand Rapids, MI: Baker Book House, 1988).

Gary Hardin, "Humility," ed. Chad Brand et al., *Holman Illustrated Bible Dictionary* (Nashville, TN: Holman Bible Publishers, 2003).

Siegfried Rudolf Dunde, "Humility," *The Encyclopedia of Christianity* (Grand Rapids, MI; Leiden, Netherlands: Wm. B. Eerdmans; Brill, 1999–2003).

Robert L. Plummer, "Meekness," ed. Chad Brand et al., *Holman Illustrated Bible Dictionary* (Nashville, TN: Holman Bible Publishers, 2003).Jefford, Clayton, Kenneth Harder, and Louis Amezaga. *Reading the Apostolic Fathers: An Introduction*. (Peabody, MA: Hendrickson Publishers, 1996).

Walter Bauer and Frederick William Danker. *A Greek-English Lexicon of the New Testament and Other Early Christian Literature* (Third Edition; based on a previous English edition by W.F. Arndt, F.W. Gingrich, and F.W. Danker; University of Chicago Press, 1957, 1979, 2000).

Merriam-Webster, Inc: *Merriam-Webster's Collegiate Dictionary*. Eleventh ed. (Springfield, MA: Merriam-Webster, Inc., 2003).

Johannes P. Louw and Eugene Albert Nida, *Greek-English Lexicon of the New Testament: Based on Semantic Domains* (New York: United Bible Societies, 1996).

James Orr, ed. *International Standard Bible Encyclopedia* (1915).

Spiros Zodhiates. *The Complete Word Study Dictionary: New Testament* (Chattanooga, TN: AMG Publishers, 1993).

Scott Bartchy, "Servant; Slave," in Geoffrey W. Bromiley, ed., *ISBE*, vol. 4 (Grand Rapids: Eerdmans, 1988).

Biblical Studies Press, *The NET Bible First Edition Notes* (Biblical Studies Press, 2006).

COUNSELING

David Powlison. *Good and Angry: Redeeming Anger, Irritation, Complaining, and Bitterness* (Greensboro, NC: New Growth Press, 2016).

David Powlison, *Seeing with New Eyes: Counseling and the Human Condition through the Lens of Scripture* (Phillipsburg, NJ: P & R Pub., 2003).

Robert Kelleman. *Gospel-Centered Counseling: How Christ Changes Lives* (Grand Rapids, MI: Zondervan, 2014).

Elyse Fitzpatrick. *Helper by Design* (Chicago: Moody Publishers, 2003).

Kenneth Boa, *Conformed to His Image: Biblical and Practical Approaches to Spiritual Formation* (Zondervan: Grand Rapids, 2001).

Jay Adams, *Christian Living in the Home* (Phillipsburg, NJ: Presbyterian and Reformed Publishing, 1972).

Tom and Chaundel Holladay. *Love-Powered Parenting: Loving Your Kids the Way Jesus Loves You* (Grand Rapids, MI: Zondervan, 2012).

Joel R. Beeke, "How Should Men Lead Their Families?" Booklet. Reformation Heritage Books.

NEW TESTAMENT

D.A. Carson, *Showing the Spirit: A Theological Exposition of 1 Corinthians 12-14* (Grand Rapids: Baker Books, 1997).

James Brennan, "The Exegesis of 1 Corinthians 13," *Irish Theological Quarterly* 21 (1954).

JOURNALS

Marius Victorinus. *Bibliotheca Scriptorum Graecorum et Romanorum Teubneriana* (Leipzig: Teubner, 1824).

"Preaching as Worship: Meditations on Expository Exultation" (*Trinity Journal* 16, 1995).

THEOLOGY
Wayne A. Grudem, *Systematic Theology: An Introduction to Biblical Doctrine* (Leicester, England; Grand Rapids, MI: Inter-Varsity Press; Zondervan Pub. House, 2004).

BACKGROUNDS
Murray J. Harris, *Slave of Christ* (Downers Grove, IL: InterVarsity Press, 1999).

John F. MacArthur. *Slave: The Hidden Truth About Your Identity in Christ* (Nashville: Thomas Nelson, 2012).

Tremper Longman. *God Is a Warrior* (Studies in Old Testament Biblical Theology Series) (Grand Rapids, MI: Zondervan Academic, 2010).

John McRay. *Paul: His Life and Teaching* (Grand Rapids, MI: Baker Publishing Group, 2003).

Everett Ferguson, *Backgrounds of Early Christianity* (2d ed.; Grand Rapids: Eerdmans, 1993).

Mitch and Zhava Galser, *The Fall Feasts of Israel* (Moody Bible Institute: Chicago, 1987).

Alexander MacLaren. *Record of Christian Work* (Moody: East Northfield, MA, 1910).

Scott Bartchy. *Mallon Chresai: First-century Slavery and the Interpretation of 1 Corinthians 7:21*, SBL Dissertation Series 11 (Missoula, MT: SBL, 1971).

Mark Cartwright. Ancient History Encyclopedia, "Slavery in the Roman World." West Sussex, UK: AHE, 2013.

Brian K. Harvey. *Daily Life in Ancient Rome: A Sourcebook* (Indianapolis, IN: Focus, 2016).

ARTICLES
Steve Saint, "Did They Have To Die?", *Christianity Today*, September 16, 1996.

Associated Press. (2012, May 19). "SpaceX Rocket Launch Aborted". Retrieved December 29, 2020, from https://www.politico.com/story/2012/05/spacex-rocket-launch-aborted-076513

From *Insurance Information Institute*. https://www.iii.org/fact-statistic/facts-statistics-identity-theft-and-cybercrime

Norman Kempster. (2016, January 28). "The Global Land Mine Crisis." Retrieved February 6, 2021, from http://menstuff.org/issues/byissue/minehistory.html#problem.

John W. Cowart. *Ephesus: A Wonder of the World* (2005). Accessed 8 February 2021. http://www.cowart.info/Ephesus/ephesus.htmlSharon Jayson. "Divorce Declining, But So is Marriage" USA Today. Published July 18, 2005. Accessed 25 February 2021. http://www.usatoday.com/news/nation/2005-07-18-cohabit-divorce_x.htm

Gary Thomas. "What Cherishing Your Spouse Really Means" September 11, 2018. Focus on the Family.

MSN Money. "How much is a homemaker worth?" (Jan 18, 2012). Archived.

TOPICAL

John Piper. *Think: The Life of the Mind and the Love of God* (Wheaton, IL: Good News Publishers/Crossway Books, 2010).

C. S. Lewis, *The Problem of Pain* (New York: Simon & Schuster, 1996).

Robert Boyd Munger; Andrea Jorgenson. *My Heart Christ's Home: A Story for Old and Young*.

Giles Buckingham Willcox. *The Pastor Amidst His Flock* (New York: American Tract Society, 1890).

C.J. Mahaney. *The Cross-Centered Life* (Colorado Springs, CO: Multnomah Books, 2009).

Robert W. Kellemen. *Gospel-Centered Counseling* (Equipping Biblical Counselors) (Grand Rapids, MI: Zondervan. 2014), 167-168.

Thomas Chalmers. *The Expulsive Power of a New Affection* (Crossway Short Classics) (Wheaton, IL: Crossway, 2020).

Abraham Kuyper. *The Work of the Holy Spirit* (Grand Rapids, MI: Eerdmans Publishing Co, 1956).

R. Kent Hughes. *Disciplines of a Godly Man* (Wheaton, IL: Crossway, 1991).

David Jeremiah. *Slaying the Giants in Your Life* (Nashville: Thomas Nelson Publisher, 2001).

Charles Spurgeon. *Evening by Evening* (New Kensington, PA: Whitaker House, 1984).

Keith and Kristyn Getty. *Sing!* (Nashville, TN: B&H Publishing Group, 2017).

A. B. Simpson, as quoted in *Once-A-Day: Walk with Jesus* (Nashville: Zondervan, 2012).

George Knight III, "Husbands and Wives as Analogues of Christ and the Church" in *Recovering Biblical Manhood and Womanhood: A Response to Evangelical Feminism,* edited by John Piper and Wayne Grudem (Wheaton, IL: Crossway Books, 1991).

Michael P. Nichols, *The Lost Art of Listening, Second Edition: How Learning to Listen Can Improve Relationships* (New York: Guilford Publications, 2009).

Charlie Shedd. *Promises to Peter* (Waco, TX.: Word, 1970).

Gavin Kendall, Gary Wickham. *Understanding Culture* (London: Sage Publications, 2001).

Jim Elliot in Elizabeth Elliot. *Shadow of the Almighty* (Peabody, MA: Hendrickson Publishers, 2008).

WENATCHEE, WASHINGTON

You may obtain this, and many other fine resources made available by Proclaim Publishers by contacting us:

Web:
proclaimpublishers.com

Email:
contact@proclaimpublishers.com

Postal Mail:
Proclaim Publishers
PO Box 2082
Wenatchee, WA 98807

Soli Deo Gloria

www.ingramcontent.com/pod-product-compliance
Lightning Source LLC
Chambersburg PA
CBHW031417150426
43191CB00006B/312